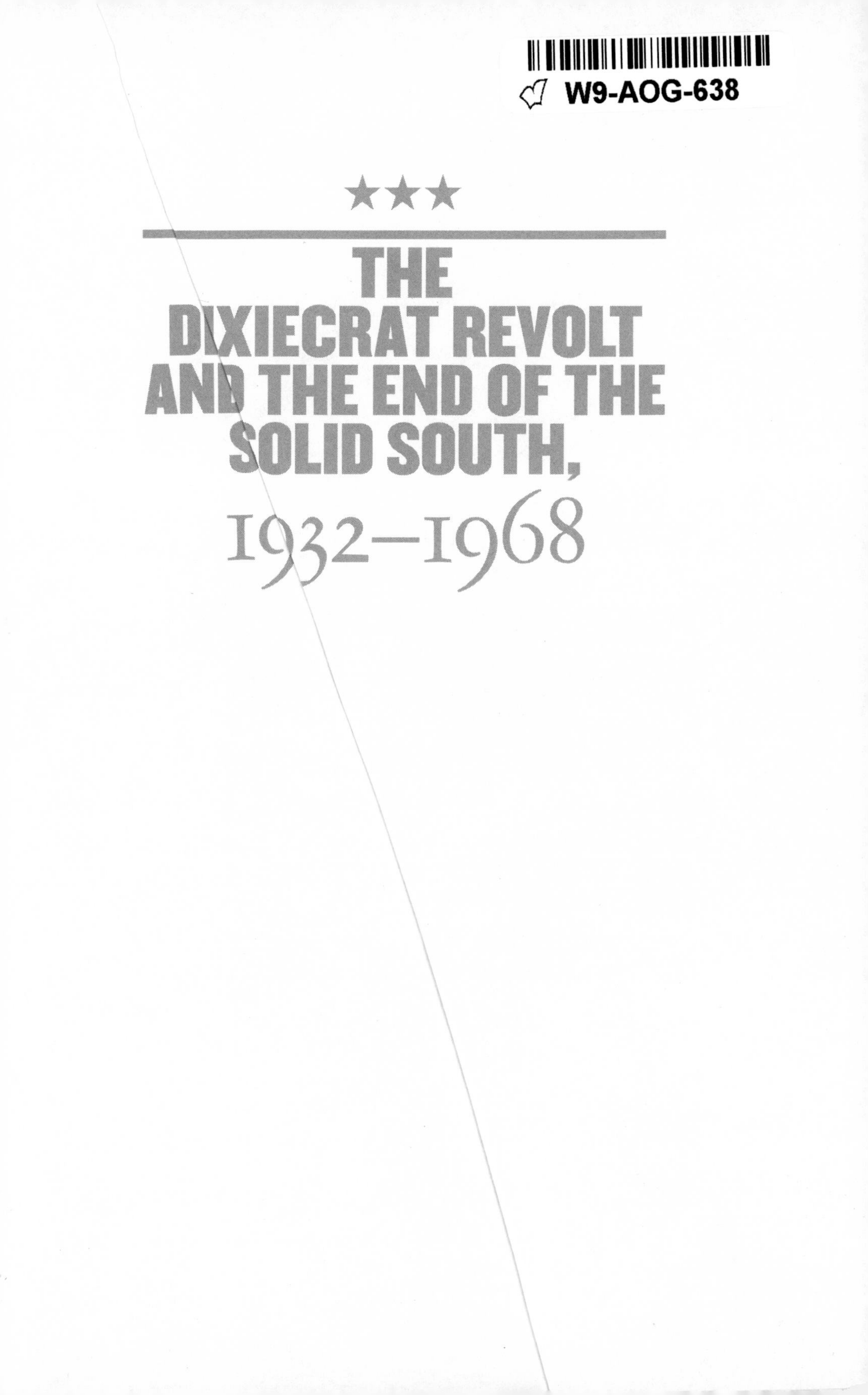

★★★

THE DIXIECRAT REVOLT AND THE END OF THE SOLID SOUTH, 1932–1968

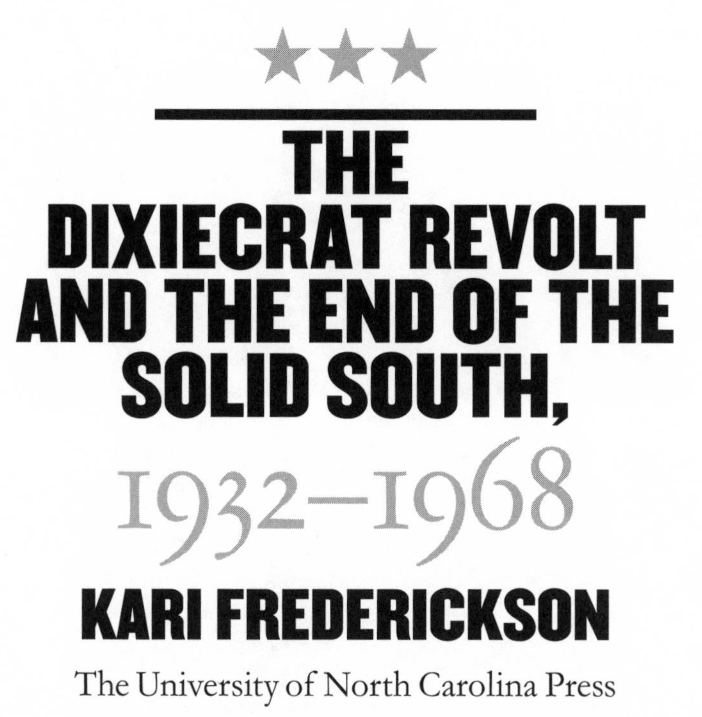

THE DIXIECRAT REVOLT AND THE END OF THE SOLID SOUTH, 1932–1968

KARI FREDERICKSON

The University of North Carolina Press

Chapel Hill and London

Manufactured in the United States of America
Set in Monotype Garamond and Champion types
by Tseng Information Systems, Inc.
The paper in this book meets the guidelines for permanence and durability of the Committee on Production Guidelines for Book Longevity of the Council on Library Resources.
Library of Congress Cataloging-in-Publication Data
Frederickson, Kari A.
The Dixiecrat revolt and the end of the Solid South, 1932–1968 /
by Kari Frederickson.
p. cm.
Originally presented as author's thesis (doctoral)—Rutgers University.
Includes bibliographical references (p.) and index.
ISBN 0-8078-2594-8 (cloth : alk. paper) — ISBN 0-8078-4910-3 (pbk. : alk. paper)
1. Southern States—Politics and government—1951– 2. Southern States—Politics and government—1865–1950. 3. States' Rights Democratic Party—History. 4. Southern States—Race relations—Political aspects. 5. Elite (Social sciences)—Southern States—Political activity—History—20th century. 6. Presidents—United States—Election—1948. 7. United States—Politics and government—1933–1945. 8. United States—Politics and government—1945–1989. I. Title.
F216.2 .F74 2001
324.273'3—dc21 00-044733

Portions of this book were previously published, in somewhat different form, in "'Dual Actions, One for Each Race': The Campaign against the Dixiecrats in South Carolina," *International Social Science Review* 72 (Spring 1997): 14–25, and "'The Slowest State, the Most Backward Community': Racial Violence in South Carolina and Federal Civil Rights Legislation," *South Carolina Historical Magazine* 98 (April 1997): 177–210, and are reprinted here with permission of the journals.

05 04 5 4 3 2

For Jeff

CONTENTS

★ ★ ★

ILLUSTRATIONS

★ ★ ★

ACKNOWLEDGMENTS

Completion of this project would not have been possible without the assistance and encouragement of an army of people. This book first began as a humble graduate seminar paper written for Professor Glen Jeansonne at the University of Wisconsin, Milwaukee, in 1989. Professor Jeansonne took an early interest in my career and has been a trusted advisor and friend ever since. He set a high standard for scholarly generosity that I try to meet with my own students. The dissertation took shape at Rutgers University under the expert direction of Professor David M. Oshinsky, who pushed me to undertake a project of broad scope. I always greatly appreciated his confidence in the project's merit and in the author, and he continues to be a source of good advice and friendship. I am also grateful to my dissertation committee—Professors William L. O'Neill, Laura D. Garrison, and Raymond Arsenault—who took time out of their summer vacations to read the final draft of the dissertation. Their criticisms and comments helped immeasurably in the revising process. Finally, how Lewis Bateman, formerly of the University of North Carolina Press, found out about this project back in 1993, before I had done any significant research, I will never know. For his early interest and his expert cultivating, I will always be grateful.

My parents, Wilbur and Annette Frederickson, and my brothers and sisters and their spouses offered regular financial and emotional support. My parents also provided access to a string of southern snowbirds—midwesterners of their generation who had migrated to the South—who willingly opened their homes to an itinerant researcher. I'd also like to thank my family for the gingerly yet regularly proffered question, "So . . . when will your book be finished?" If nothing else, the ability to finally put that question to rest pushed this project toward completion. I'm also thankful for my mother- and father-in-law, Otis and Esther Melton, South Carolina natives, who patiently indulged this midwesterner's love for southern history during family visits.

A number of people who put me up during 1993–94 as I drove my 1986 Dodge Colt throughout the South and Midwest deserve special thanks: Michelle Brattain and Andrew Milne, Virginia Steen, Laurie Tiberio and Lisa Kannenberg, Lillian Peterson and the late Bill Peterson, Eleanor Proctor, and Susan Frederickson. I also benefited greatly from the advice and support of my friends, in particular Beatrix Hoffman, Michelle Brattain and Andrew Milne, Cindy Stiles, Amy and Andy Forbes, and Nancy Rauscher.

Research for this project was supported by grants and fellowships from Rutgers University, the Harry S. Truman Library, and the Institute for Southern Studies at the University of South Carolina. It was my good fortune to have had the assistance of a number of outstanding archivists, including James Cross at Clemson University, Tara Zachary at Delta State University, and Herb Hartsook at the Modern Political Collections, University of South Carolina. Winnie Tyler of the interlibrary loan department at the University of Central Florida went above and beyond the call of duty in processing my many requests.

My former colleagues in the history department at the University of Central Florida, particularly Richard C. Crepeau, Rosalind Beiler, and Curtis Austin, made that university a fun place at which to work. They provide a model of collegiality and professionalism that continues to impress me. My present colleagues at the University of Alabama have made me feel welcome and have worked hard to make the university an exciting place for a southern historian.

This author's greatest debt is to Jeffrey Alan Melton, who took valuable time away from his own projects to read every chapter more than once. With a sharp editorial pencil, but always with good humor, he offered suggestions that greatly improved this book. It is to him that this book is fondly dedicated.

★ ★ ★

ABBREVIATIONS

AAA
Agricultural Adjustment Act

ADA
Americans for Democratic Action

CIO
Congress of Industrial Organizations

DNC
Democratic National Committee

FEPC
Committee on Fair Employment Practices

FERA
Federal Emergency Relief Act

NAACP
National Association for the Advancement of Colored People

NRA
National Recovery Administration

PCCR
President's Committee on Civil Rights

PDP
Progressive Democratic Party

SCHW
Southern Conference for Human Welfare

SDEC
State Democratic Executive Committee

SSIC
Southern States Industrial Council

WPA
Works Progress Administration

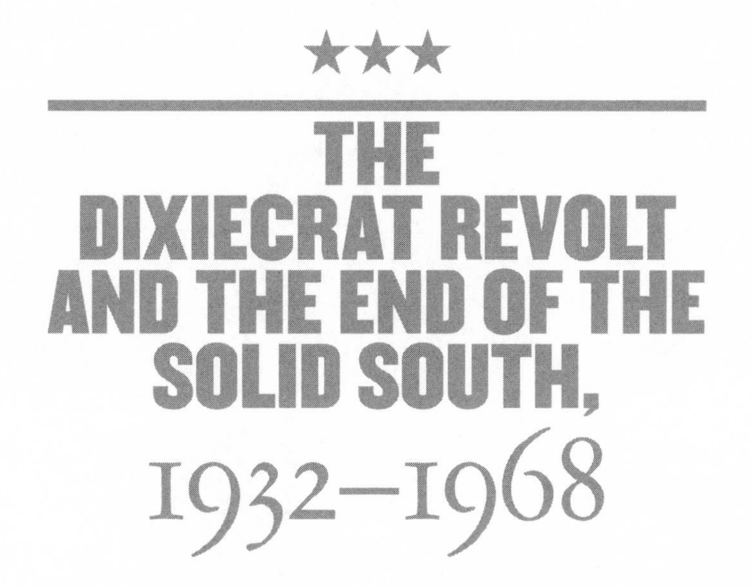
THE
DIXIECRAT REVOLT
AND THE END OF THE
SOLID SOUTH,
1932–1968

INTRODUCTION

In the light of history, the states' rights campaign of 1948 can be seen as an outgrowth of the thinking of the rednecks, the coonasses, and the hillbillies. But it was acceptable to the political elite as well.

J. OLIVER EMMERICH

Dixiecrat speech writer and publisher, McComb Enterprise-Journal

On April 8, 1996, ninety-three-year-old Strom Thurmond formally announced his candidacy for an unprecedented seventh term as U.S. senator from South Carolina. The state's "living legend" vowed to continue his fight for the cornerstones of conservatism: a strong military, a balanced budget, and a revamped welfare system. "I shall not give up on our mission to right the 40-year wrongs of liberalism," he declared.[1] Despite his popularity, many South Carolinians doubted whether the senior senator was physically up to the task of another term. Other voters chafed at the thought of turning out the venerable old gentleman. For those who had achieved voting age since the mid-1950s, Thurmond had represented them their whole lives.

Just about anyone you meet in South Carolina, it seems, has a personal anecdote about the senator or can tell you about someone who has received prompt assistance on a thorny bureaucratic matter from Thurmond's legendary staff. One story in particular illustrates the extensive reach of Thurmond's office. A friend once told me about the events surrounding the death of her grandfather, a longtime South Carolina politician, who had passed away late one night. At 6:00 A.M., barely an hour after the ambulance had taken the body away and before all immediate family members had been notified, her grandmother received a call of condolence from Senator Thurmond. "How he found out about granddaddy, we never knew," my friend exclaimed. "It wasn't even daylight yet. It was like a call from God."[2] It is hardly surprising, then, that in this conservative state with its reverence for tradition, folks should shudder at the thought of electing a new senator. By excelling at constituent contact and through sheer longevity, Thurmond has personalized the office of U.S. senator to the point where the two seem inseparable. He has become an institution.

It took Strom Thurmond almost fifty years to liberate himself from the limitations of traditional partisan politics. Along the way, he played a pivotal role in the political transformation of the South. Raised a Democrat in the one-party South, young Thurmond developed an early interest in politics, often tagging along with his father to hear rabble-rousing stump speakers in the town squares of Edgefield County. As an ambitious state legislator, Thurmond strongly supported Franklin D. Roosevelt, although like many southern Democrats, he grew impatient with what he considered the more radical aspects of the later New Deal. Thurmond won election as governor in 1946 as a moderately liberal Democrat promoting bureaucratic efficiency and industrial development. As the state's chief executive, he advocated state repeal of the poll tax and moved swiftly in 1947 to use state machinery to apprehend and prosecute a lynch mob.

Not oblivious to the escalating racial tensions in his region, Thurmond and others like him believed the South's myriad of problems to be, at heart, economic. However, unlike organizations such as the Southern Conference for Human Welfare (SCHW) and the Southern Regional Council, which linked economic and racial justice and hoped to achieve both through a combination of labor union organization and black voter registration, Thurmond advocated new industry and economic growth as the key to regional stability. The South, Thurmond argued, had long been held in an unequal, colonial status by the northern economic colossus, and only through economic parity could the region prosper and achieve racial harmony.[3] Soon Thurmond's liberalism, based on a pro-development philosophy, had diverged from the mainstream of the national Democratic Party. The South Carolina governor counted himself among a growing number of disgruntled southern Democrats who felt increasingly uncomfortable within a national party that championed the power of the state to redress grievances and ensure economic and racial justice.

Tensions came to a head in 1948 when, in an unprecedented move, President Harry Truman placed himself squarely behind civil rights legislation. Truman advocated federal protection against lynching, anti–poll tax legislation, the establishment of the permanent Fair Employment Practices Commission (FEPC), and the prohibition of segregation in interstate transportation. For the first time since Reconstruction, the status of African Americans had become a national issue. Many white southerners believed these measures signaled the beginning of an insidious campaign to destroy cherished regional "customs and institutions."

Hoping to stem this progressive tide and recover their former preeminent position within the national party ranks, a group of disgruntled southern Democrats formed the States' Rights Democratic Party and chose Strom Thurmond as their presidential candidate. Although the new party—soon nicknamed the Dixiecrats—was primarily a protest vehicle, it was not intended to be merely symbolic; the goal of the States' Rights Democrats was to upset the election bid of Harry Truman. By capturing the 127 electoral votes of the (historically) Solid South, they felt they could prevent either major party candidate from winning a majority, thus throwing the election into the House of Representatives. In the House the Dixiecrats sought to exact concessions favorable to the South, but this was not to be. The Dixiecrats won only four southern states—South Carolina, Mississippi, Louisiana, and Alabama—and 39 electoral votes. They failed to alter the outcome of the election and the future course of the Democratic Party. Nevertheless, although voters across the South did not rally en masse behind the Dixiecrat banner, the election signified an important moment in southern politics.

When political scientist V. O. Key analyzed southern politics in the late 1940s, the perverse turn-of-the-century political developments and institutions—disfranchisement, malapportionment, one-partyism, and the complex structure of Jim Crow—remained in place. Yet, Key argued, there were growing doubts about the future course of southern politics. The New Deal had sharpened class lines in the region's politics; the depression had dealt a severe blow to the traditional system of plantation agriculture, swelling the stream of black migrants north; and the war had greatly stimulated and diversified the southern economy. Even more important, in the short run, were the emergence of civil rights as an issue in national politics, the identification of the Democratic Party with that issue, and the Dixiecrat revolt of 1948. While Key stressed the importance of the presence of blacks in the South on the development of southern politics, he argued that certain socioeconomic trends would "probably . . . further free [the region] from the effects of the Negro in its politics." Key predicted the formation of a coalition between southern blacks and white southern liberals that would lead to the gradual assimilation of blacks into political life and the eventual triumph over southern conservatism. According to Key and other chroniclers, the forces of racial reaction were on the defensive. The Dixiecrat movement's failure to raise the race issue in a "compelling manner" signified the end of racism as a potent regional political weapon.[4] "Unpleasant as all this was," noted Harry Ashmore, editor of the *Arkansas Gazette,* in the wake of the 1948 election, "the Dixiecrats inadvertently performed a great service for the South by demonstrating that the race issue is no longer a certain ticket to public office for any demagogue who cares to use it."[5]

Later historians of southern politics appropriately identified the important national political implications of the Dixiecrat bolt. The Dixiecrat defection marked the exit of the South from the New Deal coalition and the reorientation of the national party toward its more liberal wing. By breaking with the Democratic Party, the Dixiecrat movement demonstrated to conservative southerners that allegiance to one party was "neither necessary nor beneficial" and thus served as the crossover point for many southern voters in their move from the Democratic to the Republican column. The election of 1948, therefore, marked the beginning, however tentative, of the two-party South and the region's political transition from a Democratic to a Republican stronghold, a process not completed until 1968.[6] These later syntheses are invaluable in identifying a singular moment in a major political transition. They correctly identify an important historic shift in conservative southern political loyalty, yet they ignore completely the very difficult, start-and-stop nature of the *process* of political change. It is tempting to read back into history, to recognize the South's transition from a majority Democratic to a majority Republican region, to note Strom Thurmond's high-profile party switch in 1964, and to draw a straight line back to the Dixiecrats. But from the vantage point of the 1940s, we see only uncertainty and confusion. Furthermore, these works present southern Democrats' disaffection as primarily the result of developments at the national level, giving scant attention to the grassroots activities of African Americans and the white working class. Only by immersing ourselves in the tumultuous events of the New Deal and postwar era can we begin to understand the meaning of the revolt for the people who staged it.

Historian Numan Bartley, in his seminal work on the rise of massive resistance organizations following the Supreme Court's 1954 decision in *Brown v. Board of Education* and in his recent major synthesis of the history of the South since World War II, draws important ideological connections between the Dixiecrats and anti–civil rights organizations in the 1950s. He further emphasizes the failure of the Dixiecrats to commit the South to political independence, thus underlining the persistence of New Deal political divisions in the region.[7] While I do not necessarily dispute Bartley's conclusions, his treatment of the Dixiecrats, situated as they are within large, sweeping narratives, begins in 1948, thus highlighting the "flash-in-the-pan" quality of a political movement whose roots ran deeper and whose impact was more lasting.[8]

The Dixiecrats were a reactionary protest organization comprised of economically conservative, segregationist southern Democrats who sought to reclaim their former prestige and ideological prominence in a party that had moved away from them. As political scientist Alexander Heard stated in his 1952 study of the political South, the Dixiecrats' strength was confined to a sector of the region.[9] The Dixiecrat movement was primarily a revolt of the Black Belt, those counties that contained the region's rich agricultural lands and large-scale plantation agriculture, the heart of the antebellum plantation South and home to the opponents of populism. The Black Belt also included those counties in which blacks outnumbered whites. Not surprisingly, maintenance of white supremacy was the area's primary political concern.[10] Following the defeat of the populists, the Black Belt factions within state governments succeeded in disfranchising black voters, diluting the potency of political dissent from poor whites, and enforcing the region's attachment to the Democratic Party. Two-party competition was anathema to Black Belt whites; it would have meant an appeal to black voters and possibly, as some feared, black rule. The ability of whites in the Black Belt to enforce regional conformity on the race issue in national politics became the South's best protection against federal interference in racial matters.

The maintenance of white supremacy and the threat of federal civil rights legislation to destroy that system was central to the formation and program of the States' Rights Democrats. The southern protest, however, was also a response to mounting agitation for racial and economic democracy at the local level. The Dixiecrats arose from and operated within a rapidly changing socioeconomic milieu stimulated by New Deal legislation and transformations brought on by World War II. Scholars recently have begun to devote more attention to the "generation before the Civil Rights Movement," those white and black southerners who in the 1930s and 1940s, energized by the promise of New Deal liberalism, created new organizations and political alliances to promote social and economic change in the South.[11] But just as economic, social, and political change in the years before *Brown* came too slowly for these groups, it came too quickly for others. For Black Belt elites, maintenance of the racial hierarchy and their own economic privilege—in particular, access to and control over natural resources and domination of a captive, low-wage labor force—were intimately intertwined. For decades following the Civil War, the southern economy had existed in isolation, cut off from the national economic mainstream, free from threats to low local wages and labor discipline.[12] New Deal programs initiated transformations that challenged the economic hegemony and control of the planter and industrial elites. Eager to feed from the rich trough of federal agricultural programs, planters were unwittingly complicit in the breakdown of the plantation system. They often refused to distribute crop reduction payments to sharecroppers and share tenants, thus effectively dislodging them from the plantation system and turning them, to borrow historian Gavin Wright's phrase, "into footloose wage laborers."[13] The war, in turn, created new economic opportunities for these workers no longer tied to the land. Labor shortages in agriculture during the war and into the late 1940s were acute. In addition, war also stirred a new race consciousness among southern blacks that frightened many southern whites.[14]

Agricultural elites were not the only ones disturbed by economic developments of the period. The New Deal's social welfare policies, wages and hours legislation, and protection for labor unions facilitated an alliance of white Black Belt and industrial leaders who shared a common conservative viewpoint.[15] In addition to planters, the Dixiecrats attracted, according to one contemporary source, the "upper crust of mill owners, oil men, . . . bankers [and] lawyers . . . who might have felt more comfortable voting Republican."[16] Thomas Sancton, writing for the *Nation,* noted that "in general the [Dixiecrats] are supported by all the investing and managing communities, from the Southern industrial metropolis to Old Man Johnson's 'furnish' store at the unnamed crossroads."[17] Men like Mississippi Delta planter Walter Sillers, Birmingham corporation lawyer Frank Dixon, Charlotte textile magazine publisher David C. Clark, and Louisiana oil and phosphate tycoon Leander Perez joined hands in common cause in an attempt to block what they termed federal interference into the rights of the states and of property owners.

"Local control"—racial and economic—became the catch phrase of the conservative elite. The Dixiecrats reserved their strongest criticism for the proposed permanent FEPC, which would outlaw discrimination based on race, religion, or national origin. To them, the FEPC violated every concept of the right of employers under the Constitution because it would remove from them decisions regarding hiring and firing and, instead, would dispatch a veritable army of federal agents throughout the South to ensure that blacks were employed in every enterprise. Out on the stump, Dixiecrat supporters regularly distorted the goals of the FEPC, equating fair hiring practices with racial quotas.[18]

In denouncing the FEPC and other civil rights measures, the States' Rights Democrats had begun to articulate a critique of the expanding liberal state increasingly responsive to interest groups such as organized labor and African Americans. Their condemnation of New Deal liberalism gained power when framed in the new and powerful language of Cold War anticommunism. States' Rights leaders warned of the possibility of a "remote, distant, mysterious" government "beyond the comprehension of the people themselves."[19] Presidential candidate Thurmond warned of a "federal police state, directed from Washington, [that] would force life on each hamlet in America to conform to a Washington patter." "American" principles were the right to "local self-government"; failure to fight for states' rights would endanger "the most precious of all human rights—the right to control and govern ourselves at home, the right of life, liberty and the pursuit of happiness."[20] Conflict arose when the institution that had protected those principles—the national Democratic Party—began to threaten them instead. Thurmond and the Dixiecrats represented a reaction to the modern welfare state that over time would reach a broader audience frightened by school desegregation decisions, fair housing laws, and race riots and eventually give rise to the backlash led by George Wallace and to the growth of the Republican Party in the South.

The Dixiecrats' failure in 1948 was in part the result of crippling ironies and internal contradictions that illustrated the difficulties of fomenting political change in a one-party region. The organization encouraged voters to question their traditional political allegiance to the national Democratic Party, yet the Dixiecrats capitalized on and manipulated party regularity, succeeding only in those states where Thurmond and Wright were listed as the regular party nominees. Leaders differed over the organization's goals. Some, like Thurmond, claimed the Dixiecrats were not a third party, insisted they had never left the Democratic Party, and hoped to use the display of Dixiecrat strength as a bargaining chip in determining the future direction of the national party. Others wanted to use the Dixiecrat machinery to create a new third party. Voters who might have supported a new party were understandably wary of the Dixiecrats' confusion and ambivalence. Ideological rifts plagued the party, with some members more comfortable than others with the rough vernacular of white supremacy. Many States' Rights supporters shared Alabama Dixiecrat Marion Rushton's desire for a well rounded and complex conservative agenda that went beyond, although did not abandon, inflammatory race baiting. "The time is gone," Rushton confided to a fellow Dixiecrat, "when we Southerners can quit thinking and simply express ourselves by shouting 'nigger' and singing 'Dixie.'"[21] In addition to these problems, the Dixiecrats suffered from a lack of funding, hasty organization, and what one newspaper called a "poverty of leadership."[22] Indeed, the South Carolina governor abruptly distanced himself from the movement shortly after the polls had closed, abandoning it to its less politically respectable members. A dearth of recognizable leaders possessing regional influence and credibility would remain a vexing obstacle throughout the duration of the States' Rights campaign.

The Dixiecrats failed to capture more states because the New Deal and the war had altered the southern political landscape in new and important ways. White southerners as a whole remained overwhelmingly united in their defense of white supremacy; however, their willingness to remain wedded to the conservative economic agenda of the Black Belt elite had weakened. Workers encouraged by New Deal labor legislation and a generation of white men who served overseas began to see the South and politics in a slightly less parochial light and to view the federal government's role in the economic life of the region in less defensive ways. Campaign rhetoric attempting to arouse the white citizenry and to explain the political crisis exposed Dixiecrats' understanding of political relations as organic. They conceived of political relations in familial ways and privileged patriarchal dominance and control above all. Such a message failed to resonate fully in a region undergoing a profound transformation and in which rival groups had come to see themselves as potential political actors.

The Dixiecrats' significance lay not in their electoral efforts, which, as others have pointed out, were a failure. Although the organization itself was far from unified and, in fact, began to unravel almost at the moment of inception, the movement nevertheless provided an impulse and a precedent. It inaugurated a highly experimental era in which conservative white southerners used the movement's organizational and ideological framework to experiment with new political institutions and new alliances in their desperate attempt to stymie racial progress and preserve power. Despite the 1948 failure, the political repercussions of resistance were significant. The Dixiecrat party broke the Black Belt's historic allegiance to the national Democratic Party. Although some Dixiecrats returned to the Democratic fold, others remained uncomfortable with the party's position on civil rights and chose to be political independents, at least in national electoral contests, in the 1950s. Dixiecrat faithful contributed the early leadership of many local and state citizen councils and served as a stepping stone to the Republican Party.

The Dixiecrats likewise affected state political contests throughout the South. The Dixiecrat campaign legitimized on a fairly grand scale the use of red baiting in combination with race baiting, a technique that was utilized with precision and effect in campaigns in Florida and North Carolina in 1950. Furthermore, historians often have pointed to the defeat of Dixiecrat presidential candidate Thurmond in the 1950 U.S. Senate Democratic primary in South Carolina and the defeat of Alabama Dixiecrats for control of their state party as proof of Dixiecrat weakness. But is that the true meaning of these races? Implicit in this assessment is the confirmation of Key's argument that race was no longer an effective campaign issue. However, these campaigns proved just the opposite; white voters rejected Dixiecrat independence because it did *not* assure effective protection against civil rights legislation, not because they were no longer aroused by the politics of race.[23] In the turbulent 1930s and 1940s, as agitation by black southerners at the grass roots, coupled with Supreme Court decisions and executive orders, threatened to erase or considerably alter the color line in the South, white southerners searched for ways to safeguard the gains of the New Deal and the economic promise of the war years while redrawing the line. The success of many New Deal and moderate legislators in presenting themselves as the most ardent defenders of white supremacy isolated the Dixiecrats and hastened their exit from the Democratic Party.

This book begins in the 1930s with an overview of the socioeconomic changes wrought by the New Deal and World War II and concludes in the immediate aftermath of the Supreme Court's 1954 decision in *Brown v. Board of Education*. Although a major goal of this work is to situate the Dixiecrats within the tumultuous ferment of the New Deal, wartime, and postwar South and to show how the increasingly self-conscious activities of the Black Belt/industrial elite were a direct response to grassroots challenges, those elite and the 1948 campaign are the book's central focus. Because this was a regional movement that operated differently in individual states, comprehensive coverage of grassroots activity is prohibitive. This study intersperses the political narrative and analysis of the national campaign with detailed coverage of the local activity in Mississippi, South Carolina, and Alabama—the flashpoints of the Dixiecrat campaign. The reasons for choosing these particular states are several. First, South Carolina and Mississippi are the home states of the Dixiecrats' presidential and vice-presidential candidates, Governors Thurmond and Fielding L. Wright, and Alabama Dixiecrats were highly influential in directing the campaign and in charting the organization's postelection future. These states also provided the Dixiecrats with their strongest support. South Carolina and Mississippi also had the largest percentage of blacks of all southern states. The story then moves on to the Dixiecrats' postelection prospects, which were exceptionally dim. The organization dissolved rather rapidly during 1949–50, due in no small part to Strom Thurmond's abandonment of it and the success of southern Democrats in Congress to stymie all civil rights legislation, thus depriving the Dixiecrats of their key issue. Although the organization per se did not survive into the 1950s, a nascent southern political independence, a disgruntlement with the national Democratic Party, did; consequently, concern over the protection of states' rights and segregation were major foci in strong Dixiecrat states in 1950 and 1952.

Strom Thurmond, not surprisingly, emerges as a central figure in this political drama. A man of keen political instincts, Thurmond also arose as a peculiar embodiment of the anxiety many white southerners felt in the late 1940s and early 1950s. Thurmond's independent political nature and, of course, his eventual switch to the Republican Party mirrored and anticipated the region's political identity crisis and transformation—in presidential politics—during this period. Thurmond's lone-wolf, almost antiestablishment, political nature meshed well with his personal life. Throughout his political career, Thurmond benefited from his ability to combine political independence and personal virility with a states' rights agenda that had as its bedrock local control over domestic institutions. His career has served as a most interesting guide into the story of southern politics in the 1940s and 1950s.

1

CHALLENGING THE LAWS OF NATURE

The New Deal and Southern Politics

As long as men live some will be in want, and all shall live in some sort of fear. To attempt to provide otherwise will meet with about as much success as an attempt to change the laws of gravitation. It is against nature and cannot be done—not even by the New Deal and its horde of crack-pot professors and communistic theorists.

WALTER SILLERS

Mississippi planter and Speaker of the Mississippi House of Representatives

To the casual observer, life in the broad, flat alluvial plains of Bolivar County in the 1930s seemed to go on pretty much as it had since the first white settlers arrived in the early nineteenth century. In this county where blacks outnumbered whites four to one, cabins once inhabited by black slaves were now filled with black and white sharecroppers and tenants who, lacking effective political voice, found themselves trapped in an economic vice from which they saw few means of escape. But to Walter Sillers, scion of a prominent Bolivar County family, proprietor of several plantations, member of the influential Delta Council, and Mississippi state legislator, the New Deal years were ominous. From his home in tiny Rosedale, Sillers fretted while New Deal Democrats in Washington, D.C., passed legislation protecting the rights of workers to organize and to bargain collectively. Quite used to having a free hand to exploit his laborers as individuals, Sillers now worried that his field hands were "easy prey for the CIO and communist organizations."[1]

Since the turn of the century, southern agricultural and industrial leaders like Walter Sillers had (with some state-by-state variations) succeeded in fashioning a relative lock on a one-party political system that disfranchised black voters and some poor whites, demanded allegiance to white supremacy, and undergirded an economic system that served their interests, which included minimal governmental interference, low wages, and limited social welfare spending.[2] For people such as Sillers and his fellow Mississippi planter Oscar Bledsoe III of Greenwood, the political and economic structure that ensured the rule of white over black merely systematized what was at heart a natural hierarchy. "The inexorable law of eternal fitness," Bledsoe confidentially proclaimed, "produces a top and bottom to everything that no man-made law can reverse."[3] The upheavals of the nation's worst economic crisis, however, initiated a decade of economic experimentation that threatened to disrupt the laws of nature, redefine economic and political relationships in the South, and undermine the iron-fisted control of men such as Sillers and Bledsoe. The Roosevelt administration's New Deal and the accompanying growth of federal power in the 1930s and 1940s threatened the South's ideal of states' rights and limited federal intervention. Although large southern agricultural operatives such as Sillers benefited from New Deal subsidies and from their control of New Deal agencies, conservative southern Democrats viewed warily the potential of New Deal programs to threaten the region's economic dependence on cheap labor while stirring the democratic ambitions of the disfranchised and undermining white supremacy. The New Deal, as one historian has noted, changed forever the relationship between southerners—both white and black—and the state.[4]

The Great Depression and the New Deal inaugurated a new era in the South's economic and political life. National focus on the South's economic rejuvenation sparked a contentious dialogue concerning the best route to lift the South out of poverty. The innovative ferment spawned by New Dealers in Washington who spoke of economic justice and parity between regions inspired southern liberals desperate to change the region's economic and political backwardness while it inflamed and threw on the defensive conservative southern leaders who believed that the region's economic salvation lay in the traditional cure of low wages to attract new industry.[5] At the national level, New Deal programs that spoke to the needs of the working classes and alleviated the misery of the poor and black drew new and powerful voting constituencies to the Democratic Party that changed the face of national politics. The creation of the Congress of Industrial Organizations (CIO) in 1935 and the prominence of organized labor and northern blacks in the New Deal coalition following the 1936 election signaled to white southern Democrats that their former position of dominance within the national party was threatened.

The 1930s delivered a wake-up call to traditional southern elites as they faced political challenges at the state and national levels. The magnitude of the economic crisis and the impact—sometimes positive, sometimes negative, sometimes merely symbolic—of New Deal programs on southern communities opened the door for liberal candidates who eschewed traditional appeals to racism for platforms focused on economic issues. Working-class white voters, buoyed by a president and a national agenda that spoke to their particular needs, found their voices and exercised their political muscle, while other white liberals reached across the color line to dedicate themselves to dismantling barriers to voting. Although no New Deal programs directly addressed the particular needs of black southerners, they nevertheless took strength and hope from New Deal liberalism and radical working-class activism and stepped up their participation in civil rights organizations, as well as Socialist- and Communist-led labor unions. These local challenges, as well as struggles over the direction of national policy, threw southern industrial and agricultural elites on the defensive in many political contests throughout the decade. Neither side could declare political victory during the New Deal years; rather, the decade marked the opening salvos in a long battle for economic and political control of the South.

★

The first fissures between the South and the national Democratic Party appeared amidst the exigencies created by the Great Depression. For three years the American people rode a downward economic spiral that by 1932 left them exhausted and desperate. During that time Americans saw personal incomes cut in half. Unemployment skyrocketed from 1.6 million in 1929 to 12.8 million in 1933, from 3 percent to 25 percent of the labor force. Farmers, already in trouble when the depression hit, faced catastrophe as commodity prices were cut in half. More than 9,000 banks closed during the period, factories and mines shut down, entire towns were abandoned, and thousands of farms were sold for debt.[6]

Compared to other regions, the South had always wallowed in poverty, and when the depression struck, it was already prostrate and suffering. A predominantly rural region, the South by 1929 was crippled by the ravages of a prolonged agricultural depression and a series of natural disasters.[7] The depression only compounded the privation endemic to the region's outdated tenant farming system. During the 1930s approximately one-quarter of all southerners and one-half of all southern farmers were tenants and sharecroppers. The depression hit them the hardest. Hurt by low commodity prices as farm income fell by half, many landlords discontinued the sharecrop furnish system, displacing hundreds of thousands of tenants and swelling the ranks of the landless.[8] Southern industry did not fare much better. During the first four years of the depression, southern manufacturing fell by 50 percent in Atlanta and New Orleans and by more than 70 percent in Birmingham, far surpassing a national manufacturing decline of one-third. Unemployment in the South exceeded the national average and overwhelmed local relief agencies.[9]

Even in relatively flush times, rural southerners suffered a poverty that was pervasive and intractable. Their personal possessions few, most lived in squalor, scratching out a meager existence in cramped, cheaply made cabins that often lacked plumbing or adequate sanitation. But the extra burdens of the depression took their toll on an already worn-out region. Mississippi congressman Frank Smith later recalled that "people were bowed low" from the privations of the depression.[10] A state report on Sumter County, South Carolina, noted that nearly 1,500 families were unemployed, hungry, and practically naked.[11] In Columbia in 1932, officials discovered some one hundred persons living at the city garbage dump.[12] Federal relief officials in the Deep South noted that approximately one-fifth of their rural clients had never owned a mattress until given one by the federal government. In addition, southern tenant families survived on an inadequate diet that rarely included fresh meat, vegetables, or fruit, and they were plagued by the diseases of the impoverished: malaria, rickets, pellagra, and hookworm.[13]

The inability or unwillingness of the federal government to act only intensified these desperate conditions. President Herbert Hoover, while more of an activist than his predecessor, was paralyzed by his personal "bootstraps" philosophy. Operating under the principle that the economy was basically sound, Hoover prescribed a hefty dose of confidence. In speech after speech he exhorted the public to keep up hope and asked businessmen to keep mills and shops open, maintain wage levels, and spread the work to avoid layoffs. In return union leaders agreed to refrain from wage demands and strikes.[14] However, as one historian has noted, "individual self-reliance, a cultural bedrock, proved to be completely ineffectual in countering personal misfortune."[15]

Clearly, by the fall of 1932 the economy was not going to cure itself; moreover, Herbert Hoover was not going to take control. Anyone, it has been argued, could have beaten Hoover in 1932. Not just anyone did, however. New York governor Franklin Delano Roosevelt, born in New York in 1882, the only child of a wealthy patrician father and an imperious mother, and a distant cousin of Theodore Roosevelt, had the advantage of a superior education at prestigious Groton School and Harvard University, followed by a stint at Columbia Law School. While Roosevelt's campaign program was vague, voters were drawn by his irrepressible confidence. Although Roosevelt had a genuine concern for the welfare of the less fortunate—the patrician's sense of noblesse oblige—he was also a shrewd judge of human nature. Roosevelt had a sure feeling for public opinion, and he won a landslide victory against Hoover. With the exception of William Howard Taft in 1912, no Republican candidate had ever been so thoroughly defeated.[16]

Franklin Roosevelt's relationship with the South had not always exhibited the prickly quality it assumed in the latter years of his administration. The South early provided him with physical and spiritual succor as well as crucial political support. Roosevelt possessed a strong personal affinity for the region and considered Georgia his adopted state. Venturing south in the mid-1920s in search of therapeutic relief for his polio-stricken legs, Roosevelt made his way to the healing waters of Warm Springs, Georgia, where he eventually acquired a farm. Warm Springs provided a welcome respite from the harried pace of Washington. The president took quickly to the Georgian countryside, his patrician upbringing not unlike that of the traditional southern squirearchy.[17]

More crucial than his appreciation for the finer qualities of southern living was Roosevelt's understanding of the importance of the South within the national Democratic Party, and he knew he needed southern support to win the presidency in 1932. National party rules gave southern Democrats virtual veto power over the party's nominee. Roosevelt also hoped to avoid the debacle of four years earlier, when five traditionally Democratic states, unable to stomach Al Smith's candidacy, had bolted the party. Seeking to avoid another split, Roosevelt worked to build a solid relationship with the region. Southern political leaders were impressed by Roosevelt, especially by his apparent desire to forge regional alliances, to mend sectional differences, and to focus on economic as opposed to social and cultural issues. With a few exceptions—U.S. Senators Huey P. Long of Louisiana and Hugo Black of Alabama, for example—traditional conservatives dominated the southern political landscape in 1932. The pragmatic and philosophically elusive Roosevelt could look forward to working with such conservative stalwarts as Mississippi's Pat

Harrison and Georgia's Walter George as well as the demagogic Ellison Durant "Cotton Ed" Smith of South Carolina, men not given to radical experimentation and who had no interest in disrupting regional power relationships.[18]

Roosevelt's attempts to address and alleviate the national economic crisis came closer than any other federal program since Reconstruction to undermining traditional social, economic, racial, and political relations in the South. Ultimately, the New Deal failed to achieve economic recovery. Though it never realized its primary objective (and even, in the case of agricultural workers, further undermined their already precarious hold on life), the New Deal initiated changes in the South's economic and social structure that by the 1980s would render the region almost unrecognizable. Southern politicians provided minimal input into New Deal administrative policy. Although southern Democrats held a powerful lock on Congress, no southerner occupied an influential position within Roosevelt's inner circle. Likewise, no southerners participated in the Brain Trust, Roosevelt's informal group of advisors drawn primarily from academia. The Cabinet included three southerners, but their influence on the development of New Deal policy was limited.[19] Nevertheless, Roosevelt enjoyed relatively strong southern congressional support through the first New Deal. Dixie Democrats held key committee chairmanships in addition to the positions of Senate majority leader and Speaker of the House during the Roosevelt years. Southerners, therefore, were responsible, through 1936, for pushing through New Deal legislation.[20] While a conservative coalition operated throughout the New Deal, generally speaking, committee chairmen cooperated with the administration.[21]

Southerners supported the president, in part, out of party loyalty but also because their destitute region needed federal relief. One historian has noted that to the vast numbers of southern families on relief, the New Deal "represented a giant, nationwide cornucopia" from which desperately needed federal aid poured.[22] A July 1933 survey conducted by the Federal Emergency Relief Agency revealed that in a seventy-county area, some 37,000 of 250,000 families (or approximately 15 percent) received federal aid.[23] By the end of the decade, New Deal relief programs had distributed nearly $2 billion in aid in the South.[24] While these measures certainly did not end the depression, Frank Smith recalled that they relieved "the sharp pockets of poverty" in small communities in the impoverished Mississippi Delta. In his hometown of Greenwood, Smith remembered that "relief from summer dust came for the first time in the hundred years of the town's existence when the WPA [Works Progress Administration] blacktopped the two main streets."[25]

Southern conservatives supported early New Deal programs because they could control them and because they personally benefited from them. Although prominent southerners were conspicuously absent from FDR's Brain Trust, southern planters and their allies occupied prominent and powerful positions in the agency established by the Agricultural Adjustment Act (AAA). Oscar Goodbar Johnston, president of the Delta and Pine Land Company, a 43,000-acre cotton plantation—the South's largest—served as comptroller for the agency and determined federal agricultural policy in the South.[26] AAA policy assisted the large planter. W. M. Garrard of the Staple Cotton Cooperative Association years later declared that the planter had "profited more under the Triple A than he has ever profited in all the years before its establishment."[27] Tenants and sharecroppers, on the other hand, suffered from the AAA's cotton reduction program because they were tossed off the land as cotton farmers cut back cultivation by 30 percent between 1932 and 1933. The full extent of tenant displacement became clear when the 1940 census revealed 192,000 fewer black and 150,000 fewer white tenants than in 1930.[28] This steady stream would become a flood by World War II, and this exodus, along with increased mechanization and depressed commodity prices, would lead to the eventual breakdown of the South's plantation system.[29]

Southern manufacturers were less successful than planters in monopolizing and controlling federal policy. FDR's plan for economic recovery, the National Industrial Recovery Act, granted industries the power to set prices and determine production levels; however, manufacturers had to adhere to a code of fair competition that included stipulations for a minimum wage and maximum hours as well as guaranteed protection of workers' right to organize unions. Despite these gains for workers, southern manufacturers won compromises on National Recovery Administration (NRA) codes that permitted regional wage differentials and allowed them to reclassify jobs to ensure segregation and racial pay scales. Determined to resist any further gains by workers, southern industrialists organized themselves into the Southern States Industrial Council (SSIC) in December 1933. The SSIC pledged to defend the region's discriminatory wage rates. Only by maintaining lower wages in relation to northern workers, the SSIC contended, could the South remain economically competitive.[30] Although they were able to bend the NRA somewhat to their will, southern industrialists nevertheless failed to thwart wages and hours legislation and the Wagner Act passed during the second New Deal.

During Roosevelt's first term, his programs and his personal charisma inspired massive support. The president's travels and speeches, his twice-weekly press conferences, and his "fireside chats" over the radio generated vitality and warmth from a once-remote White House. Indeed, Roosevelt's accessibility and ability to instill confidence in the country were two of his more powerful and enduring qualities. In turn, criticism of the New Deal during 1933 was muted or reduced to helpless carping.

The president's charisma and the New Deal initiatives slowly began to change the South's political landscape. Roosevelt gave new hope to the region's industrial workers through wages and hours legislation and collective bargaining provisions and inspired a generation of southern activists committed to social justice.[31] The decade's economic crisis and the radical reorientation of the federal government toward class issues awoke a slumbering grassroots populism and stoked the fires of political opposition within the Deep South. South Carolina millworkers let their votes do the talking by electing former mill hand Olin D. Johnston to the governor's mansion in 1934, and in 1936 they supported Johnston's efforts to elect a state legislature more responsive to liberal economic reforms.[32] Friends of organized labor gained control of the Birmingham City Commission in 1933, and the support of Alabama labor helped elected Luther Patrick to the U.S. Congress in 1936 despite a nasty campaign in which Patrick was accused of supporting racial equality and radicalism.[33] Alabama governor Bibb Graves, who defeated Birmingham attorney (and future Dixiecrat leader) Frank Dixon in 1934, became that state's New Deal advocate. In labor disputes Graves often came down on the side of organized labor. He established a new state Department of Labor in 1935 that proved more worker friendly than anything that had preceded it. When workers struck at Talladega in 1936 and at Huntsville in 1937, Graves stood by labor. In Georgia voters replaced the reactionary racist Eugene Talmadge with E. D. Rivers in 1936. Rivers went on to launch a "Little New Deal" for his state.[34] In Mississippi white voters elected the disgraced governor and "redneck liberal" Theodore Bilbo to the U.S. Senate. Bilbo ran on a platform that appealed to farmers and laborers, calling for the redistribution of wealth and unemployment insurance. He ran against the colorless and ailing incumbent Senator Hubert Stephens, who was perceived as only lukewarm toward the New Deal. If elected to the Senate, Bilbo promised to "raise more hell than Huey Long."[35]

In addition to creating the conditions that encouraged challenges to existing political and economic relations between whites, New Deal programs also began to undermine relations between blacks and whites. Although planters readily welcomed AAA subsidies, federal relief officials found that landowners and employers of agricultural labor greeted the prospect of federal relief with ambivalence and hostility. The depression had begun to break down the tenancy system, within which landlords employed agricultural workers and supported them during the off-season. During the depression many farmers welcomed government relief as a means of supporting the destitute. But at the same time, landowners complained that relief had a "demoralizing" effect on workers. They also feared that relief would create a labor shortage, which in turn would hamper their ability to keep cheap, seasonal labor tied to the land. They wanted government relief cut off at harvesting time, and the evidence suggests that Federal Emergency Relief Act (FERA) and WPA officials regularly dismissed clients from the rolls when low-wage cotton-picking jobs became available.[36]

White landowners were particularly critical of relief for African Americans. FERA investigator Lorena Hickok reported that most landlords wanted public works programs discontinued to prevent blacks from leaving the farms to seek relief work. One irate South Carolina farmer complained that "this CWA wage is buzzing in our Niggers' heads."[37] According to Hickok, whites in Savannah, Georgia, feared that the availability of federal relief would encourage a flood of African Americans to move from the countryside to the city, which would create a serious social problem. The racist attitudes of local administrators also hampered the ability of New Deal relief programs to alleviate poverty. Often state officials were reluctant to extend adequate relief, and some operated under the impression that relief was given disproportionately to African Americans. One federal reemployment director in the South told Hickok, " 'Any nigger who gets over $8 a week is a spoiled nigger, that's all.' "[38]

Nationally, despite discrimination, African Americans were overrepresented in proportion to the population in terms of receiving federal aid. In January 1935 one-quarter of all black families were on relief. They received greater proportions of aid because they faced greater poverty. The need far exceeded the receipt, however. More than half of the nation's 12 million blacks lived in rural areas during the 1930s, but fewer than 20 percent of black farmers owned the land they worked. Most were employed as tenants and wage hands with yearly incomes of less than $200.[39]

Under the AAA, tenant farmers rarely received an equitable portion of the benefit payment. Furthermore, the AAA agency adopted policies that encouraged evictions. Letters written to Roosevelt by desperate rural blacks document the abuse they received at the hands of relief officials and white landowners. Most of these letters were written anonymously for fear that physical harm or death would come to the authors should anyone discover they had written. Writing to President Roosevelt in 1935, a Reidsville, Georgia, resident reported, "the releaf officials here . . . give us black folks, each one, nothing but a few cans of pickle meet and to the white folks they give blankets, bolts of cloth and things like that."[40]

An increase in racial violence during the depression years compounded the misery of southern blacks. While the number of lynchings had declined since 1926, the depression years marked a significant reversal of this trend. Lynchings of 28 blacks were reported in 1932, 28 in 1933, 15 in 1934, and 20 in 1935.[41] The National Association for the Advancement of Colored People (NAACP) responded by stepping up the pressure for federal legislation against lynching. Numerous bills were introduced throughout the 1930s but were killed in every case by recalcitrant and filibustering southern senators. Interestingly, public opinion surveys found that 57 percent of all southerners polled favored the legislation.[42] Throughout the 1930s Roosevelt remained publicly mute on the subject, fearing southern opposition to New Deal legislation. "The Southerners by reason of the seniority rule in Congress are chairmen or occupy strategic places on most of the Senate and House committees," Roosevelt explained to NAACP national secretary Walter White. "If I come out for the anti-lynching bill now, they will block every bill I ask Congress to pass to keep America from collapsing. I just can't take that risk."[43]

African Americans naturally hoped that the programs of the New Deal would be constructed in such a way as to assist their recovery. Despite its deficiencies, however, the New Deal offered blacks more in material benefits and recognition than had any set of programs since Reconstruction. Consequently, many blacks began to vote for the Democratic Party for the first time in 1936. This was not evidence that the Roosevelt administration fulfilled the promise of its egalitarian rhetoric; rather, it reveals, more accurately, that blacks had come to expect little from governments in Washington or elsewhere and recognized that the New Deal, with all its shortcomings, was better than the Republican alternative.[44]

Despite Roosevelt's reluctance to publicly commit himself to civil rights legislation, and despite the fact that many New Deal programs in practice discriminated against African Americans, the mere fact that the programs existed and that they brought relief to even a portion of the impoverished southern black community was significant. FDR and his New Deal programs raised blacks' expectations, prompting them to participate in greater numbers in civil rights organizations.[45] Although the agenda of the 1930s NAACP would pale in comparison with the more militant tactics of the later civil rights organizations, it is important to keep in mind the challenges faced by rural black southerners during this time. In the rural areas, where most blacks lived, as one historian has noted, "only the very brave and the very foolhardy raised their voices or put their heads above the parapet."[46]

But many did raise their voices. Although the depression initially depleted membership in local NAACP branches, members slowly trickled back. During the 1930s southern branches of the NAACP grew faster than those in any other section.[47] Membership in southern branches hovered around 18,000 by the end of the decade, and by the end of World War II it had multiplied to 156,000.[48] As economic conditions improved in Louisiana, for example, dormant branches in New Orleans, Monroe, Lake Charles, and Shreveport struggled back to life.[49] Throughout the South, local NAACP branches joined together in statewide conferences that in turn fed into the national organization. NAACP special counsel Charles Houston helped rebuild the Texas organization, which ultimately won its fight to overturn that state's white primary. In South Carolina, plumber Levi Byrd from tiny Cheraw worked to link the eight hundred NAACP members in eight operating branches into the South Carolina State Conference of Branches in 1939.[50]

The creation of the CIO in 1935 and the surge of labor militancy and union organizing throughout the South reinvigorated heretofore moribund civil rights organizations, particularly in Louisiana.[51] In New Orleans both the CIO's International Longshoremen's and Warehousemen's Union and the Transport Workers Union organized strikes of black and white workers. Although ultimately only the transport workers' strike succeeded, both labor actions nevertheless alarmed city officials and state leaders. The Transport Workers Union, with a prominent Communist presence, attempted to organize white and black farmers into the Louisiana Farmers Union in 1936. Resistance was fierce; white landlords and merchants beat black organizers mercilessly.[52] One local planter told white organizer Gordon McIntire, "We don't want people interfering with our niggers. We won't have it. You keep out of here. We take care of them when they're sick and bury them when they're dead. . . . We don't mind burying societies but we won't have a union. You all let the niggers alone." McIntire was told to "get out of this parish . . . before nightfall."[53] Labor militancy filtered down to the city's NAACP branch. During the 1930s the leadership of the local branch passed from the old black professional class to a group of Young Turks from the middle and working classes who had a closer relationship with the black masses.[54]

A smaller contingent of black southerners braved extreme police and vigilante repression and joined radical organizations. The Communist Party-USA moved South in 1930 and set up headquarters in Birmingham, where party organizers hoped to find adherents among that industrial city's dispossessed. By the end of 1933 the party could boast some five hundred dues-paying members in the city.[55] In 1938 Birmingham Communists organized the Right to Vote Club, a voter education organization. The club was short lived, however, lasting only until 1940.[56] Although the Communist-backed candidates for the Alabama state senate and house were badly beaten in 1938, Alabama Communists heralded the victories of liberal congressman Luther Patrick and Senator Lister Hill, establishing in the minds of southern conservatives the specter of formidable radical foes. Although the Communist Party in Alabama would ultimately undermine its own popularity among black supporters by its participation in popular front politics of the mid- to late 1930s, such divisions were irrelevant to white conservatives. The mere presence of radical forces was enough to cause consternation among agricultural and industrial elites.[57]

Communist organizers realized greater success among the rural poor in the cotton belt, organizing the Share Cropper's Union in 1931 in Alabama's Tallapoosa County and gaining some 6,000 adherents in the Black Belt counties of Lowndes, Macon, Montgomery, and Dallas. By 1935 the union's membership topped 10,000.[58] A 1935 strike targeted some thirty-five plantations in seven Black Belt counties. Strikers won most of their demands in three counties, but elsewhere violence broke the will of the strikers. Union members were arrested and flogged; some of those arrested were turned over to angry mobs. Some simply disappeared.[59]

Emboldened by the near-annihilation of the Republican Party as a national force in the 1934 elections and by what appeared to be a mandate for the New Deal, yet clearly irritated by the fanciful yet seductive programs and panaceas to redistribute wealth and stimulate demand advocated by a number of grassroots messiahs, Roosevelt shifted the emphasis of the New Deal to programs that favored the "forgotten man" over the interests of big business.[60] Most, although not all, commentators have noted a distinct "shift to the left" in the second spate of legislation, conveniently referred to as the second New Deal. Beginning in 1935 the Roosevelt administration promoted a more forceful government intervention into the marketplace to protect the interests of the public. The result was an avalanche of legislation aimed at long-term reform: the WPA, a work relief program that surpassed its predecessors; the Social Security Act; the National Labor Relations Act; the Public Utilities Holding Company Act; the Banking Act of 1935; and the Wealth Tax Act, to name just a few. Most southern congressmen supported these new measures, and Roosevelt carried the South in the 1936 election.[61] Throughout the 1930s Roosevelt enjoyed more popularity in the South than in any other region of the country, and this support thwarted any concerted effort by potential detractors.[62] Yet congressional opposition, disorganized though it may have been, did exist from the early days of Roosevelt's administration. Conservative congressmen balanced the demands of their constituents for New Deal relief and their personal political philosophies, which championed balanced budgets and states' rights.

Conservative opposition emanated primarily from the senatorial trio of Carter Glass and Harry F. Byrd of Virginia and Josiah W. Bailey of North Carolina. Glass was an early and vigorous critic of the New Deal. A Wilsonian progressive, Glass championed the concept of a free but responsible individual and believed the welfare state threatened individual culpability. The state should simply protect the conditions of fair play and equal opportunity, he argued, and the New Deal came menacingly close to social and economic planning. Afraid that the New Deal unfairly hampered southern industry, Glass referred to the NRA Blue Eagle as a "bird of prey" that was "creating a reign of terror among thousands of struggling, small industries."[63] Bailey's conservatism dictated that he oppose both the AAA and the NRA, yet he was not above reaping political capital from the New Deal. In 1936 Bailey took credit for placing 4,000 North Carolinians in government jobs.[64] Byrd, like fellow Virginian Glass, feared increased governmental centralization and the threat the New Deal posed to states' rights and constitutional government.[65] Regularly joining Glass, Byrd, and Bailey in their opposition to New Deal legislation were southern senators Walter George of Georgia, Cotton Ed Smith and James F. Byrnes of South Carolina, and Pat Harrison of Mississippi.[66] These New Deal opponents recognized the potential relationship between New Deal reforms and civil rights, yet as long as Roosevelt made no overt moves toward supporting civil rights, they made no effort to break with the party.[67] Though some southern Democrats opposed the New Deal, even its most vocal critics preferred to remain with the party rather than encourage coalitions with Republicans.[68] Furthermore, as one historian has stated, "Until 1936 to oppose Roosevelt was to court political suicide."[69]

The changes in the Democratic Party's core constituency after 1936 disturbed conservatives more than the shifting emphasis of the second New Deal.[70] In 1936 the Democratic National Convention abolished the two-thirds rule in nominating conventions, a significant blow to southern power. This rule had been exploited successfully by the solid southern Democratic bloc in previous nominating conventions as leverage for acquiring a pro-southern presidential or vice-presidential candidate. With only a simple majority required, approval of the South became less crucial.[71] The founding of the CIO in the fall of 1935 signaled the emergence of organized labor as a serious political force, and industrial areas racked up huge majorities for the president.[72]

"The 1936 election," one scholar of the era has observed, "transformed the nation's political landscape."[73] The prominence of African Americans and organized labor in the New Deal coalition by 1936 only amplified the South's insecurity and defensiveness within a party quickly becoming overwhelmingly northern and urban. While Roosevelt did not intend to use his position to further the cause of civil rights, he could no longer ignore black voters. Roosevelt received 75 percent of the black vote in 1936, an amazing turnabout from the 1928 election, when the Democratic candidate had received no more than 25 percent.[74] The party's new composition and the South's diminishing importance threatened the region's racial status quo.

African American leaders frequently criticized Roosevelt for his lack of support for anti–poll tax and antilynching legislation (no civil rights legislation was passed during Roosevelt's twelve years in the White House) and for the deleterious effect some New Deal legislation had on black farm laborers. Still, New Deal relief programs had mitigated some of the harsher aspects of racial discrimination.[75] Their inclusion in New Deal relief and work programs prompted black voters to cast their lot with Roosevelt and the Democratic Party in 1936. A record number of black voters in South Carolina turned out to support the president in the 1936 general election, although the total number was still minuscule. In the upstate textile city of Greenville in 1939, several black civil rights organizations, the WPA's Workers Alliance, and numerous black clergy staged a voter registration campaign. Rallies in May and June drew significant crowds, and by June 1939 the number of blacks registered to vote had ballooned from 35 in late 1938 to 324. The local newspaper reported that some 900 blacks had registered to vote, and the Ku Klux Klan and local law enforcement threatened, harassed, and abused black voters and their white allies, arresting them on bogus charges and invading their homes. The repression worked; only 54 black voters and a record number of white voters cast ballots in the municipal election.[76]

In 1937 the informal conservative coalition in Congress achieved its greatest cohesiveness, angered and spurred on by Roosevelt's willingness to tamper with the Supreme Court and to interfere in local southern primary elections. Roosevelt's court-packing scheme threw conservatives together. Stymied and frustrated by a Supreme Court that for the preceding two years had invalidated New Deal measures, Roosevelt proposed to "reform" the court, no doubt in an effort to make it more amenable to New Deal legislation. His plan called for the creation of approximately fifty new federal judgeships, including six Supreme Court justices. Roosevelt had handed the perfect issue to his opponents, and Republicans deferred to their southern colleagues, who took up the cudgel to defeat the plan.[77]

Determined to overcome his setback in the court reform program and frustrated by the opposition of some conservative Democrats to recent New Deal legislation, Roosevelt moved to foster what he considered a nascent southern liberal bloc by undertaking a "purge" of conservative southern Democrats.[78] FDR's bold and profound move to wrench open the political process in the South constituted an important departure for the man who prior to 1936 had shied away from challenging white supremacy.[79] To strengthen the administration's hand, Clark Foreman, head of the Public Works Administration's power division, suggested the publication of a pamphlet detailing New Deal accomplishments in the South, which would shore up the administration's political support in the region.[80] The Roosevelt administration released the *Report on Economic Conditions of the South,* which described vividly the South's colonial relationship to northern industry, the devastating conditions of its agricultural economy, and the negative effects of its reactionary politics on the region's development. While virtually all southern leaders endorsed some of the report's specific proposals, most responded angrily and defensively. White southerners denounced it as a slur on the entire region.[81]

Roosevelt's attempts to unseat southern senators Walter George of Georgia and Cotton Ed Smith of South Carolina failed miserably. Their elections were a setback for the administration as the Democratic margin in the House fell from 229 to 93 and in the Senate from 56 to 42. With their impressive gains in 1938, Republicans were no longer interested in a coalition with disaffected Democrats. Although conservative southern Democrats often united informally with individual Republicans, any chance for some sort of party realignment along conservative/liberal lines was no longer a possibility.[82] Despite the debacles in Georgia and South Carolina, Roosevelt did enjoy some victories in the South in 1938. Alabama voters promoted New Deal congressman Lister Hill to the U.S. Senate to replace the seat vacated by liberal Hugo Black. The *Birmingham News* called Hill's election over his politically moribund challenger Thomas Heflin a victory "for the New Deal, Rooseveltism, Democracy, and the WPA."[83] In Florida voters sent liberal Claude Pepper to the Senate for his first term.[84] Still, by the end the decade, as demonstrated in the victories of conservatives George and Smith, the New Deal was beginning to show signs of age, losing steam and support, and southern voters were demonstrating the limits of their adherence to the Roosevelt agenda.

Although the *Report on Economic Conditions of the South* failed to sway white southern voters to dislodge Roosevelt's conservative opponents, it served as an impetus for the growth of grassroots political activism in the South. It inspired the formation of the SCHW in 1938 in Birmingham, an organization pledged to empowering and uplifting the region's poor, to democratizing the southern electoral process by eliminating the poll tax, and ultimately, to liberalizing the Democratic Party.[85] The SCHW attracted leading southern liberals, including University of North Carolina president Frank Porter Graham, Herman C. Nixon, and Clark Foreman, as well as more moderate southern Democrats. It also counted Communists among its members and forged close ties with the CIO. The SCHW in many ways constituted liberals' best hope and most comprehensive grassroots effort toward regional political and economic transformation.[86] Southern industrialists and right-wing organizations viciously attacked the organization, alleging that it was dominated by Communists and intent on destroying southern institutions, an accusation that would gain power as the war years drew to a close.[87]

Though relations between southern Democrats and Roosevelt grew steadily worse throughout the 1930s, on most issues white southerners continued to support the president, albeit with much variation. Only on the issue of race did southerners remain solid—not that there was ample opportunity to test this solidarity, for direct threats to the South's racial arrangement remained minimal. Despite the threats that federal initiatives posed to local southern power brokers, defections from the national party remained only threats. The South's desperate need for aid, Roosevelt's immense popularity among southern voters, and the region's formidable position within, and traditional loyalty to, the Democratic Party thwarted any organized political defection. Southern opposition to Roosevelt and the New Deal remained diffuse so long as Roosevelt's policies focused on alleviating economic distress and promoting economic recovery and not in disrupting southern race relations. Despite the growing political influence of African Americans and organized labor within the New Deal coalition after 1936, institutional barriers to racial equality remained in place in the 1930s. Unwilling to risk southern congressional opposition to New Deal programs, Roosevelt remained ambivalent toward civil rights.[88] But federal programs that initiated the dismantling of the plantation system, and discussions about economic justice that targeted the South and encouraged interracial coalitions, began slowly chipping away the foundations of southern society, foundations that would begin to crumble with the demands of wartime.

DRAWING THE COLOR LINE

World War II, Race, and the South's Political Crucible

History has taught us that we must keep our white Democratic primaries pure and unadulterated events. . . . White supremacy will be maintained in our primaries. Let the chips fall where they may.

SOUTH CAROLINA GOVERNOR OLIN D. JOHNSTON
addressing both houses of the South Carolina General Assembly, April 14, 1944

I'm a black man in South Carolina and I'm sure that there will be people who will read carefully what I've said today. . . . We serve notice upon South Carolina's demagogic, mediocre politicians . . . that threats to violence will invoke immediate court action — both state and nation.

OSCEOLA E. MCKAINE
addressing the Progressive Democratic Party state convention in Columbia, South Carolina, May 24, 1944

Reflecting on the transformation of twentieth-century southern politics from his home in northern Alabama in the 1980s, former congressman Carl Elliott pointed to the tumultuous years of World War II as an important crossroads in the South's political history. "Few of even the most liberal southern politicians took a stand on the issue of race in the first half of this century, because there was no issue on which to stand," Elliott observed. The disruptions of wartime, however, pushed racial issues to the forefront. "In the 1940s," Elliott recalled, "the line was just beginning to be drawn."[1] The potential for discord between the Black Belt South and the Democratic Party that originated during the New Deal mushroomed into full-fledged conflict during and immediately after World War II.[2]

The war unleashed forces that ultimately spun out of control, sometimes with dreadful consequences. Unstable boomtown conditions, rural labor shortages and migration, and renewed efforts by black southerners demanding economic and political justice threatened to tear the South apart. Interracial organizations founded during the New Deal years, such as the SCHW, expanded their reach across the South, building coalitions with organized labor in an attempt to democratize the southern political process. Whites intent on maintaining the color line met their efforts every step of the way with renewed violence and intimidation. The war had a transforming effect on many of the southern men who fought it, and a legion of southern veterans—black and white—returned to the South ready to continue the battle, sometimes together, but more often on opposite sides. White veterans vowed to rid their communities of corrupt political machines, to bring to southern politics the freedoms for which many of their comrades had paid dearly, and to usher in an era of modernization and development that had long eluded their region. More often than not, their definition of modernization did not include racial equality. The South convulsed as it tried to absorb the economic changes wrought by the war while maintaining some semblance of racial and political stability.

The conditions on the homefront during and immediately after World War II precipitated a decade of political turmoil that constituted an important turning point for conservative white southerners within the Democratic Party. Black Belt planters complained of labor shortages and feared loss of labor control as farmworkers, dispossessed by inequities in New Deal agriculture programs, left the plantation regions in droves to seek economic opportunities spawned by the new war industries. A renewed militancy among southern blacks emboldened by the rhetoric of the war and by their participation in the struggle for democracy, the increased voting strength of northern blacks, and a wave of racial violence that rolled across the nation during the war years and after made national accommodation to southern sensibilities increasingly difficult. The combination of Supreme Court decisions and executive orders, working in tandem with grassroots efforts, once again threw southern conservatives on the defensive.

The magnitude of the crises that rocked the domestic arena during the fifteen or so years of the Roosevelt and Truman administrations dramatically altered the role and responsibilities of the federal government and changed the face of domestic politics. Whereas Roosevelt had been willing and able to sacrifice support for civil rights for southern congressional votes during the economic crises of the 1930s, the increased political power of African Americans, the unremitting racial violence that marred the war years, and the tireless efforts of civil rights organizations to publicize these injustices spilled into the postwar era, making this previous compromise untenable. Responding to raw political realities, wartime necessity, and senseless violence, Roosevelt and Truman, acting independently of Congress, took preliminary steps toward ensuring racial and economic justice by creating the FEPC and the President's Committee on Civil Rights (PCCR). As the focus on justice moved from the economic to the racial battleground, the line Carl Elliott mentioned became more deeply etched into the regional political landscape, and southern New Deal politicians found themselves having to shore up their white supremacy credentials in the face of mounting attacks from conservatives. The postwar political arena became increasingly chaotic as liberals and moderates struggled with conservatives to determine the war's legacy for the South.

★

The war and the subsequent preparedness program brought the economic recovery that had always eluded the New Deal.[3] The South benefited materially from this program, which fostered both industrialization and urbanization. The region gorged itself on defense contracts; new shipbuilding, aircraft, and munitions plants dotted the landscape, increasing the South's industrial capacity by approximately 40 percent. Although many of these industries were not sustainable in, or applicable to, peacetime production, the degree of growth nevertheless was unprecedented. The number of manufacturing establishments grew by 20,000, jobs for production workers more than doubled, and the average worker saw a yearly salary increase of 40 percent. After reconversion, the South retained about half the wartime addition to its factory force.[4] Even Mississippi, the least industrialized of all southern states with a state government traditionally hostile to industry, created seven hundred new industrial plants during the war.[5]

Rapid, and at times reckless, urbanization accompanied industrialization. Sleepy southern towns such as Mobile, Alabama, and Panama City, Florida, overnight became overcrowded, bustling cities. Workers who ventured into southern cities for war work and economic opportunity could expect to confront inadequate housing and overburdened public services. When DuPont Chemical built a gigantic powder and explosives plant at tiny Childersburg, Alabama, population 500, some 14,000 workers descended on the town "like a cloud of locust."[6] Southern cities and towns took on a ramshackle, impermanent look as families seeking defense work took up residence in sheds, tents, gas stations, and tar paper shacks.[7] By 1942 the Mississippi Gulf Coast town of Pascagoula had become an ungainly hodgepodge of "trailer parks, rusty boarding houses, old homes with charm but limited sanitary facilities, and even tents."[8] The wartime housing shortage worsened with the conclusion of the war, as veterans anxious about postwar conditions returned to communities already stretched to their limits.

The war brought economic recovery, yet the fruits of recovery were unevenly enjoyed. The defense program's stimulation of the southern economy did not end discriminatory hiring practices. African Americans did not reap the economic benefits within the arsenal for democracy, suffering discrimination within industry, the military, government training programs, and labor unions. Those blacks able to secure employment in defense industries worked in segregated crews and were relegated to the least desirable, lowest-paying jobs.[9] In New Orleans, for example, the Brotherhood of Boilermakers, Iron Shipbuilders and Helpers of America monopolized the high-paying welding jobs for whites.[10] In 1940 Eli W. Collins, director of unemployment compensation of the Arkansas Department of Labor, informed the participants in the Little Rock Interracial Conference on the Employment Problems of Negroes that the black worker did not need "training in the fields of competition, but in those areas in which he is traditionally accepted—domestic, custodial, and agricultural work."[11] Employers often went to extremes to exclude blacks from defense jobs. Faced with a shortage of white workers, industrialists in Florida and Alabama refused to hire local blacks and instead used salary inducements to lure white workers from Mississippi.[12]

Within the military, African American men fighting in a war to protect democratic ideals overseas served in segregated units where they were regularly mistreated. Tempers flared daily on southern military training bases and in southern communities as minor confrontations between white and black soldiers threatened to escalate into larger racial conflagrations. They often did.[13] In 1944 black troops and white MPs staged a two-hour shoot-out at Mobile's Brookley Field, while that same year at Louisiana's Camp Claiborne fourteen black GIs received courts-martial for riot and mutiny after they stampeded through the camp, discharging their weapons and attacking white officers and MPs. Their leader, Private Leroy McGary, was sentenced to death.[14]

Angered by the exclusion of African Americans from industry and the discriminatory treatment of black soldiers, and frustrated by federal officials' willingness to turn a blind eye to these abuses, African American leaders pressured the Roosevelt administration to recognize and address black needs and demands. Despite their best efforts, civil rights activists had achieved little success in the 1930s. However, by 1940 blacks occupied a more propitious position economically and politically. Millions of African Americans remained underemployed despite a well-publicized manpower shortage, and black leaders exploited the defense program's need for full use of manpower to gain leverage with the administration.[15] Civil rights leaders and the black press also capitalized on the war's ideological component, pointing out the hypocrisy of a war for democracy fought by second-class citizens. The black press publicized the "Double V," the idea that African Americans were actually fighting a two-front war—a war for democracy at home as well as abroad.[16]

Conscious of their political power and the importance of their presence within the Democratic coalition, African American leaders threatened to dramatize their demands for stronger action against discrimination by staging a massive rally in Washington, D.C.[17] In response to the increased political power of northern blacks and to pressure from black leaders, and desiring to head off an embarrassing wartime protest, Roosevelt issued an executive order on June 25, 1941, that forbade discrimination in defense industries and established the FEPC. Its broadly written mandate gave it the task of overseeing "the employment of workers in defense industries, without discrimination, because of race, creed, color, or national origin."[18]

Civil rights activists hailed the creation of the committee as a great victory, but the committee in practice differed widely from the committee in theory and promise.[19] The FEPC served as a clearinghouse and investigatory agency for complaints charging employment discrimination. Unfortunately the committee lacked any power to enforce compliance and relied primarily on publicity to achieve its objectives.[20]

The fruits of FEPC efforts materialized slowly. By late spring 1942, almost one year after Roosevelt had created the committee, African Americans constituted fewer than 3 percent of all war workers. Blacks did not begin to enter defense industry jobs until late 1942, almost three years after the defense program began.[21] Not surprisingly, the FEPC faced its greatest challenges in the South, where the committee encountered discrimination not only from the general populace and private contractors but from federal agencies (staffed primarily by local personnel) as well. Nevertheless, the FEPC did achieve some victories. The committee successfully negotiated some 5,000 discrimination complaints and settled forty labor strikes.[22] While the FEPC's success could be considered modest at best, "it is perhaps remarkable under the circumstances," notes one historian, "that as much was accomplished by so few."[23]

Southern lawmakers understood that the FEPC was a wartime creation with a slim chance of surviving into the postwar era. They also knew the committee possessed little real power. Still, they recognized the intrusive precedent set by the agency and remained solid in their opposition to it. The anxiety that conservative southern whites felt over their loosening grip on economic coercion and employment control crystallized around the fight to kill the postwar FEPC. David Clark of North Carolina, publisher of the *Southern Textile Bulletin,* declared that race relations had never been better than they were in the South at that moment. The FEPC would "turn back the clock for years and Negroes will be innocent victims of the bitterness it will cause." Like most opponents, Clark regularly distorted the FEPC's proposed provisions. "Should any Negro be denied the right to room in the best hotel or to a meal in the best restaurant," Clark warned, "a heavy fine or imprisonment would confront the proprietor or manager of the hotel or restaurant."[24] Even southern liberals who had supported New Deal labor policies balked at support for a peacetime FEPC.

The greatest enemy of the FEPC in Congress was Senator Theodore "The Man" Bilbo of Mississippi. Derisively referred to as the "Prince of the Peckerwoods," the 5′ 2″ Bilbo ascended to political office as the champion of the common man. Elected to the U.S. Senate in 1934, Bilbo became one of Roosevelt's more loyal southern New Dealers, giving strong support to New Deal relief programs and the Social Security Act and, departing from other southern lawmakers, favoring the Wagner Act and the wages and hours law. Yet, like so many liberal southern politicians, Bilbo believed that progress for the working classes could be achieved only by maintaining the color bar. Bilbo became positively apoplectic in his denunciations of the FEPC. His rantings against the racial implications of the FEPC earned him a reputation as the Senate's most vitriolic white supremacist.[25] Bilbo claimed that "every Negro in America who is behind movements of this kind . . . dream[s] of social equality and inter-marriage between whites and blacks."[26] Of course, Bilbo had company. Fellow Mississippian Congressman John Rankin equated the creation of the committee with the beginnings of a Communist dictatorship.[27] Alabama governor Frank Dixon, mouthpiece of Birmingham's industrialists, accused the FEPC of seeking "to break down the principle of segregation of races, to force Negroes and white people to work together, intermingle with each other, and even to bring about the situation where white employees will have to work under Negroes."[28] In 1942 Dixon turned down a government contract to use the cotton mills in the Alabama state prison for war production because of the contract's nondiscrimination clause.[29] White business leaders across the state, from the Mobile Chamber of Commerce to the Opelika Rotary Club, applauded Dixon's firm stand.[30] Throughout the FEPC's rocky tenure, southern congressmen formed the most intractable bloc of opposition, and the FEPC ceased operating on June 30, 1946, when southern congressmen succeeded in slashing its funding.[31]

The pressure tactics used by civil rights leaders that led to the creation of the FEPC illustrated blacks' new militancy and assertiveness. During the war, NAACP membership increased ten times, and the number of chapters tripled. While the NAACP would remain the dominant civil rights organization for the next ten years, the war spawned more militant pressure tactics, such as those proposed by the March on Washington Movement. The Congress of Racial Equality, or CORE, organized in 1942, epitomized this new militancy. Eschewing the NAACP's litigation strategy for nonviolent, passive resistance, CORE's program of sit-ins and freedom rides presaged the tactics of later civil rights activists.[32] Sometimes this racial militance erupted into violence. Researchers at Fisk University recorded 242 violent racial clashes in 47 cities in 1943. The Detroit riot, the worst of these, left 34 dead and more than 700 injured. Two months later a riot in Harlem left 5 African Americans dead and 500 persons injured.[33]

Whites acknowledged, and feared, this new racial militancy. Rumors of impending racial upheaval and violence swept through the South and the nation during the war years and kept relations between the races tense. Common were rumors pertaining to the relationships between white women and black domestics, stories concerning alleged sexual improprieties by black men toward white women, and purported plots of impending race riots. Southern whites whispered about the supposed proliferation of Eleanor Clubs, inspired by first lady Eleanor Roosevelt and organized by black domestic workers. Through these clubs, whites conjectured, black servants sought to upset the racial hierarchy of domestic relations. The club's motto was reported to be "a white woman in every kitchen by 1943." Allegedly, Eleanor Clubs demanded that their members participate in subversive behavior particular to domestics. Whites claimed their black servants had been instructed by these clubs to refuse to work on Sundays, to object to serving extra people, to demand to be called "Miss" or "Mrs.," to insist on using the front door, and to take a bath in their employers' family bathtub before leaving work. Whites spread rumors of well-orchestrated campaigns of black-on-white violence. For example, whites claimed that blacks designated certain days to push white people off sidewalks and streetcars. Other fabrications centered on African American plots to massacre whites.[34]

Behind these fantastic rumors and white paranoia lay the fact that the war had brought chronic labor shortages in rural areas and had contributed to a growing sense of race consciousness among southern blacks. Historian James Cobb has noted that during the 1940s the Mississippi Delta—heralded as "planters' heaven"—experienced a 10 percent decrease in its rural black population as agricultural workers migrated to cities and towns in search of employment.[35] Oscar Johnston, president of the Delta and Pine Land Company, complained that his plantation, which once had "an average of around 850 tenant families and quite a few day workers or wage hands," by 1946 "had . . . 541 tenant families."[36] Another Mississippi planter complained to the state farm bureau that too many black farm laborers "are trying to get houses in town [and] to let their wives work in town."[37]

Black tenants who stayed behind were less disposed to tolerate ill treatment than they had been during less flush times. Though their protests were less overtly militant than northern blacks'—instead of staging sit-ins, black cotton pickers dumped stones and green bolls into their sacks before weighing—they heightened white anxiety just the same. "The day when a man could protect the grade of his cotton and assume a clean-picked crop by threatening his labor with a single-tree or a trace chain is gone forever," observed one visitor to the region. "The word spreads fast against that kind of planter nowadays and the first thing he knows, he can't get anybody to pick his cotton."[38] The social implications of labor shortages and labor control were not lost on large landowners. In a 1944 letter to the Delta Council, a powerful association of cotton growers, Richard Hopson stated that he was "confident that you are aware of the acute shortage of labor which now exists in the Delta . . . [and] that you are aware of the serious racial problem which confronts us at this time which may become more serious as time passes."[39] Planters worried about outside influences on workers who stayed on the farms. In a radio address in 1943, Walter Sillers, president of the Delta Council, warned farmers to be on the lookout for union organizers.[40] The CIO had stepped up its organizational activity in Arkansas in the early 1940s, and agents of the Farm Security Administration, a New Deal agency, were undertaking programs aimed at establishing sharecroppers and tenant farmers as independent growers.[41]

Southern planters and lawmakers used suasion and coercion to stem the tide of the rural exodus. Delta leaders held a Delta Farm Mobilization Day in 1942 that featured a parade, speakers, and a barbecue. They hoped to convince black workers to remain on the farm by "encouraging [in them] a love for the farm and . . . show[ing] the beauty and romance of farm life."[42] Other attempts to compel blacks to stay on the plantations were less neighborly. Local communities across the South passed "fight or work laws," and planters manipulated local draft boards to defer farm tenants and sharecroppers whose labor they needed.[43]

The majority of black southerners, of course, did not join the NAACP or radical civil rights organizations. Even so, the war left few unchanged. If it did not motivate them to join the movement, it at the very least prompted them to aspire to achieve something better for themselves. The change had been especially great for black veterans. Haywood Stephney, a navy veteran from Clarksdale, Mississippi, recalled that not until he served overseas did he begin to understand the damage segregation had done to him. "After seeing what some of the other world was doing then I realized how far behind I was. As we began to move and stir around and learn other ways then we had a choice—a comparison." With this point of comparison Stephney realized that, once he returned to Clarksdale, it was "going to be difficult to get me back in total darkness."[44] This point was not lost on local whites, who pointedly reminded blacks like Stephney that nothing had changed. Dabney Hammer, a highly decorated black veteran, also from Clarksdale, recalled that wartime valor and honor meant nothing to Clarksdale whites, who went out of their way to remind him that in the Mississippi Delta, he was "still a nigger."[45]

Legislation introduced during the war years compounded the growing social unrest on the homefront, further antagonized southern members of Congress, and widened the gap between the South and the Democratic Party. The Soldiers' Voting Act and an anti–poll tax bill, both introduced in 1942, impinged on racial relations, voting patterns, and political power in the South more directly than the FEPC. The anti–poll tax bill was a familiar feature by 1942, and it is not surprising that, once again, southerners defeated the bill. The Soldiers' Voting Act of 1942 attempted to facilitate voting procedures for members of the armed forces stationed outside their home states. Southern politicians feared that even this slight change would pave the way for the eventual enfranchisement of blacks. Mississippi senator James O. Eastland declared that under the terms of the bill, the federal government "would send carpetbaggers into the South to control elections." Southern Democrats succeeded in attaching an amendment to the bill that would keep the states' election machinery intact.[46]

Wartime upheavals that threatened to erase or at least alter the color line tested white southerners' New Deal loyalties. Liberal and moderate candidates continued to capture southern statehouses and to win terms in the U.S. Congress, but race had begun to rear its ugly head in state political campaigns. In Georgia, moderate Ellis Arnall gave like-minded voters hope for a better future when he defeated longtime anti-Roosevelt demagogue Eugene Talmadge in 1942. Following his impressive victory, Arnall worked to expand the franchise in Georgia by successfully securing legislative majorities to abolish the poll tax and by lowering the voting age to eighteen years.[47] In Louisiana, a state as politically complex as one was to find in the nation, Sam Houston Jones emerged victorious in a gubernatorial race in which opponent Earl Long, Huey's younger brother, tried to capitalize on the racial fears of white voters.[48] But conservative candidates did well in the congressional elections of 1942, and upon taking office, they began to dismantle systematically what was left of the New Deal, eliminating the National Resources Planning Board and the National Youth Administration and greatly emasculating the Farm Security Administration.[49]

Tired of the New Deal and anxious about wartime changes in race relations, recalcitrant southern Democrats aimed for the top and attempted to upset Roosevelt's bid for a fourth term in 1944. Governor Frank Dixon of Alabama tried to garner support for a southern defection in 1943.[50] Dixon, a Birmingham attorney, had been elected in 1938 with the support of a crazy-quilt coalition of pro– and anti–New Dealers. Once in office, however, Dixon soon disappointed his New Deal supporters, adhering closely to the antilabor agenda embraced by Birmingham's industrialists. By the end of his term, Dixon had become one of the most outspoken critics of the FEPC.[51] Joined by Louisiana governor Jones, Dixon sought unsuccessfully to enlist the support of other southern states at the Southern Governors' Conference in Tallahassee. In May 1944 a group of anti-Roosevelt Democrats known as the "Texas Regulars" captured that state's Democratic convention and named their own delegates and electoral slate. Mississippi's convention did likewise. But this was for the most part an abortive attempt, and Roosevelt remained as popular as ever with southern voters.[52]

Thwarted in their attempts to deny Roosevelt the nomination, anti-Roosevelt forces set their sights on the vice-presidential spot. By 1944 Roosevelt was in poor health, and though few doubted his chances for nomination and reelection, many questioned his ability to survive a fourth term. Given these circumstances, historian Robert Ferrell has observed, "choosing the vice-presidential candidate was tantamount to choosing the presidential successor."[53] Southern conservatives were determined that liberal Henry Wallace not be renominated. Wallace's support for the rights of organized labor and African Americans was anathema to Dixie conservatives.[54] Fearful of antagonizing the party's disparate factions, Democratic National Committee (DNC) chairman Robert F. Hannegan was determined to find an uncontroversial, inoffensive vice-presidential candidate who could foster party unity. The early front-runners were James F. Byrnes, head of the Office of Economic Stabilization, former Supreme Court justice, and former U.S. senator from South Carolina, and William O. Douglas, Supreme Court justice. Each had serious drawbacks. African Americans and organized labor would surely balk at a Byrnes candidacy, and Democratic Party insiders considered Douglas a political novice. In the end both men were jettisoned for the little-known senator from Missouri, Harry S. Truman. Above all else, Truman's ability to avoid seriously offending any crucial party constituency assured him the second spot on the ticket.[55]

African Americans responded in a lukewarm fashion to the Truman candidacy. As a senator Truman had offered weak support for civil rights legislation. Truman backed legislative efforts to fund the FEPC, but he voted against an anti–poll tax amendment in the soldiers' vote bill of 1942.[56] In an interview with the *Pittsburgh Courier,* a leading black newspaper, Truman declared his opposition to "social equality" between the races. Revealing his gullibility to wartime race rumors, Truman admitted that his daughter Margaret was not allowed to use the Washington streetcars because he had heard that blacks organized to push whites off streetcars on Thursdays.[57]

White southerners, on the other hand, were pleased with Truman. Many felt a senator from a border state that had a strong southern cultural identity would be an able and willing protector of their institutions. Ascending to the presidency on Roosevelt's death in 1945, Truman charted a tentative course on civil rights and in general pursued a policy agenda that increasingly alienated his party's left wing. Unwilling to antagonize the conservative bloc in Congress, Truman expended little political capital to save the FEPC from the political axe wielded by Dixie congressmen, and he retreated from his earlier opposition to the poll tax, stating that it "was a matter for the Southern states to work out." NAACP attorney Charles Houston resigned from his position as FEPC commissioner after Truman refused to implement FEPC directives demanding an end to racially discriminatory hiring practices by two transit companies.[58] Truman allowed the FEPC to whither away, until by 1946 it was, in the words of one historian, "out of money, out of friends, out of luck and life."[59] Southern conservatives harbored cautious optimism about the new president, taking solace in his apparent disinterest in civil rights as they faced new political challenges at the grass roots.

★

In his authoritative 1949 study of southern politics, political scientist V. O. Key observed that the destruction of the white primary "precipitated a crisis in southern politics." Key noted that the absence of any significant Republican presence in the South meant the Democratic primary functioned as the election. Although the U.S. Constitution prohibited the state from denying the vote on account of race, white southerners, since the late nineteenth century, had advanced the theory that the Democratic Party was actually a private association and, being such, could discriminate in any way it chose.[60]

In 1944, in the Texas case of *Smith v. Allwright,* the Supreme Court ruled the Texas white primary law violated the Fifteenth Amendment and was therefore unconstitutional. While the states of the Upper South acquiesced in the ruling, the decision was a political bombshell in the Deep South. White legislators across the Black Belt exchanged anxious letters hatching schemes to circumvent the decision. Mississippi congressman John Rankin warned legislators in his state to take action against the "communistic drive . . . to destroy white supremacy in the South."[61] The state legislature eventually passed a law requiring voters to swear their opposition to federal antilynching and anti–poll tax legislation and the

FEPC.[62] Alabama's former governor Frank Dixon revealed his anxiety to the head of the state party. "It is obvious," Dixon wrote, "that the only thing that has held the Democratic Party together in the South for many years past has been the thing which caused its strength in the first place, namely, white supremacy." If the national Democratic Party followed the Supreme Court's lead "through forced registration of negroes in this State, the Democratic Party will become anathema to the white people in the South."[63] In 1946 the Alabama legislature passed, and voters approved, the Boswell Amendment to the state constitution, introducing new suffrage standards that required potential voters to "read and write, understand and explain any article of the Constitution of the United States" and granted local boards the power to administer registration requirements "in as discriminatory a fashion as they saw fit."[64] But even this system was not stringent enough for many conservative white Alabamians. State Democratic Party chieftain Gessner T. McCorvey of Mobile complained that "up in North Alabama the wrong sort of Board of Registrars will register a lot of white people who have . . . no business voting."[65] Conservatives like McCorvey feared poor white voters almost as much as they feared blacks.

As Carl Elliott had stated forty years later, the line was beginning to be drawn, and many liberal white politicians, even those who had deftly sidestepped the race issue earlier, now took up the banner in defense of white supremacy. In South Carolina, millworker-turned-governor Olin D. Johnston convened a special session of the state legislature in April 1944, two weeks after the Texas decision. Determined to protect the white primary, the South Carolina General Assembly (ridiculed as "Killbillies" by *Newsweek*) repealed all state primary laws, ostensibly relegating the Democratic Party to the status of a private club with the power to determine membership qualifications.[66] In Georgia the forces of cautious moderation prevailed, at least for the time being. Governor Ellis Arnall criticized the Supreme Court ruling but took no further action to circumvent it.[67]

Georgia's Arnall aside, the impact of the ruling was felt in political campaigns throughout the region in 1944. In Alabama, where the *Smith* decision preceded the Democratic Party primary by one month, race became a factor late in the campaign for the U.S. Senate. In that contest industrialists and large agricultural interests, including the Associated Industries of Alabama, the farm bureau, Alabama Power Company, and owners of textile plants, timberlands, sawmills, and paper mills, lined up behind Birmingham state senator James A. Simpson in his effort to unseat the incumbent Lister Hill. Hill campaigned on his record as a New Deal Democrat, while Simpson championed lower corporate taxes, free textbooks, and rural electrification. Simpson was reluctant to use racist appeals but bowed to his advisors. The racial rhetoric quickly escalated, and one observer remarked that a Simpson rally in Jefferson County resembled a meeting of the Ku Klux Klan.[68] The Simpson forces received "fresh ammunition" from the *Smith* decision and made the most of it, disseminating racist propaganda through statewide magazines. Hill felt the need to respond in kind, reminding Alabama voters that "Simpson in 1927 had cast in the Alabama house the sole vote against an amendment that struck from the Alabama Code a loophole that had made it possible for mulattoes to be classified as whites after the fifth generation." Hill allowed advertisements that proclaimed "Lister Hill not only believes in white supremacy—he votes for it."[69] Hill won, but the margin of victory, according to his biographer, was "less than overwhelming."[70]

Shortly after saving the white primary in his state, South Carolina governor Olin Johnston hit the campaign trail against the incumbent senator, Cotton Ed Smith. Johnston had lost to Smith in 1938 running on his record as a New Deal governor against Smith's platform of white supremacy. Now Johnston's credentials were as strong as the aging Smith's, and he won his first term as South Carolina's senator.[71] Even Claude Pepper of Florida, arguably the South's most liberal senator, felt compelled to assure voters of his support for white supremacy. Accused by his opponents in the 1944 race of advocating social equality, Pepper condemned the court decision, declaring "the South will allow nothing to impair white supremacy." Like his more conservative colleagues, Pepper urged the state's leaders to rewrite the voting requirements in such a way as to pass constitutional muster while simultaneously denying black voters the franchise.[72] Although Pepper won reelection, he did so with only 51.8 percent of the vote against a relative unknown, barely escaping a second primary. More significantly, Pepper's support throughout the state had decreased dramatically from his 1938 victory.[73]

While the *Smith* decision prompted nervous candidates to interject race into political campaigns, it simultaneously galvanized southern blacks, sparking a fury of political activity. Despite the best efforts of white southerners to keep them from the polls, blacks registered in impressive numbers. Across the South more than a half-million African Americans registered to vote in the 1946 Democratic Party primaries.[74] In the wake of a 1946 federal district court decision that opened the Georgia Democratic primary to black voters, approximately 100,000 black Georgians registered to vote.[75] Black voter registration figures in Savannah in 1946 increased from 8,000 to 12,000, while in Augusta they tripled from 1,200 to 4,900.[76] Even in Mississippi, black activists, many of whom were veterans, orchestrated voter registration drives in an effort to unseat Senator Bilbo in 1946.[77]

For white conservatives in Alabama, the *Smith* case only underscored disturbing developments already under way in Tuskegee in the heart of the Black Belt. Charles Gomillion, a thirty-one-year-old sociology teacher at Tuskegee Institute, and several other men had organized the Tuskegee Civic Association (formerly the Tuskegee Men's Club) in 1941 and had persisted in attempting to register blacks in Macon County. The *Smith* decision energized them, and on a hot day in early July 1945 more than two hundred blacks, many of whom were middle-class government employees, showed up at the Macon County Courthouse to register. When only ten applicants had successfully registered, the Tuskegee Civic Association filed suit in state circuit court as well as in federal district court in Montgomery. Although the suit ultimately was dismissed after Probate Judge William Varner informed the court that the plaintiff had, in fact, been registered—a devious trick to forestall the suit—the specter of organized blacks pursuing their grievances in federal court was simply too threatening. By December 1947 the Macon County Board of Registrars had gone into hiding. As of early 1948 they had not registered any blacks.[78]

One of the most dramatic tales of black political awakening during this era concerned South Carolina's Progressive Democratic Party (PDP). Formally organized in May 1944, the PDP was part of a larger plan to invalidate South Carolina's white primary. Throughout the late 1940s and early 1950s, although the PDP was never strong enough to topple states' righters from power, its ability to organize a significant number of black voters and its determination in bringing its protests to the attention of national Democratic Party leaders enraged white conservatives.

The driving force behind the PDP was an ambitious young newspaper editor named John Henry McCray. Like the John Henry of legend, McCray possessed exceptional courage, strength, and stamina and provided effective civil rights leadership for South Carolina blacks until the mid-1950s. Born in Youngstown, Florida, in 1910, McCray moved with his family to Lincolnville, South Carolina, in Charleston County, when he was five years old. Like Mound Bayou in Mississippi, Lincolnville was an all-black town with a black mayor and chief of police. McCray later recalled that during his childhood he probably encountered only three or four whites a year, usually salespersons. Since both his mother and father were employed by the local government, it is not surprising that McCray developed an interest in politics. Although no black southerner could escape Jim Crow, perhaps spending his formative years shielded from whites instilled in McCray a self-confidence only too frequently crushed by the degrading strictures of segregation.

Highly intelligent and driven, McCray attended the Avery Institute in Charleston, where he was valedictorian of his graduating class in 1931. From there he went on to Talladega College in Alabama, where he studied chemistry and graduated in 1935. A gifted student, McCray turned down a scholarship to Harvard University Law School and instead chose a sales position in the Charleston office of the North Carolina Mutual Life Insurance Company. In 1939 he founded the *Charleston Lighthouse,* which in 1940 merged with the *People's Informer* of Sumter, South Carolina, to become the *Lighthouse and Informer.* McCray and the newspaper moved to Columbia in December 1941. The paper had a sworn commitment to publicize racial injustices in education, in the courts, and in politics. "Nothing was going to happen in the black community that [we] did not know about," McCray maintained.[79] The *Lighthouse and Informer* became the most influential black newspaper in South Carolina and boasted a circulation of approximately 35,000 in 1946.[80]

The idea of a separate party for African Americans first surfaced in March 1944. Barred from voting in South Carolina's white primary, hopeful that a favorable decision was shortly to come in the Texas case, and desperate to support President Roosevelt for reelection, black South Carolinians searched for a solution. The *Lighthouse and Informer* carried an editorial that proposed forming "Fourth Term for Roosevelt" Clubs, separate from the white Democratic Party.[81] It was an ingenious plan. No legal barrier existed to such an organization, plus it allowed blacks to be politically active without being associated "with the party of 'Cotton Ed' Smith, [Theodore] Bilbo and John Rankin of Mississippi and [Eugene] Talmadge of Georgia," or with the "mediocre and neglected Republican party." The organization started with the formation of local Fourth Term for Roosevelt Clubs and originally was known as the Colored Democratic Party. Almost all of the expense for the party was covered by the *Lighthouse and Informer,* although the party received its first outside funds from

John Henry McCray, leader of the South Carolina Progressive Democratic Party, ca. 1940s. Photograph courtesy of South Caroliniana Library, University of South Carolina, Columbia.

an elderly white woman who contributed $5.00 from her pension check.[82] PDP bylaws stipulated that the organization would disband once full integration into the regular state Democratic Party had been achieved.[83]

The new PDP was formally organized on May 24, 1944, when 172 delegates from thirty-nine of the state's forty-six counties attended a statewide convention at Columbia's Masonic Temple. The convention voted to send a group of delegates to the National Democratic Convention in Chicago to request eight of the eighteen seats designated for South Carolina.[84] Fully cognizant of the precarious status of his fledgling party and his own meager political credentials, McCray solicited assistance from African American congressmen William L. Dawson of Chicago and Adam Clayton Powell Jr. of New York City. Fearful that southern congressmen were conspiring to prevent the PDP from gaining an audience with national party leaders, McCray asked each man to use his influence to help the PDP gain recognition from the DNC.[85]

Already overburdened by trying to contain a possible bolt by the Texas delegation, and tied up with behind-the-scenes wheeling and dealing over the vice-presidential nomination, the National Democratic Party hoped to thwart the PDP's proposed challenge. Oscar Ewing, vice-chairman of the DNC, told McCray that a contest over seating would harm FDR's chances for a fourth term and would ultimately set back the cause of civil rights.[86] Hoping to defuse a potentially embarrassing situation, the DNC cut a deal with McCray. The party leaders, who included DNC chairman Robert Hannegan and vice-chairman Ewing, convinced McCray that any challenge posed by the PDP stood little chance of success and would be squashed on organizational technicalities. According to McCray, they reached a "gentlemen's agreement."[87] Hannegan promised McCray and the PDP that if they did not play into the hands of the Republicans, the weight of the judicial department would be thrown behind integrating the Democratic Party.[88] McCray would later be accused of co-opting his organization by refusing to make a floor fight. Given that endeavor's slim chance for success, and given the PDP's loyalty to Roosevelt and the national party, it seems unreasonable for McCray, however, to have done anything other than accept the hand dealt him by national Democratic Party leaders.

Armed with promises of assistance from the national Democratic leadership, the PDP sent a delegation to the national convention in Chicago in 1944 in an attempt to unseat South Carolina's all-white delegation in a hearing before the Credentials Subcommittee. The delegation testified that within three months of organizing, the PDP claimed 45,000 members with clubs in all but two counties.[89] Clearly impressed with the accomplishments achieved by the party in only three months, the Credentials Subcommittee nevertheless felt that representation at the national convention was a matter for the courts.[90] McCray took the decision in stride and, as promised, did not make a floor fight.[91]

Following the half-victory at the national convention in 1944, the PDP returned to South Carolina and nominated party cofounder and *Lighthouse and Informer* associate editor Osceola E. McKaine as its candidate for the U.S. Senate to run against white Democratic Party candidate Olin Johnston. McCray noted that "the convention agreed that while McKaine wouldn't win, Negro voters would have proof that their people could contest for public offices as Democrats." McKaine garnered about 4,500 votes. McCray and others contended, however, that South Carolina's complicated voting procedures and widespread polling irregularities prevented many African Americans from casting their ballots for McKaine.[92]

McCray initially had not been sold on a court challenge to the white primary.[93] He instead preferred to work independently registering and organizing African American voters.[94] But following its experience with national party leadership, and confident of party support, the PDP shifted its considerable efforts into voter registration and focused on challenging the white Democratic primary. As one PDP member would recall, Hannegan had promised that "the Department of Justice and F.B.I. would be at our disposal in all cases where intimidation, coercion, and terrorism were involved . . . with the efforts of Negroes in South Carolina to cast a ballot."[95]

McCray carefully assembled affidavits from blacks describing the obstacles whites threw up to prevent them from registering. He handed them over to the NAACP, which in turn forwarded the information to the Department of Justice.[96] But help from the federal government never materialized. In a 1946 letter, McCray reminded DNC chairman Robert Hannegan of their earlier arrangement: "At this time there are numerous affidavits on file with the Justice Department growing out of refusals of enrollment this year, 1944 and in 1942. Not only have we not had action . . . but we now understand from private sources that there will be no federal action attempted under the Smith versus Allbright [*sic*] (Texas) primary ruling." Blacks, McCray pleaded, were "desperate for an escape."[97] The federal government never provided the route.

Southern whites were especially disturbed by the fact that black voter registration efforts were boosted by the energies of the many black GIs who returned to southern communities with enhanced expectations for democracy on the homefront. When questioned by the Army Research Branch in 1944 and 1945 about their understanding of the war aims and their contribution, nearly half of all black GIs questioned "believed that they would 'have more rights and privileges' after the war."[98] Declaring that "men who faced bullets overseas deserve ballots at home," more than one hundred black veterans marched on Birmingham's courthouse in January 1946 demanding the right to register.[99] Their efforts were added to those of the SCHW, which emerged from the war determined to extend the ideals of New Deal liberalism into the postwar era and to continue its assault on the South's political system. By 1946 the SCHW had opened offices in several southern states and was focused on victory in the southern primaries. White elites also looked on warily as the CIO and the American Federation of Labor each launched union organizing drives in 1946. Liberal forces in the South looked hopefully toward the primaries of 1946, which would be the first real test of their new strength as a loose coalition.[100]

The southern political scene in 1946 exhibited a schizophrenic quality that renders easy or simple generalizations impossible. White voters sought to ensure economic stability in the postwar era and to extend protections achieved during the New Deal while preventing black political equality. Voters across the Deep South gave the nod to populist Jim Folsom in Alabama, white supremacist demagogue Eugene Talmadge in Georgia, and moderate Strom Thurmond in South Carolina. In some races, such as Folsom's successful race for governor in 1946, white supremacy appeared not to play a part at all, while it defined Talmadge's campaign. The victories of reactionaries, populists, and moderates demonstrated the instability of the postwar southern political landscape in the immediate postwar era as voters tried to balance modernization with racial inequality.

Nowhere did the enigmatic quality of postwar southern politics come through more strongly than in Alabama. Voters marked their ballots in favor of the racial status quo by approving the reactionary Boswell Amendment but turned their backs on the candidates of the industrial and Black Belt interests for the statehouse and the U.S. Senate in favor of two populist candidates from humble backgrounds. The handsome and gregarious thirty-eight-year-old veteran James E. Folsom from southeast

Alabama, an opponent of the amendment, rode into office with a 60,000-vote majority on a progressive platform that called for legislative reapportionment; allocation of more money for public schools, improved roads, and old age pensions; recognition of the rights of organized labor; and opposition to the poll tax.[101] As Folsom was preparing to take office, senior U.S. senator John Bankhead Jr. died, setting off a scramble for his replacement. Five-term congressman John Sparkman, the poor son of tenant farmers from northern Alabama who was an ardent supporter of rural electrification and a grateful recipient of CIO support, eked out a 230-vote victory over two candidates who split the state's conservative vote.[102]

But liberal advances were met at every step with fraud, intimidation, and structural inequities, such as Georgia's county-unit system. In the Peach State the dislocations of wartime and the resurgence of black political activity spurred white voters to send racist Eugene Talmadge back to the governor's mansion in a race in which neither of his opponents dared present himself as a liberal. Mississippi senator Theodore Bilbo won reelection in a campaign in which he (like Talmadge) advocated violence as a means to keep blacks from the polls. In Mississippi, ranked at the bottom of all states in black voter participation and identified by the NAACP as a serious trouble spot, barely 5,000 black citizens qualified to vote.[103] Nevertheless, fearful whites set crosses ablaze in Jackson's black neighborhoods during the 1946 primary.[104] The NAACP files contain affidavits from black citizens, many of whom were World War II veterans, who claimed they had been assaulted by whites and denied the right to vote. In Puckett, Mississippi, veteran Etoy Fletcher was accosted by four white men after he was denied registration. Fletcher reported that he was "beaten and flogged mercilessly with a large cable wire." The men allegedly told Fletcher that if he ever attempted to vote again, they would kill him.[105] In Pass Christian, Mississippi, the election commission disqualified several black men after they admitted under questioning that they supported the FEPC.[106] On the eve of the election, Bilbo challenged "every red-blooded American who believes in the superiority and integrity of the white race to get out and see that no nigger votes." The best time to do that, Bilbo advised, "is the night before" the election.[107]

The challenge faced by white liberals and blacks in their efforts to democratize the South were part of a larger nationwide struggle to define postwar liberalism. Opponents of voter registration and political organization among blacks and poor and working-class whites in the South gained strength from the growing rift within liberal ranks. Left-wing liberals found themselves increasingly under attack in the immediate postwar era as America's deteriorating relationship with the Soviet Union infused domestic politics with anticommunism. Organizations such as the SCHW and the CIO's political action committee became targets of liberal anticommunists who sought to rid the movement of Soviet sympathizers. Increasingly in 1947 and 1948, historian Patricia Sullivan has noted, "the SCHW's efforts were diverted by charges that the organization had failed to purge its ranks of Communists and Communist sympathizers."[108]

Challenging the proponents of racial and industrial democracy for the future direction of the South in 1946 were scores of white veterans who returned to southern states, created new political coalitions, and fomented "GI Revolts" that aimed to turn out entrenched political machines. Their experiences in other parts of the country and overseas had underscored the economically backward nature of southern society, and they dedicated themselves to supporting officials who promoted clean, efficient government that promised voters a safe future of economic growth but not necessarily racial democracy.[109]

Typical of these returning veterans was Sidney McMath of Arkansas. Raised in an impoverished family that lived under the tyranny of an abusive, alcoholic father, young Sidney sold papers, shined shoes, and peddled cabbages door-to-door to supplement the family's meager income. McMath joined the marines in 1940 and saw action at Guadalcanal and throughout the Pacific theater. The war was a turning point for McMath, just as it was for other southern men of his generation. He returned to Hot Springs in 1945, and in May 1946 he and a few other GIs created their own political organization, which they called the Government Improvement League. Running on a platform of honest government, they offered a slate of candidates to challenge the nominees of Garland County's political machine. Run by Mayor Leo P. McLaughlin of Hot Springs, the machine had controlled Garland County for close to twenty years, primarily through the payment of poll tax receipts. The mayor's underlings would purchase the receipts and distribute them to "loyal" voters—most often thieves, drunkards, and prostitutes—on election day. While McMath ran for prosecuting attorney and won in the Democratic primary, the others on the slate were forced to run in the general election as independents. Eventually the GIs' slate won several offices, including sheriff, tax assessor, and circuit judge, and went on to inspire GI revolts in Crittendon, Pope, and Yell Counties.[110]

Strom Thurmond of Edgefield County, South Carolina, returned from the battlefields of Europe with an agenda similar to McMath's. If Ohio fancies itself the birthplace of presidents, then Edgefield County, South Carolina, could justifiably be christened the birthplace of demagogues and political rogues. Nestled along the Savannah River on the western edge of that heart-shaped state, Edgefield County gave to the country such controversial figures as Preston S. Brooks, the U.S. congressman whose legislative accomplishments have long since been forgotten but whose vengeful caning of U.S. Senator Charles Sumner of Massachusetts is part of antebellum southern lore. Edgefield County's one-eyed son Benjamin R. "Pitchfork Ben" Tillman rode the crest of the farmers' insurgency of the late nineteenth century all the way to the governor's office and, later, to the U.S. Senate. From these lofty heights Tillman condoned lynching and used his considerable power to rewrite the South Carolina constitution, successfully disfranchising African American voters.[111]

The county's most politically enduring son, James Strom Thurmond, was born in 1902 to John William Thurmond, a successful attorney and farmer, and Eleanor Gertrude Strom Thurmond. The second of six children, young Strom enjoyed a life of relative privilege and ease and spent his formative years in a spacious country home staffed by a cook, a housekeeper, a yardman, and a driver. Thurmond's indoctrination into South Carolina politics came early. His father was a sometime politician who once served as Ben Tillman's campaign manager, and young Strom met the acerbic Tillman at the tender age of six. In those days politics and political campaigns provided one of the few sources of entertainment for isolated country folk, and Thurmond relished traveling with his father to hear the colorful stem-winders of South Carolina office seekers out on the stump. By the time he was twelve, Thurmond knew he wanted to be a politician.[112]

After graduating from Clemson College in 1923, Thurmond taught agricultural skills to high school students in McCormick, South Carolina. Committed to education, yet yearning for the excitement of public service, he ran a successful campaign for county superintendent in 1929. In addition to his new responsibilities, Thurmond studied law under his father's tutelage, passed the bar, and hung out a shingle. In 1932 he was elected to the state senate, where he proved himself a loyal Roosevelt Democrat and a cautious New Dealer. He introduced some progressive education legislation, although he proposed a loyalty oath bill for teachers as well. In a surprise move, Thurmond ran for, and was elected, circuit court judge of South Carolina in 1937.[113]

Thurmond interrupted his judicial duties to volunteer for the army and reported for active duty as a captain in April 1942. Nearly forty years old at the time, he was exempt from service; however, he wanted to serve in combat. By the time of the D-Day invasion, Thurmond had been promoted to lieutenant colonel. He took part in the invasion as a member of the Eighty-second Airborne and was wounded in a glider crash behind enemy lines. Years later, when someone asked him why he had volunteered for combat duty, he replied, "I gave up my judgeship position temporarily to come into the war and fight, not just sit behind a desk."[114] Thurmond left active duty in October 1945 and returned to the bench a decorated veteran. Seven months later, in May 1946, he resigned from the bench and announced his candidacy for governor.

Thurmond was elected over a sprawling field of ten opponents that included the incumbent governor, former and current state and national representatives, a physician, a lumberman, and a former movie stuntman—the largest and perhaps most colorful field in state history. Like McMath, Thurmond campaigned as a progressive outsider, centering his campaign on what his biographer has called "a conspiracy theory of the status quo."[115] Thurmond charged that a select coterie of legislators from tiny Barnwell County exerted an influence in state government that far exceeded their numbers. By decrying the influence of the "Barnwell Ring," which acted out of interests antithetical to the people, Thurmond presented himself as a progressive who would do the people's work. Furthermore, he posed as an FDR loyalist and lambasted an opponent for having abandoned the president in the failed revolt of 1944. He emerged victorious, winning every majority white county in the state.[116]

Given the racial violence of 1946 and the fears of many South Carolina whites, Thurmond's gubernatorial campaign was notable for the absence of appeals to white supremacy. Although in late July Thurmond did state his opposition to "mixing the races in schools, in churches, theaters, restaurants and elsewhere," this was a far cry from the virulent campaign waged by gubernatorial candidate Eugene Talmadge in neighboring Georgia.[117] In a letter to Thurmond, Osceola McKaine, black political activist from Sumter, South Carolina, field organizer for the SCHW, and cofounder of the PDP, claimed he would have voted for Thurmond in the 1946 primary "were I not disfranchised" because "not once did you raise the race issue for political purposes."[118] Compared with other southern governors, Thurmond appeared distinctly moderate, somewhere between Alabama populist James Folsom and Georgia racist Talmadge. As late as October 1947 Thurmond remained a loyal Truman man.[119]

A highly varied political landscape emerged in the postwar South as white voters sought the best method by which to safeguard the economic gains of the New Deal and war years while maintaining the racial status quo. They believed they had an ally in the president, for by 1946 Harry Truman appeared just as reluctant as his predecessor to initiate civil rights legislation.[120] However, a number of significant developments prompted the president to commit himself more firmly to the campaign for equality. The first was the Republican landslide in the 1946 congressional elections, a victory due in large part to the black vote.[121] Between 1941 and 1944 more than 1 million southern blacks had migrated to northern cities where there was no systematic denial of the franchise. African Americans had turned from the party of Lincoln and had voted overwhelmingly for Franklin Roosevelt in 1936, but they had slowly begun to return to the Republican Party, which seemed to be more amenable and sensitive to their demands.[122] The second, more dramatic, reason for Truman's turnabout was the wave of racial violence that engulfed the South in 1946. The demise of the white primary, a subsequent increase in black voter registration, and the return of black veterans to the South all combined to fuel this rash of violence. Coming as it did on the heels of a U.S. victory over tyranny in World War II, it outraged and sickened the president. In 1947 Truman declared that "we can no longer afford the luxury of a leisurely attack upon prejudice and discrimination."[123] Responding to deplorable southern conditions with a keen sense of urgency, in the late 1940s Truman took steps toward a firm commitment to equality that were unprecedented, controversial, and not without significant political consequences. With this dramatic change, Truman set the stage for a political showdown with southern Democrats.

Events in the South in 1946 and 1947 would prove pivotal to the political fortunes of Harry Truman and Strom Thurmond and to the political allegiance of many white southerners. Sickened by violent racial clashes in the wake of World War II, particularly attacks on returning black veterans; pressured by organizations such as the SCHW, the CIO–Political Action Committee, the Communist Party, the Southern Regional Council, and the NAACP to take action; and dismayed by the inability of southern communities to punish the guilty, Truman took steps to ensure federal protection for basic human rights. Some of the more dramatic incidents of postwar racial violence took place in South Carolina, making that state and its governor the focus of national attention. For Thurmond, a law-and-order moderate, the apprehension and prosecution of a group of lynchers in South Carolina in May 1947—the first mass lynching trial in U.S. history—signaled real progress and proof of the South's ability to solve its own problems. The acquittal of the mob, Thurmond believed, while perhaps disappointing, in no way justified federal intervention into what he deemed the rights of the states. The president's disregard of this jealously guarded state right set the wheels in motion for the 1948 revolt.

Much of the racial violence that scarred the immediate postwar years involved altercations between black veterans and local whites. Many of the incidents stemmed from whites' fears that blacks were no longer adhering to the protocol of Jim Crow that demanded humility and subservience. Blacks who were unwilling to work for starvation wages or who expressed dissatisfaction with substandard service from whites were labeled troublemakers and targeted for abuse. For white conservatives, what was perhaps most foreboding about these postwar confrontations was the propensity of blacks to fight back against armed white civilians and police. Nowhere was this more apparent than in Columbia, Tennessee, where in February 1946 what began as an altercation between a white radio repairman and a black customer and her son, a navy veteran, exploded into a two-day riot in which white mobs harassed the town's black citizens and the Tennessee Highway Patrol vandalized the black business district. In the end, over one hundred blacks were arrested, two of whom were killed while in police custody. After widespread protests and pressure by numerous labor and civil rights organizations, Attorney General Tom C. Clark investigated the case. No indictments were ever brought against those responsible for violating the civil rights of the black citizens.[124]

In July 1946 two black men and their wives were shot to death by a mob of armed white assailants near Monroe, Georgia. At the time of the murder, the two couples were accompanied by their employer, a local white farmer. One of the victims, Roger Malcom, had earlier stabbed a white farmer who allegedly had made advances to Malcom's wife. The other male victim, George Dorsey, a successful sharecropper, had resisted the attempts of his landlord to swindle him. A grand jury failed to return any indictments for the crimes.[125] The murders coincided with Eugene Talmadge's victory in the Georgia gubernatorial primary. In the year's most racist political campaign, Talmadge promised to restore the white primary and preserve white supremacy. In what amounted to an official sanction of voter intimidation, Talmadge stated that "if the good white people will explain it to the negroes around the state just right I don't think they will want to vote."[126] Despite Talmadge's warning to avoid the polls, an unprecedented number of African Americans voted. With ominous foreshadowing, one disgruntled white commented, "[Lynching has] got to be done to keep Mister Nigger in his place. Since the state said he could vote, there ain't been any holding him. . . . Gene told us what was happening, and what he was going to do about it. I'm sure proud he was elected."[127]

More than the violence in Columbia and Monroe, a South Carolina incident illustrated to the nation the sickening depths to which race relations in the South had sunk. On the night of February 12, 1946, U.S. Army sergeant Isaac Woodard, discharged from Camp Gordon, Georgia, boarded a bus for home in Winnsboro, South Carolina, to be reunited with his wife. Woodard had served fifteen months in the Pacific, where he had earned a battle star. An hour into the trip, the driver stopped at a drugstore, and Woodard asked the driver to wait while he used the restroom. According to Woodard, the driver cursed him, saying there was no time to stop. Woodard, by his own admission, cursed him back. "I cursed him back and told him I was a human being who could understand civil language," Woodard told a reporter. "He told me to go ahead but hurry back, which I did." When they reached Batesburg, South Carolina, the driver summoned a police officer and ordered Woodard off the bus. In his sworn affidavit, Woodard claimed that when he tried to explain the situation to the officer, the policeman struck him with his billy club. When they arrived at the police station, Woodard stated, "he started punching me in my eyes with the end of his billy" until Woodard was barely conscious. When he awoke the next morning, he could not see. Woodard was taken before the judge, who fined him "$50 or 30 days on the road." Woodard only had $44 in cash, although he did have his soldier's deposit and mustering-out paycheck, which was for $649.73. Because the blinded Woodard could not see to endorse the check, the judge returned it to him. Woodard stayed locked in the jail for the remainder of the day until he was finally taken to the veterans' hospital in Columbia.[128]

Although the assault took place in February, Woodard, permanently blinded, languished in the hospital for three months until finally, in May, news of his plight was leaked to James Hinton, president of the state

NAACP. Hinton contacted the national office and also turned the story over to John H. McCray, who was the first to publish news of Woodard's assault.[129] Despite the fact that Woodard had been discovered, his story was far from clear. By August the NAACP was still trying to ascertain accurate information on the alleged assault.[130] The organization tried without success to get information from the veterans' hospital in Columbia where Woodard had convalesced.[131] The Woodard blinding did receive national publicity, however. Actor Orson Welles took a particular interest and broadcast four separate radio shows about the case. As Walter White explained to Welles, this incident deserved special attention. "We have had many horrible cases pass through this office," White confided, "but never one worse than this, with which I am sure you will agree."[132] Relying on Woodard's affidavit and information provided by the NAACP, Welles mistakenly identified the town where Woodard was beaten as Aiken, South Carolina. In his statement Woodard claimed the police who accosted him informed him he was in Aiken. In retaliation against the actor's broadcasts, the Aiken City Council passed an ordinance barring the presentation of one of Welles's movies in a local theater, and Aiken police officers burned movie posters advertising the film.[133]

Desperate for accurate information, the NAACP hired a private investigator and also placed an advertisement in the *Columbia Record* asking for information concerning the beating.[134] Another recently discharged veteran who happened to be on the bus with Woodard saw the plea and identified Batesburg, South Carolina, as the location where Woodard was removed from the bus and taken away.[135] In late August, Lynwood Shull, chief of police of Batesburg, admitted complicity in the incident.[136]

On September 26 Attorney General Tom Clark announced that he had filed charges against the police chief, a direct result, Walter White claimed, of the publicity from Welles's show focusing on "storm trooper Shull."[137] Shull was accused of having "beaten and tortured" Isaac Woodard Jr. "in violation of a Federal Civil Rights Statute, which prohibits police and other public officials from depriving anyone of rights secured by the Constitution and the laws of the United States." Shull was charged with violating Woodard's "right to be secure in his person and immune from legal assault and battery" and "the right and privilege not to be beaten and tortured by persons exercising the authority to arrest."[138]

Shull was tried November 5, 1946. The presiding judge was Julius Waties Waring, a Charleston aristocrat. Although civil rights activists prayed for a conviction, McCray acknowledged that "many newspapermen and lawyers at the time thought Shull would receive at most a suspended sentence." But even that, it seems, was too much to ask for. The all-white jury deliberated for a mere thirty minutes before finding Shull innocent of violating Woodard's civil rights.[139]

Black leaders understood only too well the unlikelihood of a white jury convicting a chief of police; still, McCray and NAACP officials felt the prosecution had not done a thorough job. "Some of us feel . . . that the prosecution might have made its case stronger had it brought out Shull's other beatings of Negroes and their living in general terror of his force at Batesburg," McCray reasoned. He reported that Woodard cried when told of the jury's quick verdict. Denied justice in the here and now, Woodard looked to the hereafter. "Well," he sighed, "the Right One hasn't tried him [Shull] yet." Despite his faith in divine judgment, Woodard was understandably distraught over the turn of events. "I'm not mad at anybody," he informed reporters. "I just feel bad. That's all; I just feel bad."[140]

The Woodard blinding stood out among all of the horrific racial incidents of 1946. Recognizing the power of this case for catalyzing and fomenting national outrage, the NAACP made the most of it. The organization took Woodard on a nationwide tour to expose the racial discrimination and violence endemic to the South.[141] This type of promotional tour was nothing new; the NAACP and other organizations interested in publicizing racial injustice had sponsored similar events. Often circumstances dictated they feature a family member or some other person associated with the victim.[142] With Woodard, the NAACP could present northern audiences with a walking, breathing victim of southern racial injustice. Because Woodard was a veteran, because he was maimed, because his attacker was an officer of the law, and because he survived, he became an emblem of what was terribly wrong with the South.

Truman, undoubtedly angered by all acts of racial violence brought to his attention, reacted with special revulsion to Woodard's blinding, and he referred to it often in public and private when justifying his support for civil rights. The president's secretary, Matthew Connelly, later claimed that the South Carolina incident finally pushed the president into action. According to Connelly, Truman was especially upset about the Woodard attack because the president "had a special feeling for soldiers, and from that point on Truman took a different tack." Later, in his personal correspondence, Truman revealed that his commitment to civil rights went beyond political considerations. In a letter to a Kansas City friend, Truman accepted the political costs that accompanied a firm civil rights position. "I can't approve of such goings on and I shall never approve it, as long as I am here. . . . I am going to try to remedy it and if that ends up in my failure to be reelected, that failure will be in a good cause."[143]

Also outraged by such brutality, an interracial group formed in August 1946, the National Emergency Committee against Mob Violence, whose members represented civil rights, labor, and religious organizations, met with the president on September 19, 1946, to pressure him to condemn mob violence.[144] Walter White recited a long list of lynchings and assaults, concluding with the Woodard incident, after which the president allegedly exclaimed, "My God! I had no idea it was as terrible as that! We've got to do something!"[145] During the course of the meeting David K. Niles, Truman's administrative assistant, recommended the creation of a presidential committee charged with investigating the racial situation and proposing legislative solutions.[146]

In a letter to Attorney General Clark, Truman reported on his meeting with the National Emergency Committee against Mob Violence. The president expressed his "outrage" at the Woodard blinding in particular and recommended action. "I have been very much alarmed at the increased racial feeling all over the country," the president wrote, "and I am wondering if it wouldn't be well to appoint a commission to analyze the situation and have a remedy to present to the Congress." Though Truman knew that Clark was investigating the racial violence in Louisiana, Tennessee, and Georgia, the South Carolina incident convinced him that "it is going to take something more than the handling of each individual case after it happens—it is going to require the inauguration of some sort of policy to prevent such happenings."[147] On October 11, 1946, Clark suggested to the president that he create a presidential commission on civil rights by executive order.[148]

In response to pressure from civil rights advocates and the advice of his attorney general, Truman established the President's Committee on Civil Rights by executive order on December 5, 1946, as the first step in an effort to discourage "individuals who take the law into their own hands and inflict summary punishment and wreak personal vengeance" upon others. The fifteen-member committee, chaired by Charles E. Wilson, president of General Electric, included members representing industry, labor, the clergy, academia, and politics. The committee included only two southerners, both liberals: Frank Porter Graham, president of the University of North Carolina at Chapel Hill and a prominent member of the SCHW, and Dorothy Rogers Tilly of Georgia, whose causes included the Georgia Interracial Committee, the Atlanta Urban League, the Georgia Conference on Social Work, the Southern Regional Council, and the Fellowship of the Concerned. The committee's chief responsibility was to study current federal, state, and local laws and determine in what ways they might be strengthened to adequately protect the civil rights of U.S. citizens.[149]

Upon creating the committee, Truman assured Americans that civil rights were, in his words, "close to my heart." He also noted that "the deprivation of civil rights [was] not peculiar to any one region, or to any one racial or religious group." Despite these disclaimers, the committee, nevertheless, focused particularly on the current rash of problems in the South.[150]

Clearly the practice of lynching represented the most egregious example of the absence of civil rights in the South. Not surprisingly, it became a central concern of the committee. Remarkably, as the committee was getting under way, another violent racial incident rocked the South. South Carolina was the location and once again became the focus of negative national attention and disgust. A Pickens, South Carolina, lynching and subsequent trial provided yet another push for Truman's civil rights agenda. It underscored for the president and his committee the inadequacy of the current federal criminal code and the desperate need for federal protection of civil rights. The lynching and the subsequent trial served to deepen the line dividing those for racial justice and federal intervention and states' rights defenders. The acquittal of the mob and the negative reaction of white citizens to intervention by the FBI and to national interest in the trial were bleak reminders to the nation of the inability of southern communities to police themselves. To South Carolina governor Thurmond and many southern whites, however, the apprehension and prosecution of the lynch mob represented real progress.

On February 16, 1947, a twenty-five-year-old epileptic black man named Willie Earle of Greenville, South Carolina, was arrested on suspicion of robbery and assault of fifty-year-old Greenville taxi driver T. W. Brown. At 5:00 A.M. on February 17, as Brown hovered close to death (he eventually died from the wounds), Earle was spirited from his jail cell in nearby Pickens and lynched by a mob of thirty-five armed men. Ed Gilstrap, the Pickens jailer who lived with his family in another part of the jail building, claimed he did not recognize any members of the unmasked mob, although he did say that some of the men wore taxi drivers' caps. Gilstrap's daughter, who watched from a second-floor window, noted that several of the cars belonging to the mob were taxicabs. When later asked why he so readily surrendered Earle to the mob, Gilstrap responded, "They had shotguns and I danced to their music." Earle's body was found near a slaughter pen on a country road around 6:45 A.M. with shotgun wounds in the head and three gaping stab wounds in the chest.[151] Governor Thurmond reacted immediately to South Carolina's first lynching in twenty years. Condemning the crime as "a blot on the state of South Carolina," he ordered the state constabulary into action to apprehend the lynchers. As a veteran of the recent war for democracy who returned to his state advocating efficient government and law and order, and as a chief executive interested in wooing new industry to his state, Thurmond considered the lynching reprehensible. "Mob rule is against every principle for which we have so recently sacrificed so much," he stated, "and we expect to combat it with the same determination."[152] Whites and blacks applauded Thurmond's swift action. Testifying before the PCCR, FBI chief J. Edgar Hoover confirmed that Thurmond "was desirous of having this thing cleaned up and the culprits brought to justice,"[153] and black leaders commended the governor for his "very courageous action."[154]

Attorney General Tom Clark ordered the FBI to take up the Earle case on February 17, and within ten days of beginning their investigation they had secured the indictment of thirty-one men, "most of whom confessed to their participation [in the crime]."[155] Of the thirty-one men, twenty-eight were taxicab drivers. The FBI secured signed statements from twenty-six of the accused. In these statements the men described how the mob had been rounded up by taxicab company switchboard operators and dispatchers and how the procession of taxis drove into neighboring Pickens County, where Earle was being held. They also described the lynching in graphic detail, how Earle was beaten, stabbed, and finally shot in the head. Those who gave statements admitted their involvement in the crime, and eight of the twenty-six identified one man, forty-five-year-old dispatcher Roosevelt Carlos Hurd, as the trigger man.[156]

Throughout the investigation Thurmond held a firm line.[157] The governor assured liberal members of the southern community of his intent to concentrate all efforts on the conviction of the accused men.[158] On March 12, indictments for murder, conspiracy to commit murder, accessory before the fact, and accessory after the fact were returned for all defendants.[159]

Despite the actions of the governor, which held the promise of retribution for this evil crime, it was clear that community sentiment supported the accused. An anonymous informant told newsman and activist John McCray that local citizens had placed a "box at [the] cash regester asking costumers to drop somthing in the box for help pay the lyncher lawyer. . . . How can a jury be got with [that] spirit [?]"[160] The *Informer,* a black newspaper in Houston, claimed that a fund-raising drive to pay for the defense raised about $2,000 and that donation boxes had been placed in some 150 businesses throughout the Greenville area. One South Carolina newspaper confirmed that the defense was paid partly through public donations.[161]

Though many white South Carolinians abhorred the crime itself, they were more upset by federal interference in the prosecution of the lynching. South Carolina's largest newspaper, *The State,* while deploring the lynching, stated in an editorial immediately following the crime that "had the Negro . . . met his fate above the Mason-Dixon line, the tragedy probably would have been referred to simply as a murder." According to the newspaper, state officials moved swiftly and effectively to apprehend the perpetrators and needed no federal interference.[162] The newspaper strongly criticized the men who had taken the law into their own hands. "But," the *State* admonished, "it reminds those who would commit crime that had not Willie Earle, himself, violated the laws of humanity and of the State of South Carolina he would not have met such a horrible fate. If the Negro had not murdered a Greenville taxi driver, he and his victim would both be alive today, and more than 30 white men in Greenville county would not have the horror of this lynching hanging over them."[163] Many white South Carolinians presumed Earle's guilt; the lynching was unfortunate and also unnecessary because he would have been executed.[164]

The PCCR took an immediate interest in the Earle case and worked closely with the NAACP to keep the White House apprised of the situation.[165] As one of the president's assistants stated at the time, the committee was "taking [Truman] off the hot seat" by their prompt attention to the Greenville lynching.[166] Walter White wrote to Robert Carr that the Earle lynching made it all the more imperative that the committee present its report to Congress as soon as possible.[167] Robert L. Carter of the NAACP believed that Greenville, South Carolina, could serve as a laboratory for the committee. The committee, Carter argued, "should go en masse to [Greenville]" in order to gauge community sentiment toward such atrocities and "from such a testimony make some determination as to causes and reasons for this type of violence."[168] While the PCCR did not travel to Greenville, it kept close tabs on the trial's progress, and the Earle lynching came up frequently in the expert testimony given before the committee.[169]

The lynching trial opened May 13, 1947. More than four hundred curious spectators, both black and white, crowded into the dingy and sweltering Greenville County courthouse and spilled onto the sidewalk outside, all eager to witness the largest lynching trial in U.S. history. Certainly the biggest news to hit Greenville in years, the case was major news in South Carolina and was covered by several national newspapers and magazines.[170]

Presiding over the trial was thirty-seven-year-old jurist J. Robert Martin, who by all accounts did an admirable job of keeping the trial focused on the accused lynchers. Judge Martin warned defense counsel that he would not allow "racial issues" to be introduced into arguments for acquittal. Earle's guilt or innocence, the judge ruled, was immaterial to this case. He would not permit the defense counsel to propose that Earle had confessed to the mob, shortly before he himself was killed, that he had murdered taxi driver Brown.[171]

The key prosecution evidence, admitted over objections by the defense, was the confessions of the defendants to police at the time of arrest. Statement after statement detailed how the men had taken Earle from the jail and driven him out into the country, where they beat, stabbed, pistol-whipped, and finally shot him. While twenty-six of the men admitted they were present, each testified only that he "heard" Earle being beaten or had "heard" the sound of tearing flesh as someone else stabbed Earle.[172] Judge Martin later ruled that incriminating statements allegedly made by twenty-six of the defendants at the time of their arrest were to be admitted in evidence only against the persons making them. He acquitted three of the defendants on all counts, and seven defendants were acquitted on charges of murder and of being accessories after the fact. By the time the defense rested on May 19, twenty-one men still stood accused on all four counts.[173]

The lynching and subsequent trial illustrated the potential for violence and exposed the raw edges of postwar southern society. In particular, they revealed the lengths to which southern whites would go to maintain the color line that stood in danger of being erased. As taxicab drivers, these defendants were similar in station to the lower-middle-class whites studied by anthropologists in Natchez in the 1930s. The researchers concluded that white individuals placed in a subordinate position of serving black customers "achieve their superordination through direct force."[174] Furthermore, during the early postwar years of 1946 and 1947, the taxicab industry as a whole went into a slump, so even if a cabbie wanted to avoid black patrons, it was not economically feasible to do so.[175] The instability inherent in this type of employment, compounded by the fact that many of these cab drivers were veterans returning to a tight labor market and a tense racial atmosphere, heightened their propensity to wield force to maintain the color line.

Just as the political arena reflected southern whites' attempts to safeguard their economic position while resisting racial change, so too did the Earle trial become a venue at which whites sought economic security at the expense of blacks. One of the defense attorneys was John Bolt Culbertson, one of the few prominent whites in Greenville who proudly proclaimed his liberal credentials. A reporter for the *New Yorker* magazine recognized Culbertson as "one of the very few white men in these parts who shake hands with negroes and give them the prefix of Mr. or Mrs. or Miss." Culbertson addressed black veterans' groups and supported the NAACP.[176] An article in the *New Republic* barely two months prior to the trial (but unrelated to it) reported that some locals considered Culbertson's stance on the race question "mildly mad," while others expressed their opinion of his civil rights activities by burning crosses near his home. It would seem that his relatively liberal views on race would make it unlikely that he would take the case. However, Culbertson also had ties to organized labor. He was a vocal supporter of the CIO's activities in South, and he had represented several workers in compensation claims cases before the state. In the months between the lynching and the trial, Culbertson was approached by CIO organizer Jess Mitchell, himself a victim of cross burnings for his union organizing activities.[177] Two of Mitchell's sons-in-law were among the accused cab drivers.[178] Mitchell hoped that the presence of Culbertson—a man known around town as an advocate for both black civil rights and workers' rights—could convince the jury and others that this crime went beyond mere racial vigilantism to white workers' economic security.

During the course of the trial, the defense called no witnesses and presented no evidence to the jury, which consisted of eight textile workers, two salesmen, a shipping clerk, and a farmer. Defense counsel instead played to the xenophobic tendencies of the jury during closing arguments.[179] Culbertson spent as much time criticizing FBI interference in the case as he did providing a defense for the accused. He also implied that the national press covered the trial for the sole purpose of humiliating the South. Ignoring the judge's earlier warning about appealing to racial passions, Culbertson stated, "Willie Earle is dead, and I wish more like him was dead." He was severely rebuked by the judge for this prejudicial statement. The mere presence of Culbertson shifted the focus of the case from a racial lynching to a collective action by white workers. He appealed to a jury of white workers who could probably agree that cab drivers could expect a preponderance of safety on the job. Culbertson compared Willie Earle to a rabid animal, a menace to community safety. "There's a law against shooting a dog," Culbertson argued, "but if a mad dog were loose in my community, I would shoot the dog and let them prosecute me."[180] In his closing arguments, defense counsel Tom Wofford criticized "Northern interference" in the case and saddled the northern press with responsibility "for all our trouble in the South." Wofford accused the FBI of having "meddler's itch," for which there was no cure "except a verdict by jury of this kind to acquit these boys and show them it's no use meddling in Greenville County." He also claimed the trial had political importance and that the Truman administration hoped "to get votes in the North . . . by prosecuting the lynching case."[181]

The trial closed on May 21. After deliberating for a little over five hours, the jury acquitted the defendants of all charges. Judge Martin received the verdict without comment, after which he instructed the jurors where to get their $8-a-day pay and abruptly dismissed them without thanks.[182]

The PCCR and the president were deluged with letters protesting the verdict. Many demanded that the committee recommend the adoption of federal antilynching legislation. "This verdict broadcasts to the world that state action cannot be depended on to punish the crime of lynching," a Vancouver man wrote. "The state has had its opportunity and failed." Others declared South Carolina a "national disgrace."[183] Walter Reuther, president of the United Auto Workers–CIO, wrote to Truman demanding federal action to prevent another "legal farce" as happened in Greenville. "We are convinced," he wrote, "that nothing less than a federal anti-lynching law will serve to uphold justice and decency in cases of this kind." Reuther also reminded the president of the foreign policy implications of continued federal inaction. "So long as lynch mobs are permitted to murder American citizens and go unpunished, these peoples of other nations will look with skepticism on our claim that we are the most Democratic nation in the world." Another woman, distraught over the "tragic miscarriage of justice recently in South Carolina," wrote to PCCR chairman Wilson and reminded him that antilynching legislation "would be an expression of a national conscience and would have some influence toward checking such outbursts of mob violence."[184] Unfolding before their eyes, the Earle litigation served as a test case for the PCCR as it sought to find ways to use existing federal power to secure civil rights.[185] The jury's failure to convict pointed out the weakness of the current U.S. code, which focused on the responsibility of law enforcement officials and other public figures. At least one committee member, Channing Tobias of the Phelps-Stokes Fund, felt the PCCR should have reacted more forcefully with regard to the Greenville lynching in order to assure interested individuals and organizations that the committee was on the ball.[186]

The verdict had a different meaning for southern whites. Many South Carolinians recoiled from the criticism heaped on their state in the wake of the trial. They believed that justice had been served. Many, in fact, believed that the trial itself represented "progress." Walter Brown, Spartanburg businessman and advisor to Governor Thurmond, bristled at the criticism of his state and argued that federal legislation would not have made any difference in the trial's outcome. "I think it is grossly unfair, unjust and down-right outrageous for these jurymen to be held up as intolerant bigots, ignoramuses and of low mentality because they acquitted the defendants," Brown wrote. Brown's feelings about the lynching were tempered by his belief in Earle's guilt. "Like many other southerners, I was extremely disappointed in the outcome of the Greenville trial, but after all, this negro had killed a white man, and certainly if brought to trial would have been electrocuted."[187]

Shortly after the verdict was delivered, President Truman made his first public declaration of support for civil rights in an address to the annual conference of the NAACP in Washington, D.C., in June 1947. One of the president's assistants recommended that he devote only about a minute at the conclusion of the speech to a discussion of civil rights. Truman disregarded this advice. In a speech drafted in part by Robert Carr of the PCCR, Truman made evident his commitment to a vigorous pursuit of protection of civil rights. His tone was urgent. "We cannot wait another decade or another generation to remedy these evils." Probably in reference to the recent verdict, Truman asserted that the federal government must assume a stronger role in the defense of civil rights. "We cannot, any longer, await the growth of a will to action in the slowest state or the most backward community. Our national government must show the way."[188]

The PCCR presented its report, *To Secure These Rights,* to President Truman on October 29, 1947. The committee related that it had "surveyed the flaws in the nation's record and . . . found them serious." The report documented examples of violations of civil rights and urged the federal government to assume greater leadership in the protection of those rights. In an effort to deflect criticism that this was in any way a revolutionary document, the committee claimed that it believed "that the civil rights of the American people can be strengthened quickly and effectively by the normal processes of constitutional government."[189] The last section of the report enumerated the committee's recommendations, which included the enactment of antilynching, anti–poll tax, and fair employment practice legislation; legislation prohibiting discrimination or segregation in interstate transportation; and desegregation of the armed forces.[190] Upon accepting the report, Truman noted that the document's title had been taken from the Declaration of Independence. "I hope this Committee has given us as broad a document as that—an American charter of human freedom in our time. The need for such a charter was never greater than at this moment."[191] Truman wrote to committee member Dorothy Tilly and confessed that he was "confident that it [the report] will take its place among the great papers on Freedom."[192]

Southern lawmakers immediately attacked the report. Congressman L. Mendel Rivers of South Carolina called the report "a brazen and monumental insult to the Democratic South and the southern way of life for both white and colored." James P. Richards, state representative from Lancaster, South Carolina, announced that he was "opposed to the race intermingling recommendations of President Truman's civil liberties committee."[193] Civil rights activists across the country praised the committee's report as progressive and long overdue. Author and activist Lillian Smith congratulated Dorothy Tilly on the report, which she found "eloquent and profoundly moving."[194] One committee member, however, later wondered "whether the Report was not ahead of its time so far as the realities of the civil rights problems go."[195]

Black southerners, although pleased with the committee's efforts, were more circumspect. Percy Greene, editor of the *Jackson Advocate,* accurately reasoned that such reports were essentially valueless except for the dignity lent to the PCCR by the president's association. "We are in full possession of the facts," Greene wrote. "What we want to know is where, and when, do we go from here."[196]

Although he was speaking for Mississippi's black community, Greene's speculations about the future could have been uttered by many different southerners—black and white, liberal and conservative. As 1947 drew to a close, the region and the country looked ahead to the presidential election of 1948—the first presidential election since the end of the war, and the first such election in sixteen years in which Franklin D. Roosevelt would not be the Democratic Party candidate. Among his strongest supporters in 1944, white southerners had since lost some of their faith in Harry Truman. Their continued reflexive support of the national Democratic Party would very much depend on the president's actions in the wake of the PCCR's report.

Uncertainty with regard to the direction of national policy in a way mirrored the regional political scene. The stresses and strains of wartime—in particular the increasing militance of black southerners—had complicated traditional divisions within southern politics as New Deal liberals and conservatives tentatively staked out their positions in the territory of racial politics. At the same time, the war ushered in a new cadre of moderate reformers such as Sidney McMath and Strom Thurmond, whose racial politics appeared to auger something new. Just as white southerners began to question their willingness to trust the president to lead them into the postwar era, so no one could predict with any degree of certainty to whom the future political direction of the South belonged.

OUT OF THE BAG?

The Search for Southern Unity

Slap us down again Pres., slap us down again
Make us take some more, Pres., we are mice, not men
MISSISSIPPI STATES' RIGHTS SONG
ca. 1948

Despite the promises embodied in the PCCR's report, Truman remained tight-lipped regarding his future actions on civil rights. When questioned whether the committee's recommendations would find their way into his 1948 State of the Union message, the plain-talking Missourian was uncharacteristically vague. "It could be used as a foundation for part of the message," he replied, "some of it maybe."[1]

In 1948 national political realities dictated that the Democratic Party risk white southern sensibilities for the votes of urban blacks. Seemingly cast aside by the national party, southern political leaders cried foul and threatened revenge. But the caterwauling over this latest and most serious mistreatment at the hands of the president and the national party soon gave way to head scratching and stalling as southern state and congressional leaders attempted to determine the best method by which to reclaim power within the national party. Southern conservatives soon discovered a political South that was less than unified. For many Black Belt leaders, Truman's appeal to African American voters was simply the final straw in a long string of federal abuses heaped upon a beleaguered South that seemed in danger of erasing the color line. Aroused, they began engineering a strategy to deny Truman the Democratic Party's presidential nomination. Throughout the first quarter of 1948, the Black Belt coalitions within the individual Deep South states struggled for control of their respective parties and tentatively aligned themselves for some as yet unstated independent action. It was a risky venture; to bolt party ranks was to risk political suicide in the South. The process was also highly decentralized. Success in wooing party leaders and the rank and file away from the national Democratic Party depended on a number of factors and was largely determined according to the individual political cultures and fault lines of the separate southern states. In a sense, engineering the bolt from the national party was not one but eleven discrete strategies.

Amidst their political maneuvering, southern conservatives struggled to explain themselves to themselves and to white voters. In the process they crafted a political message that drew on familial and sexual metaphors to convey the magnitude of the political transformation taking place at the national level. These states' rights conservatives spoke not of shifting coalitions and changing power relationships but, rather, of bastardy, illicit liaisons, jilted lovers, and broken marriages to express their distress over their declining fortunes within the national Democratic Party and their fears regarding the potential demise of white supremacy. Their intimate rendering of political power bears testimony to the depth of their antipathy toward the president, the national party, and impending social change, an antagonism they would never fully resolve.

★

In a memorandum outlining the Democratic Party's formula for victory in 1948, presidential strategist Clark Clifford and Washington attorney James A. Rowe Jr. predicted that the election would be a three-way race between Republican candidate Thomas Dewey, governor of New York, and former secretary of agriculture Henry Wallace, who would mount a third-party effort. Party strategy was made all the more difficult by the Democrats' huge tent, under whose capacious flaps congregated "an unhappy alliance of Southern conservatives, Western Progressives and Big City labor"; the Democrats had to maintain the support of all three if they hoped to win in November. Despite this imperative, Clifford and Rowe advocated calculated risks predicated on traditional southern voting behavior. "It is inconceivable," they reasoned, "that any policy initiated by the Truman administration no matter how 'liberal' could so alienate the South in the next year that it would revolt. As always, the South can be considered safely Democratic. And in formulating national policy, it can be safely ignored." With a Republican Congress and the unlikelihood of the president getting anything through it in an election year, he did not have to "get along" with the South. Black voters, on the other hand, were more unpredictable and crucial. The Democratic Party had to make a valid commitment to civil rights or risk losing black support. Clifford and Rowe acknowledged that any efforts made to win black votes risked upsetting white southern Democrats, but, they reasoned, "that is the lesser of two evils."[2]

In December 1947 Henry Wallace declared himself the presidential candidate of the newly formed Progressive Party. He reaffirmed his strong position on civil rights by announcing a seventy-four-point program that included demands for anti–poll tax and antilynching legislation and a renewed FEPC.[3] Wallace threatened to lop off the party's left wing; to stay in the race, Truman would have to appeal to labor and minority voters. Truman's advisors agreed that African Americans might hold the balance of power in key northern cities and that there were enough black voters in fifteen northern states to swing 277 electoral votes.[4] In order to win those states, Truman would need to make a renewed and stronger commitment to civil rights.

During his State of the Union address in the first week of January 1948, Truman announced that he would deliver a special address before Congress on civil rights.[5] He assigned the task of crafting that message to Clifford; George Elsey, Clifford's assistant; and Robert Carr, executive secretary of the PCCR. The trio sought to devise a speech that occupied a middle ground between a wholehearted endorsement of the entire civil rights report and a disregard of the committee's findings.[6] Despite their essential agreement, the group haggled over what constituted "a middle ground."[7] Clifford and the others knew that even the most benign speech would "cause a terrific explosion in Congress, perhaps one of the biggest in our times."[8] But the fuse for this bomb had already been lit. Even before the president submitted his special message to Congress on civil rights, Mississippi's political leaders were already striking the match.

★

The racial passions of Mississippi's politicians always simmered just below the boiling point. Even before the president's State of the Union address, Walter Sillers, Speaker of the Mississippi House of Representatives and Delta planter, announced that if the president continued to endorse recommendations similar to those in the PCCR report, he personally would engineer the state's bolt from the national party.[9] Mississippi's U.S. Senator James Eastland, a planter from Sunflower County who, since his election in 1942, had proven the equal of the late Theodore Bilbo and Congressman John Rankin on the demagogue scale, further warned national party chieftains that southern Democrats would not support a presidential candidate bent on "destroy[ing] our social institutions." The South, he hissed, would fight all attempts by the North to "sacrifice them on the cross of political expediency."[10]

Mississippi's unassuming governor-elect, Fielding Wright, finally threw down the gauntlet on January 20, 1948. In an impassioned inaugural speech that ignited political sparks on that brisk winter morning, Wright threatened that Mississippi would possibly bolt the ticket of Truman or any other Democrat in 1948. Truman's civil rights agenda was political harassment "deliberately aimed" at the South, and he warned the national party not to take Dixie for granted. Wright regretted that Mississippi or the South should break with the Democratic Party in a national election, "but vital principles and eternal truths transcend party lines, and the day is now at hand when determined action must be taken."[11] Mississippi's political leaders responded zealously to Wright's call to arms.[12] Claiming he was not yet sufficiently informed to comment, only freshman senator John Stennis did not openly endorse Wright's plan. Roundly chastised by the *Jackson Daily News,* Stennis soon climbed onboard.[13]

Mississippi's leadership in the states' rights revolt surprised few. Even by southern standards, political scientist V. O. Key once remarked, Mississippi was in a class by itself.[14] The most rural southern state, Mississippi boasted only twelve towns whose population in 1940 exceeded 10,000; the largest of these, Jackson, the capital, had only 62,000 people. By the early 1940s Mississippi had the highest proportion of blacks in the country: 49.2 percent. Furthermore, in no area of the state did blacks make up fewer than 30 percent of the population.[15] Whites had imposed racial segregation in Mississippi during Reconstruction. Almost at the moment of emancipation, white Mississippians had so completely defined blacks' "place" in what they considered a "white man's country" that little additional legislation was required.[16] Formal political disfranchisement came with the passage of the 1890 state constitution, although extralegal measures more than actual laws prevented most black Mississippians from going to the polls.[17]

The key political issue in Mississippi with regard to national politics had always been race. Internally, other matters rose to the surface. An economic and political divide separated the flourishing Delta planter and the distressed white tenant farmer of the hills.[18] Although the 1902 primary law made it extremely difficult for a Deltan to win the governor's mansion, the 1890 constitution left legislative malapportionment in place, thus granting predominant influence in the state legislature to the white minority/black majority Delta counties. Delta solons consistently pursued fiscally conservative agendas that included regressive taxation and measures designed to promote corporate investment while opposing efforts to improve public services—including schools—for poor whites.[19]

Although the hill versus Delta conflict often resulted in lively political contests, a successful class politics could not overcome the politics of race.[20] Former governor and U.S. senator James K. Vardaman, although originally from the Delta, personified the neo-Populist animosity of the hills toward the Delta that capitalized on the racism of lower-class whites. Although whites in both the hill and the Delta agreed on the necessity of white supremacy, they differed significantly in terms of how to maintain it. Flamboyant in speech and demeanor, known as much for his florid demagoguery as for his long dark hair and billowing coattails, Vardaman campaigned for the poor white vote mounted on a lumber wagon drawn by oxen and won the devotion of this element by both his reactionary race doctrine and his progressive program of economic and social reform.[21] Vardaman's most infamous progeny was Theodore Bilbo, son of the rough and rural piney woods of southern Mississippi. Few in Mississippi then and since remained neutral on Bilbo. Deltan William Alexander Percy labeled him "a pert little monster . . . with that sort of cunning common to criminals that passes for intelligence." And, Percy acknowledged, "the people loved him." Bilbo assumed leadership of the Mississippi progressive faction after Vardaman was defeated in his bid for the U.S. Senate in 1922. For the next twenty years, until his death in 1946, the resilient Bilbo remained a lightning rod on Mississippi's political landscape as the spokesperson for the downtrodden whites. As governor he supported public education and compulsory school attendance, an equitable tax structure, prohibition, and railroad and corporate regulation, inciting what his biographer termed "the brogan and overall crowd" with his denunciations of men of wealth and privilege. More than Vardaman, Bilbo heightened Mississippi's class politics.[22]

Although poor whites and wealthy Deltans could agree on the importance of maintaining white supremacy, for the first few decades of the twentieth century, Delta politicians, according to one historian, "took a more businesslike approach to the race issue."[23] Dependent on black labor and fearful of labor shortages, Delta whites sought to protect their workers from the most violent manifestations of hill county racism that threatened to drive off black workers.[24] Increasingly though, by midcentury Black Belt whites realized that the greatest threat to racial stability in regions like the Delta were posed not by poor hill county whites but by the federal government. When the Delta leaders became increasingly obsessed with race in the postwar era, one former Bilbo supporter remarked, "They got no right to use race; that belongs to our side of the fence."[25]

In 1948 the Delta interests remained in firm control of the state legislature. Presiding over the house of representatives was red-haired Walter Sillers Jr. from Bolivar County. Sillers had served in the Mississippi House of Representatives since 1916 and had occupied the Speaker's position since 1944. The Sillers name was a familiar one in Mississippi politics, and the Speaker personified the Delta perspective. The grandson of slaveholders, Sillers's father, Walter Sr., had owned and operated several cotton plantations, which he dutifully passed to his son, and he was one of the founders of the Staple Cotton Association. The senior Sillers was also involved in state politics. He boasted of his role in banishing Republican rule from Bolivar County, served one term in the state legislature in 1886, and helped organize the first Democratic Party faction in the county. He later served as a political advisor to gentleman planter and fellow Deltan Leroy Percy in his race against Vardaman for the U.S. Senate in 1911. Walter Jr. became one of the first directors of the powerful Delta Council, which he helped found in 1935, and he served continuously, either as director, committee chair, or officer, until his death.[26] Recalled by one political associate as "a polished gentlemen" who was also impatient and arrogant, Sillers ruled the Mississippi house with an iron grip and represented the reactionary Black Belt plantation forces in Mississippi politics for several decades until his death in 1966. Years later, legislators who served with him recalled him with a measure of awe and fear. Few spoke of him with anything resembling warmth.[27]

The New Deal years were anxious ones for Sillers, who came to embody the fears of the Black Belt elite. He railed especially against wages and hours legislation and the Wagner Act, which he believed offered protection to Communists and radicals. He worried about the migration of black labor from Delta plantations during the war years, and as president of the powerful Delta Council, Sillers sent the organization's secretary Dorothy Black undercover to infiltrate meetings of the Southern Tenant

Walter Sillers Jr., Mississippi Speaker of the House and prominent Dixiecrat. Photograph courtesy of Delta State University Library, Cleveland, Mississippi.

Farmers Union.[28] The creation of the FEPC, which in Sillers's mind not only usurped the rights of employers but also threatened to drain even more labor from the countryside, only confirmed his worst fears about Communists in the federal government. Indeed, Sillers (ironically nicknamed "Red") saw Communists behind every cotton boll; he once asked a friend at the University of Mississippi to investigate possible Communist ties among students conducting a lunchroom protest. In 1948 Delta interests also controlled the governorship. Fielding Wright, from the tiny Delta hamlet of Rolling Fork, assumed the office after Thomas Bailey, who drew his support primarily from the hill region, died in office in 1946. Lieutenant Governor Wright easily won a full term as governor in the Democratic primary held in 1947.

No one, probably not even Wright himself, would have chosen the bespectacled Mississippi governor to lead the states' rights charge. Nothing in Wright's background indicated that he was temperamentally suited for such a position, and indeed he was not. Wright's disdain for the campaign trail made him a poor choice to galvanize a movement hoping to stir political passions and regional indignation. Wright, one former colleague recalled, "wasn't what you'd call a popular man. He wasn't a backslapper." Judge L. B. Porter, who served in both the house and the senate during the 1940s, observed that Wright "was not an affable fellow. . . . He was very stern even in social discussions."[29]

What was perhaps not Wright's by temperament, however, was his by birthright. Born into privilege in 1895 in Rolling Fork, Wright was the grandson of a wealthy planter and a distant relative of George Washington. Wright learned the finer elements of racial control from his father, who alternately oversaw the family plantations and served as the Sharkey County sheriff. Although his father held public office, young Fielding showed no interest in public service. In fact, he expressed disdain for the profession and once stated that he would never go into politics. His interests lay on the baseball diamond. Fielding left home at age sixteen to attend the Webb School in Bellbuckle, Tennessee, and later entered the University of Alabama, where he graduated with a degree in law in 1915. Back home, he passed the bar and entered practice with his uncle. Like so many young men of his generation, Wright cut short his career to serve in World War I. When he returned, he focused not on the rough-and-tumble of the local political scene but on the pastoral logic of the baseball diamond, playing for several semiprofessional teams in the Delta while also resuming his law practice. His taste for politics developed over time, and he was elected to the state senate in 1928 and, later, to the Mississippi House of Representatives. As a state legislator Wright quickly attached himself to the powerful Delta leaders already in office and counted himself among Bilbo's adversaries. He advocated fiscal responsibility, opposed Bilbo's proposal to construct a state printing plant for the public

Fielding L. Wright, governor of Mississippi and Dixiecrat vice-presidential candidate. Photograph courtesy of the Mississippi Department of Archives and History, Jackson.

printing of school textbooks, and worked to pass a sales tax in the 1930s to help alleviate the state's $10 million budget deficit left over from the Bilbo administration. Wright took a hiatus from politics in 1938 and accepted a position as senior partner in a Vicksburg law firm, where he amassed a considerable fortune representing oil companies. He returned to politics and was elected lieutenant governor in 1943. When Governor Thomas Bailey died in 1946, Wright ascended to the governorship, delivered his defiant speech on that frosty January morning in 1948, and waited for the other shoe to drop.[30]

With his party already beginning to splinter, Truman plunged headlong into the fray. On February 2 the president delivered to Congress a speech devoted entirely to civil rights, the first of its kind in American history. In an effort to close the gap between America's democratic ideals and reality, as well as bolster the country's international reputation and aid in the Cold War, Truman recommended a ten-point program that included establishing a permanent commission on civil rights, a joint congressional committee on civil rights, and a civil rights division in the Department of Justice; providing federal protection for voting and against lynching; establishing an FEPC to prevent unfair discrimination in employment; and prohibiting discrimination in interstate transportation facilities. "We know the way," Truman stated. "We need only the will."[31]

The white South responded shrilly and, this time, in unison.[32] Florida's Senator Claude Pepper was the only southerner who spoke favorably of the president's message. Reactions from southern governors varied in tone, although none supported the proposed legislation. Governor Millard Caldwell of Florida supported Truman's nomination regardless of his stand on civil rights, while Governor Ben Laney of Arkansas described the president's program as distasteful, unthinkable, and ridiculous. Even populist governor James E. Folsom of Alabama assailed the president and offered to challenge him for the nomination.[33] South Carolina's entire congressional delegation denounced the program, and Governor Strom Thurmond affirmed that his state was ready to fight.[34] Hoping to generate momentum for the creation of a regional movement, Fielding Wright of Mississippi called for a statewide mass meeting of Mississippi Democrats on February 12, 1948, to rally support for the states' rights cause and to lay the groundwork for a future regional meeting of "all true Jeffersonian Democrats."[35]

Facing a potential political defection from the party ranks, Truman was also deluged with mail from enraged white southerners. They accused the president of playing politics and of taking "a typically Northern, uninformed and narrow minded attitude toward things."[36] Like their elected officials, some expressed dismay and disbelief that Truman, a man from a border state, could promote the cause of civil rights. "Be a Southernor [*sic*]. You are one," one man wrote. "Stick to your colors. You are a white man. Be one."[37] An irate woman from Corinth, Mississippi, appealed to what she hoped was Truman's sympathetic appreciation of the region's race/sex taboo. "You wouldn't want your [daughter] Margaret to make a cross country trip on a bus seated by a dirty, evil smelling, loud mouthed negro man, now would you?" she asked the president. "You wouldn't want your Margaret to sleep in a Pullman section with a negro man above or below her, now would you?"[38] Above all, these correspondents sounded desperate and afraid of impending change, a change that Truman's program clearly threatened. One despondent South Carolina citizen wrote to former secretary of state and fellow South Carolinian James Byrnes that in the "small towns it's fever hot. People are scared. One man told me that he was much more afraid of Truman than of Russia."[39] Feeling alone and cornered, many white southerners were poised to strike.

Truman's proposals even prompted a response from the revived Ku Klux Klan. The night after Truman's address, 189 Klansmen met in Swainsboro, Georgia, to dedicate themselves to the protection of white womanhood. Unfortunately for the hooded order, attendance at the rally fell short of expectations. In an attempt to account for the low attendance, one Klan leader explained that "there would have been more Klansmen present but others were unable to obtain sheets."[40]

Eben Ayers, Truman's assistant press secretary, noted that in a staff meeting the day after the speech, the president appeared nonchalant and perhaps even secretly pleased with the white South's reaction. The president, he noted, thought the southern blowup inevitable and long overdue, and that it might lead to a new political realignment of conservatives and liberals in the region.[41] In his diary Truman noted that he had expected white southerners to rail against his civil rights message. Nevertheless, he wrote, "it needs to be said."[42]

Immensely unpopular with white southerners, Truman's civil rights message was generally well received among African American leaders.[43] Walter White regarded Truman's efforts on behalf of civil rights far more significant than anything Franklin Roosevelt had done. Although Roosevelt opposed blatant racial injustices, such as lynching, White acknowledged, his unwillingness to ruffle the feathers of southern lawmakers precluded any action beyond private assurances of personal support for antilynching or anti–poll tax legislation. Truman, White believed, did not bow to political pressures. Instead, reasoned White, "in his quiet Missouri fashion Harry Truman has demonstrated that he is in earnest when he says that 'we must correct the remaining imperfections in our practice of Democracy.'"[44] White, of course, conveniently overlooked any political motives Truman might have had for introducing his civil rights proposals. On the local level, James Hinton, president of the South Carolina NAACP, congratulated the president for his civil rights stance and promised that black voters (what few could vote) would reward him at the ballot box.[45]

Despite the fervor with which white southerners berated the civil rights message, by February 4 the *New York Times* was labeling the calls for a southern bolt "another Dixie flareup which would wind up with Dixie in line."[46] Indeed, the "terrific explosion" predicted by Clifford seemed more like a "sitzkrieg" as southern lawmakers hunkered down and struggled to cobble together a unified plan of action. Dixie Democrats' first opportunity to forge a regional consensus came during the first week of February at the Southern Governors' Conference in Wakulla Springs, Florida, just outside Tallahassee. The meeting originally was called to discuss plans for establishing regional southern graduate programs for African Americans, but the question of how most effectively to counter Truman's civil rights program dominated the discussions. Weakened by a 101° fever, an ailing Fielding Wright hobbled into Tallahassee determined to do battle. Having earlier issued the call for a southern revolt, the Mississippi leader advocated a hard line. Wright recommended that a "Southern Conference for *true* Democrats" meet at Jackson, Mississippi, on March 1 to draw up a plan of action.[47]

Wright's plan fell on deaf ears. The governors were united in their opposition to Truman's civil rights recommendations, yet most refused to support secession from the party. The atmosphere was tense as the governors haggled over various proposals and resolutions. James Folsom of Alabama suggested they hash out the dispute on the floor at the Democratic National Convention in July. Neither Wright's nor Folsom's proposal received a seconding motion. Into this yawning gap of gubernatorial indecision stepped Strom Thurmond with a plan calling for the creation of a committee that would seek a compromise from the president on the civil rights problem during a forty-day "cooling off" period.[48] Thurmond's motion possessed the appearance of action yet did not commit the governors to anything potentially politically damaging. It passed unanimously. The governors reasoned that if the president had catered to the liberals to keep them from following Henry Wallace, he would yield to the South under a similar threat.[49] Although the motion passed without dissent, not everyone was pleased. One of Thurmond's advisors recalled that Fielding Wright "became peeved" when Thurmond made his proposal and refused to serve on Thurmond's committee.[50]

Thurmond tried to present himself as both reasonable and defiant. His solution was comparatively moderate, and he urged white southerners to "approach the situation . . . with dignity, self-respect and restraint"; nevertheless, his tone was strident. The proposed "anti-American" civil rights measures, he declared, "would jeopardize the peace and good order which prevails" in the South. He warned the administration not to underestimate southern resolve and hinted that the South might flex its collective political muscle in the electoral college.[51] Although the governors' ultimate goal was to defuse a potentially divisive situation, Thurmond assured white southerners that they were not patsies and would demand concessions from the national party.[52] State NAACP leader James Hinton criticized Thurmond's resolution as " 'a keen disappointment to the negroes of South Carolina.' " Up to that point, Hinton claimed, blacks felt that in Thurmond, "they had a Chief Executive, free from White Supremacy attitudes and expressions, and one who would hasten the day, when Negroes in South Carolina would enjoy 'EQUALITY OF OPPORTUNITY.' " Hinton warned that governors opposing Truman "will live to REGRET THE STAND TAKEN."[53] South Carolina's tiny but active liberal community had come to expect better from its governor.

Any effective bargaining power Thurmond's committee might have had was compromised almost immediately. Not all southern governors appreciated the South Carolinian's belligerent tone. The governors of Georgia, Florida, Maryland, and Tennessee made clear they were determined to head off any southern revolt over civil rights issues.[54] Truman snuffed out any hope of reconciliation or compromise when, shortly after the governors' conference, he announced he would neither compromise any point of his civil rights plan nor discuss the issue with any southern group.[55] Snubbed by the president, Thurmond's subcommittee, which included Preston Lane of Maryland, R. Gregg Cherry of North Carolina, Ben Laney of Arkansas, and Beauford Jester of Texas, had to settle for a conference with the chairman of the DNC, Senator J. Howard McGrath of Rhode Island.

In the forty-day interim between the Southern Governors' Conference and the meeting with the national leadership, Thurmond sounded out southern congressmen and senators on the civil rights issue.[56] The responses were mixed. All respondents opposed the civil rights proposals, yet they disagreed on how to combat them. Only Senator Richard B. Russell of Georgia and Louisiana's two senators urged the governors to act independently. "Sick at heart" over Truman's "unwarranted attack," Russell reminded Thurmond that governors controlled the state party machinery and were free to instruct their electors in any way they so chose without sacrificing their party membership at the state and local levels. Russell reasoned that "if only 3 or 4 of the States did this the voice of the South would again be respected in Democratic councils." Senators John H. Overton and Allen J. Ellender of Louisiana joined Russell in advocating strong punitive action. However, the Louisiana senators cautioned, they would have to move quickly. Time was running short.[57] No senators from the Upper South commented any further than to say they opposed Truman's plan. Among southern congressmen, a wide range of opinion surfaced. Many felt a joint gubernatorial/congressional effort would produce the best results, and more respondents favored working out the problem within the familiar confines of the Democratic Party. Most praised the governors' moderate proposal but would not commit themselves to a definite plan. Again, as with the senatorial responses, the congressmen from Upper South states—Arkansas, Kentucky, Maryland, North Carolina, and Tennessee, as well as Florida—either did not respond to Thurmond's query or sent cautious replies.[58]

Despite the cooling-off period, Dixie Democrats did not forgo opportunities to retaliate against the president. The governors' self-imposed hiatus coincided with the Democratic Party's annual fund-raising event, the Jefferson-Jackson Day dinners. Held in Washington, D.C., and around the country, the dinners provided the national party with a crucial source of funds. Southern leaders took advantage of this opportunity for revenge by withholding funds and publicly embarrassing the president. South Carolina Democrats held no Jefferson-Jackson Day festivities. In Arkansas, Governor Laney announced that the $10,000 proceeds from the dinner would remain under state control until further notice. Half of the guests at the Arkansas fund-raiser departed before the radio broadcast of Truman's Jefferson-Jackson Day address. Democrats in Clark County,

Alabama, announced that they would return all mail from national party offices unopened.[59] The most widely publicized insult to the president was orchestrated by South Carolina Senator Olin Johnston. Anxious in the knowledge that African Americans would be attending the dinner, Johnston's wife, Gladys, had asked DNC chairman McGrath for assurances that she would not be seated "next to a Negro." When McGrath rebuffed her, Johnston and the entire South Carolina delegation boycotted the dinner. Because Gladys Johnston had helped plan the banquet, Johnston's table was directly in front of President Truman's podium. Johnston even hired a professional boxer to stand guard over the table to prevent anyone from sitting there.[60]

These antics, however, did not help the southerners' case when they traveled to Washington to confer with DNC chairman McGrath on February 23. During the 1½-hour meeting, a testy Thurmond did most of the talking for the southern group. One DNC official present at the meeting observed that Governors Cherry and Laney appeared relaxed and jovial and conducted themselves in a reasonable fashion. Thurmond, he noted, "was different." The South Carolina governor remained standing, "didn't smile" and "did not join in the pleasantries." Every governor present except Thurmond appeared willing to make concessions.[61] Thurmond's will won out, for the governors offered no concessions. Furthermore, McGrath and the administration stood their ground and refused to compromise the principles enunciated in the president's civil rights message.[62] As a sop, McGrath stated that he would support a platform and civil rights plank similar to the one the Democrats ran on in 1944.[63] Stymied by McGrath and the Truman administration, Thurmond bitterly warned the national party leaders that the southern states were "no longer 'in the bag.'"[64] The southern governors would reconvene to map out their strategy of resistance.

Two weeks later, on March 8, Truman raised the political stakes for white southerners when he declared his candidacy for the Democratic Party nomination.[65] The president's timing was crucial. "This should make many of the Southerners who are talking so loudly 'put up or shut up,'" the president's assistant press secretary noted.[66]

Unsuccessful in their attempt to reach a negotiated settlement with the administration, southern lawmakers returned to their states to draw up a plan of action. February's developments had proven that regional unity would be difficult, if not impossible, to achieve. As winter gave way to spring, and as white southerners reassessed the strength of their traditional political attachments, the divisions that had first appeared at the Florida meeting hardened. Southern governors remained united only in their opposition to Truman's proposals; beyond that, cohesion broke down over the appropriate response. Governors Wright, Thurmond, William Tuck of Virginia, and Laney of Arkansas leaned toward some as yet undefined independent political action. Governors Folsom, Lane, Cherry, Thompson, and Caldwell were swayed by party loyalty. By the end of April, only conservatives in Mississippi, South Carolina, and Alabama (acting contrary to the governor) appeared determined to act. Motivated by the escalating politics of race, fearful of federal intrusion, and bolstered by state parties dominated by antipopulist Black Belt/industrial coalitions, these Deep South leaders took the first tentative steps toward subregional political independence. They did not organize grassroots campaigns or attempt to build a groundswell of popular resentment clamoring for action. Such democratic measures and tactics were foreign to them. And indeed, such action would have contradicted their political philosophy that the state and national parties were capable of acting as separate entities, and that the state parties did not have to follow the dictates of the national party, even in a presidential election. Even though they worked through existing political machinery, these coalitions heightened political distinctions within their own states and underscored their increasingly conservative identity. By early May, Black Belt conservatives were holding their own states' rights convention in Mississippi, where they made common cause with their brethren in the other Deep South states.

William Tuck of Virginia was the first southern governor to act. Tuck asked the state legislature to pass a law that would allow the state convention to instruct Virginia's electors to vote for an alternate candidate should the Democratic National Convention nominate a civil rights candidate.[67] Initially supported by Senator Harry Byrd and the powerful Byrd machine, Tuck's plan seemed destined to keep Truman's name off the ballot in November.

Although Virginia was the first out of the gate, Mississippi emerged as the states' rights leader. Undaunted by his inability to effect a unified, defiant southern front at the Southern Governors' meeting in early February, and unwilling to wait for the rest of the field to get up to speed following the "cooling-off" period, Fielding Wright determined that Mississippi would carry on the fight—alone if necessary—and he immediately set to work constructing a campaign.

Governor Wright kicked off the states' rights movement with a mass meeting in Jackson on February 12, Abraham Lincoln's birthday. The *Clarion-Ledger* reported that some 4,000 "white Mississippians, blood of the Confederacy and of true Jeffersonian democracy" from the state's eighty-two counties overflowed onto two streets from Jackson's city auditorium.[68] Rebel yells rang throughout the packed arena as Mississippi's politicos excoriated President Truman, condemned the national Democratic Party, damned the civil rights legislation, and authorized a regional meeting of "True White Jeffersonian Democrats" for May 10.[69] With a minimum of confusion, the Democratic Party of Mississippi was converted into a vehicle for anti-Truman sentiment.[70]

Support for the states' rights zealots in Jackson was not unanimous. Voters in the traditional populist strongholds, young Democrats, and legislative hopefuls such as young Frank Smith, one of several veterans running in Mississippi's Democratic primary, looked askance at the states' rights takeover. Rumblings regarding the doings at Jackson resonated throughout the state. Editorials by state representative Philip E. Mullen in the *Oxford Eagle* early in the campaign expressed mixed feelings over the wisdom of Wright's threat and questioned the ability of the South to assert itself as an independent political entity. "The whole South could walk out and Truman would still get the nomination. However, we doubt any other Southern state following the course if Mississippi should be foolish enough to make such a futile gesture." Such a move ultimately would only aid the Republican Party.[71] Frank Smith later acknowledged that while he and other moderates disagreed with the states' rights revolt, they were a distinct minority. Smith soon made up his mind that he could do more good within the system than outside it and so said nothing.[72] In Mississippi the spectrum of opinion had narrowed to the point where the best moderates could do was keep quiet.

Mississippi's blacks did what little they could to voice their opposition to Wright's actions. On the eve of Wright's rally, Mississippi blacks held a statewide mass meeting, chaired by newspaper editor Percy Greene, to address the civil rights issue. They sent a telegram of endorsement to President Truman and forwarded a petition to Governor Wright and the state legislature asking them to create a permanent biracial commission to investigate racial issues.[73] They received no response.

During the alleged cooling-off period, Mississippi Democrats cranked up their states' rights effort. They opened a volunteer-staffed states' rights headquarters in Jackson on February 16, and a week later some two hundred Mississippi Democrats and supporters from nine other southern states convened in Jackson to draw up "top secret" plans for opposing Truman.[74] During the meeting, $61,500 was pledged to carry out an educational campaign in Mississippi and other states.[75] On March 1, and in the wake of the inconclusive meeting between the southern governors and DNC chairman McGrath, the Mississippi State Democratic Executive Committee (SDEC) pledged its delegates to the national convention to oppose any civil rights candidate. If the convention approved a civil rights plank in the national party platform, Mississippi's delegates planned to walk out.[76]

To direct the campaign, the Magnolia State rebels created both a Peoples' Committee of "loyal States' Rights Jeffersonian Democrats," designed to direct political organizing at the district, county, and precinct levels, and a Campaign Committee, directed to take charge of fund-raising across the state and coordinate with similar efforts in other states. Governor Wright became honorary chairman of the Peoples' Committee, and Wallace W. Wright (no relation to the governor), fifty-four-year-old president of Mississippi's largest wholesale grocery firm and powerful lobbyist whom one contemporary described as "the George Patton of Mississippi politics," was named chairperson of the Campaign Committee.[77] The State Women's Committee was captained by Mary Louise Kendall of Natchez, who resigned her post as Mississippi national Democratic committeewoman to accept the leadership of the women in the states' rights movement as it took its campaign into the state's eighty-two counties.[78] Working through networks of existing civic clubs, women served as valuable foot soldiers in the states' rights campaign, performing much of the daily canvassing and fund-raising necessary for a successful grassroots effort. The Women's Committee organized the several hundred Democratic women leaders in the state to choose states' rights delegates in the precinct elections on May 18.[79] Fund-raising consisted primarily of selling the red, white, and blue States' Rights Jeffersonian Democrat campaign buttons at local hotels and county fairs for $1.00. To galvanize women's support for the campaign, the committee held a statewide meeting, the first of its kind, at the Jackson auditorium on April 15. Designated "for Women Only," the meeting provided women the opportunity to pledge their support for states' rights.[80] In his keynote address, Governor Wright stated that the main issue in the campaign was "whether or not the majority of the people were going to let negroes run the country."[81]

The initial flurry of organizational activity culminated with simultaneous rallies in each of Mississippi's eighty-two counties on March 20. Governor Wright delivered a radio address beamed into all of the party gatherings. Wright grossly misrepresented the president's proposals, equating them with the recommendations of the PCCR, whose suggestions were, in many cases, more far-reaching than the president's. Wright urged Mississippi Democrats to "volunteer now by the hundreds and thousands" in the states' rights fight, called on them to select states' rights delegates at their precinct elections in mid-May, and invited them to attend the nationwide conference of States' Rights Democrats to be held in the Jackson auditorium on May 10. Following his speech, Mississippians attending the mass meetings across the state passed resolutions backing the stand of the Mississippi SDEC against national party leaders on the issue of civil rights.[82]

At 7:30 on Sunday morning, May 9, 1948, the day before the national states' rights meeting, as black and white Mississippians were getting out of bed and preparing for church, Governor Wright delivered a threat to the state's black citizens via a statewide radio broadcast. "It is fitting and proper on this Sabbath day of peace and quiet, of meditation and of prayer," he began, "for me to discuss with you . . . one of the gravest threats to our tranquility and our happiness." The threat he referred to was the president's proposed civil rights plan. Governor Wright hoped to correct the "maliciously false and dangerous" impression that civil rights advocates had the best interests of Mississippi blacks at heart. "The stirring up of prejudices is unfortunate for both races in the South, but more particularly for yours," he stated. "If you cast your lot with those who are your friends . . . you will reap the benefits. If you prefer to follow the leadership of the other element, I am sorry—but you will find that you will be much happier in some other state than in Mississippi."[83]

Black leaders cried foul. Percy Greene advised the NAACP national headquarters that Wright's broadcast would have serious ramifications for Mississippi's blacks.[84] The NAACP considered Wright's warning a "clear invitation to mob violence" and encouraged the Jackson, Mississippi, branch to issue an answer to Wright's address. The national headquarters recommended a meeting of black Mississippians to counter the governor's speech but later advised against it, realizing that such a meeting could endanger black lives.[85]

In Mississippi the governor assumed early the leadership role in the states' rights movement. In South Carolina activities at the grass roots moved ahead of Thurmond. In a display of what one national news magazine called "corn-pone and piney-roots politics," hundreds of Democrats in Greenwood and Jasper Counties met on February 21 and adopted resolutions condemning the president's civil rights legislative program and the national party. The resolutions also favored sending uninstructed delegates to the national convention.[86] Democrats in tiny Jasper County charged the national party with abandoning its historic "traditions and principles" and disregarding "our deep seated feelings about social segregation of the races." Jasper Countians went on record in support of almighty God, the principles of Thomas Jefferson and Andrew Jackson, the Constitution of the United States, and states' rights. Two days later, on February 23, loudspeakers mounted atop automobiles driven throughout the county drew more than 2,000 Jasper County citizens to a mass protest meeting that evening. The boisterous crowd roared its approval as the County Democratic Executive Committee voted unanimously to pull out of the national party.[87] One reporter speculated that a free hillbilly music show following the meeting may have accounted for the heightened attendance.[88] Other Black Belt counties soon followed Greenwood and Jasper.[89]

As in Mississippi, South Carolina's politics and political fault lines in the twentieth century were largely the product of geography. A fall line that zigzags across the state from northeast to southwest separates the low country from the hills. Holding approximately two-thirds of the state's total area and dominated by a large, fertile coastal plain that is part of the Black Belt that stretches across the South, the low country is home to large-scale plantation agriculture and black majorities. North of the fall line is the upcountry piedmont region, dominated by rolling red clay hills and stretching to the mountains in the northwestern portion of the state. Once populated by small farms and a few plantations, the upcountry became a magnet for New South textile industrialists attracted by the region's fast-running streams and for poor whites seeking to escape rural poverty.[90]

Class politics took hold more firmly in South Carolina than in Mississippi. When white South Carolinians, led by Benjamin Tillman, rewrote their constitution in 1895, they effectively barred blacks from the polling place but left universal white male suffrage virtually untouched. The first effective mobilizer of the white working class was Coleman Livingston Blease, who won the governorship and a seat in the U.S. Senate on a platform that effectively combined antistatism, antielitism, and racism in a way that appealed to the desires of working class men for autonomy and control in the rapidly changing world of the industrial upstate. Once in office, however, Blease did little to improve the conditions of workers' lives. With the onset of the depression, workers turned away from Bleasism and aggressively pursued state action for their own material benefit. As in so many southern states, however, legislative malapportionment worked against the interests of the working class. Under the 1895 constitution, the county became the basis from which to organize politics and representation. Each county was allowed one senator regardless of population, and rural counties outnumbered urban. As one historian has pointed out, although South Carolina millworkers succeeded in placing one of their own in the governor's mansion in the 1930s, "skewed apportionment and the fact that only half of the seats in the crucial senate were up for grabs at a time meant that the upper house would remain in the hands of low-country conservatives who were hostile to the governor and organized labor."[91] In 1948 Black Belt representatives were in firm control of the legislature and the party.

Faced with a political revolt in the provinces on one hand and an intractable national party leadership on the other, South Carolina's SDEC cast its lot with the rebels by voting on March 1 to oppose the nomination and election of Truman or any other civil rights candidate and instructing the state party to name electors committed to upholding states' rights. Thurmond, hoping to maintain control of the rebellion taking place around him, placed himself squarely at the front of the revolt, declaring that "the president has gone too far" and "I'm through with him!"[92] Thurmond created a powerful and resonant image, vowing to defend his state and region from the abuse of federal power.[93] Anti-Truman fervor continued to build in South Carolina as the May 10 States' Rights Conference in Jackson drew near. At the majority of county conventions held in late April and early May, delegates enthusiastically adopted resolutions condemning Truman and chose strident states' righters to attend the state convention later in the month.[94]

On March 13, with rebellions in Mississippi and South Carolina brewing, the southern state leaders gathered in Washington, D.C., where Thurmond's committee presented its report on the meeting with McGrath. The tone of the report was defiant. Based on its less than satisfactory meeting with McGrath, the committee could offer little hope for the future and urged "strong and effective action by Democrats everywhere."[95] The committee recommended that southerners oppose the nomination of civil rights candidates and that they withhold their electoral college votes should the national party nominate a candidate who advocated civil rights. They urged state conventions to defer the nomination of their electors for president and vice-president until after the national convention.[96] Support for the report and proposed course of action divided roughly along geographical lines. The report was approved by governors from Deep South states—Alabama, Mississippi, Texas, South Carolina, and Georgia—and by Ben Laney of Arkansas, an early states' rights advocate. Lane of Maryland refrained from voting. The governors of Florida, Kentucky, North Carolina, Louisiana, Oklahoma, Tennessee, and West Virginia did not attend the meeting.[97] As the committee's report stated, it was now up to the individual states to decide their course of action.

Although Mississippi and South Carolina took the lead in the states' rights rebellion, Alabama most dramatically illustrated the difficult position in which the states' rights/civil rights conundrum placed New Deal southern liberals. It was widely recognized in the late 1940s that Alabama's congressional delegation was the most liberal of any southern state.[98] In addition, in 1946 the state had elected populist James E. Folsom in a campaign noted for its lack of white supremacist appeals. Yet in determining what political course the state party would take in the 1948 presidential election, the conservative forces in the state emerged victorious. In Alabama the upheaval over Truman's civil rights proposals represented the latest salvo in a power struggle between the Black Belt/industrial conservatives and New Deal liberals that had been going on since the 1930s and would continue into the next decade.

Although the liberal forces, led early by Hugo Black and later by Lister Hill, had scored impressive victories in the 1930s and 1940s, the conservatives had slowly gained ground. Capitalizing on the escalating racial tensions of the war years and the Supreme Court's 1944 decision in *Smith v. Allwright,* they succeeded in passing the Boswell Amendment in 1946 and ran Birmingham senator James A. Simpson in a strong but unsuccessful race to unseat Hill in 1944. Liberals across the South desperate for New Deal ideals and programs to survive into the postwar era were heartened when "Big Jim" Folsom captured the statehouse in 1946. An effective campaigner, Folsom proved less skillful and ultimately less successful at the intricacies of governance and coalition building. He was not entirely to blame. As in South Carolina, conservatives from rural counties controlled the Alabama senate and blocked much of his program, including his attempts to revise the state constitution and to reapportion the legislature. Determined to prevent blacks from voting, conservatives likewise killed Folsom's poll tax reforms. Undeterred, the governor retaliated and exercised his power to appoint county registrars who would register blacks and poor whites.[99]

Former governor Frank Dixon was the titular head of Alabama's states' rights forces, many of whom had embarked on their political careers in the 1920s as reformers but who, as ardent defenders of white supremacy, had shifted to the political right in the 1930s and 1940s. Dixon was born in California in 1892. A nephew of Thomas Dixon, author of *The Clansman,* Dixon received an elite education, first at Phillips-Exeter Academy and, later, at Columbia University; he received his law degree from the University of Virginia. Dixon was admitted to the Alabama bar in 1917, but that same year he entered the U.S. Army and saw action overseas in World War I as an aerial observer. He was wounded in 1918 and suffered the amputation of his right leg. A decorated veteran, he received the Chevalier Legion of Honor and the Croix de Guerre with palm, as well as the Purple Heart. Dixon returned to Alabama and resumed his law practice in 1919 in Birmingham. In the 1930s he became part of Jefferson County's "good government" reform movement. He practiced law until he was elected governor in 1938.[100] Although Dixon entered office with the support of both labor and management, he soon proved himself less than supportive of the working classes and became an ardent foe of Franklin Roosevelt and the New Deal in the early 1940s. Dixon became one of the more strident opponents of the FEPC and, with Governor Sam Jones of Louisiana, attempted unsuccessfully to engineer a movement to deny the president nomination to a fourth term.

The tremendous upheavals of the war years, Dixon believed, had cast the South into a political crucible. The region had become a "crossroads democracy," threatened by the FEPC, whose activities "are helping to cause discontent and danger."[101] After leaving office in early 1943, Dixon returned to his law practice but did not retire from public life entirely, frequently speaking out on the impending dangers of an expanding federal government intent on upsetting southern race relations. As the war years wore on, and as he witnessed the challenges to the color line across the region, Dixon became increasingly alarmed that the main wartime move of Democratic Party leaders was "the fostering of a social revolution."[102] He expressed disbelief to an industrialist friend in Charlotte that North Carolinians would tolerate so liberal a man as University of North

Frank Dixon, former governor of Alabama and leading Alabama Dixiecrat. Photograph courtesy of the Alabama Department of Archives and History, Montgomery.

Carolina president Frank Porter Graham, at whose university, Dixon had been told, "white girls are forced . . . to sit beside negro men" at school assemblies.[103]

Assisting Dixon from the wings were longtime Birmingham political operative Horace Wilkinson and Birmingham's Commissioner of Public Safety Eugene "Bull" Connor. Wilkinson, whose legal career began in the 1920s, rarely held public office. He was the ultimate party insider. Unashamed to switch political sides if the moment seemed right, Wilkinson played a part in most of the major political developments in the state from the Progressive Era until his death in 1957.[104] A physically imposing and cantankerous man who also was a teetotaling Baptist who cared for his wife's disabled nephew, Wilkinson ranked among the more virulent racists in the conservative ranks. Like many other states' rights rebels, he entered public life as a progressive. Born in Birmingham in 1887, Wilkinson grew up in the nearby suburb of Woodlawn. His middle-class upbringing did not shield him from the violent clashes that were part of life in the Birmingham steel mills, and as a young man he became interested in helping the working class. After earning a law degree, he was appointed assistant attorney general and circuit court judge by progressive governor Thomas E. Kilby. As assistant attorney general, he became a vigorous opponent of the vigilantism that plagued the state. In 1919 he successfully prosecuted twenty-eight lynchers and sued the Klan. In the early 1920s he supported striking coal miners and prosecuted the lynchers of a Walker County coal miner.[105]

Holding up his finger to test the political winds, Wilkinson switched sides in the mid-1920s and aligned himself with the new governor, Bibb Graves, a former Klansman. Although he still considered himself an advocate for workers, Wilkinson became a Klan leader and defended the Klan in court. During the New Deal Wilkinson successfully installed two political cronies on the Birmingham City Commission. He became the primary dispenser of New Deal patronage in the steel town and built a powerful political machine that frequently clashed with the industrialists of Birmingham, known as the Big Mules. When the race issue heated up during the war years, Wilkinson cast aside his working-class constituency and defected to the Big Mules.[106]

Bull Connor began public life as something of a minor celebrity. Born in 1897 in Selma, in the heart of the Black Belt, Connor spent his formative years on the road with his railroad dispatcher father. At twenty-three Connor, by now married and a high school dropout, began a career as a railroad telegrapher.[107] While working in Dallas, Connor dropped by a baseball "matinee" held in a downtown storefront studio. Fans unable to attend baseball games frequented matinees, where an announcer would re-create the game using telegraph reports. On that particular day in 1921 the regular announcer had taken ill, and the manager offered Connor $5.00 to stand in and call the game. Within a year Connor had opened his own baseball matinee in Birmingham, where he called games for the Birmingham Barons. The 5′ 8″ Connor "possessed a booming voice" and a gift for "shooting the bull." A nickname was born. Looking to capitalize on his name recognition, Connor ran for the Alabama House of Representatives in 1934 as a reform candidate and won. Once in the legislature, he attached himself to conservative state senator James A. Simpson of Birmingham, ally of the Big Mules. Connor next got himself elected to the Birmingham City Commission in 1937, where he served as public safety commissioner.[108] Connor remained close to Simpson, supplying him with important information on the local political climate during Simpson's 1944 and 1946 campaigns for the U.S. Senate. Simpson used the race issue in both contests; however, it was his protégé, Connor, who in his position on the city's front line came to represent the forces of white supremacy. Connor received attention early for his efforts to uphold segregation statutes, most notably in 1938, when he forced the SCHW to conform to local custom.[109] In 1948 Connor again garnered acclaim when he arrested the Progressive Party's vice-presidential candidate, Idaho Senator Glen Taylor, for attempting to violate Birmingham's segregation laws. Even liberal senator John Sparkman praised Connor, writing that Taylor created the situation "in order to get the publicity out of it."[110]

Other leading Alabama states' rights advocates reflected the coalition's conservative outlook. Prominent within their ranks were Sidney W. Smyer, a corporation lawyer from Birmingham and former lobbyist for the Associated Industries of Alabama; Walter Givhan, former head of the Alabama Farm Bureau; Wallace Malone, prominent banker from Dothan; and textile magnate Donald Comer. The Alabama states' rights contingent rivaled Mississippi's in its degree of radicalism, its blatant white supremacism, and its willingness to abandon the national Democratic Party.

The Alabama states' righters capitalized on their control of the SDEC. Ably led by state party chairman Gessner T. McCorvey, a prominent Mobile attorney, they manipulated party rules and succeeded in wrenching control of the party machinery away from the loyalists. Shortly after

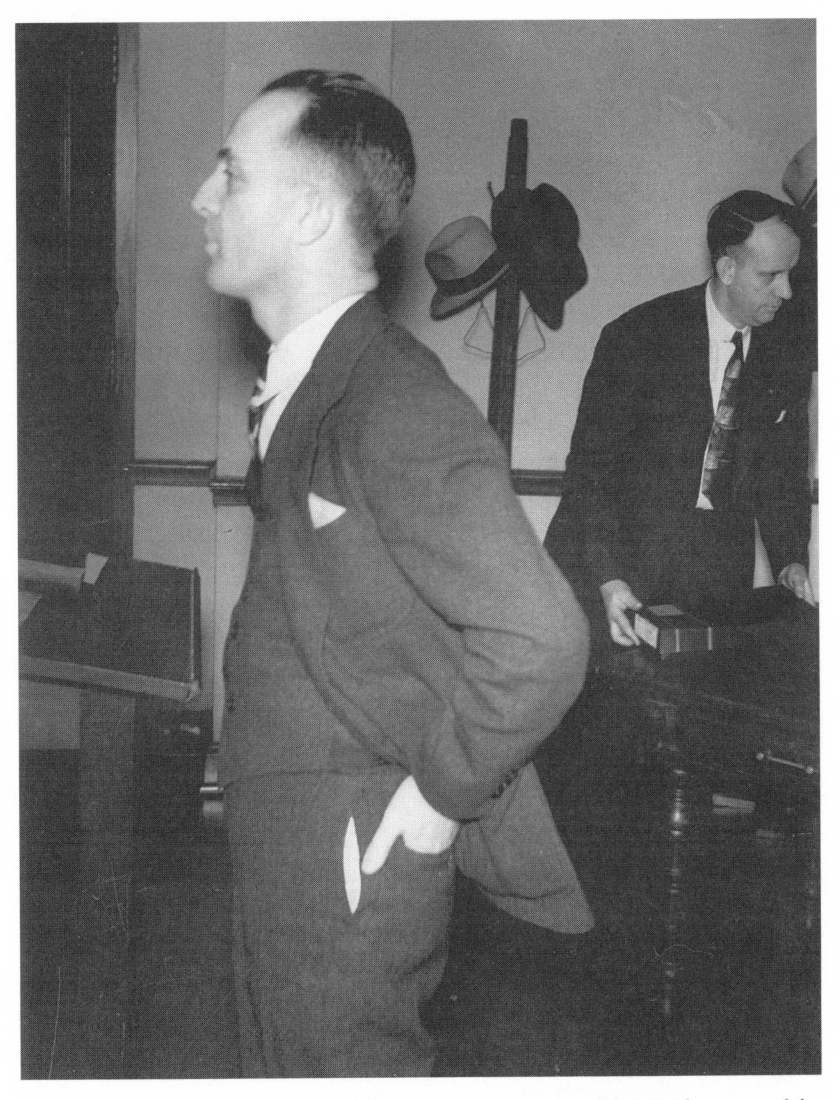

Eugene "Bull" Connor, prominent Alabama Dixiecrat, ca. 1930s. Photograph courtesy of the Alabama Department of Archives and History, Montgomery.

Truman's civil rights speech, McCorvey advocated secession from the national party unless it rejected Truman's civil rights proposals. Assisted by virulent white supremacist Wilkinson, McCorvey turned Alabama's early May primary into a states' rights referendum. Voters would choose their state and local representatives as well as the Democratic presidential electors and delegates to the national convention. McCorvey requested that all candidates for elector sign statements pledging to vote against any Democratic nominee who supported the entire civil rights program and asked that Alabama's national convention delegates pledge to walk out if a civil rights plank were adopted. By the middle of March, McCorvey and Wilkinson had received pledges from most of the candidates for elector. The campaign for delegates shaped up as a fight between those pledged to bolt the convention and those who declined to commit themselves to defect. Prominent among the antibolting loyalists were Senators Hill and Sparkman, Governor Folsom, and former governor Chauncey Sparks.[111] The loyalists, Folsom remarked, preferred "doin' our fussin' within the [Democratic] party."[112]

The national Democratic Party loyalists, with the possible exception of Folsom, found themselves in an awkward position, as they opposed the president's civil rights program just as strongly as the conservatives. Although he was the Democratic Party whip, Senator Hill had joined the southern filibuster against Truman's 1946 proposal for a permanent FEPC, and his relationship with Truman was much cooler than his relationship with FDR had been. Hill eventually relinquished his leadership position because he knew he could not support Truman's stance on civil rights. Like other New Deal liberals, he had begun the retreat as the line was being drawn.[113] Wilkinson tried to pin Hill to Truman, but Hill spoke out early against the president, proclaiming that he was "unalterably opposed" to his nomination and to the "so-called Civil Rights Program."[114]

The battle that ensued in the months between Truman's civil rights address and Alabama's primary revealed the fragility of Alabama's liberal coalition. Philosophically, Folsom was much more liberal than either of the two senators with regard to foreign policy, preferring Henry Wallace's brand of liberalism over Truman's. Folsom left just about everyone dumbfounded by offering himself as a favorite son presidential candidate in late January 1948. Most mainstream liberals considered Folsom's announcement a colossal blunder and utterly destructive to the cause of liberalism within the state.[115] Folsom's announcement further demonstrated that he did not like being in the shadow of Alabama's U.S. senators. To that end, he was plotting to unseat John Sparkman in 1948 with his choice, Phillip Hamm, and was maneuvering to challenge Lister Hill in 1950.[116]

The race for convention delegate—in which candidates were required to declare themselves for or against a walkout—was not only a contest between conservatives and liberals but a skirmish among liberals. Not wanting to defend the president, Hill had hoped to avoid any role as a delegate to the 1948 Democratic convention. His advisors had counseled him not to "get mixed up in all the politics in Alabama." Hill recognized the difficulty of championing party loyalty in the toxic political atmosphere of 1948. He did finally get involved, but only to protect himself against a challenger—possibly Folsom—in 1950. He entered his name as a delegate candidate and declared his intent to support the president, taking pains to emphasize his support for the president's foreign policy. John Sparkman, on the other hand, renounced Truman early, isolating Hill as a Truman loyalist. Sparkman, it seems, was more interested in neutralizing Folsom than in defeating the conservatives. He even considered making common cause with the conservatives in an effort to keep Folsom under control. He confided to Reese Amis of the *Huntsville Times* that he had hoped to organize a coalition comprising former governor Chauncey Sparks, Lister Hill, and conservatives Gessner McCorvey and Marion Rushton, among others, to "join with me in making an all out fight against Folsom and his whole crowd."[117] Not content to be the only Truman supporter, Hill eventually gravitated to Dwight Eisenhower. Even though he had turned his back on the president, Hill worked hard to prevent a convention walkout.

Ultimately the liberalism of Lister Hill and John Sparkman triumphed over that of James Folsom. Hill won a delegate slot; Folsom did not. Furthermore, practically every candidate Folsom supported lost. Voters simply did not respond well to a governor campaigning on a foreign policy platform. Furthermore, voters were irritated by allegations of misappropriation of funds by Folsom appointees and by charges that Folsom had fathered an illegitimate child.[118] The internecine battle left the liberals splintered and angry. Energy that could have been used to fend off the conservatives was spent fighting one another.

After the May primary and runoff, Alabama's delegation to the national convention was split almost equally between those pledged to walk out and those pledged to remain in the convention. As for the presidential electors, all eleven chosen by the voters were pledged to vote against any nominee who supported the civil rights program. It was next to impossible for the loyalists to fight against this, for they, too, opposed the president's civil rights program. Alabama law permitted only the names of candidates supported by the state's electors to appear on the ballot. Therefore, if Truman or any other Democrat supporting a civil rights plank was nominated in Philadelphia, his name would not appear on the ballot, and Democrats in Alabama would have no means to vote for the national ticket.[119] Alabama's voters had effectively approved the means of their own disfranchisement.

★

Perhaps the most daunting challenge facing the states' righters was selling themselves, and the idea of a bolt, to voters. This involved nothing less than convincing white southerners that to guarantee the preservation of their "cherished institutions" they needed to abandon the one instrument that historically had provided the bulwark against outside interference—the national Democratic Party. To subvert or, as it would turn out, manipulate party allegiance, the states' rights conservatives had to convey effectively the significance of their resistance to, and differentiate themselves from, the national party without sacrificing political legitimacy—a tricky balancing act. In the struggle to defend segregation from attack, states' rights conservatives fashioned a reactionary political message that drew on southern history, cherished regional icons, and cultural practices to explain political change and to justify their resistance.

From the moment the president first presented his civil rights message to Congress in February until the election in November 1948, states' rights conservatives waged a campaign that forced white southerners to reevaluate their long-standing allegiance to the national party. White southerners' attachment to the party was peculiarly tenacious, distinctly personal, and potentially explosive. Faced with a political situation in which the national Democratic Party aggressively courted the votes of African Americans and labor, conservatives waged a campaign designed to co-opt the allegiance of white southerners.[120] States' righters played on the South's sense of lost prestige and status, reminding white voters that one hundred years of loyalty to the Democratic Party entitled them to respect and some measure of control. Given the Democratic Party's traditional role in maintaining white supremacy and its long-standing hegemony in the South, breaking this alliance would not be easy.

Prominent conservative states' rights spokesmen used familial metaphors and gendered scenarios to play to the deep-seated fears and paranoia of white southerners and thereby explain and justify their relationship to politics and to the national Democratic Party. This close interplay of race and gender in southern society at mid-century illustrates how the potential loss of political power in the public sphere was linked to concerns regarding disruption of the private sphere—in particular, how the overreaching arm of the state threatened the most intimate of domestic arrangements. Ultimately, the language and imagery employed by states' rights dissenters throughout the South reveals much about how conservative white southerners imagined politics, power, and states' rights in the mid-twentieth-century South and, in particular, about their fears for the destruction of white supremacy.

On the hustings and in private, white conservatives explained and understood their role within the Democratic Party in familial terms. They envisioned the national party, with all its constituencies, as a family. Indeed, Arkansas governor Ben Laney exclaimed that advocacy of civil rights by the national party was exceptionally painful because it came from "our own people—our own family."[121] Within the Democratic Party, white southerners had been the dominant, masculine member, clearly a reflection of the ideal patriarchal organization of southern society. Within the greater family of the national party, different interest groups such as organized labor assumed clearly subordinate roles. Undoubtedly, white southerners expected African Americans to remain outside the political as well as the actual white family. Because the South had held the position of senior partner in the Democratic Party relationship for so long, some southern whites were not convinced their best interests were served by leaving, or bolting, the party. One congressman from South Carolina who was not in favor of bolting likened the current intraparty disagreement over civil rights to a domestic dispute that should be handled as such. The president's support of civil rights, he mused, was "like having an undesirable guest in your house," he claimed. "If you don't like him, it doesn't mean you'll pack up and leave your own home."[122]

Utilizing a familial model for politics was an easy choice for men who understood social relationships and hierarchies as natural. The rule of white over black, employers over employees, as Walter Sillers so matter-of-factly put it, was as natural as the "laws of gravitation."[123] For states' rights conservatives—many of whom had stayed tied to the land—privilege and power remained intrinsic to family and hereditary. Across most of the rural South, untouched by mechanization, the sharecropping and tenant family remained a central unit of production. The plantation operator reigned supreme over poor families, denying poor men—white and black—the opportunity to become full patriarchs in their own right. It is not surprising, then, that when black families began to leave the Delta plantations in the 1940s, planters complained not only of labor shortages but that black men were now overseeing the employment decisions of their wives, staking their own claims to familial control. Their frustrations at such a potential loss of power manifested in their political rhetoric, which played on various metaphors and scenarios of betrayal.

Given the symbolic familial relationship between the South and the national Democratic Party, the conservative bolt mimicked symbolically the severing of the bonds of matrimony, and more than one commentator referred to the southern revolt as a "divorce."[124] Just as in a real marriage or relationship, the South expected certain things from the national party. Above all, white southerners demanded fidelity. Southern whites were shocked by their sudden loss of prestige and the relative increase in power of African Americans in the party. As the dominant male partner in the political relationship, this new political arrangement symbolized a blow to their authority. In political allegories, they often assumed the role of cuckold. In mid-February 1948, as white southern Democrats were reeling from the shock of President Harry Truman's civil rights address, Mississippi's *McComb Enterprise-Journal* ran an editorial titled "Time for a Divorce," a sad tale of a husband cursed with an unfaithful wife. Although the husband had "built a lovely home and showered [his wife] with his affection and endowed her with his loyalty[,] . . . she commenced running around with Tom, Dick, and Harry." "One day Tom, Dick and Harry moved into his home, sat at his table and ordered food from his kitchen and enjoyed every luxury his home afforded. The neighbors looked on with ridicule. They laughed at him. Then one day Tom, Dick and Harry took the husband by the nap of the neck and threw him out into the mud of the street and took over his home, completely. The neighbors looked on with disgust. They had no respect for him. He was without home and standing."[125]

White southerners also often likened their new, dependent position in the national party to the status of those who possessed little or no power in society: women and children. Senator James Eastland of Mississippi warned that Truman's proposals threatened southern whites with political impotency.[126] Strom Thurmond argued that Truman's campaign against the South stemmed from the president's perception of the region as "weak," "foolish," and "meek."[127] Voicing his concern over the decline in the power of white southern Democrats, one states' rights enthusiast promoted a song he titled "The Rebel Yell." This ditty, he instructed one southern congressman, was to be sung to the tune of "Slap Her Down Again, Pa!," a song about domestic abuse. In the states' rights version, white southern Democrats assumed the role of the battered woman.

Slap us down again Pres., slap us down again
Make us take some more, Pres., we are mice, not men.
We don't have no rights, Pres., when our party's in,
Slap us down again, Pres., we will help you win.[128]

Elsewhere, others rendered the changing relationship between southern Democrats and the national party in sexual ways. One political cartoon shows both the Democratic and Republican Party nominees seeking to dance with an African American woman who seduces them with the votes she holds in her garter. The South, represented by a diminutive, donkey-faced woman dressed in nineteenth-century garb, can only watch this display from the sidelines.[129] Another crude drawing sent to Walter Sillers from a rural Mississippian depicts Harry Truman in bed with an African American man.[130] Just as miscegenation diluted bloodlines within white families, so the joining of African American interests and the Democratic Party polluted the political organism.

The concerns of states' rights conservatives for the contamination of political bloodlines and for fidelity and loss of political authority were expressed as worries about legitimacy—political and familial. J. Knox Huff, a Mississippi conservative, declared that the Truman Democrats had "reduced the South . . . to the status of illegitimate children at a family reunion."[131] William D. Workman, among others, commented that the South had been treated as "the red-haired stepchild in national Democratic party affairs."[132] Significantly, the states' righters compared themselves not just to children but to step- and illegitimate children —unwanted, ignored, and powerless. Because political authority was understood in terms of family authority and patriarchy, the removal of the dominant political partner, in this case, white southern Democrats, was akin to removing the father from the home, jeopardizing the safety of women. Given that white southerners frequently expressed fears that desegregation would ultimately require them to entertain African Americans in their homes, it is not surprising that an African American presence in their political home would yield such a dishonorable, albeit imagined and rhetorical, result. Harry C. Brown, a states' rights supporter in Charleston, enunciated this fear in a letter to Thurmond. "Would you like to see the negroes . . . admitted into our inner sanctum . . . ? If you gentlemen are looking for the negro votes which I know you gentlemen from the South aren't[,] please ask Mr. [Thomas] Dewey if he would like to have those people . . . to live in his home."[133] Although these multiple references to familial themes place the South in a variety of positions in relation to the national party, they all make explicit the central fear of states' rights conservatives: political impotency.

Within the convoluted logic of the politics of racial identity and family, the national Democratic Party's appeal to black voters was not only an insult to and a betrayal of the white South but a physical attack on the body of the South. In states' rights propaganda, "the South" was often represented as a white male. In order to acknowledge black political power, one first had to kill the dominant male figure. Dixie insurgents employed graphic and violent imagery to illustrate their point. Inverting images of racial control used in the region to keep African Americans in their "place," conservatives spoke of being slapped, gagged, choked, kidnapped, hog-tied, flogged, lynched, and stabbed by national party leaders.[134] Their campaign literature often featured a picture of a stabbing victim as representative of the South's position or dilemma. Sometimes the descriptions bordered on the grotesque, as when Mississippi congressman John Bell Williams declared that Truman "has seen fit to run a political dagger into our backs, and now he is trying to drink our blood."[135]

Having described their betrayal in violent terms, states' rights conservatives spoke of their redress in terms of personal vengeance.[136] Resistance to civil rights and encroachment by the federal government became nothing less than a test of their manhood. Although northerners expected the South to "crawl on its belly, submit and beg," white southerners declared they would not take this insult "lying down." "We must be men," one southerner claimed, "and not weaklings." Supporting the civil rights policies of the national party was unthinkable for "any red-blooded man," and failure to act on this betrayal would brand them as "less than men." Ultimately it was important merely that the South respond in some way. "Southerners respect a fighter, be his cause right or wrong," wrote William Workman. "By the same token, they loathe the faint-hearted."[137]

Strom Thurmond was particularly well suited to serve as point man in the states' rights crusade. In many ways the South Carolinian personified the gendered components of the region's reactionary states' rights political culture. Thurmond won the governorship in 1946 over a throng of candidates on a platform that positioned him as the powerful foe of a corrupt political ring. Like Ben Tillman, his political predecessor from Edgefield County, Thurmond reveled in political campaigning. In

South Carolina at this time candidates traveled together from county to county, addressing raucous mass meetings that often stretched on for hours. Thurmond thrived on this type of political debate that allowed him to take the offensive with maximum effect. He also used his veteran status to his political advantage. During one gubernatorial stump speech, Thurmond compared the "scheming, conniving, selfish men" in the South Carolina political ring with the "scheming, conniving, selfish men" who had grabbed power in Germany, Italy, and Japan. "I was willing to risk my life to stamp out such gangs in Europe," Thurmond proclaimed. "I intend to devote my future to wiping out the stench and stain with which the Barnwell ring has smeared the Government of South Carolina for, lo, these many years."[138]

In 1948 Thurmond effectively combined a fighting spirit with a well-known penchant for clean living, vigorous physical exercise, and pretty women. In the gendered discourse of South Carolina politics, Thurmond —a bachelor—portrayed himself as a virile lady's man. Whether caught lounging on Myrtle Beach with comely companions or bestowing a kiss on a local festival queen, the bachelor governor never shied away from photo opportunities that illustrated his masculinity. Thurmond's reputation as a ladies' man was widespread. Congressman William Jennings Bryan Dorn of Greenwood warned his sister about taking a job in the governor's office. "Use your own judgment," Dorn advised. "Personally, I had rather you would stay out of Strom Thurmond's office, for your own good if for no other reason. His reputation and fastness concerning women is nation-wide."[139] The governor's reputation as a sexual rascal achieved mythic proportions. Perhaps most fantastic is the tale of Thurmond's alleged relationship with Sue Logue, an Edgefield woman executed for her role in the murders of shopkeeper Davis W. Timmerman, Sheriff Wad Allen, and Deputy Sheriff W. L. Clark. Thurmond emerged a hero for his role in convincing Logue to surrender during a bloody standoff at the Logue house in 1941. More compelling, however, are the rumors of Thurmond's long affair with Logue, a woman renowned for her sexual prowess. The affair allegedly began while Thurmond campaigned for the office of county superintendent of education and continued until the day Logue was executed. The driver who transported Logue from the women's penitentiary to the death house claimed that Thurmond, then an army officer, accompanied the condemned woman, "a-huggin' and a-kissin' the whole way."[140]

Thurmond's bachelor days ended on November 7, 1947, when he mar-

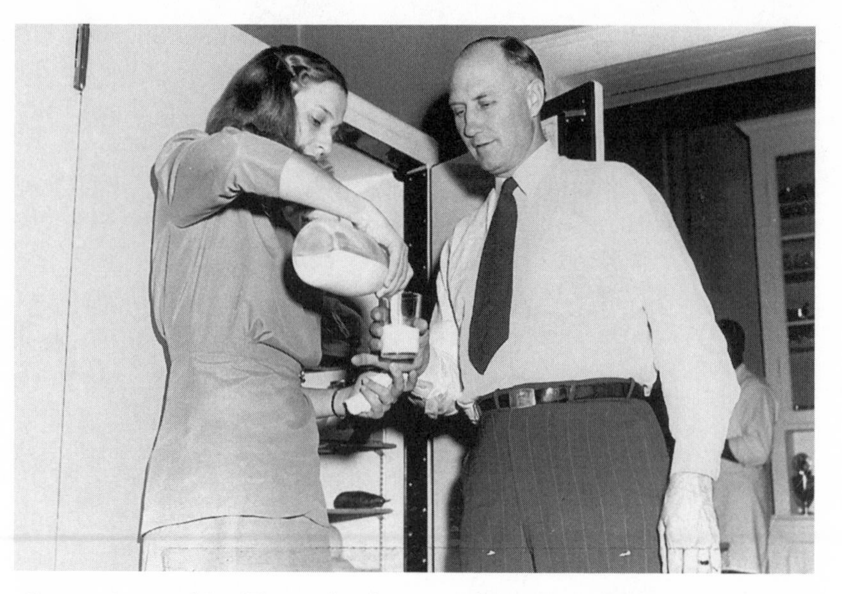

Governor Strom and Jean Thurmond in the Governor's Mansion, Columbia, South Carolina, 1948. Photograph courtesy of Special Collections, Clemson University Libraries, Clemson, South Carolina.

ried twenty-one-year-old Jean Crouch of Elko, a former Azalea Festival queen and a secretary in the governor's office. The day before their wedding, the betrothed governor, casually (albeit curiously) decked out in white gym shorts, dark socks, and wing-tip shoes, posed in a headstand for a *Life* magazine photographer. The caption read, "Virile Governor demonstrates his prowess in the mansion yard before wedding." (Before resorting to this acrobatic feat, Thurmond had asked the photographer whether he wanted to feel his muscles.) If some voters thought that the forty-four-year-old Thurmond's official retirement from the dating scene signaled a major life change, this and subsequent photo opportunities proved them wrong.[141] Amusingly, one congressman later recalled that "to most people, who didn't know about gym shorts, it looked like Thurmond had pulled off his pants, left his shoes on, and then stood on his head for the cameras."[142] Thurmond's personal countenance, then, made him a worthy leader of the battle for states' rights, a battle waged as much on the rhetorical and cultural fields as through the ballot box. As someone who combined a political outsider's fighting rhetoric with personal sexual potency, Thurmond appealed to conservative white men suffering from a self-diagnosed case of political impotency.

Governor Strom and Jean Thurmond at a carnival attraction, ca. 1940s. Photograph courtesy of Special Collections, Clemson University Libraries, Clemson, South Carolina.

Despite its power, the states' rights message did not attract all white voters. The political language crafted and employed by white conservatives competed with other dialects that had infiltrated the southern marketplace of political ideas. For most whites, the family model of politics confined them to subordinate, junior family roles. As the federal government began to reach into the South during the New Deal era, and as more white men left the South during World War II, southerners became exposed to other models that threw light on their own dysfunctional political arrangement. Motivated by the language of autonomy, independence, and modernity, these second sons of the southern political family began to strike out on their own, albeit no less committed to upholding white supremacy. Beginning in the 1930s, as southern workers began to pursue state action for their own ends, they increasingly spoke what one historian has called "a new language of Americanism," a rhetoric that allowed them to begin to transcend both the region and history. Many returning white veterans, desiring not to preserve but to oust the failed and corrupt regimes of the past, likewise conceived of politics and the state in ways that conflicted with the notions of Black Belt conservatives. And although conservatives were not speaking to them, African Americans, emboldened by their participation in the war, had begun to demand their political rights, with increasing effectiveness, using the rhetoric of freedom and liberty that at one time had been the sole preserve of whites. So as the conservative white South positioned itself to do battle with the national Democratic Party, it also was acutely aware that it was competing with rival messages at the grass roots, and in its attempt to pull white southerners back into history, it would not entirely succeed.[143]

★

On a steamy May 10, 2,500 hot and boisterous states' rights faithful drove through the Confederate flag–festooned streets of Jackson, finally converging on the municipal auditorium for the "national" states' rights conference. Although the conference organizers boasted representation from all southern states, most of the attendees were from the Deep South. With the exception of leaders from Mississippi and Alabama, however, the state officials in attendance could speak only as individuals, for most states had not yet held their conventions. With no authority to commit their states to a course of action, the conferees could accomplish little. They did not care. They had arrived in a defiant mood, determined to stand up to the insults hurled at them by the national party. Even if they could not plot any definite course, they could at least talk tough. Confident that the states' rights effort would not be in vain, Horace Wilkinson of Birmingham predicted that "when all this clouded political atmosphere has been cleared, you will find that the South has recovered from the bite . . . and it will be the dog that has died."[144]

After a rousing chorus of "Dixie," convention chairperson Governor

Ben Laney of Arkansas gaveled the meeting to order at 10:00 A.M.. "We regret the circumstances that have forced us to call this convention," Laney told the conventioneers. "We regret that the house of our fathers is divided against us."[145] Mississippi's Governor Wright greeted the delegates and set the tone for the meeting as part political rally and part historical pageant by replaying point by point the treacheries of Reconstruction. "Today," he warned, "these same forces are loose once again, straining and striving to impose their harsh will upon us." The South, he demanded, must act. "If we accept the insults and infringements upon our rights now proposed by our own party leaders, we will forever fix in their minds a conviction that whatever they wish to impose upon us, we will accept."[146]

If Wright set the somber but belligerent tone for the meeting, Strom Thurmond, who had leapfrogged over Wright to assume the leadership of the disjointed states' rights forces, recognized the opportunity to generate serious political capital from the situation and stood poised to lead the conventioneers to outrage. Voicing the personal frustration and sense of betrayal felt by many white southerners, Thurmond cautioned the national party not to take the South's indignation lightly. "The fight is on," he declared, "and we will not lay our armor down until the present leadership of the Democratic Party is repudiated and the South is again recognized as a political entity of these United States." Not only were these conservatives angry at the president for promoting civil rights. They were upset that no one was taking them seriously.

Echoing Wright, Thurmond pointed to history to justify the Deep South's stance. He reminded his audience that during the "bitter Reconstruction period . . . the slaves who had been freed as a war measure were left as a millstone around our neck." Like other white southerners, he believed that "we of the South . . . have cared and provided for the Negroes in our midst, and the progress which has been made by that race is a tribute to the efforts of Southerners, and to Southerners alone."

Like other postwar governors interested in industrial development, Thurmond attributed the South's problems to retarded regional economic development and discrimination. "Economic underprivilege in the South has known no color line," Thurmond stated. "Both races have suffered in the economic struggle to overcome artificial barriers to our recovery and growth imposed upon this part of the Nation from without," he argued. "The wonder is, not how little we have done," Thurmond speculated, "but how much we have been able to do for our people under such crushing handicaps." Conditions for blacks would improve with economic development, he contended, not with federal intervention.

He proceeded to examine the various civil rights proposals, attempting to demonstrate how each would destroy states' rights and violate the Constitution. The anti–poll tax legislation was unnecessary and dangerous. He considered the poll tax "a minor revenue measure" that "does not burden the right to vote." Only seven southern states had poll tax requirements, and he pointed out that he had advocated repeal of the tax in his home state. He feared that anti–poll tax legislation would set a precedent for federal interference in suffrage and would lead to federal "control over the ballot boxes of the Nation." Instead of opening up the franchise, Thurmond argued, anti–poll tax legislation would circumscribe it. Antilynching legislation, likewise, was superfluous, the South Carolina governor insisted, conveniently forgetting the travesty of justice in the Earle lynching, "because enlightened public opinion has virtually stamped out this crime."

Thurmond saved his strongest denunciations for the proposed permanent FEPC, which, he argued, would interfere with an employer's right to run his business. "He could be ordered to stop choosing his employees as he saw fit, and to hire someone he did not want." Segregation laws "are essential to the protection of the racial integrity and purity of the white and Negro races alike. We know that their sudden removal would do great injury to the very people sought to be benefitted." Ultimately, he warned, Truman's civil rights proposals would "force the white people of the South to accept into their business, their schools, their places of amusement, and in other public places, those they do not want to accept."[147]

The delegates quickly drafted a declaration whereby they pledged to use the electoral college to redress their grievances.[148] They scheduled a strategy meeting of all southern delegates at the national convention and agreed that southern delegates would only support strong states' rights candidates. If the Democratic Party nominee refused to repudiate the civil rights program, states' rights advocates would reconvene in Birmingham on July 17 to choose alternative candidates for president and vice-president, who would then become the official candidates of the respective state parties.[149]

The resolution did not receive unanimous support. Following the declaration, the Georgia delegation withdrew from the conference. Democratic Party state chairman James S. Peters told reporters that the Georgia delegation opposed a party bolt and the creation of a third party.[150] Georgia leaders did not want to commit themselves to a potentially suicidal political mission. Peters felt it best to "keep the opposition guessing" and allow the strategy to develop "as the battle rages." Unwilling to publicly support a party defection, Peters refused to cut all ties to the conservatives, confiding to former Alabama governor Frank Dixon that he hoped "the electors in Georgia will vote against Truman or anyone else running on a civil rights platform."[151] Gubernatorial challenger Herman Talmadge agreed with Peters. He felt it was best to fight Truman's civil rights program "step by step and not expose our hand until the proper time."[152] Although the Georgia delegation at this time opposed the creation of a third party, there remained considerable opposition to Truman within the state, and it was too soon to know how this situation would resolve itself. Privately at least, Georgia Democratic Party leaders continued to send words of encouragement to the states' rights gang. In a letter to Alabama's Wilkinson, Peters confided that he personally was still receptive to some sort of "collective action" taken by the southern states against the president.[153]

States' rights leaders reconvened in Jackson a month later at the Heidelberg Hotel and proceeded to create their campaign machinery. A five-member committee was appointed to arrange for the delegate caucus at the national convention in Philadelphia and another to organize the Birmingham convention. Looking ahead to November, the group decided to create a supervisory three-member executive committee and to hire a full-time campaign director with headquarters at Little Rock. One of the main tasks of the headquarters staff would be to familiarize themselves with the various state elections laws in order to get states' rights candidates on the ballot in each southern state. The campaign committee also approved the organization of a citizens' committee of at least twenty-five persons in each southern state and provided for the employment of three full-time liaison men to work among the eleven states. The states' rights leaders authorized newspaper releases, radio addresses, campaign buttons, and the publication of a special edition of a states' rights newspaper and approved an estimated budget of $169,000 for June and July 1948. Mississippi, the state that had pioneered the movement, contributed $10,000 to get the campaign under way, and Governor Laney pledged an additional $10,000 from Arkansas.[154]

Whether a state would take the necessary steps to free itself from the dictates of the national party ultimately depended on many factors: who controlled the state political machinery, the size of the black population and the history of the effectiveness of race as a political issue, and the strength of the Republican Party. Ultimately states' rights activists in Mississippi, South Carolina, Alabama, and Louisiana succeeded in guaranteeing their national electors against a pro–civil rights candidate. No state, however, did so without challenges.

Opposition to the states' rights movement in Mississippi resurfaced despite Wright and Sillers's control of the party. Although returns from the May 18 caucuses showed that practically all the delegates chosen to attend the state convention had signed states' rights pledges and had promised to fight the Truman administration's civil rights program, not all Mississippi Democrats went along with the pledge to withdraw from their party. Philip Mullen of Oxford, editor of the *Oxford Eagle,* member of the state legislature, delegate to the state convention, and a voice of moderation in the state, acknowledged that he and others were against Truman and the civil rights program, but that he did not believe the precinct conventions reflected the true will of the people.[155] Ned Lee, Eupora newspaperman and delegate to the state convention, likewise opposed the party bolt and claimed, "I don't see any good in forming a third political party."[156] James Ferguson, a history professor at Millsaps College, refused to take the oath as a "100 per cent true white Jeffersonian Democrat." Ferguson was defeated for a delegate's post by only one vote.[157]

By the time of the Mississippi Democratic convention on June 22, a select group of the state's Democrats had already held a caucus on June 17 to nominate state and district delegates to the Democratic National Convention.[158] The state ordered delegates to withhold their support of the national Democratic Party if Truman or any other civil rights candidate gained the presidential nomination, if the party platform included a plank advocating enactment of civil rights legislation, and/or if the party failed to adopt a plank supporting states' rights. If the delegates were forced to leave the convention or in case they were not allowed to be seated, they would proceed to Birmingham for the states' rights conference.[159]

Organizing an effective opposition to Truman's civil rights proposals was only one of several onerous problems facing white South Carolinians, who also were fighting a rear guard action on their home turf to preserve the white Democratic primary. In April 1944, in the wake of the Supreme Court's decision in *Smith v. Allwright,* then-governor Olin

Johnston had convened a special session of the South Carolina General Assembly and remarked that the Texas decision made it "absolutely necessary that we now repeal all laws pertaining to our primaries in order to maintain white supremacy." In words that sanctioned extralegal violence, Johnston further declared that if the general assembly's actions proved inadequate, white South Carolinians would "use the necessary methods to retain white supremacy in our primaries."[160] Accordingly, the general assembly stripped away all statutes, ostensibly severing the relationship between the state and the Democratic Party. The attorneys for the Richland County Democratic Executive Committee argued that by repealing all statutes pertaining to the primaries, the party had evolved into a private organization with the authority to stipulate qualifications for membership. NAACP attorney Thurgood Marshall sardonically observed that "the situation [in South Carolina] is like the state repealing all its police and letting the Elks enforce the laws."[161]

On February 21, 1947, *Elmore v. Rice* was filed in Columbia. George Elmore of Columbia, secretary of the PDP's Richland County (Columbia) club, was denied the right to register in the August 1946 Democratic primary. The complaint, filed by the NAACP, charged that Elmore and other qualified blacks had been barred from voting because of their race. The plaintiffs asked for $5,000 in damages, a judgment declaring the party's policy unconstitutional, and an order permanently barring the party from denying qualified blacks the right to vote in primary elections because of their race.[162]

Elmore was represented by the NAACP, and the suit was financed by the Negro Citizens Committee, which operated as the political action arm of the NAACP in South Carolina.[163] The *Elmore* case was heard by Judge Julius Waties Waring, who had presided at the Woodard blinding trial. On July 12, 1947, Waring shocked white South Carolinians by ruling that African Americans were entitled to enroll to vote in South Carolina Democratic primaries. Waring bluntly stated that "to say that there is any material difference in the governance of the Democratic party in this state prior to, and subsequent to, 1944, is pure sophistry." In language that outraged many white South Carolinians, Waring declared, "It is time for South Carolina to rejoin the Union. . . . Racial distinctions cannot exist in the machinery that selects the offices and lawmakers of the United States; and all citizens of this State and Country are entitled to cast a free and untrammelled ballot in our elections."[164]

Disbelief and outrage reverberated throughout much of the state's white population. The *Charleston News and Courier* predicted violence and fraud in counties where blacks outnumbered whites and feared the "return of the conditions of Reconstruction." To prevent chaos, "to save order and civilization, to prevent amalgamation of the races . . . another 'Red Shirt' campaign would be necessary."[165] U.S. Senator Burnet R. Maybank of Charleston called the decision "100 per cent wrong in principle and in law" and predicted that it would be reversed by the Supreme Court.[166]

Despite the court victory, John McCray, leader of the PDP, predicted that "the vanquished upholders of white supremacy" would resort to "assorted schemes and devices" to keep blacks from registering.[167] McCray was correct. On August 18, 1947, U.S. District Judge George Bell Timmerman granted a temporary stay of Waring's order after attorneys for the party announced they would appeal the ruling.[168] Unfortunately for white South Carolina Democrats, the Fourth U.S. Circuit Court of Appeals upheld the Waring decision.[169] Blacks continued to register for the 1948 primaries. In February 1948 party chairperson William Baskin warned executive committee members that in many counties new black registrants were outnumbering white. He was afraid black South Carolinians would control the 1948 election.[170] One national news magazine noted that in South Carolina, voter registration books were delivered to the homes of white residents at night by registration officials.[171]

The South Carolina Democratic Party appealed the U.S. Circuit Court of Appeals decision to the U.S. Supreme Court.[172] Much to their dismay, the Supreme Court on April 19, 1948, refused to review the lower court's opinion. Thurmond originally had no comment when informed of the Supreme Court's ruling. He later claimed he was "shocked" by the high court's refusal to hear the primary case. He called that decision "unsound and un-American." "Every American citizen has lost a part of his fundamental rights by this decision, and is less a free man than he was before."[173] NAACP leader James Hinton called Thurmond's remarks "below the expectancy and dignity of the office."[174]

With an acute sense of urgency, then, South Carolina's white Democrats descended on Columbia's township auditorium on May 19 for their state convention. The white delegates had much to accomplish. Not only did they have to reach a decision regarding their relationship to the national Democratic Party; they also had to devise a plan to bar black voters, vindicated by the Supreme Court and organized behind the PDP, from the August primary.

Thanks to state Democratic Party rules, Black Belt delegates and states' rights fire-eaters controlled the South Carolina convention, which burned with the fever of political rebellion. Rural conservative elites were able to use the state's legislative malapportionment to their advantage. Party rules allowed each county double the number of convention votes as it had members in the general assembly. Black Belt counties, which already benefited from overrepresentation due to black disfranchisement, enjoyed a heightened influence.[175] Following Mississippi's lead, the convention instructed its delegates not to vote for the nomination of Truman or any candidate for the presidency who supported civil rights. Instead, delegates were to cast their ballots for a favorite son candidate—Strom Thurmond. The electoral college votes then would be cast at the direction of the executive committee.[176]

To limit black participation at the polls in the August primary, the convention adopted two sets of voting rules. Blacks would be permitted to vote in the primaries by presenting registration certificates for the general election showing that they were "qualified electors." They would not, however, be admitted to party membership.[177] This stipulation deftly sidestepped the findings in the *Elmore* decision, which did not address and thus did not require South Carolina Democrats to extend party membership to African Americans. White Democrats, on the other hand, could vote in the primaries merely by enrolling on the Democratic club books. The convention also moved to require voters of both races to pledge their support for segregation and states' rights, and their opposition to proposed federal fair employment practices legislation.[178]

Undeterred by the roadblock thrown up by white Democrats, the PDP held its own convention in Columbia on May 26. Over 250 delegates from more than half of South Carolina's counties attended, although the majority were from Columbia and Charleston. Repeating their actions of 1944, the PDP voted to send a twenty-eight-member delegation to the Democratic National Convention in Philadelphia to seek representation.[179] Reports circulated around South Carolina that Henry Wallace's party was attempting to gain support among PDP members. However, PDP leadership was intensely loyal to the national Democratic Party and rejected affiliation with any third parties.[180]

As he had prior to the national convention in 1944, McCray wrote to Illinois congressman William Dawson and informed him that despite the advice of national party leaders to seek redress through the courts, "the conditions prevailing in 1944 continue in 1948." The PDP would again send a delegation to the national Democratic convention in an attempt to unseat the segregated Democratic Party.[181] McCray promptly forwarded a list of PDP delegates to national party chairman J. Howard McGrath.[182]

As in 1944, national party leaders discouraged McCray and the PDP from bringing a challenge at the convention. McCray was dismayed that the national party would simply dismiss the legitimate political claims of the PDP, an organization whose membership he estimated at around 60,000. McCray wrote, "Are we . . . to believe that the party of our choice was only kidding about a square deal for every human being everywhere? Are we now to be told that our party would prefer to boot lick at the toes of those who deliver to it hefty kicks, turning its backs upon those who do everything possible for its success . . . ? If the Democratic party does not want the votes of Negroes . . . it can say so and have its wishes on the record."[183]

African Americans were not the only South Carolina group to protest the actions of the state convention. Many whites were upset about the oath, and in response to their complaints, the party modified it slightly. The new pledge no longer required a voter to "understand" the principles of the state party or to profess belief in the "religious" separation of the races. The party also eliminated the requirement that party members work against the FEPC.[184]

Even with the modifications, some white moderates and liberals remained dissatisfied. In May, shortly after the state convention, Alice Spearman, executive director of the South Carolina Council on Human Relations, the state chapter of the Southern Regional Council, contacted John McCray for his advice on how to fight the intransigent white party. He encouraged whites who disagreed with the actions of the state Democratic Party to form a new organization that would work independently of the PDP, although their goals would be similar. Separate organizations were desirable, he asserted, because "some of the white citizens have been fed racial hocus-pocus so long" that it would take a while to turn them around and they probably would not be amenable to working with the PDP.[185] In actuality, though, the PDP was not interested in allying itself with a white organization that had no power. In arguing in favor of political independence, PDP executive secretary Arthur Clement reminded McCray that "we are interested in participation in the regular Democratic Party. Now the whites will have to determine themselves as to which group is the regular party."[186]

On June 8 some eighty interested individuals—"mostly ministers and women," according to one newspaper account—formally organized the Citizens Democratic Party. Led by Susan Fitzsimmons Allison, past president of the South Carolina League of Women Voters, and William M. Perry, a past member of the Columbia City General Election Commission and president of an electrical wholesale firm, the organization attracted a few of the state's liberal whites, including several local members of the Southern Regional Council. The biggest complaint of the Citizens Democratic Party was the oath, although it also opposed the state party's efforts to bar African Americans from party membership.[187] Cognizant of the anti-Truman sentiment engulfing the state, the fledgling organization took pains to point out that they did not endorse Truman's civil rights program; however, they did state that they would support the national party nominees.[188] The group appointed a subcommittee that met with the Democratic Party chairman and demanded that the party reconvene, repudiate the voting oath, and rewrite the primary rules in adherence to the Supreme Court white primary decisions. They further requested that the state party send delegates to Philadelphia with no instructions except an order not to walk out, and they wanted assurances that the state would support the national party in the general election. Finally, the group issued an ultimatum: If the state party did not alter its policies within ten days, the Citizens Democratic Party would select a separate delegation to challenge the regular party in Philadelphia.[189] Not surprisingly, party leaders refused to reconvene the convention or change party rules.[190] Rebuffed, the Citizens Democratic Party met again on June 29 and appointed twenty delegates to the national convention in Philadelphia.[191] Despite the decision of the state party to remain firm, six counties rebelled. Authorities in Pickens, Greenville, Darlington, Spartanburg, Laurens, and Richland Counties permitted blacks to sign party enrollment books (and thus become party members) and exempted them from the oath. Apparently the leaders in these counties were unwilling to risk an expensive lawsuit that would result if they barred blacks from party membership.[192]

By late spring the southern revolt was beginning to acquire a discernible pattern. Gubernatorial support and control of the state party machinery was crucial for a bolt to succeed. Significantly, none of the states that eventually threw their support to the states' righters faced gubernatorial elections in 1948, and therefore they were free to devote more time and energy to the rebellion. In states with gubernatorial primaries, candidates remained cagey with regard to the states' rights issue. In a region where Democratic Party politics was close to a religion, support for the states' rights insurgency could brand a candidate as disloyal, with the result being almost definite political suicide.

Conservatives in Georgia and Louisiana, two states that on the surface appeared likely candidates for insurgency, hesitated. In those states the states' rights rebellion suffered not from a lack of enthusiasm or support but from a lack of gubernatorial leadership. Promotion of the states' rights cause fell to the state legislature or to non-officeholders. Preoccupied with the power struggle that ensued following the death of newly elected governor Eugene Talmadge in December 1946, Georgians gave little thought to a states' rights bolt. Talmadge died during the period between his election and his inauguration, leaving the state without a clear successor. In 1947 and early 1948 various factions scrambled to gain control of the governor's mansion. The question of Talmadge's successor became a three-sided toss-up between the incumbent governor Ellis Arnall, the newly elected lieutenant governor M. E. Thompson, and Herman Talmadge, the son of the late governor and the probable choice of the pro-Talmadge state legislature. A ruling by the Georgia state court appointed Thompson acting governor and arranged for another primary and general election to be held in September 1948. By the spring of 1948 Thompson had been representing the Peach State at the Southern Governors' Conference sessions, and he and Talmadge were squaring off for the gubernatorial primary. Both Thompson and Talmadge opposed the president's civil rights program, yet neither was willing to break with the national party.[193] Believing strongly in the adage "like father, like son," the states' rights advocates hoped for a Talmadge victory.[194]

In Louisiana the states' rights movement, like so many other issues in that state, became ensnared in the pro-Long/anti-Long split that had existed since the political reign of Huey P. Long. The lines dividing these groups were fluid; with any given political development, a politician could easily switch allegiances.[195] As it did throughout the South, support for the states' rights movement in Louisiana had its origins in that state's opposition to the New Deal and the 1944 effort to deny a fourth term to Franklin D. Roosevelt. Led by then-governor Sam Jones, the Louisiana anti–New Dealers/states' righters considered the New Deal's expansion of the federal government's power dangerous, particularly its broadening authority over internal natural resources. That year, led by the anti-Long forces, the Louisiana delegation cast their ballots for Virginia senator Harry Byrd.

The real power behind the states' rights movement in Louisiana was Leander Perez, the swaggering political boss of mineral-rich Plaquemines Parish. Like Horace Wilkinson in Alabama, Perez did not crave high public office and was content instead to amass and wield power from his swampy fiefdom below New Orleans. Born in 1891 to an established Catholic family, Perez's first language was French. Raised in relative physical isolation in a society "in which," his biographer notes, "Christianity and its moral code were regarded as absolutes and deviations were frowned upon and punished," Perez's passions were lit not by the fire of intellectual inquiry but by the prospect of raw power—economic and political. Perez graduated from Louisiana State University in 1912 and received his law degree from Tulane in 1914. A mediocre lawyer, he struggled financially.[196] Like Wilkinson, Perez began his political career as a reform candidate, running for the Louisiana House of Representatives against the reigning boss of Plaquemines Parish in 1916. He lost but "established a reputation as a reformer." In 1919 Perez was appointed judge of the twenty-ninth judicial district and was later elected in his own right. Once in office, he set himself against the New Orleans Old Regulars, who had controlled Plaquemines, and eventually was elected district attorney, in 1924.[197] Politically connected, Perez set about establishing his financial empire. He became involved in oil, sulfur, cattle, banking, and real estate ventures; once he was financially secure, he focused on politics and eventually attached himself to Governor Huey Long. Perez became the ultimate political boss, dispensing patronage and delivering huge parish majorities to the candidates he favored.[198] Like Long, an early supporter of the New Deal, Perez eventually came to oppose Roosevelt's attempts to expand the federal government's regulatory authority over natural resources, particularly the tidelands—the oil-rich submerged land in the Gulf of Mexico that stretched from the mainland to the edge of the continental shelf.[199] It had never been legally determined whether the region belonged to the individual states or to the national government. Whoever won the right to administer the disputed territory would reap a bonanza from rental fees, royalties on production, and severance taxes. The greatest oil deposits lay off Louisiana's irregular coastline, about 38 percent of which was within the boundaries of Plaquemines and St. Bernard Parishes, Perez's bailiwick.[200] In 1946 President Truman issued Executive Proclamation 2667 that claimed the oil derived from that land as a national resource and therefore under federal control.[201] The Supreme Court ruling in *U.S. v. California* in 1947 granted control of the tidelands to the federal government. Reclaiming control of the tidelands became entwined with the Louisiana states' rights movement, and several attorneys involved in the tidelands dispute became leaders of the Louisiana states' rights organization.[202]

Opposition to the president's civil rights proposals was strong in Louisiana, yet the gubernatorial election complicated the official support for a bolt. Earl Long, former lieutenant governor and younger brother of Huey Long, had emerged as one of the top contenders following the first primary and went on to crush former governor and 1944 anti-Roosevelt leader Sam Jones in the second primary in late February.[203] Both men declared their support for states' rights. Long, who had Perez's support, further promised he would not interfere with the work of the Democratic state central committee, whose conservative faction was controlled by Perez, thus creating a power vacuum into which the states' rights conservatives would gladly step.[204]

The Democratic state central committee met on March 6 to choose delegates for the national Democratic convention to be held in July. Committeeman Perez wanted the state party to officially pledge opposition to Truman's nomination. Long controlled the committee and refused to support this proposition. Louisiana's delegation to the Philadelphia convention contained loyalists and dissenters, although the loyalists claimed the majority. In early May, Long met with the president and reassured him that he would have the support of the Pelican State at the convention and in the general election. Here Long seriously miscalculated and underestimated the public antipathy toward the president.[205]

Louisiana was well represented within the higher councils of the states' rights movement. Perez contributed not only his considerable energy and organizational skills but his enormous financial resources as well.[206] He was ably assisted by John U. Barr of New Orleans, a veteran of the struggle to nominate Harry Byrd rather than FDR in 1944. Barr, a businessman in the rope and hemp industry, had close ties with wealthy southerners through his position as an officer of the SSIC.

Both Beauford Jester of Texas and Ben Laney of Arkansas were up for reelection in 1948, a consideration that seriously colored their leadership of and participation in the states' rights crusade. Jester, an early and vocal opponent of President Truman's policies, was particularly hostile toward the federal government's position on the tidelands oil issue. Yet when push came to shove, he refused to break from the national party. In a speech delivered in late April, Jester capitulated: "No matter how aggrieved we may feel, and . . . how deep our resentment, I do not believe that Texas Democrats should bolt the Party." He concluded with a plea for unity: "Let us do our utmost to put our Democratic House in order. . . . Let us go forth to the Philadelphia Convention as a united Party."[207] In Arkansas Ben Laney considered running for a rare third term as governor, and his chances appeared uncertain. Although Laney was to become a recognized leader of the regional movement, his hold on the Democratic organization in his own state remained tenuous. Laney and state party chairman Arthur Adams were early movement supporters, yet they held little sway over other party members. In Arkansas the absence of a unified and monolithic state party organization thwarted any effective efforts to organize a bolt.[208] The disappointing developments in Texas and Arkansas underscored the primacy of the peculiarities of individual political cultures in determining the success or failure of the states' rights bolt.

★

As the outburst from southern politicians in the wake of Harry Truman's civil rights message gave way to tough political choices, states' rights advocates discovered a South that was less than united behind independent political action. Although the leaders of the revolt had not succeeded in immediately capturing the political allegiance of the Solid South, they had reason to hope. The national party's unwillingness to compromise and white southerners' almost universal opposition to Harry Truman convinced Black Belt conservatives to carry on with the fight. With their gendered political rhetoric helping to confirm their identity and with their momentum unsteady but resonant, the states' rights conservatives saw little reason to view their cause as lost. They set their sights on Philadelphia, fittingly, the birthplace of independence.

SETTING THE POSTWAR AGENDA

Civil Rights, States' Rights, and the Tale of Two Conventions

It was clear that at the family reunion we were as welcome as children whose parentage was never established.

DISGRUNTLED WHITE SOUTHERN DEMOCRAT
at the Democratic National Convention, July 1948

With an arrogance that has been rivaled only by their stupidity since they began agitating five months ago, a small group of Southerners will meet in Birmingham today.

JONATHAN DANIELS
Raleigh News and Observer, *July 17, 1948*

In early July 1948, as temperatures on the East Coast crept steadily upward, a badly splintered Democratic Party limped into Philadelphia for its first national convention since the end of World War II. Disgruntled white southerners and anxious northern liberals came itching for a floor fight on the decisive issue of civil rights and the future direction of the party in the postwar era. Were the promises of the war, particularly the commitment to democratic principles for all citizens, to be enshrined in the platform, or would conservative southerners, desperate to reclaim their prominence within national party circles, succeed in pulling the party backward?

Rising to address the hot and weary delegates on the last evening of the convention, Hubert Humphrey, the young liberal mayor from Minneapolis, made an emotional plea on behalf of racial equality. "I ask the Democratic Party to march down the high-road of progressive democracy," he pleaded. "I ask this Convention to say in unmistakable terms that we proudly hail and we courageously support our President and leader, Harry Truman, in his great fight for civil rights." Heeding his call, the delegates jumped to their feet, applauding madly. With a few well-chosen words, Humphrey suffused the heretofore moribund convention with a profound sense of purpose. Suddenly rejuvenated, the Democratic conventioneers overwhelmingly approved the civil rights plank put forth by the party's liberal wing. By most accounts, the day had been won for civil rights.[1] In reality, however, the battle for civil rights and representative democracy was lost a few days before Humphrey's speech and the famous fight on the convention floor in a series of political skirmishes that have long since been forgotten. Inspired by the words and actions of the first president to commit himself publicly to civil rights, and determined to capitalize on and extend the war's meaning into the postwar era, groups of southerners composed of African Americans, white moderates, and veterans journeyed to Philadelphia to contest the seating of the all-white delegations from the southern states. Pledging their loyalty to the national party, these challengers dared the DNC to take a meaningful stand for civil rights. Content with words over actions, platform planks over actual representation, Democratic Party leaders denied their requests. Party leaders set the tone for the postwar era by squandering this opportunity to strike a blow against oppression in the South.

If black activists felt the party failed to deliver on civil rights, states' rights partisans believed party leaders had gone too far. Southern Democrats had come to the convention determined to oppose both a civil rights plank and the nomination of President Truman. Disorganized and without a viable alternative candidate, however, they failed at both tasks. Taunted by catcalls from their fellow Democrats, delegates from Alabama and Mississippi stormed out of the convention hall in protest. Down but not out, several thousand states' rights Democrats converged on Birmingham two days later to hold their own convention. Lacking direction but not enthusiasm, the southern rebels transformed themselves into the States' Rights Democratic Party, and amidst rebel yells, jig-dancing mountain women, and portraits of Robert E. Lee, they made Strom Thurmond and Fielding Wright their presidential and vice-presidential candidates. The confusion and disorganization that characterized the Birmingham convention mirrored the States' Rights Democrats' shaky structure, a weakness the campaign ultimately would never quite overcome.

★

Throughout the first half of 1948, southern Democrats were not the only faction of that beleaguered party to oppose Truman's nomination; they were merely the most vocal. One reporter joked that the Democratic Party reminded him of "a ship beating itself to pieces on a rocky shore."[2] Northern left-wing liberals had become increasingly disillusioned with the president, whom they regarded an unworthy successor to Roosevelt. They doubted his commitment to social reform; in particular, they questioned Truman's commitment to the rights of organized labor and criticized his decision to delay action on his civil rights program until after the Democratic convention in July. Some, but by no means all, liberals had begun to chafe at Truman's increasingly strident anticommunism.

Compounding liberals' dissatisfaction was the almost universally accepted wisdom that Truman would lose in November. Henry Wallace threatened to siphon off critical support in the North, and the Republicans enjoyed a commanding lead in the polls. In the months prior to the election, the anticommunist liberal wing, led by the Americans for Democratic Action (ADA), searched desperately for a replacement candidate.[3]

The common desire to rid the party of Harry Truman made for an unlikely convergence of liberal and conservative interests around the possible nomination of popular World War II general Dwight D. Eisenhower. Conceived in March, the Eisenhower "draft" gathered momentum throughout the early spring and summer, picking up fragments of the Democratic Party's right and left wings as it rolled toward the nominating convention. By the eve of the meeting, the "Draft Eisenhower" movement was a bizarre and unworkable mélange that included big-city machine bosses Jacob Arvey of Chicago and New York mayor William O'Dwyer; the liberal anticommunist ADA; labor leaders Philip Murray of the CIO and Walter Reuther of the United Auto Workers; the three sons of Franklin Delano Roosevelt; and southern New Deal senators Claude Pepper of Florida and Lister Hill of Alabama.

Determined to prevent Truman's nomination, disgruntled southern Democrats gravitated to the Eisenhower movement in the hopes that the popular general could heal the breech in the South.[4] Realistically, had Eisenhower been nominated, the hybrid liberal-conservative coalition never would have survived the campaign. This apparently did not concern conservative southerners; by July it appeared that only an Eisenhower nomination could thwart a southern bolt. On the eve of the convention, members of Alabama's loyalist and rebel factions championed Eisenhower's nomination, as did delegations from Georgia and Virginia.[5] Strom Thurmond jumped aboard the general's bandwagon, and Governors Jester of Texas and Laney of Arkansas joined him.[6] Among leading states' righters, only Governor Wright of Mississippi and Alabama's Horace Wilkinson refused to support a possible Eisenhower candidacy.[7]

In those heady, preconvention days, Eisenhower's politics remained a mystery. No one could say for certain whether he considered himself a Democrat or a Republican, which only broadened his appeal and allowed him to be all things to all people. Southern politicians felt comfortable with what they believed were Eisenhower's compatible racial views. Senator Olin Johnston of South Carolina considered the general "extremely liberal . . . except on the race issue."[8] Alabama states' rights hard-liner Gessner McCorvey supported Eisenhower because the general "knows and understands the Southern negro and appreciates our problems."[9] The movement to draft Eisenhower came to an abrupt halt on July 5 when the general announced he "could not accept nomination for any public office or participate in partisan political contests."[10] Most of the disappointed supporters accepted Eisenhower's refusal as final.[11] Desperate to prevent Truman's nomination, however, other Eisenhower supporters, including ardent states' rights advocates, nevertheless held out hope that the general would reconsider.[12] These hangers-on abandoned all hope when, on Friday, July 9, Eisenhower gave his "final and complete" refusal to Senator Claude Pepper. Unfortunately for his supporters, the general's eleventh-hour refusal made it impossible for delegates to scare up an alternate nominee.[13] With the Eisenhower coalition blown asunder and Truman's nomination virtually guaranteed, liberal and conservative Democrats looked toward the national convention with sullen foreboding. Retreating to their respective camps, the various party factions turned their energy toward the party platform and the divisive issue of civil rights.

The fractured and fractious Democrats descended on Philadelphia for the party's national convention on July 10, resigned to nominating a candidate everyone considered a sure loser. A pall settled over the City of Brotherly Love, the oppressive gloom of the event surpassed only by the stifling midsummer heat.[14] Hotel managers anticipating a flood of free-spending conventioneers were instead plagued by hundreds of cancellations. Everyone, from taxicab drivers to newsboys, complained about sluggish business.[15] Robert Bendiner of the *Nation* commented that the event was driven more by endurance than enthusiasm.[16]

The dour mood of the Democrats contrasted sharply with the Republican bacchanalia of two weeks earlier. Also staged in Philadelphia, the Republican convention was a dapper affair with a bevy of Hollywood movie stars and a spit-and-polish presidential nominee. The road to the Republican convention had been hard fought. The chief contenders for the nomination were New York governor and 1944 Republican presidential candidate Thomas Dewey, Ohio senator Robert Taft, and former Minnesota governor Harold E. Stassen. Dewey triumphed on the third ballot and chose California governor Earl Warren as his running mate. With two attractive, progressive governors from populous states, the Republicans had assembled a formidable ticket. They also had approved a fairly liberal platform that included support for federal aid for housing and civil rights.[17]

The collapse of the Eisenhower movement dealt southern Democrats a serious setback. Unable to prevent Truman's nomination, they busied themselves in endless caucuses and meetings, desperate to devise a plan to block the adoption of a strong civil rights plank in the convention platform.[18] Four hundred southern Democrats reconvened in the ballroom of the Benjamin Franklin Hotel on Sunday, July 11, to approve their final states' rights declaration and agree on an alternate candidate. The meeting began in the afternoon and dragged on until 2:00 A.M. They vowed to work for a plank that pledged state control over elections, employment practices, segregation, and the punishment of crimes.[19]

The choice of an alternate candidate proved difficult. On the opening day of the convention, no compromise candidate had yet been found. The group considered Laney, Wright, and Thurmond and unenthusiastically settled on Laney. What little support the Arkansas governor had garnered quickly dwindled when he announced his refusal to bolt the convention if Truman were nominated.[20] Fed up with the vacillating Laney, the Georgia delegation pledged their support to favorite son Senator Richard Russell and urged other states to do likewise.[21]

The caucus painfully revealed that the states' rights movement suffered from what one southern newspaper called a "poverty of leadership." One Alabama paper observed that senators and congressmen could be found everywhere at the convention except at the states' rights caucus. This was unfortunate, according to *Montgomery Advertiser* editor Grover C. Hall Jr., for neither Strom Thurmond nor Fielding Wright cut "a commanding or even a stimulating figure."[22] A dearth of recognizable leaders possessing regional influence and credibility would remain a vexing obstacle throughout the states' rights campaign. Hall also noted that the southern caucus failed to arouse much interest or concern from the DNC. A DNC official attended the meeting but, bored, left halfway through the proceedings.[23] Ralph McGill of the *Atlanta Journal* echoed Hall's sentiments, reporting that the caucus was the laughingstock among newsmen, who referred to the southerners as "typical Cleghorns."[24] Unmindful of their less-than-heroic stature and with their strategy finally in place, Dixie Democrats anxiously anticipated the fight for states' rights on the convention floor.

While the states' rights southerners cobbled together their plan of action, across the political aisle the ADA, organized labor, and civil rights leaders worked to prevent the adoption of an anemic civil rights plank. They demanded that Truman, if nominated, commit himself to a civil rights plank derived from his earlier proposals.[25] Uncomfortably straddling the gap between southern and liberal Democrats, the Truman administration hoped to avoid a complete splintering of the party by embracing a civil rights plank similar to the one adopted in 1944.[26]

The administration won round one when the drafting committee presented a moderate civil rights plank to the full platform committee. Despite the efforts of Hubert Humphrey and former Wisconsin congressman Andrew Biemiller, the platform committee approved the tepid, ambiguous statement.[27] Civil rights leaders were understandably disappointed by the administration's apparent backpedaling on civil rights. An irate Walter White warned Chairman McGrath that "such a surrender to expediency . . . would be disastrous."[28] But the wording of the platform was not the only weapon in the battle waged on behalf of civil rights at the convention. Determined to test the depths of the national party's commitment to democracy, alternate delegates from South Carolina and Mississippi had journeyed to Philadelphia to challenge the seating of the all-white states' rights delegations. Although they would make a valiant effort, the challengers would depart Philadelphia unrecognized and disappointed by a national party more concerned with politics than with justice.

★

The Progressive Democrats and Citizen Democrats from South Carolina and pro-Truman delegates from Mississippi probably realized their chances for unseating the regular delegations were slim. Never in the history of the Democratic Party had a state delegation been denied its seat.[29] To make matters worse, the DNC appeared indifferent to the impending challenges. Indeed, Chairman McGrath claimed never to have heard of John McCray or the PDP. The DNC chairman further dampened the hopes of the challengers by announcing that it did not matter that the regular all-white delegations had pledged themselves against Truman; the Credentials Committee would decide who would be seated.[30]

Everything appeared to be going smoothly for the all-white delegations when the challengers failed to attend a preconvention meeting on July 10.[31] With no challengers in sight, the Credentials Committee voted to seat the all-white delegation from South Carolina.[32] Apparently the DNC had failed to inform the PDP of the date and time of the meeting, for the black delegation did not even arrive in Washington until late in the afternoon on July 10. John McCray successfully appealed to the Credentials Committee, and a hearing was scheduled for July 13, at which time the committee would also consider the challenges of the Citizen Democrats from South Carolina and a group of pro-Truman Mississippi Democrats.[33] Senator Johnston and Governor Thurmond both planned to be on hand to defend the seats of the all-white delegation.

The fight before the Credentials Committee took place on July 13 and lasted five hours. The Citizen Democrats of South Carolina were represented by Chairman L. A. Fletcher, a casketmaker from Leesville, South Carolina, and Dave Baker, a Columbia attorney. John McCray and Arthur J. Clement Jr. presented the Progressive Democrats' challenge, and Charles Hamilton of Aberdeen, Mississippi, and leader of the Young Democrats in the state, spoke on behalf of Mississippi's pro-Truman challengers. Representatives from the three groups urged the committee to put the war's meaning into action, and each made a concerted effort to appeal to the democratic principles of the committee members by comparing the actions of the all-white delegations to the actions of totalitarian nations. Speaking first, the Citizen Democrats demanded the disqualification of the Thurmond delegation on the grounds that it was illegally constituted because it excluded African Americans and therefore did not represent the entire population of South Carolina. They challenged the delegation on what they called "a thought-control, fascistic oath" that required voters to profess their support of racial segregation.[34] The oath, Dave Baker argued, "disenfranchised all the . . . intelligent people of South Carolina."[35] Furthermore, Thurmond's group was disloyal, while the Citizen Democrats were "willing to follow and abide by the rules of the Democratic Party . . . to vote for the nominee of the Democratic Party . . . [and] to grant franchise to all people, regardless of race, color or creed."[36] Baker turned the party's own rhetoric to his advantage and challenged the Credentials Committee to back its words with action. "Just as our government in world affairs must lend a supporting hand to every progressive and liberal element of the world," Baker conjectured, "I say that the Democratic party has got to help us in these states in particular where the progressive elements are being suppressed." If the Democratic Party was serious about promoting progressive democracy, Baker contended, let them act now. To fail to do so "will give notice to the entire nation that they are supporting the reactionary groups which have controlled and dominated South Carolina politics for so many, many years."[37]

Patriotic rhetoric aside, the Citizen Democrats were less convincing when questioned about their organization's qualifications for and particular demands regarding representation at the national convention. Baker acknowledged that only seventeen counties sent representatives to their conventions and that only four party members had traveled to the national convention, not nearly enough to replace the regular delegation. L. A. Fletcher promised that he could "round up" additional delegates if their organization was recognized. Baker and Fletcher contradicted each other with regard to the group's demands. Baker asserted that his group would not accept a partial settlement. Fletcher vacillated, at one time asking for all twenty seats, at another time agreeing to proportional representation. Flustered, he finally agreed to accept "whatever we are permitted."[38]

In contrast to the Citizen Democrats, whose last-minute organizing made it difficult for them to achieve full representation at their state convention, the PDP benefited from four years of political organizing. The PDP had held conventions at the precinct, county, and state levels. Unlike the meeting of the regular state party, all PDP conventions were "open to all races, and all people."[39] Charleston businessman Arthur J. Clement Jr. stated that the PDP likewise based its challenge on the grounds that the "delegates of the Democratic party of South Carolina were elected illegally and in defiance of all federal courts" and hence did not represent the majority of the state's citizens. Aware that the Democratic Party was bidding for the African American vote in key northern states, Clement reminded the committee that black voters "in those key and important states" supported the PDP.[40] Anticipating that the committee might consider the PDP a third party and hence unworthy of representation in Democratic Party councils, Clement informed them that members of the PDP desired to become members of the regular Democratic Party but had been barred by whites. Finally, Clement asked the committee to award the PDP proportional representation—one-third of the delegate seats.[41]

Charles Hamilton of the Young Democrats of Mississippi represented the pro-Truman Democrats of that state. Hamilton claimed his delegation was selected at a meeting following the Mississippi Democratic convention in late June and that delegates representing a majority of the state's counties attended the meeting. Hamilton declined to make public the names of his delegates, saying that if their names were published, any of their relatives holding state jobs would lose them.[42] One Mississippi newspaper later reported that several members of his delegation were former GIs.[43] Hamilton reminded the committee of the Mississippi Democratic Party's 1944 bolt. He spoke of the February states' rights mass meeting at which he had been drowned out by boos from states' righters. The Mississippi states' righters would not vote for the national party nominee come November, he contended. "They are here only as a gesture." Hamilton asked that the Credentials Committee deny the Mississippi delegation its seats unless it pledged itself to support national party nominees.[44]

Senator Olin Johnston of South Carolina, a member of the Credentials Committee, led the question-and-answer period. Johnston steered clear of the race issue and the exclusionary nature of the South Carolina state convention and focused instead on technicalities and procedural questions. He first attempted to define the PDP as a third party with no legitimate claim on delegate seats. Had not the PDP run a candidate for the U.S. Senate in 1944, coincidentally, against Johnston himself? Clement acknowledged that the PDP had indeed run Osceola McKaine for the U.S. Senate in 1944, but except for listing McKaine as their candidate for senator, the ballots of the Democratic and Progressive Democratic Parties were identical. To counter accusations that they were a third party, Clement informed the committee that the PDP planned to dissolve once it received representation in the state Democratic Party.[45] Johnston then tried to disqualify the PDP's challenge on the grounds that the black party had not held meetings in all state precincts.[46] John McCray tartly replied that "if the Senator read his own hometown papers, he would find . . . that some 200 clubs or more of your Party didn't have any meetings at all. So I don't think that would affect our case any, whatsoever." McCray reminded the committee of Waring's court decision, "which distinctly says that persons of all races desiring to belong to the Democratic Party in South Carolina should have the right to do so." According to McCray, the state Democratic Party violated Waring's decision.[47]

Strom Thurmond, representing the all-white delegation, continued Johnston's line of questioning, challenging both the PDP and the Citizen Democrats on procedural grounds. Thurmond vigorously denounced proportional representation and threatened to walk out of the convention if the challengers were seated.[48] When asked by Credentials Committee member George Vaughan, a black delegate from Missouri, whether the state Democratic Party's precinct club membership was open to African Americans, Thurmond responded that "the precinct clubs have been open, as they have in the past. We don't have any law in the primaries known in our state. The precincts were governed by the rules of the primary. As I stated, whatever decision has been handed down by the federal courts, we have complied with it." Apparently Vaughan was not satisfied with Thurmond's response and again asked him to answer the question. Thurmond snapped, "I will answer you nothing!" and stormed out of the meeting.[49]

Other committee members continued to hammer at the procedural issues. One commented that McCray and the PDP should have sought representation in the regular Democratic Party at the precinct and county levels. An exasperated McCray defended his organization, replying, "We could not belong to the club or precinct, so how could we file a case, sir, when we could not get in?" Frustrated, McCray told the committee of the case of Dillon County, South Carolina, in which eight blacks had attended their precinct meeting and were elected to the Dillon County Convention. However, the chairman of the South Carolina SDEC sent a letter to Dillon party officials informing them that under party rules, blacks could not attend club meetings and be elected delegates. The black delegates were disqualified. Hoping to avoid a confrontation with white southern Democrats, the Credentials Committee listened politely but chose ultimately to ignore the ugly facts of disfranchisement, preferring instead to blame the victims for not following proper procedures.[50]

Despite their best efforts, the challengers came up short. The Credentials Committee voted to seat the South Carolina delegation, although three members abstained. Mississippi's all-white delegation had a more difficult time. Although the committee voted that Mississippi be seated, it was by a narrow 15 to 11 margin. George Vaughan moved, and another member seconded, that the seating of the all-white Mississippi delegation be denied. The motion was defeated.[51]

The Progressive Democrats, McCray announced, were "puzzled but certainly not humiliated nor daunted" by the committee's decision. Nevertheless, he expressed disillusionment at the Credentials Committee's preference to confine itself to a narrow ruling. "It is difficult to understand the legal and moral grounds, if any, upon which these actions were based," he stated. "If this is to be the position of the Democratic Party, though confronted by rulings of our courts to the contrary, then Negroes who have so faithfully supported it and who have seen in its leadership hope for consolation and help to all our troubled people, are now confronted with an era of privation and constitutional abrogations." Despite this setback, the PDP would continue to fight for inclusion in the Democratic Party and for a Democratic victory in November. "We are certainly not relenting one step in our efforts to live freer and happier," McCray stated. "We return home geared to complete our task, as proud of our country as ever and as loyal to our convictions as ever. We plan to continue the Progressive Democratic Party in South Carolina."[52]

The states' rights delegations had survived the challenges, and as the convention opened, they stood poised for a fight on the party platform. When the convention finally got under way, white southern delegates immediately found themselves on the defensive. First, George Vaughan submitted a minority report challenging the seating of the Mississippi delegation. Supported by nine other members of the committee, the report objected to the resolutions adopted by the Mississippi state Democratic convention on June 22 that bound delegates to oppose the president or any other candidate who supported civil rights. His voice was nearly drowned out by a deafening hail of boos from Dixie delegates, but Vaughan asked that the convention bar the states' rights delegation from Mississippi. After enumerating the resolutions passed by the Mississippi state legislature, Vaughan asked that the convention accept his report, "in behalf of the 15 million Negroes of this country." Although twelve states and the District of Columbia opposed the seating of the states' rights delegation from Mississippi, the delegates accepted by voice vote the majority report of the Credentials Committee. The Mississippi states' rights forces could finally take their seats.[53] The states' rights rebels never forgave Vaughan. Later in the summer, Alabama state party chairman Gessner McCorvey used a picture of Vaughan at the Philadelphia convention in an effort to arouse white southerners. "I don't think I ever saw a human being whose picture more resembled a gorilla," McCorvey crassly wrote.[54]

The main battle, as expected, came over the wording of the platform. Former Texas governor Dan Moody, Tennessee delegate Cecil Sims, and Mississippi Speaker of the House Walter Sillers gave minority reports for the southern delegates calling for a states' rights provision. They implored the convention to return to the "fundamental principles" upon which the party was founded and to pledge to prevent the encroachment of the federal government into the domestic affairs of the states.[55]

These states' rights resolutions were followed by liberal resolutions. Andrew Biemiller, whom Truman considered a "crackpot," submitted the minority resolution of the ADA affiliates, cosponsored by Humphrey.[56] The Wisconsin delegate elicited prolonged applause when he commended Truman "for his courageous stand on the issue of civil rights." The Humphrey-Biemiller resolution called on Congress "to support our president" in guaranteeing the rights to "full and equal political participation," to "equal opportunity of employment," to "security of person," and to "equal treatment in the services and defense of our Nation."[57] Sensing the convention's momentum and hoping to capitalize on it, Humprey ascended the podium. He fervently implored the party faithful to fulfill the Democratic promise. "There will be no hedging, and there will be no watering down . . . of the instruments and the principles of the civil rights program," he promised. "There are those who say to you—we are rushing this issue of civil rights," Humphrey declared. "I say we are a hundred and seventy-two years late. . . . The time has arrived for the Democratic party to get out of the shadow of states' rights and walk forthrightly into the bright sunshine of human rights."[58]

Humphrey's articulated vision unleashed pandemonium in the convention hall. When the celebrating had subsided long enough for a vote to be recorded, the southerners were soundly beaten as the convention rebuked their minority resolution 925 to 309. Although every delegate from the South voted for it, there were only eleven votes from outside the old confederacy. Moreover, the Biemiller-Humphrey resolution passed by 651½ to 582½. Cheers and jeers filled the convention hall following the final tally. Amidst the mayhem Handy Ellis, chairperson of the Alabama delegation and leader of the walkout faction, and delegate Bull Connor, Birmingham's commissioner of public safety, attempted to get the attention of convention chairman Sam Rayburn. They wanted to capitalize on the dramatic moment and announce Alabama's withdrawal from the convention. Ellis, Connor, and several other members of the Alabama delegation perched on their seats, waving the Alabama banner. "Holler like hell, Bull—Holler!" Ellis cried. The *Montgomery Advertiser* reported that "Bull was hollering like the devil's own loudspeaker . . . [and] looked like he would like to bust. His eyes popped out. The mighty vocal cords swelled up, blue and purple and scarlet, in his open shirt." Much to the Alabamians' dismay, Rayburn failed to recognize them and, instead, recessed the convention until the evening. As he was filing out of the convention hall, a distressed Bull Connor told an assemblage of reporters, "I've always admired Sam Rayburn. I've always thought of him as a great statesman. But I hollered for five minutes. People heard me all over the hall. And when a gentleman from Texas will not recognize a delegate from Alabama—well, I just can't understand it. No, sir!"[59]

The southern rebels stood poised to strike when the convention reconvened that evening at seven o'clock. As the delegates prepared to nominate a presidential and vice-presidential candidate, Rayburn finally recognized Alabama's Handy Ellis. Ellis announced that Alabama's electors were instructed "never to cast their vote for a Republican, never to cast their vote for Harry Truman, and never to cast their vote for any candidate with a civil rights program such as adopted by the convention." He further informed the convention that half of the state's delegation was also pledged to walk out if the convention adopted a strong civil rights plank. He continued, "Without hatred and without anger, and without fear, but with disillusionment and disappointment, we are faced with the necessity of carrying out our pledges to the people of Alabama, and that we cannot with honor further participate in the proceedings of this Convention . . . we bid you good bye." Ellis and the other twelve bolters of the Alabama delegation then marched out of the convention hall, followed by the entire Mississippi delegation as the galleries booed and jeered.[60] The conductor of the sixty-piece convention band later reported that he twice had been offered "substantial sums" to play "Dixie" when the Alabama delegation walked out of the hall.[61] He declined the bribes, and the delegates filed out accompanied only by the catcalls of their fellow Democrats. As Ellis passed the Wisconsin delegation, a representative from the Dairy State bellowed, "Good riddance. We'll win in November without you." To which Ellis replied, "The hell you will. Harry Truman won't get $5.50 from the white people in Alabama to help his campaign."[62]

The departing southerners made a poor impression on the remaining delegates. "They were all rather small, shrunken-looking men," recalled Katie Louchheim, a convention delegate and later director of Women's Activities for the DNC. "Perhaps it was just my mood, but we were in an unair-conditioned hall. The men were in shirtsleeves. And they went out in a fashion that seemed to me to make them all look like little men."[63] Apparently at least one member of the Mississippi delegation anticipated encountering more than just boos. J. Oliver Emmerich, editor of the *McComb Enterprise-Journal,* recalled that Mississippi delegate Weaver Gore had a ball and knife strapped around his waist. "Look-a here," Gore said to Emmerich, revealing his weapon, "no son-of-a-bitch better put his hands on me."[64] No one did. The remaining southerners refused to accept the Truman nomination. The Georgia delegation nominated Senator Richard B. Russell, the band this time struck up a rousing version of "Dixie," and southern delegates paraded around the convention floor. Despite the southern defection, Truman gained the nomination easily. Russell eventually received 263 votes, all from the South.[65]

While the president waited offstage, conventioneers spent the next hour choosing his running mate. Alben W. Barkley, the septuagenarian Senate minority leader from Kentucky, earlier had received the nod from Truman and was nominated by acclamation. Finally, at 2:00 A.M., Truman mounted the rostrum to deliver his acceptance speech to the exhausted delegates. Public oratory had never been the president's forte; coming on the heels of rousing civil rights debates, Truman's acceptance speech, most delegates assumed, would be anticlimactic.

To everyone's surprise Truman delivered a blistering speech full of the fighting spirit that would energize his campaign in the months ahead. Lambasting the Republican platform as "a long list of promises," Truman stated he had decided to give them an opportunity to make good on them. The president announced to the shocked delegates that he would call the Republican Congress back into session on July 26. He had called the Republicans' bluff.[66]

As the convention wound down, the daunting task the bolting southerners had set for themselves was only beginning to take shape. In just a few short days they would converge on Birmingham to chart the next stage of their protest. If their experience at the national convention prof-

Governor Strom Thurmond at the Democratic National Convention, Philadelphia, July 1948.
Photograph courtesy of Special Collections, Clemson University Libraries,
Clemson, South Carolina.

fered any indication of what they could expect in the months ahead, they must have anticipated the Birmingham meeting with some foreboding. Lacking both a clear leader and a well-articulated plan, and harassed by national party liberals and organized minority factions on their home turf, states' rights southerners were quickly discovering that fomenting a revolution would be more difficult than they had originally thought.

★

"The chips are down. The die is cast," a defiant Fielding Wright wrote to former Alabama governor Frank Dixon. "We must make Birmingham the beginning of our . . . fight to save the South."[67] Two days later, several thousand determined white southerners journeyed to that industrial metropolis for the culmination of the protest that had begun five months earlier. An event that should have marked the high point of solidarity instead exposed some of the problems that would plague the states' rights forces for the next three and a half months.

Their common opposition to Harry Truman and his civil rights program aside, states' rights leaders achieved unanimity on little else. Disagreements over strategy and confusion over what the Birmingham convention had actually accomplished left many supporters dissatisfied. Birmingham also exposed the ideological gulfs among individual rebels, revealing yet another division within the southern political spectrum. Some states' rights supporters such as Strom Thurmond complained of "extremists" within their ranks and agonized over how to promote states' rights and segregation without resorting to blatantly racist language and ideology. The more moderate Dixie rebels found themselves in a bind, aware that the racist political language of the last half-century was becoming a liability outside their core constituency in the postwar era. But lacking a broader, more encompassing conservative agenda that would appeal to voters outside the Deep South, and desperate for support, the more moderate members readily joined their radical brothers in the gutter of white supremacy.

★

Bruised but not beaten, some 6,000 rebellious southern Democrats descended on Birmingham's Municipal Auditorium on Saturday, July 17, determined to avenge their defeat at the Philadelphia convention. Ironically, the convention hall that in 1938 had been the site of the landmark meeting of the integrationist SCHW hosted the self-appointed gatekeepers of white supremacy ten years later.[68] The meeting originally was scheduled to be held in a hotel conference room that could accommodate three hundred persons. By Friday afternoon, organizers recognized that thousands of white southerners desired to attend the convention, so they switched the location to the city's red brick auditorium. This sudden change of plans left the auditorium's staff with barely twenty-four hours to prepare for the event. The hall's large wrestling ring was dismantled and replaced by a speaker's platform. Hoping to avoid a "sectional atmosphere," the arrangements committee requested decorations that were strictly Americana. Auditorium employees festooned the walls with red, white, and blue bunting, and American flags stood like sentries at the hall's entrance. The more partisan delegates, however, happily discovered a flag company, conveniently located down the street from the auditorium, that was gladly selling scores of Confederate flags.

Fortunately for the financially strapped states' rights forces, the auditorium had been furnished free of charge, and the Birmingham Chamber of Commerce offered to replenish the conventioneers' energy with a steady supply of soft drinks and sandwiches. Organizers hired a band and made special lighting and wiring arrangements to accommodate the nearly 150 news personnel expected to be on hand to cover the event. Conference leaders must have been pleased with the attention their movement was garnering from the media. The convention was broadcast over the three major radio networks, and the National Broadcasting Company televised the proceedings.[69] Putting the sound thrashing they had received in the City of Brotherly Love behind them, the states' righters reveled in the growing enthusiasm and strength on their home turf. The battle had been joined.

Delegates seasonally attired in "shirt-sleeves and broad-brimmed hats" began pouring into the Magic City on Friday, July 16. Although convention organizers bragged that representatives from thirteen southern states attended the event, the majority of the delegates came from Mississippi, South Carolina, and Alabama. Like the prior states' rights meetings and caucuses, the Birmingham convention exhibited the "y'all come" atmosphere of a revival meeting. There were no qualifications for attending the conference, and anyone who cared to attend was granted entrance. Just about anyone could acquire a delegate's badge, one conventioneer noted, "just so [long as] they're Believers." But few political movements survive on messianic zeal alone. Unfortunately for states' rights supporters, most of the delegates were political novices, small-time officeholders, or curious observers with no official standing in the Democratic Party. The Virginia delegation consisted of four students from the University of Virginia and a young woman who had stopped off in Birmingham on her way home from New Orleans. A Kentucky-born Alabamian was the sole representative of the Blue Grass State.[70]

The most prominent figures at Birmingham were Strom Thurmond, Fielding Wright, former Alabama governor Frank Dixon, Mississippi senators James Eastland and John Stennis, Mississippi congressmen John Bell Williams and William Colmer, and former governors Hugh White of Mississippi and Sam Jones of Louisiana. Aside from the Mississippi contingent, politicians of national renown stayed away. Senator Richard B. Russell of Georgia, who received 263 votes from southern delegates at the Philadelphia convention, let it be known that he did not wish to be nominated by the Birmingham convention. Other southern leaders, such as Governor Ben Laney of Arkansas, Governor Beauford Jester of Texas, and Governor William Tuck of Virginia, who had supported the movement back in February, declined to attend.[71] Even a few recognized States' Rights leaders approached the conference with ambivalence. As late as July 16, reports circulated that Thurmond felt the conclave was being held too soon, and that neither he nor any other member of the South Carolina convention delegation planned to attend.[72]

Alabama States' Rights leaders established campaign headquarters at the Tutwiler Hotel and had begun planning the conference Thursday evening. Messages exchanged between the convention headquarters and local States' Rights leaders remained vague as to the purpose of the meeting. As late as the day before the conference, it remained unclear whether the States' Rights Democrats would name their own candidates for president and vice-president or, instead, work to convince the presidential electors in the individual southern states to withhold their votes from President Truman in an attempt to deny either candidate a majority and thus throw the election into the House of Representatives.[73] The last-minute conference details were finalized on Friday evening by a steering committee composed of Fielding Wright, fellow Mississippian Wallace Wright, Horace Wilkinson, Sidney Smyer, and Frank Dixon from Alabama.[74] The steering committee represented the movement's more radical elements and was responsible for determining the direction and setting the mood of the conference. Considering the personalities involved, the tone promised to be strident.

By the time Alabama state Democratic Party chairman Gessner T.

McCorvey called the convention to order at 11:00 A.M., delegates had packed the 6,000-seat hall to the rafters, with the exception of an upper-level gallery normally reserved for blacks. That area remained empty. Hundreds of fervent followers milled along the sidewalks outside, following the proceedings on an outdoor sound system.[75] Police Chief Floyd Eddins told the *Birmingham News* it was the largest crowd ever gathered in and around the auditorium.[76] Mixing with the states' rights faithful were ten picketers representing Henry Wallace's Progressive Party. Hopelessly outnumbered, they quietly departed as the conference got under way.[77]

Despite the hour-long delay, their amateur status, and the 90° heat, the conferees whooped it up like seasoned professionals. College students from Alabama, Tennessee, Georgia, Virginia, and Mississippi who had caravanned to Birmingham to participate in the conference provided much of the energy and color during the proceedings. Among them were seventy-five students from the University of Mississippi who, reflecting the socioeconomic ties of many of the states' rights supporters, came decked out in black planters' hats and carried the Confederate flag. Treated as if they were state dignitaries, the students had the honor of a state highway patrol escort that led them to the Alabama border.[78]

At the conclusion of his opening remarks, McCorvey yielded the microphone to the Reverend John Buchanan, a Baptist preacher from Birmingham, who asked God to "purge from [the delegates'] hearts all prejudice." Following the invocation, Metropolitan Opera star Ruby Mercer sang the "Star Spangled Banner" and "Dixie" as the audience cheered, clapped, stomped their feet, and sang along. Adopted by the southern crowd as one of their own, Mercer later told reporters she was actually a registered New York Republican.[79] Convention chairman Walter Sillers told the cheering crowd that "we are here to warn that group who claims to be the Democratic party that principles still prevail in this land" and that he would fight for states' rights "until doomsday." Senator Stennis of Mississippi and Frank Upchurch from the Florida delegation followed with preliminary speeches that castigated Truman and his civil rights program. With the crowd sufficiently aroused, Chairman Sillers finally turned the podium over to Frank Dixon for the keynote address.[80]

Dixon set the tone for the convention and the campaign by emphasizing the very issue that had sparked the revolt: race. Speaking to the enthusiastic throng, he grossly misrepresented Truman's civil rights proposals and accused the president of "trying to enforce a social revolution in the South." Dixon warned that Truman meant to eliminate segregation in the public and private schools "from grade schools through colleges." Black schoolteachers would soon have charge over their white children, which would inevitably lead to an increase "in immorality, in vice [and] in crime." Truman, he charged, supported the desegregation of public transportation, housing, restaurants, theaters, beauty shops, swimming pools, and ball games. Racial intermingling, he predicted, would only foster hostility, bitterness, and violence.

Dixon continued his harangue against the president by attacking the other civil rights proposals. He warned that the creation of a permanent FEPC would require all businesses to meet racial hiring quotas, and that elimination of the poll tax would result in mass registration of ignorant, uneducated, unqualified blacks. An antilynching law was unnecessary, Dixon argued, because "we . . . know that there is no lynching in the South." "Government is a dangerous thing," Dixon warned, and he implored his white southern brethren to protect basic democratic principles to guard against the establishment of a police state. Failure to fight Truman's "vicious program" would inevitably "reduce us to the status of a mongrel, inferior race, mixed in blood, our Anglo-Saxon heritage a mockery."[81]

The convention floor erupted in a wild celebration that lasted almost as long as the speech itself. "The floor was a surging sea of frenzy and the crowd in the galleries were cheering," one newsmagazine reported. Confederate flags waved wildly, and one college student paraded down the aisles carrying aloft a huge portrait of Robert E. Lee.[82] The bedlam lasted nearly twenty minutes before Chairman Sillers gaveled the crowd back to order. The morning's final speaker, Lloyd E. Price, a vile, race baiting state representative from Texas, pinned the blame for the country's race problems on New Englanders who had first brought the "howling, screaming savages" to the New World from Africa.[83] On this low note, the convention convened for lunch. One Alabama newspaper reported that during these racist harangues, the American Broadcasting Company had ceased broadcasting the convention because "it was too inflammatory."[84]

While the teeming crowd cheered on Dixon and the other speakers, states' rights insiders worked feverishly to produce a presidential candidate. As late as noon on the day of the convention, political reporters predicted Governor Laney and Governor Thurmond would be the presidential and vice-presidential candidates, although some picked Fielding

Wright for the second spot. This plan soon went awry. Like Thurmond, Laney had his doubts about attending the conference. One newspaper reported that on his way home to Arkansas from the Philadelphia convention, Laney told reporters in Cincinnati that neither he nor any of the Arkansas delegates would go to Birmingham. By the time he reached St. Louis, he had changed both his mind and his train and was on his way to Alabama. Laney arrived in Birmingham on Friday, checked into his hotel, and never left his suite for the duration of the convention. During the noon recess he formally withdrew his name from consideration for the presidential nomination. He felt the best hope for defeating the civil rights plank was through the state Democratic organizations, not a third party.[85]

In lieu of this development, states' rights leaders turned their attention to Thurmond, who initially had not planned to attend. The South Carolina governor had been detained on state business and did not arrive in Birmingham until late Saturday morning. While the conventioneers were enjoying lunch, Fielding Wright, Laney, and Thurmond remained closeted in conference. States' rights leaders appealed to Thurmond to accept the official command of the organization. Though he felt the convention had been organized too hastily, Thurmond agreed to accept the states' rights mantle by the time the caucus reconvened at 2:30 P.M.[86] Apparently Thurmond made this decision during, not before, this closed-door conference. His closest political allies did not accompany him to the convention and were surprised by his decision. In an interview given more than forty years later, Thurmond advisor and Charleston attorney Robert Figg stated that had he gone with the South Carolina governor to Birmingham, he would have advised Thurmond against accepting the nomination. At the time, some observers in the Palmetto State saw Thurmond's candidacy as a public relations ploy designed to improve his chances in the 1950 U.S. Senate Democratic primary. In later years Thurmond denied this accusation.[87]

Alabama Governor James Folsom gave a brief welcoming speech to open the convention's afternoon session, providing one of the gathering's more awkward moments. The rebellious crowd greeted Folsom with lukewarm applause. The Alabama governor was on record as opposing Truman's civil rights proposals but had remained within the loyalist camp and had steadfastly refused to bolt the party. In his address Folsom criticized the president but offered no words of support for the bolters.

Following Folsom's speech Horace Wilkinson delivered the report of the resolutions committee. The eight-point "Statement of Principles" affirmed their belief in the Constitution as "the greatest charter of human liberty" and their opposition to "the elimination of segregation, the repeal of miscegenation statutes, the control of private employment by federal bureaucrats called for by the misnamed civil rights program." The committee's resolutions were unanimously adopted by the delegates, and the floor erupted in a boisterous demonstration of support. The audience howled and stomped its feet when seventy-nine-year-old Beulah Waller, nicknamed "the wool hat woman of Byron, Georgia," expressed her enthusiasm for states' rights by performing an impromptu jig on the auditorium stage.[88]

Indicative of the confusion that permeated the states' rights effort, the statement declared that "the Birmingham conference . . . did not form a new party and did not nominate anyone for any office." Unwilling to sever themselves completely from the national Democratic Party, the States' Rights Democrats merely "recommended" that the state Democratic parties nominate Thurmond and Wright "as candidates for President and Vice-President of their State Democratic Parties."[89] Nevertheless, the events in Birmingham bore the marks of the birth of a new political party. At least one of the South's ardent states' rights newspapers reported as much.[90] Throughout the course of the presidential campaign, leading states' righters would adamantly maintain that neither Thurmond nor Wright were nominees and that the Birmingham conference did not herald the formation of a new party. Speaking in Jackson shortly after returning from the convention, Fielding Wright commented, "We were recommended to the Democratic parties in the various states as men suitable to be president and vice-president."[91] Thurmond promptly contradicted Wright but said that "all those matters will be cleared up."[92] Confusion over what actually had transpired in Birmingham would plague the campaign in the ensuing months.

Finally, around 6:00 P.M., the zealous, rebellious southerners proceeded to formally nominate Strom Thurmond and Fielding Wright as the party's presidential and vice-presidential candidates. Some states' rights supporters in Florida, Alabama, and his home state of Mississippi had wanted Wright for the top position. Demonstrating a self-awareness uncharacteristic of politicians, Wright had discouraged this, saying, "I do not feel that I am a man of sufficient political stature to accept such a nomination."[93] Strom Thurmond operated under no such personal misgivings.

When it was his turn to speak, Thurmond strode to the platform to the tune of "Dixie" under the escort of the American and Confederate battle flags, followed by a portrait of General Robert E. Lee and the South Carolina flag.[94] He reminded the audience of how "for our loyalty to the party we have been stabbed in the back by a president who has betrayed every principle of the Democratic party in his desire to win at any cost." He warned his audience that the enactment of Truman's civil rights proposals would "lead to a police state." He predicted that "if the anti-poll tax laws are passed, it won't be long until there are bayonets around your ballot boxes." In an attempt to repackage the rough discourse of white supremacy and thus assume a broader appeal, Thurmond declared his desire to focus the campaign on the constitutional question of states' rights. Unfortunately, he could only distance himself so far and soon returned to extremist language to rally the segregationists. "There's not enough troops in the Army to force the southern people to break down segregation and admit the Negro race into our theaters, into our swimming pools, into schools and into our homes," Thurmond shouted to thunderous applause.[95]

The conventioneers next clarified their intention to win the 127 electoral college votes of the Solid South, thus preventing either Republican Party nominee Thomas Dewey or Harry Truman from winning the 266 electoral college votes necessary. The election would then move to the House of Representatives, where the South possessed 11 of the 48 votes. Southern Democrats reasoned that they could deadlock the election until either party agreed to abandon its civil rights plank. States' rights leaders believed that they could then barter for a compromise candidate. The conference came to a close at 7:00 P.M. In a mere eight hours the southerners had engineered a rebellion.

The States' Rights Democrats based their strategy on two assumptions that revealed their regional chauvinism. Above all, they believed that Truman could not win the election without the support of the South. They believed that the Republicans would probably win an outright electoral majority. If this happened, they would still have proven the South's political importance. Thus having demonstrated its power, the South would then resume its dominant position in the national party. Secondly, they assumed that the South was still capable of asserting itself as a separate political entity and that the civil rights/states' rights issue had sufficient appeal to create such sectional unity. The success of this strategy relied on their ability to convince the uncommitted states to pledge their electors to the States' Rights candidates. The adoption of Thurmond and Wright as the Democratic Party nominees in Mississippi, Alabama, and South Carolina would be a simple formality. Consequently, this meant that Truman would not appear on the ballot as the Democratic candidate in these states. However, the difficulty states' rights supporters had encountered in the early months of 1948 should have warned them that achieving unity in the presidential election would prove extremely difficult.

The States' Rights Democrats based their strategy on the ideas of sixty-nine-year-old Birmingham attorney and author Charles Wallace Collins. In his 1947 book *Whither Solid South?,* which had become a "must read" among southern leaders, Collins urged southern politicians to use the electoral college to wage war against their political enemies.[96] Collins argued that the South could protect its institutions by creating a regional party, which could be accomplished by taking control of the state Democratic Party organizations.[97]

Since the turn of the century, Black Belt elites in the Deep South had successfully exploited the structural inequities of their state political systems to their advantage. This election would be no different. Not the democratic process, but obsolete election laws and the arcane process of selecting presidential electors had made a states' rights victory possible. Only seven states required that presidential electors be nominated in primaries. The majority of other electors were handpicked by party officials. In Alabama, Georgia, Kentucky, South Carolina, Tennessee, and Virginia the party organization was the legal agency charged with nominating the electors who would theoretically choose the president. In Alabama the Democratic hierarchy had already named its slate of electors, all of whom were opposed to President Truman. Mississippi and Texas were among the numerous states that chose their candidates for electors in conventions—a system that usually gives the politicians in control of the party machinery a dominant voice. Alabama, Mississippi, and Louisiana did not require that the names of presidential and vice-presidential candidates appear on the ballot. In South Carolina each party printed its own ballots and decided whether the names of the actual candidates would appear.[98] Rather than test the popularity of their message through the democratic channel of an unfettered election, States' Rights elites sought to manipulate the system they had worked diligently to perfect and perpetuate. But here they faced an irony that would come back to haunt them repeatedly: the electoral process that had been used to bind white southerners to the national Democratic Party now had to be used to undo, or in the very least undermine, that tie.

The Birmingham convention and the nomination of the States' Rights Democratic Party candidates received a mixed response from supporters and opponents alike. Despite Thurmond's professed attempts to redirect the focus to the constitutional issue of states' rights, States' Rights Democrats relied on racism and the fear of desegregation to arouse white passions. In the end, the Birmingham convention—and later, the States' Rights Democrats' presidential campaign—could not escape the shrill appeal to white supremacy embodied in Dixon's speech and the "Statement of Principles." The presence of numerous well-known hatemongers at the convention further hampered the States' Rights Democrats' bid for respectability. Gerald L. K. Smith, a former lieutenant to Louisiana senator Huey P. Long, virulent anti-Semite, and leader of the Christian Nationalist Party, attended the conference under the pseudonym S. Goodyear. Smith told reporters he had offered Thurmond his support; the South Carolina governor denied having met with Smith and subsequently spurned Smith's offer of aid, declaring that the States' Righters did not invite or need the support of "rabble-rousers who use race prejudice and class hatred to inflame our people."[99] Also making the rounds on the convention floor was former Oklahoma governor "Alfalfa Bill" Murray, who boasted to anyone who cared to listen that he was "the man who introduced Jim Crow in Oklahoma."[100] Rounding out the list of the undesirables were J. E. Perkins, anti-Semitic author of *The Jews Have Got the Atom Bomb;* J. B. Stoner, founder of the Anti-Jewish Party; and Jessie Welch Jenkins, president of the national Patrick Henry Organization, which wanted to abolish both the Democratic and the Republican Parties.[101]

The convention received mixed reviews from southern newspapers. *The State* in South Carolina reserved immediate judgment. It believed, however, that the decision to meet in Birmingham had been too hasty and that "a program for Southern protest would rest on firmer ground if it came from a Southwide meeting preceded by county and state conventions."[102] The *Jackson Clarion-Ledger,* on the other hand, reported enthusiastically on the convention, as did the *Shreveport Times* and the *Shreveport Journal.*[103] A prominent Alabama paper described the convention as an "ugly carnival scene" at which delegates "shouted 'nigger' and burned President Truman in effigy." States' righters would have to abandon the tactics of "wild and crude" white supremacists like Birmingham attorney

Horace Wilkinson and adopt a more sophisticated system of beliefs and tactics if the movement was to win support outside the South. "We cannot win friends," the *Montgomery Advertiser* wrote, "by hoarse blasphemies and the appearance of unreasoning obstinacy."[104] Southern newspapers with regional influence such as the *Atlanta Constitution,* the *News and Observer* of Raleigh, and the *Richmond Times-Dispatch* severely criticized the gathering.[105]

Thurmond's nomination, however, mitigated or at least complicated outsiders' negative assessment of the southern party. In an editorial immediately following the Birmingham meeting, the *New York Times* said the States' Right platform illustrated a lack of "good sense" but regarded Thurmond's nomination as politically astute.[106] John M. Lofton Jr. of the *New York Star* labeled Thurmond a "Dixie Paradox" who "embodies in one personality the Old South and the New." Both New York papers were impressed by Thurmond's opposition to the poll tax, his abhorrence of mob violence and his action in the Earle lynching, his support of a minimum wage and maximum hour law, and his support for industrialization and for the removal of discriminatory regional freight rates.[107] The most colorful attempt to reconcile Thurmond's relatively moderate gubernatorial policies with the unseemly aspects of the states' rights cause came from Baltimore editor and critic H. L. Mencken. The curmudgeonly Mencken considered Thurmond "the best of all the [presidential] candidates" but lamented that "all the worst morons in the South are for him."[108] John Ed Pearce of Kentucky's *Louisville Courier-Journal,* however, was less enamored of the South Carolinian. He noted that Thurmond's racism differed from that of the more outspoken white supremacists in style but not in substance. "On the platform Mr. Thurmond and his fellow travelers shout of Americanism, our way of life, the right to choose one's associates, Communism, Reds. But they mean Nigger. Mr. Thurmond, of course, never says the word; he's not the type."[109] Throughout the campaign, Thurmond differentiated between himself and people like Wright and Wilkinson; nevertheless, he was willing to make common cause with them.

States' Rights leaders from South Carolina, Mississippi, Alabama, Florida, Texas, Louisiana, and Arkansas reconvened a week later in Atlanta to create an organizational machine and to map out a campaign strategy. They adopted "States' Rights Democrats" as the official party name; established various campaign committees, including a veterans' committee and a women's division; and authorized the publication of a weekly campaign newspaper. The States' Righters scheduled the official start of the campaign for August 11 at a Houston, Texas, rally where Thurmond and Wright would formally accept the nomination. Judge Merritt H. Gibson of Longview, Texas, was appointed campaign director, and George C. Wallace of Jackson, Mississippi, was named campaign treasurer. The national headquarters would open a few days before the Houston convention, on August 9, at the Heidelberg Hotel in Jackson, Mississippi, with subsidiary offices to be opened later in Columbia, South Carolina, and Washington, D.C.[110] The States' Rights Democrats revealed that they would work to place their candidates on the general election ballots in the forty-eight states. The principal campaign efforts, however, would be concentrated in the fifteen southern states.[111]

Between the Birmingham and Houston conferences, states' rights rebels in South Carolina, Mississippi, and Alabama took the necessary steps to distance themselves from the national party and to cement support for Thurmond and Wright. Alabama Democrats had the least amount of work to do, as voters there had bound their electors to oppose any civil rights candidate during the May primary. Alabama leader Marion Rushton resigned as the state DNC representative on July 23 and informed the national party chairman not to expect any financial support from his state. On July 29 Alabama's eleven electors convened and pledged their votes to Thurmond and Wright.[112] Unless Dewey could work a miracle, the presidential election in Alabama was effectively over.

In Mississippi, Governor Wright reconvened the temporarily recessed state Democratic convention on August 3, where with little discussion the delegates systematically pledged the state's nine presidential electors to support the Thurmond-Wright ticket in the electoral college. Supportive student groups from the University of Mississippi, Mississippi Southern College, Mississippi State College, and Hinds Junior College attended the convention. A small group of students from the University of Mississippi, however, objected to their school's contingent, stating that the States' Rights representatives did not express the "majority opinion of politically conscious Ole Miss students."[113] Approximately twenty-five students from Millsaps College and Vanderbilt University in Tennessee attended the meeting in protest and occupied a space under a banner that read "Opponents of States' Rights." Millsaps College student George Maddox of McComb, Mississippi, in an address before the convention, accused Mississippi Democrats of hypocrisy for claiming Truman's civil rights program was a violation of states' rights while supporting other types of federal intervention. "You have never objected to flood control programs, subsidies for farmers and education, and TVA or any of the other things the government has brought in to your profit." Maddox attacked the state's outmoded voting system and precinct conventions as undemocratic. He further reminded the crowd that Mississippi was one-half black and that blacks were discriminated against. Following these remarks, the crowd roundly booed Maddox, with particularly rowdy catcalls coming from the large crowd of college students. Maddox was followed by a Vanderbilt student who accused the states' righters of "setting the South back by attempting to stop anti-segregation laws."[114]

Thurmond returned home to a state still in turmoil over the white Democratic primary. South Carolina's primary was scheduled for August 10, yet exactly who would be permitted to vote in it remained in dispute. Most South Carolina counties continued to defy Judge Waring's 1947 ruling in *Elmore v. Rice,* which had opened the Democratic primary to African Americans. In reaction, the NAACP filed suit in *Brown v. Baskin* on July 8. The plaintiff this time was David Brown, a black man from Beaufort, South Carolina, located on the southernmost tip of the Carolina coast. Following an order from South Carolina SDEC chairman Baskin, the Beaufort County Election Committee had purged Brown's name from the party enrollment book. Judge Waring issued a temporary restraining order barring the party from racial discrimination and scheduled a hearing on July 16, forcing many in the South Carolina delegation to leave the Democratic National Convention in Philadelphia. Waring granted Brown's petition and ordered South Carolina Democrats to enroll blacks and grant them full participation in party affairs. He threatened party leaders with prison sentences if they failed to comply. Clearly fed up with the machinations of party leaders and speaking in no uncertain terms, Waring declared, "The time has come when racial discrimination in political affairs must stop." Turning to the plaintiff, Waring remarked apologetically, "It is a disgrace and shame when you must come into a court and ask a judge to tell you you are an American."[115] On July 19, shortly after the Birmingham rally, Waring ordered enrollment books open through July 31 and demanded that the South Carolina Democratic Party's voters' oath be abolished.[116] Following Waring's ruling, Baskin announced on July 23 that the voting oath was eliminated and ordered county chairpersons to enroll all qualified electors regardless of race.[117]

South Carolina's white Democrats hoped to follow the lead of Alabama and Mississippi by committing their electors to Thurmond and

Wright. Unfortunately, the South Carolina SDEC was not scheduled to decide the matter until August 17. This could be potentially embarrassing to Thurmond, who planned to accept the States' Rights Democratic Party's nomination at Houston on August 11. To avoid this situation, Baskin solicited assurances from all committee members that they planned to support the governor.[118]

The States' Rights campaign would not officially begin until after the Houston convention, yet rules governing independent parties in the individual states forced the southern candidates to start ahead of schedule. Thurmond chose the annual Watermelon Festival in Cherryville, North Carolina, on July 31 as the site of his first campaign speech. The relaxed atmosphere of the folksy gathering belied the trouble States' Rights supporters would encounter in the Tarheel State and in other southern states in the ensuing months. North Carolina had been demonstrably cool to the states' rights revolt. Democrats in this state were reluctant to sign on to the states' rights cause in part because the state Republican Party there was rather strong, and any split in the Democratic Party could mean Dewey would carry the state.[119] Consequently, States' Righters had failed to gain control of the state party machinery and were forced to qualify as an independent party by the August 3 deadline.

In his address Thurmond contrasted the festival's celebration of small-town life with the horrors and intrusions that would accompany an expanded federal government. Thurmond predicted that the civil rights program was only the first step toward the creation of "a totalitarian, socialistic government." To enforce his program, Thurmond warned, "the President has directed that a nationwide Federal police system be set up." This alleged police force would fan out across the countryside "to police elections; to meddle in private business affairs; to spy into their private records; to intervene in private law suits; [and] to keep people in a state of fear and intimidation." The national party leaders had "chosen the South as a whipping boy," but the region could not "take this whipping any longer." It was time to "stand up and fight."[120] Thurmond urged the festival crowd to sign and circulate petitions for his party and to return them to J. E. Baker of Burlington.[121] Baker, president of Baker-Cammack Hosiery Mills and a regional vice-president of the SSIC for Maryland, Virginia, North Carolina, and South Carolina, was supervising the party's efforts in the state.

State party leaders and the state board of elections worked together to deny the States' Rights candidates a place on the North Carolina ballot.

In early August the States' Rights committee in North Carolina handed in petitions with more than 18,000 names requesting a place on the ballot for the Thurmond-Wright ticket. However, the state election board rejected the petitions, citing noncompliance with the rules and regulations of the board and insufficient time for county boards to check the names.[122] The North Carolina States' Righters brought their case before Wake Forest Superior Court Judge W. C. Harris, hoping to have the board of elections ruling invalidated. The States' Righters contended that the board's decree that required a new party to secure as petitioners 10,000 registered voters who had not voted in a primary that year was illegal and unreasonable.[123] Judge Harris agreed and ruled that the States' Rights Democratic Party was entitled to a place on the North Carolina general election ballot.[124] The North Carolina Supreme Court ruled on September 8 and affirmed the lower court's decision that ordered the state board of elections to recognize the States' Rights ticket.[125]

The States' Righters' were destined to repeat their North Carolina experience in a number of other southern states. Where they could not gain control of the Democratic Party machinery, they were forced to petition for a spot on the ballot. Despite their ultimate victory in winning a place on the North Carolina ballot, court fights drained the hastily constructed local organizations of time and effort. Furthermore, these efforts were orchestrated by political novices whose lack of experience, resources, and time hardly guaranteed success. The North Carolina campaign heralded an inauspicious start to the states' rights campaign. Although the North Carolina forces had gathered 18,000 signatures quickly in a supposedly cool state, their prolonged—albeit victorious—court battle foreshadowed a difficult road ahead.

★

"With their minds on Washington and their memories on Gettysburg," the *Houston Post* reported, insurgent Dixie Democrats rolled into Houston on August 11 to officially launch the campaign.[126] Delegations from Mississippi, Louisiana, Kentucky, South Carolina, North Carolina, Oklahoma, Tennessee, Virginia, Florida, Texas, Alabama, Arkansas, and Georgia packed the city's coliseum to witness Strom Thurmond and Fielding Wright formally accept the nomination of the States' Rights Democratic Party. Newspaper estimates placed the number of attendees between 6,000 and 10,000. By all accounts the second convention was a boisterous affair, with plenty of Confederate flags and rebel yells to accompany the countless rounds of "Dixie."[127] One student of the movement has noted that the Houston meeting was the largest political gathering in that hall since the Democratic National Convention nominated Al Smith there in 1928, coincidentally the only other nomination to split the solid Democratic South.[128]

The candidates played on themes that would soon become standard Cold War rhetoric. Wright warned of the possibility of a "remote, distant, mysterious" government "beyond the comprehension of the people themselves." He decried the power of organized minority groups as "a cowardly thing" and "a disgrace to America." Wright concluded, "Only a return to American principles, to local self-government, can halt the unseemly spectacle we are now witnessing."

Addressing the enthusiastic conventioneers, Thurmond ominously predicted that "the proposed federal police state, directed from Washington, will force life on each hamlet in America to conform to a Washington patter." Failure to join the fight for states' rights would endanger "the most precious of all human rights—the right to control and govern ourselves at home, the right of life, liberty and the pursuit of happiness."[129] The audience went wild. "With a band blaring, rebel yells sounding through the big convention hall and scores of banners of all kinds waving—including Confederate flags," one newspaper reported, "the steaming delegates snake-danced, churned, and paraded through the jam-packed aisles for more than five minutes after the conclusion of Governor Thurmond's address."[130]

The enthusiasm unleashed on the convention floor temporarily masked the challenges ahead. The reality remained that only Mississippi, South Carolina, and Alabama had endorsed the States' Rights candidates. Nowhere else in the South had the respective state organizations been obliged by earlier action to pledge their support to the southern nominees. All other party committees had condemned Truman and the civil rights program, yet none had taken definite steps toward independence. Consequently, Thurmond and Wright hoped that they could persuade these uncommitted states to support electors pledged to the States' Rights candidates.[131]

At a press conference following the Houston convention, the undaunted Thurmond confidently predicted that the States' Rights candidates would receive more than one hundred electoral votes.[132] Thurmond admitted that this would be difficult, primarily because the States' Rights Democrats had gotten off to a late start. As it would turn out, time, or rather, lack of it, was only one of several obstacles confronting the States' Rights Democrats. The problems originally encountered in Birmingham, both organizational and ideological, would eventually become obvious and insurmountable, but just how much damage the States' Rights Democrats would inflict before it was all over was anybody's guess until late in the campaign.

THE DIXIECRAT PRESIDENTIAL CAMPAIGN

The time is gone . . . when we Southerners can quit thinking and simply express ourselves by shouting "nigger" and singing Dixie.

MARION RUSHTON

chairman of the Alabama States' Rights Democrats Executive Committee, August 1948

On August 9, on the eve of the Houston convention, the headquarters of the States' Rights Democratic Party officially opened in Jackson, Mississippi. Subsidiary campaign offices in Columbia, South Carolina, and Washington, D.C., flew into action a few weeks later. With the basic campaign machinery in place, the States' Rights forces quickly focused their energies on capturing the Democratic Party organizations in individual southern states. Control of these apparatuses offered the best hope for success by bringing organizational and financial benefits and instant political credibility. The southern rebels—by this time nicknamed "Dixiecrats" by an enterprising North Carolina journalist—understood that to win the Democratic Party label in the one-party South was to be assured of victory. They had barely two months either to convince the remaining southern state parties to pledge uncommitted electors to the Thurmond-Wright ticket or to secure, usually through petitions, a place for the States' Rights Party on the state ballot as an independent party. Many of the electors were to be appointed at state conventions scheduled to meet in August and September. The Dixiecrats had to act quickly.

The campaign was a curious spectacle in a tumultuous presidential election. The Dixiecrats found themselves trapped by a political history their predecessors had conceived and from which many of them had long benefited. By lashing the defense of white supremacy and states' rights to the fortunes of the Democratic Party, and by demonizing the Republican

Campaign flyer for the States' Rights Democratic Party. Photograph courtesy of Special Collections, Clemson University Libraries, Clemson, South Carolina.

Party, southern conservatives had fostered a deeply rooted allegiance that they themselves would now have to undermine and manipulate. Despite their best efforts to enunciate a political message that melded traditional historical animosities with racial and gender anxieties, the States' Rights Democrats in the end captured only four states.

Ultimately the fate of the Dixiecrats rested on the strength of the Black Belt coalitions within the individual states. Where those factions were weak, the Dixiecrats lost. Their fortunes turned on a number of variables, including the potential of Republicans to benefit from a split among Democrats and the degree to which New Deal political alignments had infiltrated state party dynamics and mitigated the appeal to white supremacy and conservative economic philosophy. The campaign suffered from inadequate funding, faulty organization, critical strategic inconsistencies, and ill-defined long-range goals. Where the Dixiecrats failed to capture the state party machinery, as in North Carolina, the campaign fell to political amateurs with little experience and no political power. More often than they would have liked, the States' Rights forces had to resort to time-consuming court action to ensure a place on the ballot. In spite of such hardships, the Dixiecrat ticket eventually appeared on ballots in thirteen states.[1]

With the fortunes of States Righters so intimately tied to the decisions of the state party conventions and the Democratic Party label, and with their wholly inadequate grassroots effort, the election should have been declared unofficially over by the end of September. It seemed unlikely that the States' Rights Party would win the Solid South; however, no one could measure with any degree of certainty the extent of the political damage it would do. The uncertain outcomes in states such as Florida and Georgia, as well as the threat of Republican voters in Virginia and Tennessee, made the Dixiecrats' role of political spoiler viable. Because their strategy involved capturing the Democratic Party electors in each state, the Dixiecrats did not put forth much effort where they ran as a third party, thus making it difficult to gauge the strength of their message. Perhaps only in states such as Florida, North Carolina, Georgia, and Arkansas, where southern whites had the opportunity to make a clear choice between their racial politics and their historic political allegiance, would the Dixiecrats' appeal be truly tested.

★

The Dixiecrats' unwillingness to try their luck as a third party meant that efforts to seize control of the presidential electors from individual states would conform to preexisting intrastate political rivalries. The States' Rights Democrats held out little hope for the Upper South, and indeed, they fared badly there. They failed to qualify for the ballot in Missouri. In Maryland, where Governor Preston Lane had been demonstrably cool to the movement since February, supporters of Thurmond and Wright were forced to write the names of the eight electors on their ballots.[2]

Arkansas was a political wild card. The rich fertile lands of the Mississippi Delta along the state's eastern edge were home to plantation agriculture and the site of intense, violent labor activity by the sharecroppers' union in the 1930s. White inhabitants of the region placed a high value on labor control and the defense of white supremacy, and the Dixiecrats counted on exploiting these issues. Governor Benjamin Laney led the States' Rights forces in Arkansas. The grandson of slaveowners, Laney had been born and raised in the tiny community of Cooterneck in Ouachita County. His family was of modest means until oil was discovered on their land in 1922. By the time he was elected mayor of Camden, Arkansas, Laney possessed a diverse economic portfolio; he owned a number of feed, grocery, and hardware stores and had interests in the oil business and in cotton gins. Elected governor in 1944 and again in

1946, Laney was a fiscal and racial conservative who supported the enabling legislation for Arkansas's 1944 antiunion right-to-work amendment and enjoyed the support of the Delta.[3] But the political influence of the Arkansas Delta was unlike its Mississippi counterpart. Dixiecrat forces in Arkansas had no ready-made faction upon which to graft themselves. Arkansas politics, as V. O. Key noted, was "the one-party system in its most undefiled and undiluted form."[4] The cleavage between the hills and the lowlands exploited by Governor Jeff Davis was a thing of the past. Political factions were intensely personal and transient. Thus the political culture in Arkansas worked against Laney, the outgoing governor, successfully controlling the 1948 state convention. Once Laney left office, an entirely new political dynamic rose to take his place. It was, Key noted, the politics of the moment. The moment did not belong to the Dixiecrats.

Arkansas politics in 1948 turned on the question of road construction, not race. Sidney McMath, leader of the state's 1946 GI revolts, ran on a moderately progressive platform that emphasized infrastructure development. McMath received the support of former governor Carl Bailey, while Laney stood behind candidate Jack Holt, a former attorney general. McMath beat Holt in the runoff primary by a slim majority. While Holt was Laney's choice and the more virulent race baiter, McMath did not shy away from the topic and declared his opposition to Truman's civil rights program as well. But the voting distribution did not indicate a clear pattern. Holt did not win overwhelmingly in the Delta, and McMath failed to carry many predominantly white rural counties.[5]

Arkansas Dixiecrats worked feverishly to produce a States' Rights majority at the state Democratic convention scheduled to meet in Little Rock on September 23. The odds were long. Although both former governor Bailey and gubernatorial nominee McMath opposed the federal extension of protection for civil rights, they nevertheless campaigned against the bolters and on behalf of the national ticket.[6] Furthermore, Arkansas political history dictated that the incoming governor typically dominated the convention.[7] Working with Dixiecrat Laney was John Daggett of Marianna, executive director of the Arkansas Free Enterprise Association, an organization comprised of large planters and Little Rock corporation executives, who regularly lobbied the state legislature on behalf of restrictive labor legislation. In 1944 the Free Enterprise Association had been largely responsible for the passage of the state's right-to-work constitutional amendment. Daggett had taken the lead in the Arkansas states' rights movement, heading a delegation from the Arkansas plantation counties to the May conference in Jackson.[8]

Laney's involvement in the states' rights revolt had been schizophrenic, reflecting his uncertainty regarding the radicalism of leaders such as Wright of Mississippi and Wilkinson of Alabama. He had attended the Birmingham convention but had remained in his hotel room. Nevertheless, he chaired the States' Rights executive committee and was a member of the organization's steering committee. He did not support the Dixiecrats' third party efforts, believing that the organization lacked money and credibility.[9] Laney's qualified support of the Dixiecrat effort was emblematic of the weakness of the movement as a whole.

Hoping to shore up support before the convention, Thurmond journeyed to Marianna in late August to deliver his first major address as an official presidential candidate. He cautioned that the "subversive" civil rights proposals would "force mingling of the races on our trains and busses, in our restaurants, in our theaters, in our schools, and who knows where in the future." Emphasizing themes that would dominate his campaign, Thurmond warned that these were "evil days." Describing a federal government bent on taking control away from local power brokers, he tailored his message not for the masses but for the employers of low-wage, segregated labor. Under FEPC provisions, he counseled, "employers . . . could be hauled before a federal inquisition by anyone who failed to get a job or a promotion." The fair hiring provisions of an FEPC law would be manipulated by "communists . . . [who] could place their agents in every factory and defense industry in America."[10]

Despite Thurmond's impassioned rhetoric, the Dixiecrats faced certain defeat at the Arkansas convention. Wanting to avoid a major embarrassment, the States' Rights Democrats abandoned their planned convention fight altogether and instead secured a spot on the Arkansas ballot as a third party, which was as good as admitting defeat. Neither Daggett nor Laney was willing to risk political alienation.[11] Laney distanced himself from the third party effort, thus leaving the Dixiecrats to flounder more than a month before the election.

The significant threat of the Republican Party checked Dixiecrat fortunes in Virginia and Tennessee. In the Old Dominion, which had been first out of the gate in the states' rights revolt, the state party had sixty days following the national convention to reconvene and instruct its electors. Shortly before the sixty-day deadline, States' Rights Democrats moved to win a spot on the ballot as a third party. Although state leaders did not embrace the Dixiecrats, as in many southern states nearly every major political figure in Virginia tried to distance himself from the president, but few rushed to embrace the Dixiecrats. Eventually, however, three relatively well known Democrats supported Thurmond.[12] Despite the Dixiecrats' third-party status, many Democrats feared that Thurmond had the potential to pull in 20 percent of the state's popular vote, which could put Virginia in the Republican column. Thurmond remained hopeful about his chances in the state and delivered five major speeches there in October to "large and enthusiastic" crowds. He received critical tacit approval. Mrs. Harry F. Byrd, wife of the U.S. senator, and Robert O. Norris Jr., president pro tempore of the state senate, attended a States' Rights fund-raiser. Although Governor William Tuck did not publicly endorse Thurmond, neither did he brush him off, even going so far as to introduce Thurmond in glowing terms at one states' rights event. As election day drew near, one Gallup poll showed Thurmond's support hovering around 10 percent of the popular vote.[13]

In Tennessee, another state with a significant Republican minority, Thurmond likewise threatened to dilute the potential Democratic vote. Dixiecrat prospects became tied to the declining fortunes of Memphis machine boss E. H. Crump. Both suffered a major setback in early August when Crump's candidates for senatorial and gubernatorial nominations were defeated. The popular and liberal congressman Estes Kefauver trounced Crump's candidate for the senatorial nomination, and former governor Gordon Browning defeated the incumbent James N. McCord, the Crump favorite.[14] Crump announced in October that he would support the state party's congressional nominees, although he would not endorse Truman. He also declared that he would support the Dixiecrats, but his political capital had been spent by this time.[15] Despite the reluctance of the state party to support the Dixiecrats, boisterous crowds greeted Thurmond at rallies in late October, and Tennessee's electoral status was listed as undecided on the eve of the election, as most political observers agreed that the Dixiecrats could poll a sufficient number of voters to throw the state to Thomas Dewey.

The Dixiecrats' chances were most promising in the Deep South states, where from mid-August through mid-September they appeared to be on a course to capture the electoral votes not only of Mississippi, South Carolina, and Alabama, but also Georgia, Louisiana, and possibly Texas and Florida. By mid-September the national Democrats appeared to be in danger of losing Texas. Reporters assessed the contest as a three-man race, and Florida had split its electoral votes between Truman and Thurmond. Herman Talmadge's victory in Georgia's gubernatorial primary in September appeared to assure a States' Rights coup in the Peach State, and Earl Long's fence-sitting in Louisiana provided the perfect opportunity for Dixiecrat Leander Perez to engineer a States' Rights takeover.[16]

Florida's chaotic, disordered political landscape differed from Arkansas's only by degrees. As in Arkansas, politics in the Sunshine State during the first half of the twentieth century remained relatively untainted by ideology and issues. The state's large size, sparse settlement, and geographical and economic diversity promoted a fragmented political culture in which candidates won through the force of their personalities or because of geographical ties. By the late 1940s Florida was in the midst of a significant demographic and political transformation. Heavy migration from the Midwest and East in the postwar years profoundly affected the state's political life as most of the new arrivals settled in cities in the state's central and southern regions, fostering an urban-rural cleavage and fertile ground for the growth of the Republican Party. Indeed, by the late 1940s, Florida already boasted a healthy contingent of "presidential Republicans," who gave Thomas Dewey nearly 30 percent of the popular vote in 1944.[17]

Although the state's rapidly changing demographics had given Florida a more cosmopolitan image than that of its Deep South neighbors, Florida's rural counties fostered some of the region's most exploitive and violent labor and race relations. In the 1920s rampaging whites had wiped out the black neighborhoods in Perry and Ocoee and destroyed the black town of Rosewood. In 1946, in what historians have termed Florida's "Little Scottsboro," Sheriff Willis McCall of Lake County shot two unarmed black prisoners accused of raping a white woman but whose real offense had been an unwillingness to work as low-paid fruit pickers. Florida also proved hostile to labor unions. CIO organizers sent to Orange County to enlist fruit pickers in 1937 were harassed by Klan members who worked with the complicity of local law enforcement, and in 1944 Florida joined Arkansas in passing a right-to-work amendment.[18]

Within the Democratic Party a growing disenchantment with the liberalism of Senator Claude Pepper surfaced in the presidential election of 1948 and melded with the states' rights revolt. Elected in 1938 as a Roosevelt liberal, Pepper had been steadily losing support and barely eked out a reelection victory against a relative unknown in the 1944 Democratic Party primary. Pepper's conciliatory attitude toward the Soviet Union in particular was increasingly out of step with the views of his more conservative constituents. Although Pepper was severely critical of the president's foreign policy and had even been in the forefront of the Eisenhower boom, the senator was above all else a loyalist and would not desert the party over civil rights. The States' Rights faction drew primarily from the state's Black Belt counties and was led by longtime Pepper antagonist Frank Upchurch, a former state senator and lawyer from St. Augustine. Backing the States' Rights effort was a group known as the Associated Industries of Florida, the political arm of the state's business community. The Associated Industries had long been critical of Pepper's liberalism, particularly his support for the rights of organized labor, and had worked in tandem with DuPont Corporation financier Ed Ball in the failed attempt to oust Pepper in 1944.[19] As of August 26, half of Florida's eight electors chosen in the primary were lined up behind the Dixiecrats.[20] On September 3 *Miami Herald* publisher Reuben Clein sought to disqualify the electors in Florida because they had not pledged to cast their votes for President Truman. On September 8 Circuit Judge Miles W. Lewis ruled that presidential electors were free to vote as they pleased in the electoral college.[21]

Under Florida election law the ballots carried only the names of the electors of the Democratic and Republican Parties and not the names of the presidential candidates themselves. New parties could be added to the ballot only after they had convinced 5 percent of the voters to change their affiliation. Under pressure from the States' Rights forces, the state legislature overwhelmingly approved a change in the election law that would allow Truman, Dewey, and Thurmond—but not Progressive Party candidate Henry Wallace—on the ballot. The presidential candidates would be listed without party designation. The committee further decided that the eight Democratic electors would be divided by preference between Thurmond and Truman and that additional electors would be chosen to fill out each slate.[22] A poll taken in mid-October revealed that about a third of Florida's Democratic leaders favored Thurmond, and the Dixiecrat candidate remained hopeful of his chances in the Sunshine State.[23]

States' Rights forces faced stiff opposition in Texas, the home of the 1944 party desertion; nevertheless, Dixiecrat supporters made sufficient noise to cause political observers to characterize the presidential contest as a three-man race as election day drew near.[24] The stigma of disloyalty plagued those who sought to engineer another revolt, and Texans emerged from the national convention evenly divided between pro- and anti-Truman forces.[25] With twenty-three electoral votes, Texas was a tantalizing political prize for the States' Rights crowd, but Dixiecrats in the Lone Star State faced stiff opposition from Governor Beauford Jester and the Texas SDEC. In early August the state party certified Truman and Barkley as the party nominees and rejected a demand from States' Righters for a statewide referendum in the August 28 primary that would allow the voters to determine whether Texas's Democratic electors would be pledged to Thurmond or to Truman.[26] Temporarily derailed, the Dixiecrats rallied and looked ahead to the Democratic primary on August 28 and the state convention in Fort Worth on September 14, when they hoped to recoup their losses.[27] But the Texas Dixiecrats hedged their bets. Meeting in Dallas on September 8, the Dixiecrats laid the groundwork to assure that, should their effort to overtake the state convention fail, Thurmond and Wright would still appear on the November ballot. They chose presidential electors who would be submitted as a slate prior to the filing deadline of September 17, only a few days after the convention.[28]

Political tempers ran hot at the stormy and contentious convention in Fort Worth. Despite support for a revolt in some of the larger Texas counties, the dominant loyalist faction succeeded in branding the States' Rights Democratic Party and candidates as insurgents and scratched Dixiecrats from the state's three most populous counties from the party rolls. Those delegates and delegations from five other counties stormed out of the meeting carrying Thurmond banners and Confederate flags. Having failed to capture the state convention, the States' Rights forces switched to plan B and qualified the States' Rights electors as an independent party for the November election.[29]

Louisiana and Georgia presented the States' Rights forces with their best hopes for success in the Deep South. In Louisiana the Dixiecrat effort continued despite Governor Earl Long's lack of support and succeeded in part because of his negligence. Plaquemines Parish boss Leander Perez had led an enthusiastic fifteen-member delegation to the Birmingham convention. Anti-Long forces in Shreveport began recruiting States' Rights followers from Caddo and Bossier Parishes, while New Orleans industrialist John U. Barr, general manager of Federal Fibre Mills in New Orleans and regional vice-president of the SSIC, organized States' Rights forces in the Crescent City.[30] On July 20 Louisiana's States' Rights leaders held mass meetings throughout the state to rally support for the Dixiecrats and to organize a petition drive to place Thurmond-Wright electors on the ballot as a third-party slate. On August 4 zealous Dixiecrats from throughout the state, including representatives from each of Louisiana's eight congressional districts, flocked to Baton Rouge's Heidelberg Hotel for a two-hour strategy meeting. Led by Barr and Shreveport attorney W. Scott Wilkinson, a major financial supporter of anti-Long New Orleans mayor Chep Morrison, the group formally endorsed the Thurmond-Wright ticket, created a statewide organization, and chose the Statue of Liberty as the emblem of the Louisiana States' Rights Democratic Party.[31]

Several members of the state's congressional delegation threw their support to the Dixiecrats as the Louisiana campaign gathered momentum. U.S. Representative Otto Passman declared that the time had come for all "true Southerners to stand up and be counted," and he urged Governor Long to take the appropriate measures to secure a spot for Thurmond and Wright on the Louisiana ballot. Congressman James Domengeaux called U.S. Senator Allen Ellender a "sorry spectacle" for his unwillingness to take a public stand for states' rights. "I suppose Senator Ellender would have dined with Sherman as he marched through Georgia," Domengeaux mused. Congressman F. Edward Hebert publicly endorsed the States' Rights ticket and predicted that Thurmond and Wright would carry the state.[32] Within three weeks the Louisiana Dixiecrats had successfully completed their petition drive and qualified a slate of Thurmond-Wright electors for the November ballot.[33] The Louisiana Dixiecrats headed into September determined to take their campaign, in the words of one student of the movement, to "every crossroad and bayou bank."[34] Throughout August, Governor Long said little about the States' Rights movement. He was preoccupied with the tight race for the U.S. Senate between his nephew Russell Long and Robert Kennon, a judge from Minden, Louisiana. The primary, scheduled for August 31, was to fill the unexpired term of Senator Overton, recently deceased. Into this and various other primary contests was injected a bitter factional struggle between Long supporters and detractors. Russell Long defeated Kennon by a narrow margin in the primary, but the Long faction lost in several other races.[35]

With their candidates safely on the ballot, Louisiana Dixiecrats took crucial steps to guarantee victory by manipulating traditional political symbols. Familiar with the habits of Pelican State voters, States' Rights supporters lamented the fact that Thurmond and Wright would appear not under the traditional rooster symbol of the Louisiana Democratic Party but, rather, under the unfamiliar Statue of Liberty emblem. Perez estimated that in any given election at least 100,000 Louisianans automatically voted for the candidates listed under the rooster. Unwilling to cede this advantage, Perez maneuvered to capture the rooster for the States' Rights candidates. Arguing that the state and national Democratic Parties were separate entities with their own unique symbols, he pointed out that the state party used the rooster while the national party favored the donkey. Therefore, if the state Democratic Party rejected the national Democratic presidential nominee, it might then name its own candidate, who would, of course, run under the rooster emblem.[36]

Perez moved quickly and quietly, lining up votes among his cronies on the Democratic state central committee. He planned to seize the party symbols at a routine meeting on September 10 in which several members who planned to be absent had given their proxies to their more conservative colleagues. Privy to Perez's plans, Governor Long conferred secretly with his forces in a late-night strategy session on September 9. Although Long feared that Perez's plan would antagonize the Truman administration and jeopardize Russell Long's chances in his race for the U.S. Senate, Long and Perez finally reached a compromise. Long agreed not to attend the upcoming party meeting and gave Perez his proxy. In return Perez promised not to oppose a plan to place President Truman on the ballot by petition. Long did not want to antagonize his in-state enemies, but he also sought to minimize any friction with the Truman administration. By avoiding the meeting, Long could still gain access to the White House should Truman win the election.[37]

Perez's rooster grab went smoothly. At the September 10 meeting, following routine business, Perez introduced a motion pledging Louisiana's ten Democratic presidential electors to the Dixiecrat ticket and listing Thurmond and Wright, as well as all other Democratic Party nominees for national, state, district, and local offices, beneath the venerable rooster. The choice, Perez stated, was simple: they either "lie down supinely and see the resurrection of carpetbagging in the South" or endorse the States' Rights Democrats.[38] The committee adopted Perez's resolution by a unanimous vote.[39]

DNC officials cried foul. McGrath's assistant, William Primm, declared that "one must go behind the 'iron curtain' of eastern Europe" to find a similarly undemocratic process.[40] Chairman McGrath demanded that Governor Long restore Truman and Barkley to their places on the Democratic ticket. For a moment it appeared that the president's only recourse in Louisiana was to run as a write-in candidate. Voters wishing to support the president would have to write in the names of all ten presidential electors.

After a long public silence on the States' Rights cabal, Governor Long finally summoned a special session of the state legislature on September 21 to enact laws enabling the Truman-Barkley ticket to be placed on the November ballot by petition. Honoring their prior agreement, Perez made no move to block this legislation, provided it did not award the rooster to Truman.[41] The real debate on the bill took place at a closed-door conference that included U.S. Senator Ellender, Long, Perez, and state representative Henry C. Sevier, chairperson of the state central committee. The new law permitted a slate of Truman-Barkley electors to be placed on the ballot by petition of one hundred signatures but denied the slate the use of the word "Democratic" as well as the rooster symbol. Truman would appear beneath the unfamiliar donkey. Fearful the split in the Democratic Party might aid Republican opposition to Russell Long, the governor demanded that the bill permit all statewide Democratic candidates to appear on both the Democratic/Dixiecrat ticket and the Truman-Barkley ticket. A few candidates, Leander Perez and Edward Hebert, for example, chose not to have their names listed on the Truman-Barkley ticket.[42]

An American Federation of Labor official from Baton Rouge launched the Truman petition effort. Two other federation officials, both from Lake Charles and both members of the Democratic state central committee, filed a suit to restrain the secretary of state from printing ballots listing Thurmond and Wright as the Democratic Party candidates. The suit alleged that the September 10 meeting of the committee had been convened under false pretenses. Notices for the meeting indicated that only routine matters would be discussed. Assuming they would not be missing anything important, the members affiliated with the labor organization did not attend the meeting and sent proxies. State district court judge Charles Holcombe issued a temporary restraining order on the secretary of state but shortly thereafter allowed a suspensive appeal under which the secretary could proceed with the printing of ballots. The state supreme court refused to hear the case immediately, and the suit was withdrawn. Despondent, Truman supporters urged Louisiana voters to "stamp the 'donkey.'"[43]

With the intraparty struggle resolved and the various barnyard symbols designated, the outcome of the presidential election in Louisiana was all but decided. Support for the president was so thin that the national Democratic Party did not even open a campaign office in New Orleans. Only five hundred persons turned out to meet vice-presidential candidate Alben Barkley when he visited the Crescent City, the paltriest attendance of his southern speaking tour.[44]

Because the success of States' Rights supporters to control the state party machinery often turned on the sympathies of the governor, Dixiecrats waited with anticipation for Georgia's September 8 gubernatorial primary between acting governor M. E. Thompson and Herman Talmadge. Both men publicly opposed Truman's civil rights program; however, neither Thompson nor Talmadge publicly supported a bolt because neither wanted to be accused of party disloyalty.[45] States' Rights leaders throughout the region nevertheless prayed for a Talmadge victory. Like his father, Talmadge championed white supremacy and supported the restoration of the white primary, declaring that "the fight I am making is a white man's fight to keep Georgia a white man's state."[46] He promised Georgians a primary "as white as we can have" and denounced Truman's "oppressive, communistic, anti-South legislation."[47]

Thompson found himself on the wrong side of the issues in 1948. The anti-Talmadge faction of the Georgia Democratic Party had aligned itself with the liberal wing of the national party, and Thompson was one of the few southern Democrats actively supporting President Truman. Furthermore, Thompson had vetoed the white primary bill in 1947 and had received many black votes in 1946. In addition, two of Georgia's best-known liberal politicians, Ellis Arnall and E. D. Rivers, actively supported him.[48] Despite his opposition to the president's civil rights program and his own proposals to reinstate the white primary and strengthen the county unit system, white Georgians committed to the racial status quo viewed Thompson with suspicion.

Much to the delight of Dixiecrat supporters across the South, Talmadge won the primary. They believed this boded well for the Georgia States' Rights movement because in addition to the ideological similarities between the Dixiecrats and Talmadge, the new governor was a distant cousin to Strom Thurmond. Talmadge's mother was a Thurmond from Edgefield County, South Carolina. Talmadge contended, however, that he and Thurmond were not close, having only met when they were governors.[49] Wallace Malone, Dixiecrat leader and bank president from Dothan, Alabama, made it fairly clear that the States' Rights movement expected support from Talmadge now that he had wrested control of the state from the more liberal Thompson forces. Malone had made financial contributions to Talmadge's campaign, and he reminded Talmadge of their quid pro quo. The Dixiecrats, he bluntly told the governor-elect, were "counting on Georgia's twelve votes."[50]

The day after Talmadge's victory, some thirty men from Augusta organized the Savannah Valley Thurmond-Wright Club. Led by Ed L. Willingham Jr., an "insurance, oil, and auto-finance man" from Augusta, the organization declared its intention to win a spot for the States' Rights candidates on the Georgia ballot.[51] Clearly, though, they hoped that the governor-elect would engineer a takeover of the state Democratic Party and tie the party's electors to the States' Rights cause.

The Dixiecrats' hope was short lived, however. They had barely any time to savor the victory when Talmadge made it clear that he would not engineer a states' rights coup; instead, he acknowledged that the Georgia SDEC would select the electors for the Democratic Party ticket.[52] Nevertheless, the political scene in Georgia remained confused for much of September. Despite Talmadge's apparent distancing from the States' Righters, party leader Charles Bloch of Macon and Talmadge wheelhorse Roy V. Harris of Augusta announced that Georgia's presidential electors would be instructed to vote against any candidate supporting federal civil rights legislation. On September 14 the *Augusta Chronicle* explained how, through some maneuvering, Georgia's twelve electoral votes eventually would go to Thurmond and Wright.[53] On September 17 the *Atlanta Journal* predicted that the Georgia ballot would most likely omit the names of Truman and Barkley. The twelve electors would not be instructed regarding candidates but would be pledged specifically to support candidates who opposed enactment of the civil rights program.[54] The *New York Times* likewise believed Georgia would appoint uninstructed electors. The *Times* reasoned that choosing uninstructed electors would strengthen Georgia's bargaining position within national Democratic Party politics. Should Truman desperately need Georgia's twelve votes, they could barter. Should the president be beaten, Georgia could vote for him without providing crucial support and thus avoid the label of "bolter."[55] Despite their hostility toward Truman, leaders of the Talmadge faction warned their supporters not to join the Dixiecrats. Such action would leave the state party machinery to Governor Thompson and former governors Rivers and Arnall.[56]

Like many, Talmadge insiders considered Dewey a sure winner and were looking down the road to state elections in 1950. Talmadge floor leader J. Robert Elliott of Columbus (who later would be appointed to the federal bench by President John F. Kennedy) reminded his cronies that "the Georgia situation is our primary concern . . . the Georgia situation in *1950*. By September 1950, Dewey will have been in office almost two years and his popularity and that of the Republican party will have waned. Many of our own people who support him [in 1948] will be turning back to the traditional party of the South. The question of party regularity will then rise to haunt those who may have deprived the people of the State of the opportunity to vote the regular Party ticket." Putting Truman's name on the ballot would not constitute an endorsement. "On the other hand, if we deny [Georgians] the *chance* of voting for [Truman], we will antagonize many [voters]." The Talmadge faction could avoid this rancor. "Let the names of the candidates appear and let there be no attempt at dictation. This is the only sure way to maintain Party regularity [and] will eliminate ghosts in 1950."[57]

Dixiecrat leaders felt Georgia slipping away. Alabama party chief Gessner McCorvey wrote to Talmadge on September 21 seeking his commitment to the cause. Appealing to Talmadge as a "Southern white man," McCorvey tried to convince the governor-elect that Georgia was key to persuading the other southern states to follow.[58] States' rights advocates also knew they were working against the clock. Delayed action of the Georgia SDEC on certifying the state's electors would close the door to any Democratic slate other than the one picked by the committee. Georgia's election rules held that candidates for electors must be certified thirty days prior to the general election, in this case by October 2.[59]

Leaders of the Talmadge faction met in Atlanta on September 22 and tentatively decided to nominate twelve uninstructed electors.[60] The next day Thurmond arrived in Augusta for an evening States' Rights rally that received a big buildup in the local paper. Some 4,000 cheering, flag-waving states' rights faithful from Georgia and neighboring South Carolina packed Municipal Auditorium to hear Thurmond blast "power-mad politicians" who had "sacrificed their birthright for votes of the minorities." He urged the Georgia SDEC to pledge their electors to the States' Rights candidates.[61]

Hoping to snuff out any pro-Thurmond contagion and to preempt the rumored plans of the Talmadge-controlled SDEC to appoint uninstructed electors, Governor Thompson convened a special session of the legislature on September 27. Thompson wanted the legislature to pass a measure that would permit the names of presidential and vice-presidential candidates of all parties to appear on the November ballot but that would also bar unpledged electors. Thompson said he hoped such measures would clarify in the voters' minds for whom they were voting and would make sure the electors could not "traffic and trade" in the electoral college. He also wanted to force the Talmadge-aligned electors to pledge themselves to Truman and Barkley. Should the Talmadge group fail to do this, friends of Thompson or of organized labor might seek to place a set of electors pledged to Truman on the ballot, thereby wresting control of the state party away from the governor-elect.[62]

Failing to win the electors for Truman and Barkley, the special session proved a defeat for Thompson. The state senate voted on September 29 and the house on October 1 to leave Georgia electors free to cast their ballots for any presidential candidate they pleased. One state senator told reporters that he believed that "electors should be at liberty to trade." Further, the senate's bill separated the presidential electors from those of the other Democratic Party candidates, thus making it possible for Georgians to vote the straight Democratic ticket for state offices and for another party's presidential candidate.[63] Finally, lawmakers amended that part of the law requiring thirty days' advance certification of candidates to allow more time for contestants to qualify for the ballot.[64]

States' Rights advocates remained hopeful, for the individual electors still had to be appointed by the Talmadge-dominated Georgia SDEC. Many hoped that the committee, although barred from instructing the electors, would choose individuals with Dixiecrat leanings. In the October 2 meeting the committee appointed twelve electors "verbally" pledged but not legally bound to support President Truman should he receive a majority of the popular votes cast in the state.[65]

Although they publicly proclaimed victory, States' Rights leaders privately mourned the loss of Georgia. James Peters, chairperson of the Georgia SDEC, tried to assuage the hurt feelings of the Dixiecrats, assuring one States' Rights leader that although uninstructed electors had been named, "Thurmond and Wright will carry Georgia."[66] White Georgians' invective toward Truman was strong, but was it virulent enough to cause voters to abandon party loyalty? Fearful that a wholesale endorsement of the States' Rights Party would place them in an anomalous position within state politics in 1950, the Talmadge faction chose to play it safe. State leaders charted a middle course that allowed them to champion states rights' principles without completely abandoning the national party. Peters continued to send letters of encouragement to States' Rights leaders, and he reported to DNC chairperson McGrath that the States' Rights forces would triumph in Georgia.[67] One pro-Truman elector in Georgia even accused Peters and others of secretly aiding the States' Rights effort.[68] But on the same day that he wrote McGrath, Peters confided to a fellow Georgian that although the president "had insulted every Southern white man, . . . President Truman is not the Democratic party, and I suspect that most voters in the end will feel their loyalty to the Party is stronger than the resentment towards President Truman."[69] Peters was less duplicitous than uncertain of how white voters would react when forced to choose between their racial principles and their traditional political allegiance.

Thurmond felt betrayed by Talmadge. He complained that prior to Georgia's primary, Talmadge had told him that the Georgia Democratic Party would appoint uninstructed delegates and that after the general election those electors would be instructed to support Thurmond and Wright. Thurmond further claimed that Roy Harris, "Talmadge's right-hand man," had told him Georgia Democrats would oppose any candidate who favored the civil rights program. That, Thurmond whined, "was equivalent to saying that they would support us."[70]

Herman Talmadge remained cagey throughout the entire election. Appearing on the TV news program "Meet the Press" in early October, Talmadge skillfully avoided showing his hand. The Georgia governor-elect denied that his organization had any connection to the Dixiecrats, and he refused to predict the outcome of the presidential election. He conceded that "the people of Georgia are bitterly opposed to the President's civil rights program" but that they were faithful Democrats. White Georgians, he concluded, were torn. When asked whom he would support, the youthful governor-elect answered repeatedly, "I'm not supporting anyone except Herman Talmadge as candidate for governor."[71] Talmadge's memoirs reveal little about his decision not to engineer a states' rights coup. Talmadge eventually voted for Thurmond, but he remained officially neutral in the campaign.[72] Thus Herman Talmadge executed a delicate balancing act. Focused on preserving power within his state, he avoided the label of "bolter"; however, by voting for Thurmond he could still claim the power of the states' rights mantle.

On October 7 supporters of the Georgia States' Rights Democrats converted the Savannah Valley Thurmond-Wright Club into the Georgia States' Rights Party. On October 13 some three hundred States' Rights delegates, many of whom were identified in local newspapers as Talmadge supporters, gathered in Augusta and chose presidential electors for the general election ballot.[73] Hoping to salvage something from the Georgia debacle, Thurmond addressed a States' Rights rally in Macon on October 19.[74] Despite the decision of the Talmadge organization, Georgia remained an unknown political quantity on the eve of the election. Although Herman Talmadge did not commit his organization to engineering a States' Rights revolt, members of his coalition publicly supported the Dixiecrats. Furthermore, as of October 27 no member of Georgia's congressional delegation had come out for Truman. Finally, on October 29, U.S. Senator Richard Russell and five of the state's ten congressmen declared they would vote, if not exactly for the president, for the electoral nominees certified by the Democratic Party of Georgia. However, Russell asserted, "I do not consider myself bound to support the Communistic plank of the Democratic national platform which is mislabeled civil rights," and he would continue to fight any civil rights legislation.[75] As the election drew near, political observers considered the contest in Georgia a three-way race. Truman was expected to receive a plurality of the popular vote, but because of a peculiarity in the Georgia law, it was possible that the final decision on the electoral vote would not be determined until well after election day. State law required a majority rather than a plurality of the popular vote for electors. When a majority was lacking, the decision was left to the state legislature.[76] Although the Talmadge-dominated group had proven that they were not inclined to bolt, the Dixiecrats still clung to the hope that they would swing the state to Thurmond after the fact.

Clearly the success of the Dixiecrat movement depended primarily on the ability of States' Rights activists to gain control of state party machinery. In the states where they were unsuccessful, the Dixiecrats were forced to run a third-party campaign, something they were organizationally and philosophically ill equipped to do. For Democrats who had long benefited from their ability to manipulate the system, identifying themselves as a third party in a one-party region was an irony they could not appreciate. From its inception the States' Rights revolt was rife with internal discord, and third-party status in some states pushed forward disagreements over the organization's ultimate goals. Were they merely staging a protest vote, or were they indeed creating a new political party? Their inconsistent message and conflicting motivations left voters confused as well. Those who might have been receptive to a third party received no assurances from the Dixiecrats that they would be around once the polling stations closed.

Inadequate funding proved a major hurdle to mounting an effective third-party effort. The national campaign was financed by contributions from the states, each of which was assigned a quota of $10,000 for each electoral vote.[77] In late October party leaders reported contributions totaling a mere $158,975. More than half came from Mississippi Dixiecrats. This figure covered only the funds that came into the headquarters and did not represent funds raised by state organizations. The largest single contribution came from banker Wallace Malone of Dothan, Alabama, for $3,500. As far as can be ascertained from existing financial documents, the Dixiecrat campaign survived primarily on small, individual contributions.[78]

Throughout the campaign the Dixiecrats were hounded by accusations of financial support from corporate interests, particularly oil companies. Leading the charge against the Dixiecrats were Ralph McGill of the *Atlanta Constitution* and John Ed Pearce of the *Louisville Courier-Journal*. No existing financial documents, however, reveal contributions from oil interests. Clearly, though, the individual Dixiecrats possessed conservative economic interests and had extensive corporate connections. While planters constituted an important party constituency, so did utility executives, bankers, and industrialists. Fielding Wright and Ben Laney of Arkansas had ties to the oil industry, and local representatives of large corporations were among the Dixiecrat leaders. Both Houston attorney and Texas Dixiecrat Palmer Bradley and Alabama Dixiecrat Gessner McCorvey of Mobile had Standard Oil of New Jersey for a client. McCorvey also represented Humble Oil (a Standard subsidiary), Gulf Oil, Magnolia Petroleum, and Tennessee Coal and Iron (United States Steel). Marion Rushton, chairperson of the Alabama Dixiecrats, represented Chase National Bank, Buckeye Cotton Oil, and the Capital Fertilizer Company. Former governor Frank Dixon was an attorney for the Associated Industries of Alabama and the National Association of Manufacturers representative in the state; Dixiecrat and Judge Eugene Blease of South Carolina represented the South Carolina Power Company. North Carolina Dixiecrat David Clark published the *Southern Textile Bulletin,* while the major Dixiecrat organ in Alabama was *Alabama,* a "newsmagazine" and the mouthpiece of the Big Mules. One newsmagazine reported that officials of the Mississippi Power and Light Company contributed $5,000 to the May convention held in Jackson.[79]

Thurmond deflected charges of corporate control and insisted that "not a dime" of oil money had passed through his hands.[80] Thurmond acknowledged that although the Dixiecrats considered the tidelands oil question "a matter for the states just as we consider so-called civil rights legislation . . . to be reserved to the states," neither he nor the party had been unduly influenced by oil industry money. His accusers, Thurmond contended, merely desired to smear the movement.[81] Countering the *New York Times* claim that the Dixiecrats were funded by big money donors, Fielding Wright insisted they were supported almost exclusively "by individual southern citizens."[82] In their denunciations of ties to large donors and corporate interests, the Dixiecrats tried to portray the revolt as a spontaneous grassroots movement. Both Wright and Thurmond conveniently forgot that Houston oil executive H. R. Cullen and Humble Oil Company had flown Thurmond to the Houston convention in a private plane and had chartered a special train for the Mississippi delegation.[83]

If the Dixiecrats did indeed receive major contributions from the oil interests, it certainly was not reflected in their campaign efforts. Unlike the major party candidates, Thurmond did not travel in his own campaign train and often relied on local volunteers to transport him to and from speaking engagements.[84] The shoestring budget made it difficult for the party to finance extensive efforts in the individual southern states, which meant that most voters would get only limited exposure to the candidates. The Dixiecrat campaign dollar was used sparingly in states where the Democratic leaders refused to join the States' Rights fight.[85]

Time constraints and a paucity of experience in managing a campaign of this magnitude also proved to be critical factors. Outside the Dixiecrat strongholds, the campaign fell to political amateurs, "successful young businessmen who are more at home at Rotary and Kiwanis luncheons than in smoke-filled rooms."[86] The results were often disappointing.[87] When the Dixiecrats' national campaign office opened on August 9, States' Rights organizers in the various states had barely three months to organize an offensive. The candidates and their supporters readily acknowledged this handicap. One Florida Dixiecrat leader told Thurmond that the major weakness of the Dixiecrats was "that we were trying to do a job in a matter of months that would have required a minimum of four years."[88]

Problems arose with the presidential and vice-presidential candidates themselves. Fielding Wright abhorred campaigning, and it showed. Dixiecrat speechwriter J. Oliver Emmerich, publisher of the *McComb Enterprise-Journal,* frequently accompanied Wright on the stump. Years later he described a typical Wright campaign outing to New Orleans.

Emmerich recalled with bemusement how, as their train approached the New Orleans station, Wright became nervous at the sight of the crowd awaiting his arrival. Anxious, he quietly slipped out the back of the train and climbed, undetected, into a waiting taxicab. Wright bristled at campaign fuss and hoopla. "It irritated him," Emmerich remarked years later. "He was a shy man."

Thurmond and Wright "were just as different as daylight and dark," Emmerich later mused. He recalled how Thurmond, a natural campaigner, thrived on the crowds and the campaign motorcades preceded by wailing police sirens. "Thurmond got a big kick out of it," Emmerich recalled.[89] But Thurmond's love of the campaign trail, the pressing crowds, and the blaring marching bands arose from political egocentrism rather than a desire to build a viable and lasting political movement. Thurmond's independent political tendencies made him a good spokesman for white southerners angry at what they saw as abuse at the hands of the national party; these same tendencies also made him difficult to manage as a candidate. He frequently bypassed the Jackson office altogether when arranging his personal appearances and disregarded speeches written for him by public relations staff, preferring instead to use his own writers. Thurmond dashed from town square to town square throughout the South, sometimes delivering as many as five speeches a day. Campaign director Judge Merritt Gibson remarked bitterly that the Dixiecrat candidate wanted to greet voters in every little "pigtrail" in the South. Significantly, Thurmond clashed with the other Dixiecrat leaders over the movement's ultimate goal. Throughout the campaign, Thurmond avoided any hint that the political effort he was spearheading had a shelf life longer than the presidential election, while the Jackson office wanted their candidate to serve as point man for a new political movement.[90]

Candidate management issues belied deeper rifts within the Dixiecrat ranks over ideology and goals. Although his subsequent political career made him the poster boy for white supremacy, a closer look at Thurmond's gubernatorial politics and policies places him somewhere between the "good government" position of Arkansas's Sidney McMath and the rabid race baiting of Alabama's Horace Wilkinson. Thurmond came closer, politically, to returning veterans seeking to turn out the corrupt machines and usher in an era of industrial development and modernization. His 1946 campaign had been remarkably free of racist appeals. As governor he helped design and push through the general assembly legislation creating a governmental reorganization commission, which was responsible for streamlining government agencies. Furthermore, he consistently urged abolition of the state's poll tax, advocated legislation to provide secret ballots in the general election, championed the creation of a personnel merit system for state government, and had moved quickly to apprehend the lynchers of Willie Earle. Once in office, Thurmond focused on modernization. He threw open the doors of the governor's mansion to visiting industrialists and undertook an intense campaign to promote industrial development and economic growth in South Carolina. A firm adherent to the dictum that a rising tide raises all boats, Thurmond heartily believed that the South's racial dilemma would be solved through economic growth and modernization, not through federal interference. Thurmond and his advisors clearly distinguished between their brand of conservatism and what they referred to as "the reactionary and conservative background" of the Alabama and Mississippi Dixiecrats.[91] Thurmond's racism drew from a well-worn paternalism that stressed responsibility for black southerners. However, victory demanded that Thurmond maintain the support of the more radical elements within the movement.

Ever since he vaulted to the front of the revolt in February, Thurmond remained convinced that the states' rights effort represented nothing more than a temporary protest whose ultimate goal was to reassert white southerners' control of the national party. But despite his acknowledgment of the temporary nature of his assignment, Thurmond felt the need to develop positions on other national issues, such as labor relations, foreign policy, education, agriculture, and the atomic bomb. Of course, no one ever asked him his opinion on these subjects. In comparison with the relative simplicity of the defense of segregation, Thurmond confided to an advisor that developing a more comprehensive platform would be "pretty difficult."[92] Nevertheless, in elaborating on states' rights and the dangers of federal intrusion into racial matters, the Dixiecrats began to develop a language and a philosophy that melded unease over racial integration and an expanding state with Cold War fears, a conjunction that would find its ultimate success in the 1960s.

White southerners' concerns about civil rights and intrusions of the federal government into southern racial arrangements multiplied when considered part of what they viewed as the larger postwar Communist menace. Dixiecrats articulated their objections to civil rights legislation in terms of its anti-American features. Antilynching and anti–poll tax measures, they believed, encroached on individual liberty and freedom,

*Dixiecrat presidential candidate Strom Thurmond (*second from left*) poses with veterans in Columbia, South Carolina. Photograph courtesy of Special Collections, Clemson University Libraries, Clemson, South Carolina.*

abrogating local self-government.[93] Seemingly ignorant of the grotesque irony, Dixiecrat campaign literature warned that an individual "charged with participation in a lynching could be dragged away from his home and taken to a distant place [where] he would be at the mercy of the paid prosecutors of the Federal Government."[94] Most objectionable to Dixiecrats such as Thurmond was the proposed FEPC, which would outlaw employment discrimination based on race, religion, or national origin. Dixiecrats charged that the FEPC was patterned after a Soviet law authored by Joseph Stalin in the 1920s and was therefore proof that Communist spies had infiltrated the U.S. government. The FEPC, they argued, violated the rights of employers under the Constitution because it would remove from the employer decisions regarding hiring and firing and would instead dispatch a veritable army of federal agents throughout the South to ensure that blacks were employed in every enterprise. Thurmond warned that Communists would use the proposed FEPC provisions to force "their agents and saboteurs into every tool and die room, every machine shop and every industrial plant and laboratory, atomic or otherwise, in America."[95]

Equally important, the proposed FEPC threatened to upset the local control of southern labor. Dixiecrat denunciations of the FEPC were meant for the ears of employers, not employees. A. P. Shoemaker, manager of a hotel on Mississippi's Gulf Coast, complained to Congressman William C. Colmer that the proposed FEPC was encouraging local blacks to pursue jobs above their traditional "station." He related how surprised his clerk was to see a particular female job applicant, "because [she] was one of the members of the Ethiopian race, one of the products of the FEPC to which we are so bitterly opposed." The audacity of this black woman shocked the hotel's white employees. Shoemaker continued, "My secretary did not believe it could possibly be a negro that would have that much nerve to apply for this type of job down South."[96] Black Belt plantation operators such as Mississippi's Walter Sillers and industrialists like Louisiana's John U. Barr likewise understood the benefits of job segregation. The proposed FEPC would, in the words of the Alabama Chamber of Commerce, "strike at the fundamental rights of an employer in the selection of his employees in the operation of his own business."[97]

States' Rights campaign events reflected the reactionary nature of the organization as well as its elitism, confirming that the Dixiecrats were not a spontaneous grassroots organization but, rather, a creation of elites intent on protecting their own privilege. The Dixiecrats' preferred modus operandi—capturing control of existing state party organizations—illustrated their disdain for grassroots politics, and their rallies reflected this perspective. Throughout the South, Dixiecrat functions became staged affirmations of privilege, historical pageants at which attendees dressed in the garb of the Old South or resurrected the symbols of the violent period known as Redemption, during which white Democrats overthrew the Reconstruction governments. Young male Dixiecrat supporters dressed as Confederate generals or donned planters' hats, while in Abbeville, South Carolina, women attending a meeting of the South Carolina Democratic Party's women's division dressed in red shirts, reminiscent of the violent campaigns of 1876. One newspaper reported that guests at the meeting included "women who remember the Reconstruction period and the strenuous campaign which ended the rule of the carpet-baggers."[98] States' Rights rallies opened to the strains of "Dixie," and supporters hoisted pictures of Robert E. Lee and Jefferson Davis in conjunction with the likeness of Thurmond and Wright. The Confederate battle flag became a popular symbol of the southern States' Rights resistance and regularly dotted Dixiecrat rallies and adorned Thurmond's motorcades. One supporter even wrote to Thurmond to request "the Dixiecrat flag."[99]

The adoption of the flag as the unofficial party symbol sparked considerable debate. Ralph McGill spoke out against southerners who "prostitute the Confederate Flag and the song 'Dixie' to their own uses." *Birmingham Post* columnist John Temple Graves, on the other hand, claimed the time had come "for a proud Dixie-singing, Confederate flag-waving South that will stand up for all that's best of its own, and do it in the spirit of no Lost Cause or secession but of a new place to be won in our land of the free and home of the brave."[100]

Perhaps the Dixiecrats' most significant stumbling block concerned a political paradox of their own making. The white South's ability to defend itself against federal intrusion into race relations had always rested on its dominant position within the national Democratic Party, a position of seniority ensured by white southerners' intense political allegiance. The desire to recapture this prestige and power had prompted the Dixiecrat revolt. In order to succeed, the States' Rights Party hoped to capitalize on its regularity, yet it needed to differentiate itself from the national party and to encourage white southerners to resist political change occurring at the national level. In a region where deviation from the Democratic Party typically spelled political suicide, Thurmond and the Dixiecrats struggled to overcome their status as party bolters. Thurmond angrily reminded one supporter to "explain to everyone you meet the fact that Governor Wright and I are the *official nominees* of the *regular Democratic party of South Carolina,* just as we are the official nominees of the regular Democratic parties of Alabama, Louisiana, and Mississippi."[101] Although individual Dixiecrats could agree on the efficacy of working through the state party machinery, they disagreed on the long-term goal of the organization they had hastily created. Organizers and supporters alike differed on whether the States' Rights Democratic Party would continue to exist as a viable protest vehicle or separate party after the election. In order to be taken seriously, some campaign strategists, particularly in Mississippi and Alabama, felt that they needed at least to appear committed to carrying on the fight after the election, to prove to voters that, as one Dixiecrat staffer confided, "the States' Rights movement is not a flash-in-the-pan."[102] Some, such as campaign chairman Merritt Gibson, felt that while the Dixiecrat campaign could help restore the South to power within the Democratic Party, so, too, could it serve as the foundation for a new party that would attract conservative elements from both major parties. Among themselves the more radical Dixiecrats acknowledged that, indeed, they were philosophically closer to the Republicans. For them the States' Rights Democratic Party represented a means to creating a more viable two-party system in the South.[103] Finally, the Dixiecrats had to defend themselves against the charge that by injecting themselves into the campaign, they had diluted the strength of not only the national Democratic Party but of state Democratic parties and had thus made a Republican victory more likely.[104]

★

Loyal Democrats roundly condemned the aims and ideological focus of the new States' Rights Democratic Party, yet many believed the Dixiecrat revolt would benefit the South if it resulted in the permanent exodus of conservatives from the party and fostered the creation of a two-party system.[105] The upheavals of the New Deal and war years had revitalized groups around which liberal southern state Democratic Parties could grow. Most visible among those committed to democratizing the South were members of the SCHW and left-wing CIO affiliates, who, along with a small group of black and white liberals, endured intimidation and physical assault while enthusiastically campaigning for Henry Wallace and the Progressive Party. But they were not the only southerners longing for political change. The presence of contesting delegations at the Philadelphia convention demonstrated the existence of a small but persistent moderate white Democratic constituency in the Deep South, loyal to the national party and ready to challenge the entrenched political elite. Joining them was a highly organized African American political organization wary of Wallace's third-party candidacy and desperate for national recognition and assistance. In the end, President Truman, leaders of the DNC, and loyal Democrats within Dixiecrat-controlled states were unwilling and often unable to challenge the Dixiecrat cabal and to further the cause of two-party politics in the South. Aware of the violence that met the Wallace caravan at nearly every stop and hoping to prevent more states from breaking away, Truman avoided the South during his campaign tour.[106] He calculated that he could win the election without the South, yet he hedged his bets, endeavoring to contain the bolt by not further antagonizing the loyal states. The greatest push to hasten the exit of conservatives from the Democratic Party in the interest of creating a two-party system should have come from loyal congressmen and senators within the Dixiecrat states, but personal prejudice and political realities prevented them from acting. Vehemently opposed to civil rights legislation, loath to tie themselves to the president, and often constrained by party rules, loyal New Deal Democrats such as Senators Lister Hill and John Sparkman in Alabama and Olin D. Johnston in South Carolina chose instead to sit out the election, only occasionally making bland and feeble statements about party loyalty.

In Alabama, control of the presidential electors had been decided prior to the Philadelphia convention. Despite the Dixiecrats' lock on state political power, their effort there did not proceed uncontested in the remaining months of the campaign. The States' Rights movement received little support and often keen opposition from Alabama newspapers. Neither the *Birmingham News* nor the *Montgomery Advertiser,* the state's largest papers, supported the Dixiecrats, referring to the States' Rights Party as politically "bankrupt." Several other papers, including the *Huntsville Times,* supported the Republican Dewey.[107]

No sooner had the Birmingham convention closed than a movement was afoot to place Truman electors on the November ballot. "If Mrs. Harry Truman were a registered Alabama voter," *Montgomery Advertiser* editor Grover Hall wrote, "there would be no way possible for her to vote for her husband in November."[108] Support for the president was thin; nevertheless, many Alabamians resented being denied the opportunity to vote for him. Governor Folsom received letters from irate citizens incensed that the president would not appear on the ballot.[109] Many voters apparently regretted, or conveniently forgot, their complicity in their own disfranchisement. The decision to eliminate Truman from the ballot altogether had been made during the May primary. The voters, Hall wrote, "feel somehow gypped." He advocated presenting a full choice of electors to Alabama voters to avoid a lot of "needless belly-aching."[110]

The effort on behalf of the Truman electors was initiated by state senator Joseph Langan of Mobile, spokesman for Alabama labor and one of Governor Folsom's few supporters during the 1947 legislative session. Langan threatened court action if Truman electors were barred from the ballot. More than fifty Alabama labor leaders met on August 15 to pledge their support of the Truman electors. Led by high-ranking officials of the Alabama Federation of Labor, the Alabama CIO, and the Alabama Brotherhood of Railway Workers, the meeting adopted a resolution condemning the "dictatorial tactics and objectives" of the Alabama Dixiecrats designed "to confuse and mislead the people . . . into unconsciously contributing to the election of a Republican president."[111] Langan organized a statewide rally of "loyal Democrats" in Montgomery the following day. Of the two hundred persons expected, approximately thirty-five showed up, most of whom were labor leaders. The *Montgomery Advertiser*'s front-page photo of the meeting revealed row upon row of empty chairs. Despite the small turnout, the Truman supporters planned to reconvene in Birmingham to choose electors for the November ballot. In the absence of a groundswell of support, and not relishing a court fight, Langan soon rescinded his threat to seek a court order.[112]

The Truman electors movement remained dormant until October 7, when Governor Folsom, who had been strongly critical of the president during the first half of the year and who at one time had offered himself as a favorite son presidential candidate, pledged his support. Until this time Folsom had argued that the issue was one for the state legislature to decide and had been content to "let those that done it undone it."[113] The governor's endorsement ended a long public silence on the issue. Folsom further intimated that *he* possibly would seek court action to bind the state's electors to Truman. To this threat state party leader McCorvey brashly replied that three of the eleven electors were ready to go to jail for contempt if necessary before they would vote for Truman. The following week Folsom announced that he would file a suit with "the proper authorities" and pledged to pursue the case to the U.S. Supreme Court if necessary.[114] To avoid a court battle, loyalist Democrats contemplated calling a special session of the state legislature to consider ways to place Truman electors on the ballot. But this plan fizzled because the Dixiecrat forces had the loyalists in a bind. According to Alabama law, anyone who failed to support the electors duly chosen in a Democratic primary—in this case, the Dixiecrat electors—risked being barred from the party's next primary.[115] Senators Lister Hill and John Sparkman, along with members of the congressional delegation, eventually announced that they would vote for the Democratic electors (in this case, Thurmond and Wright), though they refused to campaign for the ticket.[116]

After placing himself squarely, if belatedly, in the Truman camp, Folsom campaigned for the unpopular president in the last week and a half of the campaign. Hoping to head off Republican gains in his state, the governor went to northern Alabama, where Dewey appeared most threatening. A natural campaigner, Folsom hit the hustings with the Strawberry Pickers, a string band that had accompanied him on the campaign trail since 1946. Absent from the 1948 campaign, though, was John Stiefelmeyer, whose job it had been to pass around the "suds bucket" during the campaign stops. Stiefelmeyer informed the governor that he was a Dewey man.[117]

Governor Folsom sponsored a pro-Truman rally on November 1 at the state capitol. Speaking to a crowd of about five hundred, Folsom railed against the "manipulation" perpetrated by "three dozen" men meeting in "smoke filled rooms" that "took away the rights of three million persons." He then instructed Alabamians to "vote under the Rooster"—the straight Democratic ticket. He told the crowd that although this would mean voting for the States' Rights electors, proposed court action could compel those eleven electors to vote for Truman. Later, in a statewide radio broadcast, Folsom neglected to mention the importance of the pending lawsuit and simply told listeners, "When you go to the polls and vote the straight Democratic ticket it will be counted for the president."[118] Alabama's congressional delegation offered mixed support. While all pledged their support for the "Democratic ticket," they varied in their willingness to speak out on behalf of the Dixiecrats. Senators Hill and Sparkman kept their distances, as did Congressmen Carter Manasco, Edward deGraffenreid, and Bob Jones. Congressman Laurie C. Battle from Birmingham offered his assistance, as did Albert Rains from Gadsden and George Grant from Alabama's second district.[119] Certainly, many voters could not truly know to whom Democratic votes would go.

Mississippi Dixiecrats encountered the least resistance; the campaign, for the most part, had been won by early August. Vice-presidential candidate Wright spent the balance of the campaign touring neighboring states in an attempt to win uninstructed delegates to the Dixiecrat banner. Mississippi's congressional delegation solidly backed the States' Rights takeover. The ground on which one could challenge the States' Rights forces was rapidly receding. After witnessing Mississippi's walkout at the Democratic convention, Frank Smith wrote to Philip Mullen and secretly encouraged him to organize a slate of Truman electors. Mullen was skeptical that such a move would garner any support. "There is no way you can rationalize with [white Mississippians] after nigger has been yelled," he lamented.[120] Despite warnings from Congressman John Stennis, a relative liberal by Mississippi standards, that he would be "contaminated" by the effort, Mullen proceeded to gather a group of students from the University of Mississippi from among whom they would choose electors. Before they could present their slate of electors, however, a group of nine students from Mississippi State College—Dixiecrat supporters all—qualified themselves as pro-Truman electors on September 17. Mullen's group nevertheless qualified for the ballot and awaited the election, which they viewed as a "tremendous opportunity" to "take the party over for real democratic purposes and for human rights."[121]

Among the Dixiecrat states, South Carolina experienced the strongest and best-organized anti-Dixiecrat, pro-Truman effort, led by the PDP and the Citizen Democrats. Even within the state party itself, opposition arose to the hijacking of the electors. Representatives from the majority white upstate counties, where New Deal labor policies had aided working-class whites, opposed the move. One representative demanded that voters be given a choice and urged the committee to put out a party ballot carrying two slates of electors, one pledged to the States' Rights Democratic ticket and one pledged to the national Democratic ticket. During the tumultuous seven-hour meeting, committee members debated whether by instructing their electors to vote for Thurmond and Wright they had formally severed their ties with the national party. Dissenters feared that such an action would cost members of their congressional delegation their seniority.[122] After the state Democratic Party had formally endorsed Thurmond and Wright as its nominees, Thurmond made it known that he supported placing Truman electors on the ballot—just not as Democratic Party electors.[123]

The South Carolina Dixiecrat headquarters opened in Columbia on August 25. States' Rights committees were organized in every county, and a woman's committee, directed by Mrs. Nathaniel Gist Gee, formed in early October. Gee, a former teacher at Winthrop College in Rock Hill, was the wife of the great-nephew of Confederate brigadier general S. R. Gist.[124] To raise funds for the campaign, the South Carolina committee assessed a quota of $1,000 for each member of the general assembly from each county. Campaign strategists reminded their workers that "no white man or woman in South Carolina should be satisfied until he or she HAS DONE ALL for this cause."[125] Although the States' Rights Democrats enjoyed wide support throughout the state, funds trickled into the office. As of October 30, the eve of the election, the state office had received only $68,895.83 in total contributions, far short of the $170,000 goal they had set for the state.[126]

Almost from the start of the campaign, even the strongest Dixiecrat paper in the state, the *Charleston News and Courier,* acknowledged Thurmond's slim chances for outright victory and recognized that they could only send a protest vote.[127] The *Columbia Record,* the closest thing to a liberal white viewpoint in South Carolina, labeled the Dixiecrat effort futile. "If the South wants to make its protest meaningful and effective," the *Record* claimed, "it will have to shift not from the Democratic Party to the Dixiecrat splinter party but to the Republican Party."[128] Despite the Dixiecrats' lock on the state party machinery, South Carolina was less than solid behind the organization. Geographically speaking, discontent with the Dixiecrats centered in the majority white upstate counties. State party leaders listened anxiously to rumors that select counties were planning to withdraw from the state party but hoped to remain affiliated with the national party.[129] Upstate newspapers leveled harsh criticism on the Dixiecrats. The *Spartanburg Herald* called the movement "top heavy" and questioned the organization's claims of grassroots support, while the *Anderson Independent* labeled the movement "backward-looking, reactionary, and self-seeking."[130]

South Carolina Dixiecrats lacked the vocal support of the state's most renowned public figure, James F. Byrnes. Throughout 1948 the former senator, Supreme Court justice, secretary of state, and presidential confidante remained tight lipped and aloof despite numerous entreaties to involve himself in the movement. Privately Byrnes expressed concern regarding federal encroachment on the rights of the states and seemed to support southern independent action, admitting to one confidante that "the South must put itself in the position where its power is felt and where it can no longer be relied upon to furnish the electoral votes necessary to the success of the Democratic party regardless of the policies of the party."[131]

South Carolina's congressional delegation gave Thurmond mixed support. Senator Olin Johnston, a veteran New Dealer who depended on the support of South Carolina labor, announced on August 9 that he would not bolt the regular party, although he did not enthusiastically support the president. Political observers speculated that Johnston expected Thurmond to challenge him in 1950 and hoped to tarnish the governor with a charge of disloyalty.[132] Senator Burnet Maybank, whose strongest support came from the low country and Black Belt counties, announced his tacit support for the States' Rights candidates, as did the rest of the state's congressional delegation, with Congressman L. Mendel Rivers of Charleston among the most vocal.[133]

White South Carolinians did not necessarily believe Thurmond and Wright could win; nevertheless, they saw value in voting for them as a protest action. C. P. Ryan, a physician from Jasper County, bluntly reasoned that "anybody in the South . . . who doesn't vote the States' Rights

Protest Action

ticket is a plain jackass."[134] Even if the average white citizen did not think Thurmond could win, at least one avid supporter hoped he would. The governor's twenty-two-year-old wife, Jean, was excited by the possibility of being first lady. When interviewed by Charles Parmer of the *Washington Post,* Jean Thurmond said that if she should spend the "next four years in the White House, I shall certainly serve grits there." Grits were not the only southern tradition Jean Thurmond hoped to transport to the nation's capital. She told Parmer she would staff the White House with "a group of very faithful Negroes" who currently served the Thurmonds in the governor's mansion in Columbia.[135]

The independent challenges to the South Carolina Dixiecrats got under way shortly after the kickoff of the States' Rights campaign. The Citizen Democrats opened their state headquarters at the Wade Hampton Hotel in Columbia on August 30 and immediately began work to prepare a Truman-Barkley ticket of electors for the November ballot.[136] Aware that their best chance for success depended on support from the DNC, state party representatives met with national chairman Howard McGrath for nearly an hour on September 2. Following the meeting McGrath announced that because "the Dixiecrats are a fourth party movement, deliberately designed by their leaders to aid the Republican party," the DNC would recognize and support the new party pledged to the national Democratic ticket.[137] McGrath further warned southern Democratic Party office seekers that they risked losing their party status if they supported the Dixiecrat presidential ticket, and that prominent Dixiecrats risked forfeiting their spot on the DNC.[138]

Although the DNC encouraged and recognized the pro-Truman party organizations in Mississippi and South Carolina as official Truman electors and as representatives to the DNC, the committee admitted that it had no authority to expel from the party any "duly elected legislators" who might choose to support Thurmond.[139] It could, however, deny them recognition as members of the DNC. Both Thurmond and Marion Rushton of Alabama, who had represented their states on the national committee, had tried to resign, but their respective state committees had refused to accept their resignations. McGrath's assistant William Primm commented that "if these people think they can fight the national party ticket and then come in and ask that they be seated or recognized by the national committee, they are mistaken."[140] Beyond recognizing the new party organizations and sending them small campaign grants, the DNC and the Truman administration approached the Dixiecrat defection with ambivalence and detachment.[141] Clark Clifford later recalled that the president was willing to sacrifice the Dixiecrat states, confident that he would carry the South despite the defections. Clifford advised the president further that "Negro votes in the crucial states will more than cancel out any votes [you] may lose" in the Dixiecrat-controlled states.[142] Aware that maintaining party harmony and keeping the remaining states in the Democratic column required a delicate touch, Truman by and large avoided the South during the campaign and gave no overt encouragement to loyalist factions within the captive states.

The PDP had been turned back at Philadelphia; nevertheless, the group returned to South Carolina determined to continue the fight for civil rights. Despite Judge Waring's July decision, registration restrictions against African Americans continued. John McCray told the *Columbia Record* that he possessed affidavits of voting registration violations in Marion, Marlboro, and Chesterfield Counties charging that registrars required blacks either to present registration certificates or to submit to the regulations necessary to obtain these certificates. Some reported that they had to show poll tax receipts and be able to read and interpret the Constitution to enroll in the party books, prerequisites that violated Waring's order. McCray further claimed that white persons in those counties were able to enroll by merely signing their names in the books.[143] Despite these obstacles, African Americans made considerable gains in some counties. The county chairman of Beaufort reported on August 3 that nearly one-third of that county's enrolled voters were black, and that 1,226 names were added to the party's books during the extended enrollment period ordered by Judge Waring. During the extension only sixty-five whites enrolled.[144] Nearly 30,000 blacks voted in the state's mid-August primary.[145]

After the enrollment books were officially closed, McCray and the PDP focused on the November election. The outspoken black leader did not shy away from denigrating the Dixiecrats' campaign as "the worst hate campaign ever to disgrace America" and Strom Thurmond as "the rabble-rousing . . . inciter of the Ku Klux Klan."[146] Even though the national party had turned its back on the PDP in Philadelphia, McCray still considered the Democratic Party black southerners' best hope. "If President Truman loses we can . . . kiss Civil Rights goodbye," he declared.[147] At a speech in Orangeburg, he discouraged black South Carolinians from supporting Henry Wallace and the Progressive Party, whom he believed had no hope of winning and thus no power to change the situation in the South.[148]

The PDP appointed field captains who fanned out throughout the state's black communities in a "Re-elect Truman" campaign to solicit vote pledges and money to be used to get voters to the polls in November. Although the organization fell short of its goal to get 100,000 black citizens to pledge their vote and $1.00, McCray did receive petitions and pledges of money for the president. Most of the signers contributed $1.00; some, only 25 cents. H. B. Sharon of Horry County, who contributed $5.00 to the campaign, wrote, "I am a Truman man. I wants to stand by the man that stand for me."[149]

McCray remained firm in his opposition to joining forces with the Citizen Democrats as he felt they were not as yet recognized as the state Democratic Party. To align with them at this point, McCray felt, would be self-defeating. Further, the explosive nature of racial politics in South Carolina worked against interracial coalition politics. Any cooperation between the white and black groups would surely be exploited by the Dixiecrats. Indeed, McCray urged black South Carolinians to boycott a Truman rally in Columbia in October because he believed that Dixiecrats were bribing blacks to attend in order to discredit the national Democratic Party.[150]

No one believed that the loyalist organizations in Mississippi and South Carolina would successfully deliver their states from the clutches of the Dixiecrats. Not unreasonably, however, members of the Citizen Democrats and the pro-Truman group in Mississippi hoped that the DNC and the Truman administration would continue to nurture these nascent political organizations as part of a larger commitment to the growth of legitimate, indigenous, and more liberal Democratic southern politics. But for Truman to have interfered in state political organizations would have been political suicide, raising the specter of federal intrusion into state institutions, thus adding fuel to the Dixiecrat fire. Any hope that these new organizations would have of replacing the Dixiecrat groups lay with officeholders and activists interested in remaining loyal to the national party. Unfortunately, these political leaders preferred to keep their heads down and wait out the election, loath to lash themselves to Truman.

★

On the morning of November 2, 1948, States' Rights Democratic Party presidential candidate Strom Thurmond and his wife, Jean, traveled to the Edgefield courthouse to vote. Thurmond maintained the posture of confident candidate, posing for the cameras as he dropped his ballot into the ballot box. After voting, he and Jean drove back to Columbia to await the results.[151]

The presidential election of 1948 has nearly attained the status of a legend. Harry Truman was elected to a term in his own right, defying the predictions of most pundits, who considered him a sure loser. Less surprising was the performance of the States' Rights Democrats, who came in a distant third in the popular and electoral votes. Although the Dixiecrat leaders claimed that from its inception the movement was national, in fact it was exclusively southern. The Dixiecrats received one-fifth of the popular vote in the South, and 98.8 percent of the total Dixiecrat vote was from the South. They carried the four states in which they were listed as the Democratic Party candidates—Alabama, Mississippi, South Carolina, and Louisiana. Truman carried the remaining southern states. The Dixiecrats received one or more votes in only nine states outside the Deep South, and their greatest success of those nine came in the border state of Kentucky, where they garnered 1.3 percent of the total votes cast. The percentages of votes for the Dixiecrats were, in Alabama, 79.8; Arkansas, 16.5; Florida, 10.3; Georgia, 20.3; Louisiana, 49.1; Mississippi, 87.2; North Carolina, 8.8; South Carolina, 72.0; Tennessee, 13.4; Texas, 9.3; Virginia, 10.4.[152]

Those states with the highest percentages of blacks gave Thurmond his largest margins of victory. Furthermore, the States' Rights Democrats were confined not only to the South but (with a few notable exceptions) to the Black Belt region, an area that had previously been most loyal to the Democratic Party because it had never interfered with southern race relations. Studies have confirmed that within a state, counties with a high proportion of blacks tended to vote more heavily for Thurmond, while those with fewer blacks supported Truman. Whites living in areas with a large black population were more responsive to the Dixiecrats' warnings of impending integration than were whites living in areas with a relatively small black population.[153]

South Carolina provides a good illustration of Dixiecrat strengths and weaknesses. In his study of presidential voting in South Carolina, political scientist Donald Fowler found that in the twenty-six counties in the coastal plains or low country area (counties with the highest proportions of blacks) sixteen ranked in the top one-half of all counties for Thurmond. The South Carolina governor fared less well in the piedmont, or upstate, region, where fewer blacks resided. Of twenty counties in the piedmont, thirteen ranked in the upper twenty-three counties in percentage of vote for President Truman. Thurmond captured every county in the state but two: Anderson and Spartanburg, which had low percentages of blacks and significant percentages of textile workers, who were less inclined to be motivated by the Dixiecrats' economically conservative message.[154]

Where the States' Rights Democrats were forced to run as a third party, their fortunes declined considerably. Nevertheless, Thurmond carried three counties in northern Florida, three in the Arkansas delta, two in Tennessee, and twelve in Georgia. The Dixiecrats also made a respectable showing (though short of a plurality) in eastern Texas and southern North Carolina.[155]

Political commentators rushed to deliver post mortem appraisals of what one journalist termed "one of the most conspicuous failures in American political history."[156] True, the Dixiecrats had not achieved their immediate goal of capturing the electoral votes of the Solid South. Traditional political allegiances, fear of party reprisals, intrastate political challenges, and New Deal political inroads kept many voters from supporting the reactionary movement. A year after the election, political scientist V. O. Key Jr. wrote the Dixiecrats' epitaph, saying that their electoral failure represented the last gasp of the Old South, the end of the political power of white supremacist appeals. But analysts who hoped to consign the Dixiecrats to history's dustbin were speaking prematurely. For in spite of its failure at the polls, which historian Numan Bartley has labeled "decisive," the Dixiecrat effort had profound meaning for the South and southern politics. The Dixiecrats' racially charged states' rights agenda would influence numerous political contests in 1950. Support for the Dixiecrats—and disgust with the policies of the national Democratic Party—was stronger than historians have acknowledged, and while New Deal political divisions held, their strength faltered in the face of the increasing vigor of racial politics in the postwar era.[157]

The true strength of Dixiecrat support has been obscured by the Dixiecrats' own strategy. The tenacity of Democratic Party attachments dictated that the Dixiecrats work through state political parties and insist on maintaining the Democratic Party label. In Georgia and Florida, for example, the Dixiecrats had to run as third-party candidates. It is worth noting that in Georgia, Thurmond received over 20 percent of the popular vote. While this was far short of victory and most certainly a disappointment to the States' Rights forces, it indicates a healthy degree of dissatisfaction with the national party and a breakdown in Democratic Party allegiance, no small concern in the rural South. Traditional political loyalty proved to be a major obstacle confronting the Dixiecrats throughout the campaign; for 20 percent of the voters of one state to reject their historic political affiliation and separate their racial politics from their political identity reveals the persistent power of the States' Rights message.

★

Strom Thurmond would later recall fondly his run for the presidency. The Dixiecrats' greatest service, he declared, had been "to pull four states away from the national Democratic Party and show the sky wouldn't fall. Ever since then the South has been independent."[158] While not entirely accurate, Thurmond had touched on something. The Dixiecrats' exercise in political independence, no matter how circumscribed, would serve as a model and a lesson during the next presidential election. Given Strom Thurmond's considerable political skills and longevity, his role in the revival of the Republican Party in the South in the 1960s and its subsequent ascendancy in the 1980s and 1990s, and historians' obsession with "origins," it is tempting to draw a direct line between Thurmond's Dixiecrats and the modern Republican Party. While it is, of course, essential to ponder political developments and recognize fundamental links, it is perhaps more important to remember that historical figures acting in the postwar era were obviously coming from a very different perspective. Although the Dixiecrats did lay some of the groundwork for the two-party South, at the time that is not what they had set out to do. Indeed, as will be shown in the following chapter, Strom Thurmond quickly distanced himself from the Dixiecrats as the votes were being counted. Examination of the Dixiecrat campaign and its results reveals a crucial irony of southern political development: The Dixiecrats sought to recapture lost prestige and power within a party that seemed to be moving away from them. Guided by their own sense of historic loyalty, they attempted to coopt party allegiance. But the mere act of staging a revolt in effect led them to create something new and, as a result, sever forever the relationship between the Black Belt and the national party.

THE CAUSE LOST

The Decline of the Dixiecrat Movement, 1949–1950

I must . . . concede that [Olin] Johnston needs a sound beating, but I also must maintain that he does not deserve it from [Strom] Thurmond.

MODJESKA MONTIETH SIMKINS

South Carolina businesswoman and political activist, 1950

"We shall win that civil rights battle just as we won the election," declared a confident Truman in the wake of his upset victory.[1] Many voters likewise believed Harry Truman's election constituted a mandate on civil rights, and they expected the Eighty-first Congress to heed the message.[2] Senator Hubert Humphrey of Minnesota, new head of the ADA, whose last-minute plea at the national convention had so upset southern conservatives, predicted that Congress would pass the entire Truman program if those who had endorsed civil rights planks at the 1948 Democratic and Republican conventions were "sincere and honest." Members of Congress who reneged on their promises of support, he continued, would "face a lot of trouble in the days ahead."[3]

Many liberals echoed the sentiments of one NAACP leader that Truman's victory represented "a great achievement for democracy [and] a death knell for Dixiecrats," and they waited impatiently for the Dixiecrats to disappear.[4] The States' Rights organization survived the transition into the postelection era, but during the next two years it suffered from the same problems that plagued it in 1948. Almost before the last votes were counted, Strom Thurmond abandoned the organization to its more radical leaders in preparation for his run for the U.S. Senate in 1950, giving credence to critics who believed that his candidacy had been a public relations ploy for national exposure. Lacking the purpose and momentum of a national election, the directionless organization floundered in its attempts to attach itself at the state level. The strength of the States' Rights movement was tested in 1950 in a series of elections interpreted as battles between liberal and conservative forces for the future of the South. The results were mixed. Although the Dixiecrats lost in strategic political contests in South Carolina and Alabama, their opponents unequivocally defended segregation and distanced themselves from the president—effectively usurping the Dixiecrat message of white supremacy while still adhering to a New Deal philosophy. No longer tied to Truman, southern leaders who had passively supported the national Democratic Party in 1948 were free to run on their own records, which demonstrated their firm, effective opposition to civil rights legislation. Their successful melding of New Deal economic achievements with pledges to maintain the racial status quo guaranteed that the color line would be protected in the postwar South.

The Dixiecrats' failure in the 1950 elections demonstrated the difficulty of breaking traditional voting habits in anything other than presidential elections. It was more difficult for Dixiecrat candidates to challenge indigenous southern officeholders with strong segregationist credentials than it was to convince voters to turn away from Harry Truman. But a close look at the elections themselves demonstrates the degree to which the Dixiecrats had poisoned the well of postwar southern politics by forcing candidates who had come into office on platforms of economic liberalism to slug it out with the Dixiecrat candidates for the title of most ardent defender of racial segregation. The fallout from the elections would have disastrous consequences for black civil rights.

★

The party status of wayward southern Democrats remained an open question in the wake of Truman's victory. The president's assistant press secretary Eben Ayers noted in his diary only days after the contest that the president initially favored taking a hard line against party bolters. "I don't want any fringes in the Democratic party," Truman declared in a staff meeting. "No Wallacites and no States' Righters."[5] Many hoped Truman would work to deny southern congressmen committee chairmanships and patronage power and thus make it easier to pass civil rights legislation. In a radio broadcast from Paris on November 8, Eleanor Roosevelt infuriated many white southerners when she urged party leaders to expel the Dixiecrats from the Democratic Party.[6] Some analysts speculated, however, that any attempt by the administration to withhold patronage would result in another southern rebellion.[7] A former senator, Truman remained sensitive to Congress's protection of its prerogatives and acknowledged that the granting of committee chairmanships was a congressional, not a presidential, privilege.[8] Furthermore, the president was eager to consolidate congressional gains and to win passage of his legislative program. The threat of a coalition of Republicans and southern Democrats in Congress curbed any vengeful tendencies Truman might have exercised.

Loyal southern Democrats, while hostile toward the Dixiecrats, believed that punishing the States' Rights supporters could boomerang in the Dixiecrats' favor in future elections. In a region that viewed even the slightest perception of interference of local elections from outsiders with suspicion, a perceived slight could work against the loyalists. South Carolina senator Olin Johnston, who along with many others believed Thurmond planned to challenge him in 1950, worried that "if the [DNC] should try to punish . . . Thurmond, it might react to his advantage."[9] One Truman loyalist in the state commented that for national leaders simply to ignore Thurmond would be "just about the worse [*sic*] treatment you can give a politician."[10]

Ironically, not only did Dixiecrats in Congress go unpunished, but because of congressional seniority rules, States' Rights supporters secured committee assignments that directly impinged on civil rights legislation. Mississippi senator and outspoken Dixiecrat James Eastland took over as chairman of the judiciary subcommittee on civil rights. From this lofty position he could wreak havoc on the administration's civil rights program, with the exception of FEPC and anti–poll tax bills. Eastland surprised no one when, on January 28, he announced that he would filibuster any attempt to limit debate on civil rights legislation.[11] John Stennis, Mississippi's other senator, headed a Rules Committee subcommittee that oversaw anti–poll tax legislation. William Colmer, congressman from Mississippi, was appointed to the House Rules Committee.[12] Whatever his personal feelings, the president refrained from taking any obviously punitive actions or petty potshots. As Truman told one supporter, he had "tried [his] best to keep personalities out of the campaign and to stick strictly to issues."[13] Truman apparently could not resist all opportunities for personal revenge and publicly snubbed the South Carolina governor during the inaugural parade. As Strom and Jean Thurmond rode past the presidential reviewing stand, Strom waved his hat at the president. Truman, stone-faced, nodded curtly and turned away. After the Thurmonds had passed, the president laughed with his entourage.[14] Although Truman denied having done this, the alleged brush-off was big news in South Carolina and inflamed anti-Truman passions there.[15]

In his State of the Union address delivered the first week of January 1949, the president introduced his legislative agenda that collectively came to be known as the Fair Deal, a comprehensive program comprised of proposals rehabilitated from his first term, including plans for public housing, public power development, and health care reform, and new demands such as the repeal of the antilabor Taft-Hartley legislation.[16] Once again the president asked for civil rights legislation. Progress, he declared, depended on "faith in our domestic institutions," and that "faith is embodied in the promise of equal rights and equal opportunities which the founders of our Republic proclaimed to their countrymen and to the whole world."[17]

Harry Truman's Fair Deal proposals convinced States' Rights Democrats that the national Democratic Party had moved even farther from its original principles. The struggle, they declared, must continue. But the disagreements over strategies and goals that had hindered the States' Rights organization during the 1948 campaign spilled over into the post-election era and multiplied exponentially. Minimal cohesion had been achieved during the presidential campaign primarily because all factions were dedicated ultimately to securing votes for Thurmond. With that focus gone and with no discernible leadership, the organization's tenuous unity began to crumble altogether. Many political observers were surprised the Dixiecrats continued to function at all. The *Atlanta Journal* reported that 90 percent of 150 southern daily newspaper editors polled predicted the States' Rights Democrats would fold following the election, which was no cynical prediction, considering that many of these papers remained sympathetic to the States' Rights cause.[18]

In the weeks prior to the election, however, Alabama and Mississippi Dixiecrats began laying the groundwork for a permanent organization. Many States' Righters agreed with attorney Charles W. Collins, author of *Whither Solid South?* and the Dixiecrats' tactician, that Thurmond's campaign had created the basis for a new political party. Dixiecrat leaders convened in Memphis about a week before the election and agreed to continue the fight for "constitutional government and individual liberty" after the election.[19] Although Thurmond vowed publicly to continue to fight for states' rights principles, he proved unwilling to maintain any close affiliation with the movement he had led only a few months ago.[20] The South Carolina governor sent mixed messages to his fellow Dixiecrats. Thurmond wrote to Alabama's Horace Wilkinson in mid-November that he supported the creation of a permanent States' Rights organization to fight all civil rights legislation and promised his active support.[21] To others he refused to commit to any postelection activity and instead counseled patience.[22]

States' Rights leaders, minus Thurmond, shook off their defeat and convened in Birmingham in mid-December 1948 and again in January 1949 to chart their postelection activity. Members, including Barr of New Orleans and Dixon of Alabama, remained divided over whether to create a new party or to organize themselves into a nonpartisan lobbying group. They did little more than plan. The group voted to create a non-profit states' rights institute in Washington with the vague mission of "spreading" states' rights principles. They eventually decided to postpone the opening of the institute, choosing instead to focus their energies on defeating the civil rights legislation pending in Congress.[23]

Thurmond's distancing act gave some influential States' Righters pause. *Birmingham Post* columnist and States' Rights proponent John Temple Graves urged Thurmond to regain control of the movement. "You are the titular leader of the movement . . . and it was for you that more than a million people cast their vote," he pleaded. Furthermore, Thurmond represented the movement's best hope "because you stand for a liberalism . . . that set[s] you apart from most of the leadership."[24] Thurmond admitted to Graves that although the future of the States' Rights movement was important to him, he had "many serious questions" concerning its future course.[25] Clearly, Thurmond was biding his time. With the conclusion of his protest candidacy, he hoped to lay low, anticipating his run for the Senate in 1950. Unwilling to disassociate himself completely from the movement he had, in fact, helped create, he nevertheless wanted to maintain his distance from the more strident members.

With mixed emotions, States' Righters watched as all attempts to pass civil rights legislation in 1949 and 1950 succumbed to congressional deadlock. Although the House voted in January 1949 to curtail the power of the Rules Committee to bottle up legislation through debate, the Senate remained a graveyard for the various civil rights bills, and southern Democrats once again proved themselves most effective through the use of the filibuster. The Senate spent the early months of 1949 wrangling over measures designed to limit debate and the possibility of filibuster.[26] Liberal Democrats in the Senate moved slowly, much to the consternation of civil rights activists.[27] Senate Democratic leaders were caught in a "triangular squeeze" among Republican efforts to promote civil rights legislation, southern Democrats' fierce opposition to any revision of the cloture rule, and the increasingly incessant demands from civil rights groups to amend the rules from a two-thirds to a majority requirement for cloture. The White House, not wishing to jeopardize its relationship with the new Congress, steered clear of this parliamentary debacle. Unwilling to take the lead, the administration avoided civil rights groups demanding action. Presidential assistant Philleo Nash advised, "I know of nothing we could say at this point [to civil rights groups], except that the matter is entirely congressional. This would be so unsatisfactory that I am sure it is better to say nothing."[28]

In private the president remained determined to pursue his civil rights agenda. In a letter to his brother, Vivian, Truman intimated that he expected all bills except the one authorizing a permanent FEPC to pass. When his brother suggested that he sacrifice FEPC legislation, Truman disagreed. The FEPC, Truman argued, "has to be carried to its conclusion," and he stated that he expected "to put the whole [civil rights] program over before I leave this office because it is right."[29] Nevertheless, the administration failed to get any of its desired civil rights legislation passed. Anti–poll tax, antilynching, voting rights, and FEPC measures went down to defeat.[30] In June 1949 congressional watchers reported that the president's program had been "quietly scuttled" by Democratic leaders in Congress who simply buried it in committees, a device that allowed responsibility to be spread widely. The NAACP referred to this method of killing legislation as a "back-door filibuster."[31] By late summer of 1949 little hope remained for any of Truman's civil rights program. The president conceded defeat in October and "agreed to postpone civil rights until the next session," angering many activists. By the summer of 1950 Truman publicly supported civil rights but was unable to bend Congress to his will. In 1951 congressional committees again failed to report on any civil rights measures.[32] Civil rights groups were despondent.[33]

In early February 1949 Dixiecrat delegates from twelve states assembled in Birmingham for another strategy session. Both Thurmond and Fielding Wright were scheduled to attend; however, only the Mississippi governor showed up.[34] The group officially changed its name to the National States' Rights Committee and declared that although it was not a political party, it hoped to have some impact in the 1952 and 1956 presidential elections.[35] Anticipating a repeat of the 1948 revolt in the upcoming presidential election, Alabama's Horace Wilkinson wrote urgently to Frank Dixon that "we should not lose any time organizing a Democratic club in every precinct of Alabama."[36] From their posts in the Deep South, the Dixiecrats watched the congressional fight over Truman's civil rights program with mixed feelings. One Texas Dixiecrat expressed concern that if the southern filibuster proved successful, "our states' rights movement will be more or less left out on a limb because our 'issue' will disappear."[37]

On May 10, 1949, the Dixiecrats held their second annual convention in Jackson, where they created a permanent organization and adopted a constitution, an administrative structure, and a program of action. Again Thurmond stayed away. In an effort to provide some direction for future activities, the organization proceeded to define itself as a states' rights lobbying group whose major goal was to work for a states' rights amendment to the Constitution. The proposed amendment read like a conservative manifesto. It would "preserve local self-government, [and] check the trend toward centralization of power in Washington," and it affirmed that state law predominates over federal in the areas of education, voting rights, race relations, and labor relations. Any federal funding for education "shall be administered exclusively by the states." The amendment would require Congress to settle the national debt and would prohibit deficit spending. Finally, the amendment would prohibit the "nationalization of labor, business, industry or the professions" and would thus provide "a constitutional bar to communism and socialism."[38] The organization had articulated its goals, yet it still lacked the machinery with which to carry them out. Staffing the Washington office posed a problem.[39] Ben Laney and Frank Dixon both declined the position. Outspoken Louisiana millionaire Leander Perez finally assumed the post in August 1949, much to the chagrin of states' rights stalwarts such as Birmingham's John Temple Graves, who rightly placed Perez in the extremist faction.[40]

Thurmond refrained from commenting on the action taken in Jackson. With his eye on the 1950 Democratic primary, he hoped to maintain the support of the States' Rights faithful while running for the U.S. Senate. Thurmond advisor Robert Figg, a Charleston attorney, warned Thurmond that the States' Rights group was trying "to draw a fine line of distinction between a national party and a national organization which the average citizen will not appreciate, but it does permit those interested in it to remain good Democrats in their state organizations at least while believing in the objectives of the National States' Rights Committee." He advised Thurmond to pull back from the inner workings of the States' Rights group in order to "keep from being put in an anomalous position in State politics." Figg worried that if too many South Carolina voters affiliated themselves with the States' Rights organization, "they might not feel qualified to enroll and vote in the Democratic primary next summer."[41] Spartanburg businessman Walter Brown counseled Thurmond likewise to keep his distance from the States' Rights forces, whose proposals he labeled "screwy." Brown understood that Thurmond did not want to be accused of "running out on your crowd"; nevertheless, Brown feared that continued close association with the National States' Rights organization might tarnish Thurmond's reputation.[42] Thurmond concurred and continued to keep his distance.[43]

While the Dixiecrats attempted to cobble together a national organization, the pro-Truman groups in South Carolina and Mississippi, organized during the 1948 presidential campaign, struggled to extend their organizations across their respective states. In Mississippi they reorganized the party from the ground up. Some six hundred loyal white Mississippi Democrats held a mass meeting in July and appointed temporary county chairmen and state officials who called precinct meetings, county conventions, and a state convention. They adopted a statement of principles that endorsed the 1948 Democratic Party platform "with the exception of the civil rights proposal." They declared the States' Rights Party dead and suggested the group "bury their malodorous corpse, seek forgiveness and recognize they can't always fool the real Democrats by appeals to fear and prejudice." Governor Wright denounced the convention of Truman Democrats in a radio address. States' Rights canvassers were sent to leaders warning them to stay away from the meeting; college students were told unofficially by their professors that if they attended, they would not be allowed to graduate.[44]

At a meeting in late July, South Carolina loyalists announced their plans to challenge the Dixiecrat forces for control of the state's Democratic Party by organizing their own competing meetings at the precinct, county, and state levels in 1950. The loyal Democrats sought to create a liberal political coalition and to build loyalist support in every county through Democratic Voters Leagues.[45] Supporters of the national Democratic Party knew they had to work quickly because the States' Rights element was far more organized. According to one loyalist insider, the national Democratic Party had representation in only three counties.[46] One Columbia columnist indicated that "the political strength of the States' Righters and the Truman Democrats is scarcely to be compared; in any election the States' Righters could win, hands down. The Truman Democrats would hardly make a showing."[47]

The question remained, though, concerning who would represent the southern states within the national Democratic Party councils. The DNC was not so quick to forgive and forget the Dixiecrat betrayal. In January 1949 the DNC purged Dixiecrat leaders from the national party. The *Jackson Clarion-Ledger* was quick to report, however, that the replacements made by the national committee in Mississippi applied only to the national level and did not affect state party activities.[48] DNC Chairman McGrath and the president met with pro-Truman Democrats from Mississippi in mid-January and again in May to discuss federal patronage in the state.[49] Philip Mullen of Oxford, vice-chairman of the Mississippi group, reported that the president sanctioned the cleavage in the state Democratic parties. Mullen claimed the president declared that "a two-party system in Mississippi would be a good thing," and McGrath promised to recognize the loyalist organization as the official state party of Mississippi. According to Mullen, Truman stated, "If the Democratic National Committee fails to recognize the pro-Truman group in Mississippi, I will get a committee that will." The pro-Truman group vowed to challenge the reelection of Mississippi's seven congressmen in 1950. As for patronage, the *New York Times* reported that the strong Dixiecrats would get no jobs, the pro-Truman Democrats would get some rewards, and members of Congress who were neither strong States' Rights Democrats nor fervid Truman Democrats would get consideration.[50]

The DNC was scheduled to meet on August 24 to choose a successor to McGrath, who had accepted the position of U.S. attorney general. The Louisiana and Mississippi delegates had not been invited. McGrath stated on August 14 that the pro-Truman Democrats who had been recognized previously by the DNC as national committeeman and committeewoman from South Carolina would "probably be the only ones present" from the Dixiecrat states.[51] Fielding Wright felt that the national representatives from Mississippi, though uninvited, should attend the meeting of the DNC anyway.

Without consulting his fellow South Carolina pro-Trumanites, Ashton Williams, the acting national committeeman, offered to resign in favor of Senator Burnet Maybank provided the States' Rights forces elected the senior senator as national committeeman from South Carolina and the state party realigned itself with the national Democratic Party. Maybank, like other southern senators, had hedged his bet during the past election; not in the forefront of Dixiecrat activity, he nevertheless did not support Truman. The SDEC agreed to Ashton's plan. Dominated by Dixiecrats, the state committee met on August 18, accepted Thurmond's resignation as national committeeman, and elected Maybank.[52] Double-crossed, the pro-Truman Democrats met on August 19 and elected Baptist minister and temperance advocate Maxie C. Collins to replace Williams as their choice for national committeeman.[53]

The State of Columbia predicted that "serious party division has been ended" with Maybank's election. "If the pro-Truman committeemen are seated (as they surely would have been had the developments of the last few days not taken place) then the breach is widened, and the position of the old line party in national affairs further confused." Williams's resignation "took his colleagues of the pro-Truman group by surprise and somewhat left them in the lurch."[54] Williams claimed he made a deal with the States' Rights group because he felt the pro-Truman organization did not have "any conception of what is necessary to restore the Democratic Party to power in South Carolina." He also cited the fact that there were no "responsible political leaders" associated with the pro-Truman movement.[55]

On August 23 the DNC's Credentials Committee met to take testimony from disloyal state party leaders regarding their activities during the 1948 campaign. Maxie Collins testified that since the election, the loyalists had been working to strengthen their organization.[56] The Mississippi committeeman and -woman, J. B. Snider, editor of the *Clarksdale Daily Press,* and Mrs. Hermes Gautier, proudly stated that they had supported Thurmond and Wright in the 1948 election. Nevertheless, Snider declared, "We were duly elected [by our state party]. We feel we have a right to be seated on this committee."[57] Anne Agnew, national committeewoman from South Carolina, stated that although she did not openly support Truman, neither did she actively work for the Dixiecrats.[58] Snider, Gautier, and Agnew were promptly purged from the ranks of the national committee, along with Dixiecrats William H. Talbot of Louisiana and Marion Rushton of Alabama. Maybank was approved but did not take his seat because he had been instructed by the state to refuse unless Agnew was also recognized. The DNC recognized neither Collins nor

Susan Allison, South Carolina's pro-Truman representatives. Truman approved the action taken by the DNC and agreed with McGrath that Dixiecrats had no place on the party's national committee. The president addressed the DNC on August 24 and invited "dissident Southern Democrats to return to the party fold," but only on the basis of the party platform.[59]

The State claimed that in seating Maybank, the DNC had "recognized the State Democratic party of South Carolina as being 'the' Democratic party in South Carolina and that by not recognizing either Mr. Collins or Mrs. Allison that they have 'looked over the heads' of the so-called pro-Truman forces in the state."[60] Meanwhile the pro-Truman Democrats were considering possible court action for national party recognition.[61] Regarding the party split, Olin Johnston predicted that all would be cleared up after the 1950 state convention.[62] Shortly after the DNC debacle, the pro-Truman group in South Carolina quickly disintegrated. Undermined by its own members and lacking support from political heavyweights, the committee decided against holding separate precinct meetings, county or state conventions, or separate primaries in 1950 but chose instead to fight Dixiecrats for control of the regular precinct meetings. One leader of the Democratic Party loyalists stated, "The people will decide whether they want to be Democrats, States' Righters, or Republicans. They can not belong to two parties at the same time, but each individual voter has a right to decide for himself to which party he will belong."[63]

While Thurmond attempted to bide his time until the 1950 Democratic primary, another South Carolinian slowly moved into the states' rights spotlight. Former U.S. senator and Supreme Court justice James Byrnes began to lash out publicly in 1949 at the Fair Deal and the growth of the welfare state.[64] At a speech at Washington and Lee University, Byrnes warned that some of the proposed federal programs threatened to turn the individual into "an economic slave pulling an oar in the galley of the state."[65] By October Byrnes intimated that he was seriously considering a run for the South Carolina governorship in 1950.[66] Byrnes's declarations energized the States' Righters, who hoped that the South Carolina luminary would "give their bandwagon a strong shove," although Byrnes warily kept his distance from the Dixiecrats.[67] Not everyone was thrilled with Byrnes's assumption of the states' rights mantle.[68] Marion Wright, president of the Southern Regional Council and a South Carolina native, referred to Byrnes as "a [Eugene] Talmadge without the red galluses."[69] The White House was particularly worried about Byrnes, who to a degree far greater than Thurmond, commanded regional, even national, respect. They believed he was masterminding a scheme to swing many southern states to Dwight Eisenhower should he oppose Truman or some other New Dealer in 1952.[70]

A States' Rights steering committee met in February 1950 to map out a three-year plan. The group's immediate focus was the 1950 elections. They hoped to organize States' Rights Committees of 100,000 members each in the thirteen southern states. Membership would be $1.00 per person. They divided the southern states into three areas, with a field organizer assigned to each area to assist the state groups. The committee authorized publication of *The States' Righter,* a bimonthly newspaper, and estimated an annual budget of $200,000 based on a projected annual income of $350,000 to be raised from selling subscriptions to the newspaper and from the annual dues.[71]

Thurmond continued to have misgivings about the future of the States' Rights organization. He declined to attend the February meeting and told Wallace Wright that he doubted "seriously the advisability of launching at this time the program that has been outlined." Thurmond, clearly uninterested in leading the movement toward a new political organization, believed that the "proposed organization will appear to the public as another political party set-up, and this will cause many in public office and public life to avoid active affiliation with it." For Thurmond, the lessons of 1948 were clear. "The political strength of the States' Rights [effort] in 1948 was the support given to it by the Democratic party organizations in the states which it carried, and it made little political headway in those states whose Democratic organizations did not support it." Therefore, Thurmond argued, the States' Rights organization should work within the state party organizations and should not create a new party. He believed that southern voters would resent "any outside organization" that would try to tell them how to vote. Moreover, Thurmond felt that concerted action should wait until the 1952 presidential election. "Until that time I think we should confine our activities to our own states."[72] Although Thurmond was unwilling to assume a leadership role in a postelection organization, he maintained loose ties to the States' Rights group.

★

The 1950 midterm elections in the Deep South became a referendum on Harry Truman's Fair Deal as well as a test of Dixiecrat strength.[73] It was difficult to predict how well the States' Righters would do. In spite of the declining fortunes of the Dixiecrats, a Gallup poll in April 1950 demonstrated that nearly a quarter of white southern voters wanted to see them put up a presidential candidate in 1952.[74] Political pundits watched southern state elections closely to determine whether white southerners' dissatisfaction with the national Democratic Party would translate into political change at the state level.

The election results present a complicated picture of the politics of race and class in the South during the period between the New Deal and post-*Brown* eras. In Alabama and South Carolina, where despite Strom Thurmond's attempts to distance himself from the States' Rights organization, there were clear Dixiecrat and national Democratic Party loyalist candidates, the Dixiecrats were defeated. Historians and political scientists have generally interpreted these outcomes as New Deal/Fair Deal victories, illustrations of the persistence of New Deal voting alliances and the triumph of economic interests over racism, and victories for party regularity over political independence and impotency. But if class sympathies determined the outcomes, it was a class politics heavily compromised by race baiting. In Alabama and South Carolina, Democrats who remained loyal in 1948 were now free of Truman and could run on their own records, consistently emphasizing their roles in defeating Truman's civil rights legislation. Democratic Party loyalist candidates in those states won in large measure because they succeeded in presenting themselves as the most able protectors of segregation and pointed proudly to the recent scuttling of the president's civil rights proposals in Congress. Voters rejected the path of political uncertainty promised by the Dixiecrats for the assurances of protection against civil rights legislation that came with Democratic Party representation. In addition, the defeats of liberal incumbent senators in North Carolina and Florida who refused to don the white supremacy mantle were clear, decisive rebukes for New Deal liberalism. Although they did not present their campaigns as clearly pitched battles between loyalists and Dixiecrats, the conservative victors in those two states enjoyed strong support from States' Rights forces.

The first major test of States' Rights strength came in Alabama, where a fierce battle raged for control of the SDEC, the party's governing body and the organization responsible for engineering the state's 1948 Dixiecrat revolt. Although Alabama was also choosing a governor in its May 2 primary, the States' Rights organization concentrated on the race for the seventy-two seats on the committee.[75] States' Rights leaders appointed

Tom Abernethy, a member of the SDEC from the fourth district, a 1948 Dixiecrat elector, and the editor of the *Talladega Daily Home,* campaign chairman. The Dixiecrats began rallying their forces statewide in mid-March. The election issue was simple, Abernethy declared: "Alabama must decide . . . whether she will be bound or free—bound to Trumanism and its civil rights program or free to stand for her self respect."[76] Some States' Rights faithful hoped the experience of 1948 would move the South toward two-party competition. At a States' Rights banquet in April, keynote speaker John Temple Graves urged listeners "not [to] wince anymore when we hear the word 'Republican.' Hell trembled for us once at the hideous name. That was because of the race problem." Blind partisanship was a thing of the past, Graves declared.[77] Despite their enthusiasm, the States' Righters were in trouble from the beginning of the campaign because they were unable to field eight candidates in every district. They faced their stiffest challenges in northern Alabama, where there were few States' Rights enthusiasts. The *Birmingham News* estimated that the loyalist candidates outnumbered the States' Rights candidates almost three to two.[78]

In addition to the Alabama SDEC elections there was a free-for-all gubernatorial race with a fifteen-man field. Leading contenders for the state's top spot included former governor Chauncey Sparks (loyalist); Gordon Persons, president of the public service commission (loyalist); former lieutenant governor and Dixiecrat Handy Ellis; and Birmingham police commissioner Bull Connor, the top States' Rights candidate. Persons assailed the president's civil rights program but came out strongly for fighting these proposals within the party. He warned that Alabama and the South could not afford to "change to new and untried" methods or "experiment on such crucial issues." Reassuring a Montgomery audience, Persons reaffirmed his support for states' rights. "I want no change in our present segregation laws. I am against the FEPC in any manner, shape or form." He also believed there was "no need" for federal antilynching legislation.[79]

The Alabama election received national attention. Unlike in 1948, the loyalists in the 1950 election enjoyed vigorous support from the state's congressional delegation, especially Senators Lister Hill and John Sparkman and Congressmen Albert Rains, Bob Jones, Edward deGraffenreid, and Carl Elliott, as well as support from the state's labor unions.[80] It was a bitterly fought campaign in which the loyalists occupied the stronger position. No longer tied to Truman's civil rights program as they had been in 1948, they campaigned vigorously on their records in Congress. They pointed with equal degrees of confidence and pride to their roles in defeating the president's civil rights program and fighting for New Deal/Fair Deal economic programs.[81]

Loyalists reminded Alabama voters of the benefits of party allegiance. Their radio announcements combined class-based appeals with racism. Of seventeen radio spots approved by Senator Hill, fully one-third emphasized the importance of Democratic Party membership in defeating civil rights legislation.[82] Loyalists effectively distanced themselves from the president. Sparkman stated, "Being a Democrat doesn't mean you have to agree with President Truman on everything. President Truman is not the issue—it is, 'Do I want to be a Dixiecrat or a Democrat?' "[83] At a major loyalist rally at the Temple Theater in Birmingham a week before the election, Senators Hill and Sparkman appealed to both the class and race interests of the audience. Hill told the crowd of approximately 2,000 how the Dixiecrats, whom he identified as large landowners and closet Republicans, had opposed the Tennessee Valley Authority, Social Security, and farm programs. Senator Sparkman added, "You haven't heard of any civil rights legislation enacted into law and it wasn't any Dixiecrat in Alabama that prevented it from being done."[84]

The Dixiecrats found it practically impossible to counter the effectiveness of the loyalists' arguments that the best way to protect segregation was through membership in the Democratic Party. Abernethy warned that the FEPC would "take jobs from white workers and give them to Negro workers."[85] Marking one of the campaign's low points, Wilkinson said he would "rather die fighting for States' Rights than live on Truman Boulevard in nigger heaven."[86] The *Birmingham News* reported that the Dixiecrat forces were using telephone "smear" tactics to sway votes in the closing days of the campaign. Apparently an anonymous caller masquerading as a representative of an African American employment agency called unsuspecting small merchants in remote areas to ask how many blacks they employed. The caller then told the unsuspecting merchants that unless the Dixiecrats won, they would be required to hire more blacks under an FEPC law.[87]

The loyalists emerged victorious, capturing thirty-eight seats to the Dixiecrats' twenty-six; one seat was uncommitted, and seven seats were headed toward a runoff election.[88] Significantly, the Dixiecrats had not been crushed by the Democratic Party machine. Considering the political firepower arrayed against the Dixiecrats, who ran on an empty platform, the loyalists' margin of victory appeared somewhat anemic, and the Alabama press was unimpressed with the magnitude of the loyalist victory. The *Birmingham News* noted that "the States' Righters made enough of a showing to make it seem probable that they will go on with their fight."[89] In the runoff election held on May 30, the Dixiecrats won two seats; the loyalists gained five, giving them a forty-three to twenty-eight majority over the Dixiecrats, with one member uncommitted.[90] The loyalists achieved clear-cut victories in the northern majority white districts, while the States' Righters won decisively in the Black Belt. In the remainder of the districts, the results were inconclusive.[91]

Six hundred cheering faithful convened at the third annual States' Rights convention on May 10, 1950, in Jackson. Vowing to "Fight thru to '52," they voted unanimously to undertake a two-year campaign of "ringing doorbells at the grass-roots level to bring our cause home to the people." The convention approved a nine-point resolution that denounced FEPC legislation and urged fidelity to a states' rights program. Fourteen states had sent delegates, but the majority of participants were from Mississippi, Alabama, South Carolina, Texas, and Louisiana. After much deliberation and consultation, Thurmond attended the meeting and delivered a brief speech.[92] He told the audience that "as an announced candidate for the United States Senate this year I am going to tell the people of South Carolina that if they believe in what President Truman stands for, then don't vote for me."[93] Although he had eschewed leadership of any independent States' Rights group, Thurmond nevertheless believed he could garner political support by addressing the convention and reaffirming his support for states' rights principles.

Around the South, numerous elections captured national attention as pitched battles between States' Rights and New Deal forces. Florida held its primary on May 2, and the U.S. Senate race between incumbent Senator Claude Pepper and Representative George Smathers attracted national attention as a referendum on New Deal liberalism. Pepper, first elected to the Senate in 1936, had established a strong New Deal/Fair Deal record. The Florida senator regularly supported minimum wage and maximum hours bills and compulsory health insurance, and he was moderate on civil rights legislation. Although he supported segregation, Pepper was far from a race baiter. He had been a leader in the Eisenhower boom of 1948; however, after the general refused to consider nomination, and after his own brief stint as a presidential contender had been rejected, Pepper was one of the few officeholders in the South who stumped for the president. George Smathers served as U.S. district attorney for Florida's southern district before being elected to the U.S. House of Representatives in 1946. During the campaign, he succeeded in presenting Pepper as a Communist sympathizer and a threat to segregation, frequently referring to the senator as "Red Pepper." Pepper, Smathers claimed, was "an apologist for Stalin, an associate of fellow travelers and a sponsor for Communist front organizations."[94] Pepper's counterattacks were too little, too late, and Smathers went on to crush him by more than 60,000 votes.[95]

In North Carolina, incumbent Democratic senator Frank Porter Graham faced a stiff challenge in the runoff primary with Willis Smith. Graham, a relative newcomer to party politics, had never held elective office and had been serving as the president of the University of North Carolina when Governor Kerr Scott appointed him to fulfill the term of Joseph Melville Broughton, who had died in March 1949. Graham brought to the office a long history of commitment to social activism and involvement in left-wing causes. As a member of the PCCR, he was particularly vulnerable on the segregation issue. Smith, a former Speaker of the North Carolina House of Representatives and former president of the American Bar Association, was returning to politics after a nineteen-year hiatus. A "progressive conservative," Smith was the type of candidate around whom the anti-Graham forces could coalesce.[96]

Energized by Smathers's victory in Florida, Smith focused his attack on Graham's activist past, challenging his support for the FEPC in particular and exploiting and distorting Graham's moderate racial views. Smith's local campaign committees employed stunts designed to frighten white voters. For example, Smith supporters hired blacks dressed in flashy clothes and conspicuous jewelry to drive through small towns in eastern North Carolina with a "Graham for Senate" banner affixed to the automobile. Flyers and advertisements showed African American soldiers dancing with white women with a caption explaining that Graham supported this type of behavior. Another ad exclaimed, "WHITE PEOPLE WAKE UP!" Did they want "Negroes working beside you, your wife and daughters in your mills and factories? Negroes eating beside you in all public eating places? Negroes riding beside you, your wife and your daughters in buses, cabs, and trains? Negroes sleeping in the same hotels and rooming houses?" As with the Pepper campaign in Florida, the Graham forces were slow to respond to the barrage of attacks on their candidate, and Willis won with a 20,000-vote margin.[97]

Although States' Rights forces had not played a dominant role in the Florida and North Carolina campaigns, States' Rights advocates across the South interpreted the outcomes as victories for their side. An insurance agent from Tennessee wrote to presidential assistant Charles Ross in late June that he should remind the president of the outcome of the senatorial elections in North Carolina and Florida. "These two elections give clear indication that the States' Rights cause is far from being dead."[98] Walter Sillers, Mississippi's Speaker of the House, wrote to Thurmond that the "elections in Florida and North Carolina should convince the most so-called ultra-conservatist that the main issue in the South today is RACIAL."[99] Dixiecrat assistance in the campaigns was not entirely absent. In North Carolina, Dixiecrat leader and textile industry publisher David C. Clark, a Smith supporter, was accused by many in the Graham camp of having distributed some of the more virulently racist campaign materials.

The States' Rights forces fared better in South Carolina, where they demonstrated impressive strength at the precinct, county, and state conventions in April and May. The elections were billed as a showdown between the Dixiecrat forces and the Truman supporters for control of the party. In reality, however, there was no contest. At the county conventions held on April 3, a majority of the state's forty-six biennial conventions came out against the national party and its civil rights platform; thirteen specifically endorsed the state party's 1948 stand against the national party.[100] *The State* reported that the county conventions demonstrated that within the state party the states' rights group remained dominant "and that within its framework our policies would be formed."[101] At the state convention held April 19, South Carolina Democrats reaffirmed their allegiance to states' rights and declared they would " 'beat no retreat' from the stands taken two years ago."[102]

In addition to capturing the local and state conventions, the Thurmond forces in the legislature also took steps to curb the state's burgeoning ranks of registered black voters when it passed a new primary election bill in mid-April to go into effect for the primary in July. The state had been operating without a primary election law since 1944, when South Carolina repealed all of its statutes relating to primaries and sought to regulate the Democratic Party as a private club. The new law required prospective voters to "both read and write" any section of the 1895 state constitution submitted to them by registration officials. The literacy requirement would be waived if the voter owned property worth at least

$300. Formerly a citizen could vote in party primaries after merely signing the club rolls.[103] The *New York Times* estimated that the new state law would reduce black voter registration by at least 50 percent.[104]

In late spring South Carolinians took up the task of choosing both a governor and a U.S. senator. James Byrnes formally announced his gubernatorial candidacy on January 14, 1950. If it had been possible, white South Carolinians probably would have bestowed the office of governor on James Byrnes rather than be bothered with the election.[105] "These are dangerous times in the South for us," a Charleston man wrote Byrnes, and dangerous times called for strong leaders. As George W. McFadden of Clarendon County wrote to Byrnes, "You're the man."[106] The seventy-year-old Byrnes was the fourth candidate to announce for the Democratic primary. He was challenged by Thomas H. Pope of Newberry, Speaker of the state house of representatives; Lester L. Bates, an insurance company executive and Columbia City councilman; and Maurice A. Stone, a lumberman from Florence. In his prepared address, Byrnes noted that when he retired from public life in 1947, he had no intention to return. However, "the trend of political events [has] caused me to express my views of policies affecting the state and nation."[107] When asked during a news conference to comment on the Byrnes candidacy, Truman shot back that Byrnes "was a free agent and could do as he damn pleased."[108]

The gubernatorial race was Byrnes's to lose. The most interesting variable seemed to be whether he would win a majority of the votes to avoid a runoff. The contest to watch in South Carolina became the U.S. Senate Democratic primary, which pitted incumbent Senator Olin Johnston against Strom Thurmond. During the fiercely fought campaign, the candidates, according to a Columbia newspaper, "vied for the title of racial segregation's sincerest champion."[109] Historians have downplayed or ignored entirely the volatility and significance of segregation as a crucial issue in the South Carolina campaign.[110] They have also overlooked a highly significant and ironic element: In a campaign where each candidate strove to present himself as the most able protector of white supremacy and segregation, organized black voters, united behind PDP leader John McCray, held the balance of power in the election. Ultimately the campaign and a highly volatile political atmosphere would have serious ramifications for South Carolina blacks.

Few were surprised when Thurmond finally announced his candidacy for the U.S. Senate in the late spring of 1950.[111] Some of South Carolina's more astute political observers believed his 1948 presidential campaign had been a thinly disguised attempt to gain national exposure and a trial run for the 1950 Senate race.[112] Thurmond immediately made political independence from Washington a major campaign issue. In reference to Johnston's loyalty to the national Democrats in 1948 Thurmond declared, "If honored with a seat in the senate, I will not be one kind of Democrat in Washington and another kind of Democrat in South Carolina." He was entering the race, he stated, because the NAACP "and other bloc organizations have been encouraged by the rulings of a turncoat federal judge who has forced into our primary thousands of voters who do not believe in the principles of the Democratic Party of South Carolina." He vowed to "fight for Americanism and against socialism; for the right of the people of a state to govern themselves and against further centralization of power in the national government; and for the right of South Carolinians to choose who is to represent them in the senate without interference and dictation from far-away bosses who seek to control the government of the United States by having puppets instead of men in the Congress."[113]

Although the candidates debated their positions on other topics such as the Marshall Plan, segregation quickly assumed prominence. From May until the Democratic primary on July 11, the candidates went at each other hammer and tongs, each trying to besmirch the segregationist credentials of the other, no small task for either man. Both were well qualified. As South Carolina's governor and U.S. senator, Olin Johnston had proven himself a strong friend of white supremacy. In April 1944, in the wake of the U.S. Supreme Court decision that opened the Texas all-white Democratic primary to black voters, Governor Johnston summoned a special session of the South Carolina General Assembly to take steps to protect the white primary. Under Johnston's leadership, the general assembly repealed all statutes that specifically pertained to primary elections.[114] As a U.S. senator, Johnston proved himself an ardent foe of President Truman's civil rights program.[115]

Many white southerners as well as seasoned political commentators made connections between the Pepper-Smathers contest, the Graham-Smith contest, and the Johnston-Thurmond contest, as well as the South Carolina gubernatorial primary. States' Rights conservatives hoped the races in Florida and North Carolina signified an anti–New Deal contagion that eventually would sweep into South Carolina. One advertisement used by the Thurmond campaign shows a baseball game with the caption, "The South is Pitching! Strike 1 was Pepper; Strike 2 was

Graham; Strike Three will be Johnston . . . and Truman's Force Program will be OUT!"[116] Thurmond's advisor Robert Figg hoped that Thurmond could capitalize on the "successful outcome of the North Carolina second primary."[117]

The campaign's format made the contest that much more explosive. Following an age-old tradition, all candidates for office in 1950 campaigned together during a five-and-a-half-week tour that took them to every county in the state. This precipitated some potentially combative and physical encounters between the senatorial candidates. Once the campaign was under way, Thurmond wasted no time attacking Johnston's record on segregation. Because Johnston had not supported the Dixiecrats in 1948, Thurmond referred to the senator as Truman's "fair-headed" boy, accusing Johnston of pandering to Truman and abandoning the state. He criticized Johnston for failing to use his office to fight the desegregation of the armed forces in 1948 and argued that Johnston's support for federal aid to education would give the federal government license to interfere in state schools. Thurmond also criticized Johnston's record as governor and accused him of running a pardon racket that released some 3,000 dangerous criminals onto South Carolina's streets. Playing on voter fear, Thurmond gave crime a black face. He told audiences of an incident from 1947 when a black male convict, Dave Dunham, pardoned by Johnston, attacked a white veteran from Chester County. Said Thurmond, "Dave Dunham was the instrument of death but in reality it was the pardon racket which ended the life of this young Chester County veteran."[118]

During the first month of the tour, Johnston ignored Thurmond's personal attacks, preferring to run his campaign on what he called "Christian principles."[119] Johnston defended his segregationist record, citing his opposition to the FEPC and to other aspects of Truman's civil rights program.[120] He reminded audiences how he protected the white primary in South Carolina and asserted that "I am not for the races mixing because God did not mix them himself."[121] He defended his position on federal aid to education, claiming that instead of threatening schools with desegregation, the money actually allowed southern states to build truly equal schools for African Americans. This would allow states to stave off court-ordered desegregation.[122] The Supreme Court's decisions in the civil rights cases *Sweatt v. Painter* and *McLaurin v. Oklahoma Board of Regents* in early June inadvertently strengthened Johnston's position. The Court did not overturn the separate-but-equal doctrine, but it demanded equalization of educational facilities, a potentially costly endeavor for southern states.[123] Following the court's decision, Johnston declared, "In view of the present chaotic condition of the state's finances it is obvious that South Carolina cannot afford to provide separate and equal school facilities for both races."[124]

Each candidate probed for weaknesses in his segregationist foe. Neither missed an opportunity to vilify Federal Judge Waring of Charleston, who had opened South Carolina's white Democratic primary to black voters in 1947. Next to kissing babies, demonizing the judge and his northern wife had become a South Carolina campaign ritual. Thurmond claimed that the Warings were avid Johnston supporters. Johnston vowed to work for the judge's impeachment.[125] By late June both candidates were aggressively race baiting. Johnston set the first trap when he accused Thurmond of breaking down segregation by appointing an African American doctor, T. Carl McFall, to the Advisory Council of the South Carolina Medical Association. In his campaign advertisements, Johnston proclaimed that this appointment illustrated how, under Thurmond's governorship, the state was experiencing its first desegregation since Reconstruction. Johnston also brought up a letter Thurmond had sent to William Hastie, governor of the Virgin Islands. Unaware that Hastie was black, Thurmond's office had sent him an invitation to stay in the governor's mansion should he ever come to Columbia.[126] Thurmond insisted the letter was an administrative error.

To win white votes, each candidate sought to prove himself sufficiently segregationist, yet each kept a wary eye on African American voters. Both Johnston and Thurmond were well aware of the potential of this significant minority voting bloc. By 1950 there were approximately 73,000 registered black voters in South Carolina, and the PDP could boast chapters in the majority of the state's counties, with many counties organized down to the precinct level.[127] Strom Thurmond's advisors and political allies, in particular gubernatorial candidate Byrnes, kept close tabs on the PDP and worried about the potential strength of the black vote. Correspondence among these politicians describes voter education meetings organized by the PDP and other political action groups. According to their reports and to sample ballots circulated by the PDP, neither Byrnes nor Thurmond could expect African American support. Their advisors were especially concerned that a combination of unified black and labor electorates could spell trouble for these candidates.[128]

While Johnston never actively or overtly cultivated black votes, both camps generally agreed that blacks favored him over Thurmond. Although black voters were well aware of Johnston's dismal civil rights record, they championed Johnston's support of New Deal and Fair Deal labor and economic policies aimed to assist the working class and the poor. Furthermore, blacks were intensely loyal to the national Democratic Party. Black voters wagered that they had absolutely nothing to gain by voting for Thurmond, whose maverick tendencies and Dixiecrat candidacy left them cold. The Dixiecrats, John McCray once commented "offer Negroes nothing but [hard] times . . . , trouble, bloodshed, death, and terror."[129] There was no chance the PDP would support Thurmond, yet African Americans were hardly excited or energized by the prospect of voting for Johnston. Possibly they would have declined to support either. But as the primary season heated up, John McCray was indicted for libel. This case, which involved McCray's publication of allegations of consensual sex between a black man and a white teenager, set off a series of events that eventually landed McCray on a chain gang and destroyed the *Lighthouse and Informer,* the state's leading black newspaper. African Americans interpreted McCray's indictment as a politically motivated attempt by the Thurmond forces to intimidate them and thus minimize the impact of the black vote. Incensed, organized black voters threw their support to Olin Johnston. This example illustrates with distressing clarity the toxic political atmosphere that enveloped the South in the wake of the Dixiecrat campaign. Even if Thurmond did not have a hand in McCray's indictment, black voters believed he did and voted accordingly. Thurmond did, in fact, try to capitalize on the case by tying Johnston to the black journalist and to the alleged libeling of a white woman, thereby elevating himself as the protector of white womanhood.

John McCray's indictment for libel in January 1950 stemmed from a rape case a few months earlier. On August 9, 1949, the *Greenwood Index-Journal* reported that a search was under way for a black male suspected of robbery and attempted rape of a sixteen-year-old white girl, the daughter of a politically prominent Greenwood citizen. According to the newspaper, Greenwood police were looking for a "husky," "strongly built" black male.[130] The next day police identified the wanted man as Willie Tolbert Jr., a twenty-five-year old, 5′ 9″, 150-pound black man from Greenwood. A city employee, married with one child, Tolbert had served two prior prison terms for purse snatching and petty larceny.[131] He eluded police for three days. After a massive manhunt that covered Greenwood and neighboring Laurens County and included 100 law enforcement officials, 1,000 private citizens, a pack of bloodhounds, and three airplanes, Tolbert surrendered to police at his home on August 11.[132] Tolbert's NAACP attorney Harold Boulware stated that his client categorically denied all charges. Boulware did not elaborate on Tolbert's version of the incident, but he did indicate that his client's statement varied greatly from the newspaper account. The Greenwood County prosecutor claimed that Tolbert admitted that he twice raped the girl.[133]

Willie Tolbert's trial began on September 12 and lasted one day. The state presented seven witnesses, including an FBI agent, the white teenage girl, and her eighteen-year-old white male companion.[134] The physical evidence indicated sexual intercourse had occurred, although no definitive match to the male suspect or another partner was possible.[135] The highlight of the trial came late in the afternoon when the girl took the stand. The teenager testified that she and her date had been to a movie and a local hangout for something to eat. After driving around, they pulled off the road and parked the car. They had been there less than five minutes, according to both their statements, when the girl spotted a black male, allegedly Tolbert, approaching the car. She locked her door, and her companion tried to start the car. Before he could do so, Tolbert had opened the door on the driver's side and pushed the boy over, taking the car keys. The girl jumped out and ran. Tolbert overtook her and caught her by the arm. Both the boy and the girl testified that Tolbert put his hand around her throat and threatened to kill the girl if the white boy advanced on him. Tolbert held her by the neck and walked her back to the car. Then, she testified to a tense and silent courtroom, he kissed her and boasted, "Now, don't say you've never been kissed by a Negro in South Carolina." He put his hand on her dress and started lifting it, she testified, but her white companion knocked Tolbert's hand away. She broke away and ran, but the black man again caught her. This time he told them he would let them alone if they gave him some money.

Tolbert forced the couple back into the car. Then he told them if they engaged in the sexual act, he would let them alone. The girl testified that, in her opinion, Tolbert hoped that by forcing the white boy to have sex with the girl, he could then implicate him in the rape he planned to commit. The couple climbed into the backseat, and Tolbert knelt on the front seat to watch them. Meanwhile, they had whispered to each other that they would fake the act. Tolbert turned on the light, she said, saw they were faking, and ordered the boy out of the car.

Again Tolbert caught the girl by the throat, she said, and told her escort that he would kill her if the boy resisted. The white boy testified that he walked around the car, dazed, searching, he claimed, for a stick or a rock. He tried to get the car keys out of Tolbert's pocket, he said, but Tolbert threatened to hit the girl. At this point Tolbert raped her. She became most frightened, she testified, when Tolbert threatened to impregnate her.

Afterward Tolbert got behind the wheel and ordered the young man into the front seat and the girl into the back, and the three took off on a wild ride that covered two counties at breakneck speed. All the while Tolbert threatened to wreck the car and kill them all if anyone attempted to move or get away. During the ride he stopped twice for gas and cigarettes. The girl had allegedly written the word "Help" in lipstick on the outside of the car, but none of the three gas station attendants had noticed it. However, the attendants later testified that they had seen the threesome that night. After two hours Tolbert returned to the spot where he had originally approached the couple. According to the girl, as Tolbert left them he boasted, "Some Negro will die for this, but it won't be me."[136] In their statements, neither the girl nor her companion mentioned a weapon.

The teenager's testimony regarding the events of August 9 was nothing less than fantastic. Perhaps most disturbing was the scripted quality of her "recollection" of Tolbert's comments regarding the alleged rape. According to her testimony and to the words she attributed to Tolbert, this was not an act of power, violence, humiliation, or rage but one of sexual desire. Her testimony made it apparent that Tolbert understood the social taboos and lethal consequences that stemmed from sexual relations between a black man and a white woman, but as her story demonstrated, he was willing to risk death just to have her. Indeed, the white teenager declared that Tolbert wanted nothing less than to force her to bear his child. Her testimony closely resembled southern whites' collective fantasies and fears about African American men. Having been raised in the South, the girl must have known that such an account would play well to a small-town jury. Tolbert did not take the stand in his own defense. The white male jury took only ten minutes to convict Tolbert of rape, and the judge imposed the sentence: death by electrocution.[137] No appeal was filed on Tolbert's behalf, and he was executed on October 28, 1949.[138]

Following Tolbert's conviction but prior to his execution, two newspapers—the *Lighthouse and Informer* and the *Anderson Independent*—published similar stories about his case. The *Lighthouse and Informer* piece, written by editor John McCray, was based on an earlier meeting between Tolbert and his NAACP attorney.[139] The story for the *Anderson Independent* was written by Associated Press reporter Deling Booth, who was granted an interview with Tolbert the night before his execution. Both journalists reported that Tolbert maintained his innocence. Tolbert told both men that he had been with the young couple that night and that they had asked him to find them some whiskey. Although he admitted to having sex with the young woman, Tolbert insisted that it had been consensual. Indeed, he claimed that the girl's date had offered her to Tolbert after the white couple had sexual relations in the backseat of their car.[140]

On January 4, 1950, the Greenwood County grand jury indicted McCray and Booth for criminal libel. The indictments, which were brought by the county solicitor, who happened to be the girl's father, charged both men with maliciously publishing false and defamatory statements with the intent to injure the reputation of the girl.[141] Neither journalist published the girl's name, but the grand jury held that the stories nonetheless defamed her character in the eyes of those who had been in the courtroom and who knew her identity. The *Chicago Defender* closely followed the case, which it considered a clear "challenge to the freedom of the press, one of the most fundamental principles of our democratic system."[142] Booth had the resources of the Associated Press at his disposal, and his case never came to trial. John McCray, however, would eventually pay a substantial fine and serve time on a county chain gang.

McCray's first concern was whether he could receive a fair trial in Greenwood County. This problem ostensibly was solved when McCray was granted a change of venue to neighboring Newberry County. McCray had presented affidavits from local Greenwood citizens stating that due to the nature of the crime for which Tolbert was convicted, in their opinion McCray could not receive a fair trial.[143]

But even with a change of venue, McCray's chances for exoneration appeared slim.[144] NAACP litigator Thurgood Marshall and the Legal Defense Fund provided research assistance and helped prepare the case for trial, but all parties agreed that their best chances for acquittal from an all-white jury lay with a local white defense attorney.[145] Not surprisingly, McCray encountered difficulty locating suitable counsel. He confided to one friend that the white attorneys he contacted were reluctant to go up against the victim's politically well-connected family.[146] One attorney confirmed McCray's suspicions by agreeing that few white lawyers in South Carolina would even attempt to defend in court the statements printed in McCray's article. Even if he could find a white attorney to represent him, conviction was almost a foregone conclusion. Where the reputation of a white woman was involved, a jury would be more apt to bring a verdict that stemmed from their passions and prejudices rather than law.[147] Finally, on the advice of counsel, McCray pleaded guilty on June 19, 1950, to the charge of criminal libel. It was the opinion of Marshall and others that should this case make it to trial, McCray would almost surely be convicted and would end up serving a year on a chain gang. Marshall and others believed that whoever was behind this case intended to incarcerate McCray, remove him from the political scene, and subsequently destroy the *Lighthouse and Informer.* They believed that if McCray pleaded guilty, he at least would stay out of jail and could continue publishing the newspaper. As it turned out, McCray was fined $3,000 and given a suspended sentence with three years' probation. McCray also had to publish a statement proclaiming his guilty plea and his sentence on the front page of the *Lighthouse and Informer.*[148]

In August 1951 McCray's parole was revoked after he traveled to Illinois to deliver a political speech. Under the terms of his parole, he was not allowed to leave the state without permission. McCray maintained that he had received permission. His case was appealed to the state supreme court, which affirmed revocation and ordered McCray into the custody of the Newberry County chain gang, where he served time from November 11 until December 18, 1952. NAACP legal counsel Jack Greenberg speculated that then-governor James Byrnes, angered by the *Lighthouse and Informer*'s support of the Clarendon County school desegregation cases, engineered the revocation of McCray's parole in an effort to destroy the newspaper.[149]

Because of McCray's prominence as the head of the PDP and as the editor of the state's leading black newspaper, the black community regarded his indictment and inevitable guilty plea as political persecution. In their opinion, McCray's predicament was the result of a thinly disguised attempt at intimidation and disfranchisement. Because of the political position of the girl's family, many blacks believed that the indictment had been engineered by Thurmond's forces to intimidate them, destroy the *Lighthouse and Informer,* keep them from the polls, and thus prevent them from casting their votes for Johnston. Whether McCray's indictment was politically motivated or not is a moot point. What is important is the perception of the African American community. From the moment of his indictment until his guilty plea, the African American community, in South Carolina and nationwide, rallied around McCray. Aware of the importance of the *Lighthouse and Informer* as a political vehicle, members of the black press around the country swung into action. The National Negro Press Association and a host of publishers of prominent black newspapers such as the *Pittsburgh Courier,* the *Chicago Defender,* and the *Norfolk Journal and Guide* organized the Lighthouse Defense Committee to offer guidance and financial support. They collected several thousand dollars for McCray's defense and fine, which had grown to about $10,000.[150] In South Carolina McCray utilized the extensive PDP network to raise funds. He received contributions from individual black business owners, teachers' associations, and fraternal organizations.[151] PDP county clubs, local NAACP chapters, and community and church groups proclaimed John H. McCray days and held mass meetings, teach-ins, and rallies designed to educate the black citizenry and to collect funds. Lists of contributors from these events indicate that most were able to donate a dollar or two, no doubt at great personal sacrifice.[152] Even a group of eighth graders from a Florence, South Carolina, high school contributed $10 to McCray's defense.[153]

This coming together of the African American community was fueled by a collective sense of outrage at this perceived attempt at intimidation. Supporters wrote long, heartfelt messages of hope to McCray and placed his legal troubles in the context of their larger struggle for political freedom. Most believed that his indictment was a setup and that he was being persecuted because of his influential position within their community.[154] McCray and other African American leaders were convinced that the Greenwood case had ties to the race between Johnston and Thurmond. Political activist Modjeska Simkins and others attributed McCray's indictment to Thurmond's Dixiecrat supporters, and she implored blacks to vote for Johnston. She reminded black voters that while Olin Johnston was hardly a palatable choice, Thurmond's Dixiecrats had organized for the sole purpose of opposing civil rights. Johnston was the lesser of two evils. Simkins admitted that Johnston's campaign race baiting was contemptuous. However, she insisted that Thurmond forced Johnston into a corner. She and other African American leaders were not blind to political realities. "While it is most unfortunate" that Johnston engaged in race baiting, she claimed, it would have been "political suicide" for him to allow Thurmond's charges to go unanswered. In her opinion, South Carolinians' best hope of ridding state politics of "the Negro question" was for blacks to vote and defeat Thurmond.[155] McCray later mused that for black voters, the choice in the 1950 election was between two snakes, one three feet long and another six feet long. They chose the smaller snake.[156]

Thurmond did not pass up the opportunity to take political advantage of the libel case. In June he ran an advertisement claiming that Johnston was in the Greenwood courtroom when McCray—identified in the ad as a defamer of white womanhood and an enemy of Strom Thurmond—requested and received a change of venue in his case, implying that Johnston had somehow intervened on behalf of defendant McCray.[157] The Greenwood newspaper published a front-page denunciation from the judge in the McCray case concerning this advertisement. The judge vehemently denied that Senator Johnston had discussed McCray's case with him, and in a later campaign advertisement, Johnston denied that he had tried to help McCray.[158]

The outcome of the election surprised many. Johnston defeated Thurmond by a margin of approximately 30,000 votes.[159] Contemporary analysts and historians agree that Johnston benefited from the relatively solid vote of labor, particularly textile workers in the upstate region, and African Americans.[160] Approximately 40,000 black South Carolinians voted, and they voted overwhelmingly for Johnston.[161] Returns from predominantly black precincts in Charleston and Columbia support this contention.[162] Thurmond's advisors generally felt that black voters also cut into their comfort margin in the rural Black Belt counties, an area where their candidate historically had done well. Thurmond's forces conceded that they had underestimated the level of African American organization in rural precincts.[163] The evidence suggests that while Thurmond received the majority of the white Black Belt vote, he did less well in those rural counties that supported strong Progressive Democrat organizations.[164]

Olin Johnston had been one of Franklin Roosevelt's most staunch southern supporters, yet his victory over Strom Thurmond, like the victory of the loyalists in Alabama, illustrated how far New Deal politicians in the South had strayed from the platforms of the 1930s and the great extent to which the political atmosphere had been poisoned by the politics of race. Trumpeting their records of opposition to civil rights, and no longer tied to Harry Truman, Johnston and the Alabama loyalists defeated their Dixiecrat rivals by convincing the white voters that party loyalty in congressional elections was the best means by which to safeguard their economic and their racial interests. Technically, the Dixiecrats had lost the battles of 1950, but they had inflicted considerable damage along the way. In the long run, southern politics in general and southern blacks in particular were the real losers, as race once again dominated southern political contests.

To almost no one's surprise, James Byrnes won the South Carolina governorship by a huge margin of almost 150,000 votes. His victory was interpreted as a significant defeat for Truman, and South Carolina's new governor appeared to be the perfect choice to inherit the leadership of the states' rights forces. This was good news for states' rights supporters, for by the end of 1950 the National States' Rights Organization was in serious trouble. The defeat of the Dixiecrat candidates in 1950 had effectively nailed the coffin shut on the formal movement. Furthermore, the organization's fund-raising schemes had not proved profitable, and the major cost of maintaining the office had fallen to Louisiana, Mississippi, Alabama, and Texas.[165] In December Frank Dixon informed Wallace Wright that Alabama's states' rights organization had disintegrated and that the state therefore would not be capable of contributing to the maintenance of the national office.[166] Hardcore Dixiecrats would continue efforts to resuscitate the organization—to no avail. Any further attempts at independence from the national Democratic Party would be left to the individual southern states to decide for themselves.

7

CUT FREE FROM THE MOORINGS

Presidential Politics in the South in the 1950s and 1960s

We have always classed ourselves as Democrats, but have voted Republican lately. But I would classify myself as independent.

ANONYMOUS MISSISSIPPI FARM WOMAN

1967

As the 1952 presidential election drew near, Mrs. Claude H. Girardeau, custodian of the Confederate relic room in Columbia, South Carolina, puzzled over the candidates. Once again, as in 1948, loyal white southern Democrats like Girardeau struggled with the clash of traditional voting habits, ingrained political deference, and an uncompromising stand on segregation. Proudly declaring herself an unreconstructed rebel, Girardeau recalled fondly how as a child she had seen Wade Hampton's Red Shirts march through Camden during the closing days of Reconstruction and how this had shaped her political allegiances. "I'll vote like [Governor] Jimmy Byrnes tells me to," she said. "But if he votes for a Republican, then I won't." She continued, "If I vote for Stevenson, the Democrat, I vote for a candidate favorable to the FEPC, and I am opposed to that. And if I vote for General Eisenhower, I'll be voting for a Republican, and I am still a rebel," she said as she considered her options. "I just don't know," she sighed. "Maybe I won't vote."[1]

In the early 1950s the fear of a general assault on southern schools became more widespread as the civil rights court cases began, piece by piece, to erode the South's wall of segregation. Southern whites concerned about federal encroachment into the rights of the states searched desperately for a solution. As the presidential election neared, many longed for an alternative to the national Democratic Party, which, they believed, remained unresponsive and insensitive to the region's demands.

Crippled by dwindling finances and an equally diminished reputation, the National States' Rights Organization proved incapable of providing the necessary leadership to unhappy southern conservatives. States' rights advocates across the South turned instead to South Carolina governor James Byrnes for direction. Addressing the annual Southern Governors' Conference in Hot Springs, Arkansas, Byrnes articulated a position that ardent states' righters would follow for the next several years. Proclaiming a course of political independence in presidential elections, Byrnes declared the South owed no loyalty to party or candidate. He warned that "in 1952 Southerners will look beyond the wrappings to see what's in the [political] package."[2] Following his lead, many states' rights advocates refused to return to the national Democratic Party fold, although they stopped short of creating a separate political organization. Instead, former Dixiecrats and other states' rights enthusiasts confined their activities to their particular states and attempted to maintain independence from the decisions made at the Democratic National Convention. Unwilling to support national party nominee Adlai Stevenson, averse to resurrecting the Dixiecrat organization, and not yet ready to join the Republicans, states' rights advocates became presidential Republicans, organizing independent parties to promote Dwight Eisenhower's candidacy.

The staging ground in the fight for states' rights changed dramatically following the Supreme Court's decision in *Brown v. Board of Education* in 1954. No longer confined to the ballot box, states' rights defenders went to work in communities throughout the South, organizing at the grass roots to forestall desegregation orders. The most powerful of these massive resistance organizations was the White Citizens' Councils, which by the end of 1955 claimed chapters in every southern state. After the court decision, southern politics and white southern life successfully and intensely focused on race and the defense of segregation. The organized resistance to federal encroachment into the rights of the states that had begun with the Dixiecrat campaign spread with a terrible fury and did not abate until well into the next decade.

★

The National States' Rights Organization drew its last official breaths just as the NAACP's civil rights strategy was gaining momentum. The Supreme

Court had found in the NAACP's favor in the *McLaurin* and *Sweatt* suits in 1950 that mandated equal facilities for black students. In December the NAACP filed suit in *Briggs v. Elliott,* a Clarendon County, South Carolina, case that directly attacked the "separate" provision in the separate-but-equal doctrine established in *Plessy v. Ferguson* (1896). Aware that the tide was turning against them, southern lawmakers scrambled to delay, or in some cases prepare for, the inevitable.

In 1951 Byrnes successfully lobbied for a 3 percent sales tax and a $75 million bond issue to fund a massive school building program to equalize black schools in an effort to stave off court-ordered desegregation. "South Carolina need have no fear that white children and colored children will be forced to attend the same school," Byrnes declared in late January 1951 in his first message to the state legislature. "The white people will see to it that innocent colored people will not be denied an education because of selfish politicians and misguided agitators."[3] Lobbying before the South Carolina Education Association in March, Byrnes argued that the state should improve black schools "because it is right" but also because "it is wise in view of the suit."[4] With the Clarendon County case already before the federal courts, Byrnes hedged his bets. In 1952 the state legislature approved a measure, to be presented as a referendum to voters in November, to close the state's public schools if the Supreme Court overturned *Plessy*.[5]

Governors across the South took strong stands in defense of segregation. In April 1951 Mississippi's Fielding Wright declared that his state would protect racial segregation "regardless of costs or consequences."[6] Georgia's Herman Talmadge, recently elected to a full four-year term in 1950, likewise emerged as one of the region's staunchest defenders of segregation and states' rights. A *New York Times* correspondent would later dub Talmadge "the South's foremost spokesman of 'white supremacy.'"[7] Following the *Sweatt, Henderson,* and *McLaurin* decisions, Talmadge declared, "As long as I am Governor, Negroes will not be admitted to white schools."[8] In 1951 the Georgia legislature approved an appropriations bill that denied funds to any desegregated public college or university.[9]

Many white southerners anticipated that the 1952 presidential election would be as contentious as the 1948 race. It was unclear, though, to whom disgruntled southern Democrats could turn. The National States' Rights Organization disintegrated as the more moderate membership turned away. By May 1951 Birmingham columnist John Temple Graves had disassociated himself from the States' Rights organization entirely and confided to Thurmond his feeling that the group should disband: "I am certain . . . that only harm can come . . . from further association with Laney, Perez, Wilkinson, and company, and that this is the only way to get those albatrosses from our necks." Although he was unwilling to publicly express his displeasure with the States' Rights group, Thurmond assured Graves that "you and I think a great deal alike."[10] *The State* newspaper, once an avid supporter, admitted that "the States' Rights movement . . . needs heavy shots of vitamins and vitality if it is to be of any assistance in the American scene" in 1952.[11] That desperately needed revitalization never came, and the National States' Rights Organization quietly folded, unceremoniously closing its Washington bureau in August 1952.[12]

Thurmond retired to his private law practice in Aiken, South Carolina, following his loss to Senator Olin Johnston in 1950. He eschewed any public association with the states' rights movement, telling one supporter that "since I am now out of politics and practicing law, it will be incumbent upon some of these persons who are Governors or Senators to take the lead in the movement this time."[13] Despite his new life as a private citizen and his disavowal of formal association with the Dixiecrats, Thurmond nevertheless continued his involvement in South Carolina states' rights activity. In particular he oversaw the administration of more than $18,000 remaining from the 1948 Dixiecrat campaign earmarked to promote "states' rights principles." He announced that the money would be used "to reaffirm Southern political independence."[14] Thurmond also worked to get the state's new governor, James Byrnes, to assume leadership of the movement, probably in an effort to separate the states' rights movement from its present discredited leadership.[15] Thurmond had not slipped quietly into political retirement; he was simply regrouping.

Thurmond wanted Byrnes to "[point] the way for our people" in 1952.[16] Byrnes responded that while he appreciated Thurmond's sentiments, "I will not seek such leadership. I am sure no effort will be made to thrust it upon me; but should I be urged to assume the role of leadership, either as a candidate for national office or without being a candidate, I would decline to assume that role."[17] Thurmond nevertheless believed that Byrnes would assume leadership of the states' rights movement "at the appropriate time."[18] He wrote to Horace Wilkinson that "Governor Byrnes is a man of national prestige and we are extremely anxious for him to be active and I feel confident now that he will be."[19]

Despite his coolness to the official states' rights organization, Byrnes was recognized as the "South's chief strategist."[20] He spent much of

Governor James F. Byrnes of South Carolina. Photograph courtesy of Special Collections, Clemson University Libraries, Clemson, South Carolina.

1952 traveling across the South, addressing state legislatures and private groups on the importance of states' rights and political independence. Speaking at the annual Southern Governors' Conference in Gatlinburg, Tennessee, in late 1951, Byrnes stated flatly his opposition to another term for Truman and acknowledged the possibility of another southern revolt, depending on the nominee.[21] In a speech to a joint session of Georgia's general assembly in early February 1952, Byrnes declared that "we must let the leaders of all political parties know that the electoral vote of the South [can] no longer be taken for granted." He promoted Richard Russell's candidacy and urged all white southerners to "stand up and fight."[22] Political writer Jack Bell acknowledged that Byrnes planned to "fight to the last ditch," and unlike the 1948 effort, "his will be no heedless half-effective bolt."[23] *The State* noted that "if a revolt [in 1952] becomes necessary, plans should be laid more carefully, with official delegates from the several southern states attending. They should be appointed by the Democratic party in each state. Then the movement would be tied in with the existing organization."[24]

Mississippi continued to be a stronghold of states' rights support. In May 1951 Fielding Wright advocated a repeat of the 1948 revolt, with supporters to be drawn from both the Republicans and the Democrats. Speaking before the National Cottonseed Products Association, the Mississippi governor advocated the creation of a third party based on "states' rights and Americanism." Wright declared, "The old traditional Republican party is too reactionary to inspire confidence. The present party in power has lost the confidence of the American people and I am convinced will not be returned to office." He suggested the southern states attend the Democratic National Convention "and demand all socialistic planks and those repugnant to the South be deleted." They should also hold their state conventions in recess should they need to reconvene to reinstruct their electors. Although supportive of a third party effort, Wright announced that he was through with politics when his term ended in January 1952.[25] The Mississippi SDEC met in June 1951 and reaffirmed its opposition to President Truman, and all candidates for the 1951 gubernatorial primary pledged allegiance to the states' rights movement. Former governor Hugh White, who had served his first term in the 1930s, was elected to a second term on a campaign that opposed the FEPC and all other civil rights legislation and supported states' rights and industrial development. He also succeeded in presenting himself as the strongest segregationist candidate. Following the election, Wright confided to Thurmond that Mississippi would be "safe" with governor-elect White.[26]

The states' righters' strategy in 1952 depended in part on whether Harry Truman would run again for president. Although Truman had written in his diary on April 16, 1950, that he was "not a candidate for nomination by the Democratic Convention" in 1952, he remained silent on the question for the first few months of the election year.[27] The president approached several individuals in his search for a successor, including Chief Justice Fred Vinson and General Dwight Eisenhower. Neither expressed interest.[28] Truman announced on March 29, 1952, that he would not accept another nomination for president, breaking the Democratic field wide open.[29] The leading contenders included Senator Estes Kefauver of Tennessee, whom Truman privately nicknamed "Cow Fever" and ridiculed as a "demagogic dumb bell"; Senator Richard Russell of Georgia, the strong favorite among southern Democrats and whom Truman considered a man of "ability and brains . . . but . . . poison to Northern Democrats and honest liberals"; Adlai Stevenson, the intelligent and urbane governor of Illinois; Vice-President Alben Barkley, respected by many Americans but regarded as too old at age seventy-four; and Governor Averell Harriman of New York, whom the president considered "the ablest of them all," but a man whose Wall Street credentials and immense wealth threatened to alienate the party's working-class constituency.[30] Not surprisingly, most southern conservatives rallied behind Russell.[31]

With a smaller field of candidates, the Republicans anticipated a much tighter race for convention delegates. Senator Robert A. Taft of Ohio was the early front-runner but anticipated a strong challenge from Harold Stassen. On January 7, from the headquarters of the North Atlantic Treaty Organization in France, Eisenhower announced that he would accept but would not seek the Republican nomination.[32]

Eisenhower emerged early as the choice of many Alabama states' rights supporters. Shortly after the general threw his hat into the ring, Dixiecrat leader Gessner McCorvey unveiled a plan by which "Southern state Democrats [would] nominate their presidential electors prior to national conventions of national parties and pledge them to the general." According to McCorvey, "If one of the major political parties then comes along later and nominates the same man . . . that will be perfectly all right. We will let them share with us the glory of electing a president." Although he stopped short of personally endorsing Eisenhower, Frank Dixon predicted that the state would vote Republican if the general was the nominee.[33]

Even before the national party candidates were chosen, however, southern politicians, often led by former Dixiecrats, were actively taking steps to free their states from any obligations to the national Democratic Party while still remaining within the state Democratic Party, which still wielded the political power in the state. Alabama Dixiecrats faced the toughest challenge. The loyalists were determined to maintain a firm grasp on the reins of power following their 1950 SDEC primary victory. Senator Lister Hill threw down the gauntlet to states' righters early, insisting that the "mandate" Alabama voters sent in 1950, when they elected loyalists, be carried out in 1952. He and other loyalists strongly believed that they needed to ensure against a repeat of 1948.[34]

The Alabama SDEC was scheduled to meet in late January to make arrangements to support the 1952 Democratic nominees from "top to bottom." Specifically, the loyalists wanted to institute a pledge to bind electors and delegates to support the national party nominee.[35] Dixiecrat Roger Snyder, a Birmingham lawyer and member of the SDEC, announced that he would introduce a states' rights resolution "allowing white Democrats of Alabama the privilege to vote as they please for presidential electors."[36] In a preemptive strike, Dixiecrat Horace Wilkinson brought suit against the SDEC a little more than a week before the meeting. Wilkinson asked the court to enjoin the SDEC from requiring elector candidates in the spring primaries to pledge their support to the national party nominee.[37] On January 24 the Alabama Supreme Court rejected Wilkinson's motion.[38]

The Alabama SDEC gathered for the showdown on January 26. During the roll call the States' Righters on the committee stood and waved Confederate flags. Senators Hill and Sparkman, and Representatives Rains, Jones, and Elliott, all party regulars, were on hand to support the loyalists. As expected, the loyalists introduced the pledge to bind electors to the national party nominees; the committee adopted it by a nearly 2 to 1 margin.[39] The *Birmingham News* called the pledge "unwise in practical procedure and unsound in basic principle."[40] Several county committees refused to require candidates for county office in the spring primaries to sign the oath adopted by the state.[41]

Following the convention, Dixiecrat Sidney Smyer threatened that the Alabama States' Rights supporters would stage another revolt "if the nominees and platforms of both major parties are obnoxious to the South." He said that Alabama should have an independent presidential elector slate just in case.[42] Smyer spoke prematurely, for the Dixiecrats first tried to capture control of the state's Democratic electors by challenging the legality of the pledge. On January 30 Ed Blair, publisher of the *Pell City News-Aegis* and a 1948 Dixiecrat elector, attempted to qualify as a candidate for presidential elector without pledging support to the Democratic nominees for president and vice-president.[43] The Alabama Dixiecrats won an early victory when an Alabama circuit court invalidated the loyalty oath for presidential electors. In a decision that applied only to electors, the court held that the oath violated the U.S. Constitution, which provides that electors shall vote for candidates of their choice. The loyalists promptly appealed the decision to the Alabama Supreme Court.[44] Unwilling to wait for the state supreme court's decision, the

Dixiecrats moved to circumvent the oath. On February 12 McCorvey filed as a presidential elector candidate in the May 6 primary using a newly printed Dixiecrat form that omitted the national party loyalty pledge.[45] Wilkinson announced shortly thereafter that the Dixiecrats had a slate of eleven electors, seven of whom were Dixiecrat electors from 1948, who had refused to sign the pledge.

On February 29 the Alabama Supreme Court ruled in favor of the Dixiecrats, upholding the lower court, 5 to 2. It declared that candidates for presidential elector could run in the Democratic primary without promising to support the national party nominee.[46] McCorvey announced that the decision "clears the way for Alabama to withhold its electoral vote from Harry Truman or anyone selected by him." U.S. Senator Lister Hill warned voters that "the decision would impair, if not destroy, party government and defeat the will of the people of Alabama expressed in the Democratic primaries of 1950. It is to be deplored."[47] On March 10 a circuit court panel issued a writ of mandamus directing the state party chairman to certify the eleven-member Dixiecrat elector slate in the May 6 primary.[48] A couple of the Dixiecrat candidates for presidential electors in Alabama declared that they would possibly vote for the Republican nominee. One man even swore under oath that he would be willing to steal votes to prevent Truman's nomination.[49] As in 1948, the Solid South was in political disarray.

On April 3 Alabama Democrat loyalists won their fight in the U.S. Supreme Court, which reversed the Alabama lower court's decision knocking out the loyalty pledge. The court ruled that the oath was indeed constitutional and that presidential elector candidates could be required to pledge party loyalty. A despondent McCorvey noted that "naturally that ruling takes a lot of steam out of us."[50] In a last-ditch effort to get the Dixiecrat slate of presidential elector candidates on the Democratic primary ballot, Wilkinson appealed to the Alabama Supreme Court on April 4, asking the state court to circumvent the U.S. Supreme Court by ruling that the loyalty oath violated the state constitution. The state supreme court refused to consider Wilkinson's motion until it had received the formal opinion of the U.S. Supreme Court.[51] The request was effectively denied.

With the loyalty pledge secured, Alabama state party leaders called for unity. With Truman out of the race, many felt it was now feasible for the loyalists and the Dixiecrats to reconcile their differences.[52] Many Dixiecrats balked. Wilkinson said Truman's withdrawal as a candidate would not change the position of Alabama Dixiecrats. "Our fight has been not only against Truman, but against anyone who advocates Truman's civil rights program."[53] Approximately a dozen Alabama Dixiecrats met in Montgomery on April 24 and decided against organizing a slate of independent electors for the May primary. Following the advice of South Carolina governor Byrnes, they agreed to "hold their fire" until they knew who the nominees for the two parties would be. Several Dixiecrats could not wait that long and stated that they were fairly certain they would be voting Republican in November.[54] To no one's surprise, the Alabama Democratic primary produced an unopposed slate of electors pledged to support the national nominee.[55] At the state party caucus on May 27, however, the Democrats failed to unite the delegates in a solid front behind one candidate; thirteen lined up for Russell and nine for Kefauver.[56]

The other former Dixiecrat states were more successful in freeing themselves from the dictates of the national party. South Carolina's Democratic convention met on April 16 and "left the door wide open for [another] bolt." The convention threw its support behind Russell and adopted a resolution in which the party "reserve[d] the right to determine its course in the general election" based on the actions taken at the national convention. The delegates voted to hold another state convention the second week in August following the national convention. In his keynote address Byrnes declared his fidelity to "principles and not . . . party labels. I want to know what is in the platform of the Republican party as well as in the platform of the Democratic party."[57] The state took a wait-and-see attitude but clearly reserved for itself the right to act contrary to the national convention should the delegates so desire. Byrnes stated on the eve of the convention that South Carolina might go Republican in November if the Democratic presidential candidate proved unacceptable.[58]

Mississippi's state Democratic Party convention, held June 26, likewise supported Russell and voted to attend the national convention but not to bind its representatives to support any candidate chosen by the national convention. Should Russell fail to get the nomination, and if the nominee were not acceptable to the delegation, Mississippi Democrats would reconvene the state convention and choose their own presidential ticket.[59] The convention recessed until August 5, when it would either ratify or reject the national party nominees and platform. Addressing the convention, Governor White warned, "The States' Righters would again become a third party as in 1948 rather than accept a civil rights . . .

platform and nominees pledged to it."[60] Mississippi Democrats declared their state party "a free and independent political party and as such is fighting for the sound principles of Jeffersonian Democracy and States' Rights. Ours is a fight for sacred principles—not a fight for any man."[61]

Ultimately six southern states—South Carolina, Louisiana, Mississippi, Georgia, Texas, and Virginia—agreed to reconvene their conventions after the Democratic National Convention. Between the state and national conventions, Byrnes continued his fight on behalf of southern political independence. Addressing the Delta Council in Cleveland, Mississippi, the heart of Dixiecrat country, he declared that unless southern Democrats received "sympathetic consideration" from the national party, they should support a third party candidate. Byrnes went on to praise the million-plus voters who supported the Dixiecrats in 1948.[62] Thurmond remained publicly silent.

Aware of a potentially significant independent vote, the national Republican Party welcomed the disgruntled Dixiecrats. At a Lincoln Day rally of Alabama Republicans in Birmingham in early February, Republican national chairman Guy Gabrielson made a strong bid to win Alabama Dixiecrats over to the GOP. Gabrielson intimated that nothing separated Dixiecrats from Republicans, other than simple semantics. "Our friends call themselves States' Righters and we call ourselves Republicans. But they oppose corruption in government, and so do we," he declared. "We want the Dixiecrats to vote for our candidate. The Dixiecrat movement is an anti-Truman movement. The Dixiecrat party believes in states' rights. That's what the Republican Party believes in."[63] Dissident Democrats, though, were not so readily accepted by the state Republican parties, who jealously guarded the reigns of power and resented the Dixiecrats as "one-shot Republicans" who would do nothing to help strengthen the party at the grass roots.[64]

The Republicans poured into Chicago the first week of July for their nominating convention. Probably more than in any past election, white southerners felt they had a stake in the outcome of the Republican convention. Although Taft entered as the front-runner, Eisenhower dominated the first ballot, 845 delegates to 280.[65]

The Windy City also played host to the Democrats, whose convention opened on July 21. To prevent a repeat of 1948, the convention adopted a loyalty pledge, which stated, "No delegate shall be seated unless he shall give assurance . . . that he will exert every honorable means available to him in any official capacity he may have to provide that the nominees of the convention for president and vice president through their names or those of electors pledged to them, appear on the election ballot under the heading, name or designation of the Democratic party." Southern delegates strongly opposed the pledge and predicted another bolt. Unlike in 1948, the national party leaders took pains to appease southern conservatives. Convention chairman Frank McKinney defused a potential rebellion by announcing that no attempt would be made to oust delegations refusing to abide by the loyalty oath.[66] In the end only representatives from Louisiana, South Carolina, and Virginia refused to sign the pledge, and they nonetheless participated fully in the convention, which ultimately approved a watered-down civil rights plank and nominated Adlai Stevenson for president and Alabama senator John Sparkman as his running mate.[67] The Democrats had avoided the panic and bolt of 1948; the threat of Eisenhower's conservative appeal forced the more liberal wing of the party to accept concessions in the interest of unity.

Shortly after the convention, Alabama Dixiecrat and Birmingham attorney Sidney Smyer conceded he did not think the Dixiecrats would fight the Stevenson ticket or put up any opposition.[68] Alabama Dixiecrats recognized the futility of opposing a Democratic ticket that carried the state's U.S. senator. But having made the break in 1948, many could not go back. Instead, several prominent Alabama Dixiecrats threw their lot in with the Republican Party. Tom Abernethy of Talladega, a 1948 Dixiecrat elector and 1950 States' Rights campaign chairperson, announced early in 1952 that he planned to stump the state for Eisenhower. He resigned his position on the SDEC in late July.[69] A number of other influential Dixiecrats eventually threw their support to the general, including state chairman Gessner McCorvey, textile magnate Donald Comer, Dothan banker Wallace Malone, and Montgomery construction king Winton M. Blount, who would later serve as Richard Nixon's postmaster general.[70] Aside from Abernethy, though, there was not a wholesale switch of Dixiecrats to membership in the Republican Party. The bonds of local party loyalty and the power of the state Democratic Party were too intense to allow a wholesale resignation. Furthermore, even had they wanted to join the Republicans, former Dixiecrats were not always welcomed by the preexisting state Republican organizations, which were fairly moribund bodies in the late 1940s and early 1950s. Assessing the state of southern politics in 1949, V. O. Key had little good to say about the leaders of the southern Republican parties, whom he referred to as "palace or bureaucratic politicians" more concerned with patronage than with keeping in contact with Republican voters. Most Republican leaders in southern states, Key noted, "are overwhelmed by the futility of it all, but they keep the faith in a quiet spirit of dedication not unlike that of the Britisher who, although living in the jungle surrounded by heathen, dresses for dinner."[71]

South Carolina Democrats reconvened their state convention on August 6 and unenthusiastically supported the national party nominees. Despite his alienation from the national Democratic Party, Byrnes refused to engineer a revolt akin to the one in 1948. Without Byrnes's leadership, the impetus for another takeover fizzled. The governor, nevertheless, distanced himself from the Democratic Party candidates. He criticized the national party platform and refused to commit himself to voting for the Democratic candidates. Some states' rights advocates at the convention moved that the party support the Eisenhower-Nixon ticket. Byrnes disagreed, arguing that it would not be right for the state Democratic Party to pledge its electors to the Republican candidates. The convention left the door open, however, by assuring party members that no one would be punished for supporting Eisenhower in the general election. Byrnes later told reporters that the vote supporting the Stevenson-Sparkman ticket did not reflect the true strength of the Eisenhower backers.[72]

That same day, shortly after the convention voted to support Stevenson and Sparkman, South Carolinians for Eisenhower launched their movement to collect 10,000 signatures to place presidential electors pledged to Eisenhower and Nixon on the general election ballot as an independent ticket. Byrnes signed the petition on August 13 but claimed he did not yet know for whom he would vote.[73] The movement, spearheaded by a little-known Columbia attorney, garnered the support of many South Carolina Dixiecrats.[74] Petitions with 53,000 signatures asking for an independent Eisenhower ballot were filed with the South Carolina secretary of state on September 3.[75] Byrnes finally came out for Eisenhower on September 18. In a prepared speech the governor declared, "I shall place loyalty to my country above loyalty to a political party and vote for General Dwight D. Eisenhower."[76] Strom Thurmond, silent, remained in the shadows.

South Carolina independents were backed by a national independent organization, Citizens for Eisenhower, and were assured that the candidate would campaign in the South. The state chapter of Citizens for Eisenhower and the South Carolina Eisenhower group agreed to pool their resources in an effort to carry the state for the general.[77] As in Alabama, those states' righters who wished to support Eisenhower steered clear of the state Republican Party, which in South Carolina suffered from years of disarray. When Eisenhower visited the state in late September, it was at the request of the independents, the stronger and better-organized group.[78] Recognizing the power of traditional political allegiances, even the regular state Republican Party encouraged voters to support the independent slate, since they knew they would be unsuccessful in pulling in any votes on the Republican ballot.[79] *The State* went to great lengths to assure voters that voting independent was not the same as voting Republican.[80]

States' rights forces in Mississippi also agreed to run Eisenhower on an independent ticket, although Governor Hugh White backed the national party candidates.[81] As in South Carolina, this display of party loyalty and acquiescence masked discontent with the national party platform. The absence of a wholesale rejection of the Democratic nominees was due more to the fact that Stevenson simply did not engender sufficient hatred to foment a political revolt on the scale of the 1948 Dixiecrat campaign. In Louisiana, Eisenhower supporter and Dixiecrat Leander Perez tried once again to "capture the rooster" for an independent slate. This time his efforts failed, and the Louisiana state central committee awarded the vote-getting chanticleer to the Stevenson-Sparkman ticket.[82] Perez threw his considerable influence and finances behind Louisiana's bipartisan statewide group called Americans for Eisenhower. Also endorsing Eisenhower in Louisiana were anti-Long governor Robert Kennon and former governor and Dixiecrat Sam Jones.[83] Relatively quiet throughout the campaign, in his first public statement regarding the presidential campaign, private citizen Thurmond announced on November 2 from his home in Aiken that he would support Eisenhower.[84]

The national Republican Party recognized this opportunity to make serious inroads into the South, and Eisenhower gladly accepted invitations from state Republican parties and independent organizations in a number of southern states.[85] One of the Republican candidate's biggest campaign stops was in Columbia, where an estimated 50,000 people crowded onto the statehouse lawn to hear him. From atop the speaker's platform, the general rose to his feet when the band struck up "Dixie." "I always stand when they play that song," the general said matter-of-factly. The crowd cheered.[86] The switch was on.

If the Dixiecrat movement failed in its 1948 attempt to defeat Truman, it in no uncertain terms began the transformation of southern politics, although the road to a two-party South was far from smooth. The 1952 presidential election confirmed voting trends that had been set in motion in 1948 and established new patterns that would continue throughout the 1960s. Stevenson carried every state in the Deep South, but Eisenhower made profound inroads into the traditionally solid Democratic territory and captured Florida, Oklahoma, Tennessee, Texas, and Virginia. The Republicans added new support from voters in the South's swelling urban and suburban populations to their traditional bailiwicks in the Upper South. This metropolitan Republicanism had first appeared in 1948 and would prove the most durable over the next two decades. Eisenhower also pulled in a surprising number of voters from the Black Belt region, the Dixiecrat stronghold. Throughout the Deep South, but especially in Georgia, South Carolina, and Mississippi, there was a strong correlation between counties that supported the Dixiecrats and those that endorsed Eisenhower. Although it had been unable to institutionalize itself at the state level, the Dixiecrat movement had effectively loosened the moorings of southern political allegiance at the national level, weakening the custom of automatically supporting Democratic Party nominees. The Dixiecrats had, after all, accomplished something: the national party could no longer take the South for granted.

Despite definite Republican gains in the 1952 presidential election, declarations heralding the demise of the one-party South were premature, or at least they underestimated the time required for such an immense shift in political identity. However, to undervalue the significance of this transformation powered by the Dixiecrat movement distorts political history. The Republican Party would make few electoral inroads beneath the presidential level until the early 1960s.[87] White southerners were firmly committed to a period of flux, however, and those concerned with the maintenance of segregation spent the 1950s in a search for the best political alternative. In late 1953, one year into the Eisenhower administration, South Carolina newspaperman William Workman polled some sixty persons who had played active roles in the independent movement to elect Eisenhower. Respondents were asked whether they thought independents should maintain their own organization, join the state Republican Party, or resume affiliation with the Democratic Party of South Carolina. Those polled overwhelmingly believed that South Carolinians who had supported the president should remain independent, although not a few still wished to maintain their standing within the Democratic

Party. As one respondent stated, "South Carolinians for Eisenhower organization should be kept intact, not as a third party, but as a framework, ready for prompt expansion in case of eventualities in 1956."[88]

★

From the late 1940s to the early 1950s, the NAACP had been carefully choosing cases with which to challenge head-on the separate-but-equal doctrine enunciated in *Plessy v. Ferguson*. The U.S. Supreme Court consolidated five related school desegregation cases under the title *Brown v. Board of Education of Topeka, Kansas,* and handed down its decision on May 17, 1954. Speaking for a unanimous court, Chief Justice Earl Warren posed the crucial question: "Does segregation of children in public schools solely on the basis of race, even though the physical facilities and other 'tangible' factors may be equal, deprive the children of the minority group of equal educational opportunities? We believe it does." Addressing himself directly to *Plessy,* Warren continued: "We conclude that in the field of public education the doctrine of 'separate but equal' has no place. Separate educational facilities are inherently unequal."[89] This momentous decision, delivered on what came to be known as Black Monday to many white southerners, effectively destroyed the constitutional foundation for segregation and changed forever southern race relations.

Given the monumental nature of the ruling, the reaction in the South was defiant. Senator James Eastland's comments were uncharacteristically tempered, albeit resolute. Southerners would not abide the court's decision, he declared, and "will take whatever steps are necessary to retain segregation in education."[90] Senator Maybank of South Carolina admitted he was "shocked" by the ruling, which he called "a shameful political rather than a judicial decision."[91] A strong states' rights newspaper in Charleston commented, "We receive the decision with distaste and apprehension. But it is too late to secede and start another war between the states. Other means must be sought to live within the laws of our country."[92] Columbia's *The State* pleaded for "no excitement between the races" and counseled "calm deliberation," while the *Clarion-Ledger* in Jackson encouraged Mississippians' to tackle the problem of desegregation with "wisdom, courage, faith and determination."[93] The court was not yet through with the South, however. One year later, in April 1955, the court reconvened to hear arguments regarding the timetable and methods for the execution of the ruling.

As historian Numan Bartley succinctly stated, the "*Brown* decision focused race politics in the South." In the 1954 gubernatorial races in Georgia and South Carolina, two states in the forefront of resistance to segregation in the pre-*Brown* era, the defense of segregation dominated campaign oratory.[94] Voters in Mississippi and Louisiana would have to wait until 1955 and 1956, respectively, to choose new state officials. Louisiana's state legislature, however, created the Joint Legislative Committee to Maintain Segregation that began drawing up plans to fight orders to desegregate.[95] Other state legislatures soon followed suit, creating committees and passing laws to prevent the enforcement of desegregation. In South Carolina the Gressette Committee, chaired by state senator Marion Gressette, had been strategizing since 1951, so by the time the court handed down its decree, the committee had devised countless obstacles to subvert it.[96]

While the efforts of southern legislators to circumvent the law were disturbing, perhaps more sinister was the explosion of grassroots resistance organizations in communities across the Deep South. Angered by the persistence of African American parents petitioning local school boards to desegregate, these groups retaliated with economic reprisals and physical violence. Led by the White Citizens' Councils but encompassing a myriad of groups, the massive resistance movement articulated and channeled white anxiety and effectively aided elected officials in delaying the implementation of desegregation orders for a decade.

The first citizens' council was organized in Sunflower County, Mississippi—the home of Senator James Eastland—in July 1954. By the end of the following year, the massive resistance movement claimed 250,000 members, with organizations in every southern state, though Mississippi's Association of Citizens' Councils dwarfed all other state confederations. Like the Dixiecrats, the councils were strongest in Black Belt towns, and in some states they strongly influenced state politics.[97] Council membership reflected a community cross-section, and former Dixiecrats, many of whom were connected to industrial and plantation interests, frequently occupied positions of power. Mississippi circuit judge Thomas Pickens Brady of Brookhaven, chairman of the Dixiecrat party's speaker's bureau, published a widely circulated book titled *Black Monday* and became one of the councils' more sought-after spokespersons. In a speech before the Citizens' Council of Indianola, Mississippi, Brady spelled out the horrors of integration to an anxious white audience. History had proven, Brady declared, that "the black blood swallows up [the white], and with it goes this deterioration. It blows out the light within a white man's brain."[98] Walter C. Givhan, a Safford, Alabama, planter; spokesperson for the State Farm Bureau; and a 1948 Dixiecrat elector, sat on the board of directors and eventually became executive secretary of the Citizens' Councils of Alabama in 1958. Birmingham attorney and prominent Dixiecrat Sidney Smyer was also an influential council member.[99] Leander Perez helped found the Association of Citizens' Councils of Louisiana, and New Orleans industrialist and Dixiecrat founder John U. Barr was elected president of the Federation for Constitutional Government, a regional organization initiated by Senator Eastland, whose goal was to coordinate the activities of the state resistance groups.[100] South Carolina Citizens' Council leaders Farley Smith, Emory Rogers, and Micah Jenkins were all strong Thurmond supporters. Furthermore, the councils in South Carolina received financial assistance from the states' rights fund—money left over from the 1948 campaign that was earmarked for states' rights activities.[101]

In 1954 Strom Thurmond recovered from his defeat to Johnston and regained his mastery of the art of political timing. Thurmond's triumphant return to public life coincided perfectly with the uproar over *Brown*. In September 1954, well after the state Democratic Party primaries, Senator Burnet Maybank died suddenly of a heart attack. In a meeting held only hours after Maybank's funeral, the South Carolina SDEC named state senator Edgar Brown of Barnwell, a powerful national Democratic Party loyalist, as the U.S. Senate nominee instead of convening a special primary election. South Carolina Democrats reacted immediately with anger. Capitalizing on this wave of public outrage, Thurmond declared himself a write-in candidate on September 7. He further announced that, if elected, he would resign from office before the 1956 Democratic primary, allowing South Carolina voters to choose a senator to serve the remaining four years of the term. With this bold stroke, Thurmond once again transformed himself into a candidate of "the people," the political outsider bravely challenging the draconian dictates of the state Democratic Party, which had—behind closed doors—cheated them of their rightful voice. To a group of white southerners still reeling from a Supreme Court decision they considered unjust and oppressive, this was an exhilarating development. In just two months, despite the obvious practical obstacles facing a write-in candidate, Thurmond engineered a huge upset victory. He won an astounding 63 percent of the votes and was easily reelected in 1956. After his election, advisor Walter Brown recommended that Thurmond "drop the 'J'" from his name. "'Strom Thurmond' sounds like a people's Senator, while the 'J' is just a little stilted," Brown advised.[102] Thurmond agreed. As for being "the people's Senator," Thurmond quickly demonstrated *which* people he represented when he became a leading figure in the massive resistance movement. He was one of the authors of the 1956 Southern Manifesto, which eventually was signed by a majority of southern congressmen and senators. It declared the *Brown* decision "a clear abuse of judicial power" and commended "the motives of States which have declared the intention to resist forced integration by any lawful means."[103]

If the *Brown* decision rejuvenated the states' rights cause, it dampened the support of former Dixiecrats for Republican presidential candidates. In a 1955 follow-up questionnaire to Eisenhower supporters, William Workman asked various South Carolinians to assess Eisenhower's strength in the Deep South. Most respondents agreed that Eisenhower had suffered some setbacks, primarily because of the race issue.[104] But where would the disgruntled Democrats turn? To many, the only safe path was the path of independence. In his 1956 reelection bid, Eisenhower gained votes in the peripheral South but lost some of the support he had gained in the Black Belt in 1952, although he swung Louisiana into the Republican column. In all four of the states that had supported the Dixiecrats in 1948, states' rights electors pledged to Harry F. Byrd, U.S. senator from Virginia, and Mississippi congressman John Bell Williams were on the ballot. For the most part, the states' rights candidates drew Black Belt support that had gone to Eisenhower in 1952. Deep South voters apparently blamed the new Republican chief justice Earl Warren for the *Brown* decision and were upset about the support given the plaintiff's case by Herbert Brownell, Eisenhower's attorney general.[105]

In 1960 Louisiana and Texas returned to the Democratic fold, but Democratic Party candidate John F. Kennedy lost the electoral college votes of Mississippi and half of Alabama, which went to independent electors. Political scientist Alexander Lamis points out that civil rights was not a major issue in the 1960 campaign and that Kennedy and Nixon held similar positions on the issue. Furthermore, in the aftermath of Little Rock, civil rights was more closely identified with the Republican Party. Finally, Kennedy's choice of Texas senator Lyndon B. Johnson as vice-president offered a conciliatory gesture to the Democratic Party's southern wing.[106]

Republican gains among white southern voters in presidential races were virtually solidified with President Johnson's embrace of civil rights.

In 1964 Johnson won every state in the Union except Arizona and the Deep South. Republican candidate Barry Goldwater, in his effort to "hunt where the ducks are," instituted the "Southern Strategy" aimed at the conservative region. Strom Thurmond campaigned strenuously for the Arizona senator, and Thurmond himself switched allegiance to the Republican Party. Two years later Thurmond was elected as a Republican senator in South Carolina.[107] Goldwater's strength in the South correlated with the black population in those states—very similar to the Dixiecrat trend. In the 1950s, whites had split along class lines: the middle- and upper-class white suburbanites supported the Republican nominees, rural whites supported independent states' rights candidates, and urban working-class whites stuck with the Democrats. In 1964 the race issue obliterated class differences. The side effect of the Goldwater landslide in Dixie had been the election of seven new Republican congressmen—the first since Reconstruction. This renewed Republican regional vitality, however, was tenuous. In Mississippi, for example, the state Republican Party put up challengers in four of five house districts, and Republican congressman Prentiss Walker, elected in 1964, challenged U.S. Senator James Eastland for his seat. All efforts failed.[108] White voters disenchanted with the national Democratic Party were not ready to fully embrace the Republicans. When asked about his party affiliation, one seventy-year-old white farmer told the interviewer, "You kinda help me out and give me some ideas; everything has gone out of sight. Don't know what to say. Democrats have always been high; things are out of sight now."[109]

As the 1968 election drew near, southern defections from the national Democratic Party peaked. President Johnson committed himself to dismantling what remained of Jim Crow through his Great Society programs, the Civil Rights Act of 1964, and the Voting Rights Act of 1965, which significantly increased black voter registration throughout the South. Much of the angry white working-class South turned to the candidacy of Alabama governor George C. Wallace and the American Independent Party, hoping to deadlock the election in the electoral college and force the decision into the House of Representatives, just as in 1948. They failed just the same, but combined with voters who supported Republican nominee Richard Nixon, 80 percent of the white electorate rejected the national Democratic Party nominee, Hubert Humphrey. Together Nixon and Wallace virtually annihilated the Democratic presence in presidential voting in the South. Wallace captured the votes of

Black Belt and traditional working-class white Democrats, and Nixon received solid support from whites in the cities and suburbs.[110] Capitalizing on whites' anger and sense of betrayal over potential and actual racial change, Goldwater, Nixon, and Wallace tapped into the same core of Deep South voters that had supported Thurmond in 1948.[111]

★

By all accounts the Dixiecrats' play for political power failed. Indeed it is easier to dismiss them as Confederate-battle-flag-waving political malcontents than to determine their impact. But in assessing the Dixiecrats' importance in terms of southern political history, it is perhaps necessary to separate the men from the message and to identify the mere act of political rebellion—status quo and reactionary though it was—as significant. As some historians and political scientists have noted, the politics of economic class took root in the South during the 1930s and 1940s and persisted into the 1950s. Amidst the economic upheavals engendered by the Great Depression and World War II, the predominantly white hill counties and working-class white urban precincts joined forces and succeeded in electing numerous economic liberals to southern statehouses and Congress.[112] Feeling increasingly uncomfortable within the national Democratic Party and within state politics as well, Black Belt whites, wedded to a political philosophy that melded economic conservatism and white supremacy, nevertheless remained within the national party fold so long as the party maintained the racial status quo. President Truman's embrace of civil rights legislation in 1948, in addition to the local civil rights agitation they witnessed firsthand, constituted the last straw for Black Belt whites as well as for a number of economically conservative industrial and agricultural elites who felt that a permanent FEPC threatened their ability to exploit both black and white labor. Hill county and urban working-class whites, while strongly opposed to all civil rights legislation, nevertheless still identified with the national party that had addressed their basic economic needs. For these voters the hardships of the Great Depression and the gains of the New Deal and World War II were close enough, and the civil rights threat posed by Truman's agenda not yet immediate enough, to prompt them to abandon the national Democratic Party. The threat was more than strong enough for whites in the Black Belt, however. Perched atop a platform of racial and economic conservatism, the Dixiecrats led the exodus of Black Belt whites from the solid Democratic South. The Dixiecrats' insistence on maintaining the Democratic Party label in the 1948 election and their rhetorical strategies to assure voters of their political legitimacy demonstrate how difficult this process of political transformation would be. However constrained and manipulated their protest, it provided an outlet for white anxiety and the first tentative steps toward significant and lasting regional political change.

With this revolt, then, the Dixiecrats precipitated the weakening of the Democratic Party's grip on presidential elections in the Deep South. Furthermore, the 1948 campaign laid the foundation, if only in presidential voting, for the creation of a two-party region. While the more durable factor of presidential Republicanism was the support of affluent urban and suburban whites, the Republicans in 1952 gained adherents among former Dixiecrats in the Black Belt as well. Until the mid-1960s the Black Belt vote remained wildly unpredictable and unstable, attaching itself to the national candidate—Eisenhower in 1952, Byrd in 1956, Nixon in 1960, Goldwater in 1964, and Wallace in 1968—who presented himself as the most ardent defender of states' rights.

Finally, the Dixiecrats and, in particular, Strom Thurmond initiated a national political discussion on the dangers of an expansive federal government and on interest group politics that threatened issues of "local control." This conservatism gained credence among a wider audience following the civil rights and Great Society legislation of the 1960s, and it fueled George Wallace's presidential campaigns in the 1960s and 1970s and the Reagan revolution and the rise of the Christian right in the 1980s. Indeed, Thurmond's ploy in the 1950 senatorial campaign to paint himself as a political independent while portraying opponent Olin Johnston as a Washington insider eerily foreshadowed the anti-incumbency fervor of the 1990s. When a majority of South Carolina voters in November 1996 walked into the voting booth and pulled the lever for Thurmond, honoring him with another term as their senator, they may have recalled his earlier pledge to "fight the forty-year wrongs of liberalism." Who better to fight that war than the man who had fired the first shot?

NOTES

ABBREVIATIONS

In addition to the abbreviations used in the text, the following abbreviations appear in the notes.

ADAH
: Alabama Department of Archives and History, Montgomery

CU
: Clemson University Libraries, Clemson University, Clemson, S.C.

DNC Papers
: Democratic National Committee Papers

DSU
: Charles W. Capps Jr. Archives, Delta State University, Cleveland, Miss.

EU
: Robert Woodruff Library, Emory University, Atlanta, Ga.

HSTL
: Harry S. Truman Library, Independence, Mo.

MDAH
: Mississippi Department of Archives and History, Jackson

MOHP
: Mississippi Oral History Project

MSU
: Mitchell Memorial Library, Mississippi State University, Starkville

NAACP Papers
: Papers of the National Association for the Advancement of Colored People, Library of Congress, Washington, D.C.

NAACP Papers (mf)
: Papers of the National Association for the Advancement of Colored People, microfilm collection

OF
: Official Files

PCCR Papers
: Papers of the President's Committee on Civil Rights

PDOHI
: Progressive Democrats Oral History Interviews, Dacus Library, Winthrop University, Rock Hill, S.C.

PPF

President's Personal Files, Harry S. Truman Papers

PSF

President's Secretary's Files, Harry S. Truman Papers

SCCHR Papers

South Carolina Council on Human Relations Papers

SCL

South Caroliniana Library, University of South Carolina, Columbia

UA

William Stanley Hoole Special Collections Library, University of Alabama, Tuscaloosa

UGA

Richard B. Russell Library for Political Research and Studies, University of Georgia, Athens

USM

McCain Library and Archives, University of Southern Mississippi, Hattiesburg.

WHCF

White House Central Files, Harry S. Truman Library, Independence, Mo.

INTRODUCTION

1. *The State,* April 9, 1996.

2. Anonymous interview with author, Columbia, S.C., June 20, 1996.

3. "Motion of J. Strom Thurmond, Governor of South Carolina, at Southern Governors' Conference," February 7, 1948, States' Rights Democrats file, box 2, Workman Papers, SCL.

4. Quote in Key, *Southern Politics,* 671. Also see Ader, "Why the Dixiecrats Failed" and *Dixiecrat Movement;* Lemmon, "Ideology of the 'Dixiecrat' Movement," 162–71; Carleton, "Dilemma of the Democrats."

5. Ashmore, "South's Year of Decision," 2.

6. See Heard, *Two-Party South?;* Havard, *Changing Politics of the South;* Garson, *Politics of Sectionalism;* Bartley and Graham, *Southern Politics and the Second Reconstruction;* Bass and DeVries, *Transformation of Southern Politics;* Lamis, *Two-Party South.* The 1948 election was what V. O. Key later defined as a "critical" election, that is, one in which there is a high incidence of involvement and a subsequent realignment that seems to persist for several succeeding elections. See Key, "Theory of Critical Elections."

7. Numan V. Bartley, *Rise of Massive Resistance,* 17–20, 32–37, and *New South,* 74–104.

8. A fourth book, Nadine Cohodas's *Strom Thurmond and the Politics of Southern Change,* devotes two chapters to Thurmond's Dixiecrat candidacy. With chapter titles such as "Irreversible Course" and "Candidate by Default," Cohodas presents Thurmond very much as a man upon whom history was thrust. She gives little attention to regional transformations, and thus Thurmond's connection to other Dixiecrats appears happenstance and illogical.

9. Heard, *Two-Party South?,* 25.

10. Key, *Southern Politics,* 5–10.

11. Egerton, *Speak Now against the Day;* Sullivan, *Days of Hope;* Fairclough, *Race and Democracy;* Kelley, *Hammer and Hoe.*

12. Wright, *Old South, New South,* 260.

13. Ibid., 199.

14. Ibid., 241.

15. Key, *Southern Politics,* 329.

16. "Southern Revolt," 24.

17. Sancton, "White Supremacy," 97.

18. See, for example, J. Strom Thurmond, address, Memphis, Tennessee, October 21, 1948, file 163, Speeches Series, Subseries A, General File, Thurmond Papers, CU.

19. Address of Fielding Wright, August 11, 1948, Houston, Texas, in *States' Rights Information and Speakers' Handbook.*

20. Address of J. Strom Thurmond, August 11, 1948, in ibid.

21. Quoted in Garson, *Politics of Sectionalism,* 286.

22. *Montgomery Advertiser,* July 14, 1948.

23. In his influential book *Southern Governors and Civil Rights,* political scientist Earl Black argues that southern politicians "gave relatively little attention to racial matters" in elections during the years 1950–54. Although Black examines only gubernatorial races, one can safely assume his contention that "racial segregation was of relatively little import as an overt campaign issue in the early 1950s" held for other electoral races as well. See Black, *Southern Governors and Civil Rights,* chap. 3, quotes on 29, 45.

CHAPTER ONE

1. Walter Sillers to John Rankin, October 10, 1942, file 32, box 22, Sillers Papers, DSU.

2. Sullivan, *Days of Hope,* 3.

3. Oscar Bledsoe III, "The Political Aspect of the Delta and the Plantation System," typed statement, May 1942, file 23, box 14, Sillers Papers, DSU.

4. Schulman, *From Cotton Belt to Sun Belt,* 46.

5. Ibid., 23.

6. Leuchtenburg, *Roosevelt and the New Deal,* 1; McElvaine, *Great Depression,* 43–48.

7. Grantham, *South in Modern America,* 116; Mertz, *Southern Rural Poverty,* 1–19. Per capita income in the twelve southeastern states in 1929 was $368, compared with a national average of $703. Cotton prices in the South dipped to a miserable 6 cents per pound in 1933, plummeting from an all-time high of 36 cents per pound in 1919. In addition to economic catastrophe, the South suffered through the boll weevil infestation of the mid-1920s, the Mississippi River flood of 1927, and a drought in the Southwest in 1930 and 1931.

8. Mertz, *Southern Rural Poverty,* 5–6, 11–15. Tenantry and cropping were most extensive in cotton farming, which accounted for 60 percent of all agriculture.

9. Lofton, "Social and Economic History of Columbia, South Carolina," 68–71; Sullivan, *Days of Hope,* 21.

10. Frank Smith, *Congressman from Mississippi,* 39.

11. Hayes, "South Carolina and the New Deal," 5.

12. Lofton, "Social and Economic History of Columbia, South Carolina," 71.

13. Mertz, *Southern Rural Poverty,* 11–13.

14. Albert U. Romasco, "Hoover-Roosevelt and the Great Depression: A Historiographic Inquiry into a Perennial Comparison," in Braeman, Bremner, and Brody, *New Deal,* 3–26. For Herbert Hoover, see Hoff, *Herbert Hoover.*

15. Sullivan, *Days of Hope,* 22.

16. Leuchtenburg, *Roosevelt and the New Deal,* 17. For Roosevelt's early years, see Schlesinger, *Age of Roosevelt,* 317–43.

17. For a description and analysis of Franklin Roosevelt's early relationship with the South, see Freidel, *FDR and the South,* 1–33; Jasper B. Shannon, "Presidential Politics in the South," in Cole and Hallowell, *Southern Political Scene,* 466.

18. Interestingly, Roosevelt's future nemesis Huey Long was largely responsible for holding portions of the South for FDR in 1932. For information on Roosevelt's nomination at the 1932 Democratic National Convention, see Freidel, *Franklin D. Roosevelt,* 291–311; Leuchtenburg, *Roosevelt and the New Deal,* 4–8; McElvaine, *Great Depression,* 123–34; Freidel, *FDR and the South,* 2; Grantham, *South in Modern America,* 118; Schlesinger, *Age of Roosevelt,* 276–77. On the 1928 bolt, see Key, *Southern Politics,* 317–29.

19. Freidel, *FDR and the South,* 42–43.

20. Grantham, *South in Modern America,* 122–23; Tindall, *Emergence of the New South,* 608–11.

21. Freidel, *FDR and the South,* 2, 46; Patterson, "Conservative Coalition," 760.

22. Freidel, *FDR and the South,* 48; see also Sullivan, *Days of Hope,* 3.

23. Mertz, *Southern Rural Poverty,* 45–46.

24. Tindall, *Emergence of the New South,* 476.

25. Frank Smith, *Congressman from Mississippi,* 21, 22.

26. Schulman, *From Cotton Belt to Sun Belt,* 16, 44; Robson, "Mississippi Farm Bureau through Depression and War," 257.

27. W. M. Garrard to C. C. Smith, March 1, 1943, file 7B, box 29, Sillers Papers, DSU.

28. Census data summarized in Myrdal, *American Dilemma,* 253. For cotton acreage figures, see Schulman, *From Cotton Belt to Sun Belt,* 17.

29. For the flaws in, and abuses of, the AAA, see Mertz, *Southern Rural Poverty,* 23–44; Raymond Wolters, "The New Deal and the Negro," in Braeman, Bremner, and Brody, *New Deal,* 174–75. For the transformation of southern agriculture and rural life, see Daniel, *Breaking the Land;* Fite, *Cotton Fields No More;* Kirby, *Rural Worlds Lost.*

30. Schulman, *From Cotton Belt to Sun Belt,* 22–23; Sullivan, *Days of Hope,* 24; Tindall, *Emergence of the New South,* 444–45.

31. Sullivan, *Days of Hope,* 92–101.

32. Simon, *Fabric of Defeat,* 182–83.

33. Norrell, "Labor at the Ballot Box," 211, 213. Norrell notes, however, that despite these victories, labor's vote was split.

34. Numan V. Bartley, *Creation of Modern Georgia,* 190–92; Rogers et al., *Alabama,* 500.

35. Swain, *Pat Harrison,* 78; Chester M. Morgan, *Redneck Liberal,* 64.

36. Lorena Hickok to Harry L. Hopkins, February 10, 1934, in Lowitt and Beasley, *One Third of a Nation,* 185; Mertz, *Southern Rural Poverty,* 48–49.

37. Lorena Hickok to Harry L. Hopkins, February 8, 1934, in Lowitt and Beasley, *One Third of a Nation,* 183.

38. Lorena Hickok to Harry L. Hopkins, January 16, 1934, in ibid., 151; Mertz, *Southern Rural Poverty,* 48–56.

39. Tindall, *Emergence of the New South,* 549–50; McElvaine, *Great Depression,* 189.

40. Quoted in McElvaine, *Great Depression,* 189–90.

41. Ibid., 187; Tindall, *Emergence of the New South,* 550.

42. Tindall, *Emergence of the New South,* 554. Seventy-two percent of all polled nationwide favored antilynching legislation.

43. White, *Man Called White,* 169–70.

44. Raymond Wolters, "The New Deal and the Negro," in Braeman, Bremner, and Brody, *New Deal,* 170–71.

45. Fairclough, *Race and Democracy,* 44.

46. Ibid., xvii.

47. Autrey, "National Association for the Advancement of Colored People in Alabama," 178.

48. Sullivan, *Days of Hope,* 141.

49. Fairclough, *Race and Democracy,* 46–47.

50. Sullivan, *Days of Hope,* 141–42.

51. Fairclough, *Race and Democracy,* 46–50.

52. Ibid., 51.

53. Ibid., 52–53.

54. Ibid., 50.

55. Kelley, *Hammer and Hoe,* 33.

56. Ibid., 182, 184.

57. Ibid., 177–78.

58. Ibid., 54, 163.

59. Ibid., 161–62.

60. Leuchtenburg, *Roosevelt and the New Deal,* 114–17; McElvaine, *Great Depression,* 229. For challenges to Roosevelt, see Leuchtenburg, *Roosevelt and the New Deal,* chap. 5; Brinkley, *Voices of Protest.*

61. Grantham, *South in Modern America,* 124–25.

62. Tindall, *Emergence of the New South,* 607–8.

63. Koeniger, "Carter Glass and the NRA," 355.

64. Tindall, *Emergence of the New South,* 611; Patterson, "Failure of Party Realignment," 611.

65. Tindall, *Emergence of the New South,* 612; Koeniger, "Carter Glass and the NRA."

66. Patterson, "Conservative Coalition," 757–59. Patterson notes that Pat Harrison and James Byrnes were early New Deal supporters who consistently voted against the New Deal after 1937.

67. Freidel, *FDR and the South,* 72–73. Other New Deal opponents included, in the House, Edward E. Cox (D-Ga.), Howard Smith (D-Va.), William J. Driver (D-Ark.), J. Bayard Clark (D-N.C.), Martin Dies Jr. (D-Tex.), Carle E. Mapes (R-Mich.), J. Will

Taylor (R-Tenn.), Donald H. McLean (R-N.J.), and in the Senate, Charles L. McNary (Oreg.), Arthur Vandenburg (Mich.), Henry Cabot Lodge (Mass.), Warren R. Austin (Vt.), and Hiram W. Johnson (Calif.), all Republicans. Democratic senators opposed to the New Deal included Edward R. Burke (Nebr.), Peter G. Gerry (R.I.), Walter George (Ga.), Cotton Ed Smith (S.C.), Pat Harrison (Miss.), and James F. Byrnes (S.C.).

68. Patterson, "Failure of Party Realignment," 616–17.

69. Tindall, *Emergence of the New South,* 618.

70. Patterson, "Conservative Coalition," 766–67.

71. Garson, *Politics of Sectionalism,* 7.

72. Zieger, *CIO,* 39–41.

73. Sullivan, *Days of Hope,* 61.

74. Billington, *Political South,* 76–77; Lamis, *Two-Party South,* 7. The economic appeal of the New Deal undermined the Republican loyalty of black voters outside the South, and this shift of northern blacks to the Democratic Party occurred while the black migration from the South was in full swing.

75. Leuchtenburg, *Roosevelt and the New Deal,* 184–85; Tindall, *Emergence of the New South,* 556.

76. Sullivan, *Days of Hope,* 145–46.

77. According to the plan, once a judge reached the age of seventy, and provided he had served more than ten years on the bench, if he waited more than six months to retire, Roosevelt could appoint an additional justice. See Leuchtenburg, *Roosevelt and the New Deal,* 231–38; Tindall, *Emergence of the New South,* 620; Freidel, *FDR and the South,* 92–95.

78. Freidel, *FDR and the South,* 99–101.

79. Sullivan, *Days of Hope,* 70.

80. Mertz, *Southern Rural Poverty,* 231–33.

81. Alan Brinkley, "The New Deal and Southern Politics," in Cobb and Namorato, *New Deal and the South,* 107.

82. Patterson, "Failure of Party Realignment," 612, 616; Shannon, "Presidential Politics in the South: 1938," pts. 1 and 2.

83. Quoted in Hamilton, *Lister Hill,* 84.

84. Ibid., 84–85.

85. Sullivan, *Days of Hope,* 67, 70.

86. Schulman, *From Cotton Belt to Sun Belt,* 43.

87. Kelley, *Hammer and Hoe,* 188–89.

88. Garson, *Politics of Sectionalism,* 12; Patterson, "Failure of Party Realignment," "Conservative Coalition," and *Congressional Conservatism and the New Deal;* Moore, "Conservative Coalition in the United States Senate."

CHAPTER TWO

1. Elliott and D'Orso, *Cost of Courage,* 114.

2. Tindall, *Emergence of the New South,* 694.

3. Neuchterlein, "Politics of Civil Rights," 172.

4. "In all . . . from 1939 to 1947, the number of manufacturing establishments grew from 26,516 to 42,739," and the number of production workers more than doubled,

from 1.3 million in 1939 to 2.8 million in 1943 "and remained at 2,032,000 in 1947" (Tindall, *Emergence of the New South,* 700–701). See also Hon, "South in the War Economy"; Schulman, *From Cotton Belt to Sun Belt,* 72.

5. Behel, "Mississippi Homefront during World War II," 20.

6. Rogers et al., *Alabama,* 511.

7. C. Calvin Smith, *War and Wartime Changes,* 23.

8. Behel, "Mississippi Homefront during World War II," 20, 29.

9. Dalfiume, " 'Forgotten Years,' " 91; Sitkoff, "Racial Militancy," 665; Reed, "FEPC and the Federal Agencies in the South," 43; Kesselman, *Social Politics of FEPC,* 11.

10. Fairclough, *Race and Democracy,* 85.

11. Quoted in C. Calvin Smith, *War and Wartime Changes,* 77.

12. Finkle, "Conservative Aims," 699. Also see Kesselman, *Social Politics of FEPC,* 6; Behel, "Mississippi Homefront during World War II," 42.

13. Sitkoff, "Racial Militancy," 668.

14. Rogers et al., *Alabama,* 514; Fairclough, *Race and Democracy,* 78.

15. Neuchterlein, "Politics of Civil Rights," 176.

16. Dalfiume, " 'Forgotten Years,' " 94–95; Finkle, "Conservative Aims," 693.

17. Garfinkel, *When Negroes March,* 8; Ruchames, *Race, Jobs, and Politics,* 3–21; Kesselman, *Social Politics of FEPC,* 13–15, 93–97.

18. Executive Order 8802, June 25, 1941, quoted in Neuchterlein, "Politics of Civil Rights," 176.

19. Sitkoff, "Racial Militancy," 666.

20. Neuchterlein, "Politics of Civil Rights," 176.

21. Finkle, "Conservative Aims," 700.

22. Neuchterlein, "Politics of Civil Rights," 180.

23. Reed, "FEPC and the Federal Agencies in the South," 54.

24. *Southern Textile Bulletin,* February 1, 1946, 26.

25. On Bilbo's New Deal liberalism, see Chester M. Morgan, *Redneck Liberal,* esp. 70–76, 174; on Bilbo and the FEPC, see Bailey, "Theodore G. Bilbo and the Fair Employment Practices Controversy."

26. Quoted in Ruchames, *Race, Jobs, and Politics,* 94.

27. Tindall, *Emergence of the New South,* 715; Neuchterlein, "Politics of Civil Rights," 180.

28. Sancton, "Trouble in Dixie II," 50; *New York Times,* July 24, 1942, quoted in Kesselman, *Social Politics of FEPC,* 167.

29. Kesselman, *Social Politics of FEPC,* 167.

30. See Defense Supplies Corporation files, Gubernatorial Papers, Dixon Papers, ADAH.

31. Reed, *Seedtime for the Modern Civil Rights Movement,* 340–43; Neuchterlein, "Politics of Civil Rights," 189; Tindall, *Emergence of the New South,* 715.

32. On CORE, see Meier and Rudwick, *CORE.*

33. Sitkoff, "Racial Militancy," 671, 674–75.

34. For wartime race rumors, see Odum, *Race and Rumors of Race;* Sancton, "Trouble in Dixie I."

35. Cobb, *Most Southern Place on Earth,* 198.

36. Oscar Johnston to Walter Sillers, April 24, 1947, file 14, box 32, Sillers Papers, DSU.

37. Fred Young to Ransom Aldrich, February 25, 1943, file 7B, box 29, ibid.

38. Quoted in Cobb, *Most Southern Place on Earth,* 203.

39. Quoted in Lemann, *Promised Land,* 49–50. Also see Dorothy Lee Black to Walter Sillers, March 13, 1943, file 7B, box 29, Sillers Papers, DSU.

40. Walter Sillers, radio address transcript, April 21, 1943, file 11, box 1, Sillers Papers, DSU.

41. C. Calvin Smith, *War and Wartime Changes,* 78.

42. William H. Mounger Jr. to Walter Sillers, June 23, 1942, file 1, box 15, Sillers Papers, DSU.

43. Minutes, Special Labor Committee, Delta Council, November 23, 1942, in file 14, box 14, ibid.; Brooks, "From Hitler and Tojo to Talmadge and Jim Crow," 102.

44. Quoted in Neil R. McMillen, "How Mississippi's Black Veterans Remember World War II," in McMillen, *Remaking Dixie,* 102–3.

45. Quoted in ibid., 103.

46. Garson, *Politics of Sectionalism,* 42–46.

47. Sullivan, *Days of Hope,* 203; Brooks, "From Hitler and Tojo to Talmadge and Jim Crow," 149.

48. Fairclough, *Race and Democracy,* 36.

49. Hamby, *Beyond the New Deal,* 30.

50. Garson, *Politics of Sectionalism,* 94–95; Jones, "Will Dixie Bolt the New Deal?," 20–21, 42, 45.

51. Rogers et al., *Alabama,* 501.

52. Tindall, *Emergence of the New South,* 727–28; Sancton, "Trouble in Dixie II." A Gallup poll taken in the summer of 1943 showed that 80 percent of southern voters favored Roosevelt in 1944.

53. Ferrell, *Choosing Truman,* 3; Heaster, "Who's on Second," 156–57.

54. Partin, "Roosevelt, Byrnes, and the 1944 Vice-Presidential Nomination," 88; Tindall, *Emergence of the New South,* 728.

55. Tindall, *Emergence of the New South,* 728; McCoy, *Presidency of Harry S. Truman,* 7–8; Berman, *Politics of Civil Rights,* 16–17.

56. Berman, *Politics of Civil Rights,* 16.

57. Ibid., 15–16, 19–20.

58. Sullivan, *Days of Hope,* 223–24.

59. Ibid., 23–30; quotation from Egerton, *Speak Now against the Day,* 217.

60. *Smith v. Allwright,* 321 U.S. 649 (1944); Key, *Southern Politics,* 619.

61. John Rankin to Walter Sillers, file 32, box 22, Sillers Papers, DSU.

62. Moon, *Balance of Power,* 183.

63. Frank Dixon to Gessner McCorvey, October 12, 1944, file 24, box 1, Personal Papers, Dixon Papers, ADAH.

64. Key, *Southern Politics,* 571–72; Barnard, *Dixiecrats and Democrats,* 61–62, 127–28; Moon, *Balance of Power,* 182–83. A federal court in Mobile declared the Boswell Amendment unconstitutional in early 1949.

65. Gessner T. McCorvey to Frank Dixon, file 24, box 1, Personal Papers, Dixon Papers, ADAH.

66. *Elmore v. Rice,* 72 Fed. Supp. 516 (1947); South Carolina *House Journal,* 1944, 115–57; *Newsweek,* May 1, 1944, 33. See Key, *Southern Politics,* 625–43. Federal district courts soon found this and other measures to be unconstitutional.

67. Sullivan, *Days of Hope,* 203.

68. Hamilton, *Lister Hill,* 120, 123.

69. Ibid., 125–26.

70. Ibid., 126.

71. Simon, *Fabric of Defeat,* 232.

72. Pepper quoted in Clark, "Road to Defeat," 61.

73. Clark, "Road to Defeat," 65.

74. Sullivan, *Days of Hope,* 218–19.

75. Numan V. Bartley, *Creation of Modern Georgia,* 201.

76. Sullivan, *Days of Hope,* 202.

77. Brooks, "From Hitler and Tojo to Talmadge and Jim Crow," 34.

78. Norrell, *Reaping the Whirlwind,* 41, 59–78.

79. For information on McCray's early life, see John McCray interview, tape, January 11, 1986, PDOHI. Also see John McCray to Arthur Clement, August 4, 1952, McCray file, Clement Papers, SCL.

80. John McCray to Peter C. Kelly, April 1, 1946, file 6, box 1, McCray Papers, SCL.

81. John McCray to I. DeQuincey Newman, December 20, 1967, McCray file, Clement Papers, SCL.

82. See John McCray to Dr. J. G. Stuart, May 13, 1944, box 4; John McCray to Arthur Clement, May 14, 1945, file 13, box 3; John McCray, typescript editorial for *Lighthouse and Informer,* "Explanation of the Plan for 'Beating the Primary,'" April 2, 1944, file 3, box 1; press release, ca. 1944, file 23, box 4, all in McCray Papers, SCL. See also John H. McCray to I. DeQuincey Newman, December 20, 1967, McCray file, Clement Papers, SCL.

83. Borsos, "Support for the National Democratic Party," 23.

84. McCray, "Explanation of the Plan for 'Beating the Primary,'" April 2, 1944, file 3, box 1; press release, ca. 1944, file 23, box 4; and John McCray to "Fellow citizens," June 4, 1944, file 21, box 2, all in McCray Papers, SCL; John H. McCray to I. DeQuincey Newman, December 20, 1967, McCray file, Clement Papers, SCL. Prior to the convention, the PDP proposed to the state Democratic Party that it include eight black delegates of the state's eighteen to the national convention. When that proposal was turned down, the PDP decided to send its own delegates. See John McCray to Winchester Smith, May 10, 1944, box 4, McCray Papers, SCL. See also John McCray to William L. Dawson, June 22, 1944; John McCray to Adam Clayton Powell Jr., June 21, 1944; Nat J. Humphries to Herbert L. Bruce, June 19, 1944; Robert E. Hannegan to John McCray, June 29, 1944, file 21, box 2; and typed manuscript, "The Whys, Whats and Wherefores of Progressive Democratic Party," ca. 1945, box 4, all in McCray Papers, SCL.

85. John McCray to Adam Clayton Powell, June 8, 21, 1944, and John McCray to William L. Dawson, June 22, 1944, file 21, box 2, McCray Papers, SCL.

86. Telegram, Oscar R. Ewing to John McCray, July 7, 1944, file 22, box 2, McCray Papers, SCL.

87. John McCray, "A Report from the State Chairman," July 26, 1944, ibid.

88. John McCray interview, January 11, 1986, PDOHI.

89. Transcript, "Meeting of the Progressive Democratic Party of South Carolina with Subcommittee of Democratic National Committee," July 17, 1944, p. 4, box 1, Records of Meetings, DNC Papers, HSTL.

90. PDP, press release, July 19, 1944, file 22, box 2, McCray Papers, SCL. The subcommittee ruled that the PDP had not had enough time for thorough organization that would have allowed it to hold all precinct and ward meetings.

91. John McCray, "A Report from the State Chairman," July 26, 1944, box 2, McCray Papers, SCL.

92. John McCray to "Fellow Citizen," September 1, 1944, file 22, ibid. See also McCray to I. DeQuincey Newman, December 20, 1967, McCray file, Clement Papers, SCL.

93. In 1944 he wrote, "We [the PDP] are not opposed to the court action . . . but frankly, court decision or no decision, it shall be a very long time before we (colored) can participate in elections[,] . . . and in our position as leaders, I don't think we treat our people justly when we lead them to the altar of life sacrifice and lay the groundwork for violence upon them." See John McCray to Rev. W. Mc??, April 27, 1944, box 4, McCray Papers, SCL.

94. John McCray to Arthur J. Clement, August 11, 1946, and Arthur J. Clement to John McCray, July 16, September 25, 1946, file 13, box 3, ibid.

95. L. Howard Bennett to John McCray, November 1, 1946, box 3, ibid.

96. See, for example, S. A. Williams to John McCray, June 4, August 5, 1946; John McCray to William J. Ellis, August 7, 1946; George Chism to John McCray, September 19, 1945; John McCray to Julian L. Morgan, December 22, 1945; and Theron L. Caudle to James Hinton, January 5, 1946, all in box 4, ibid.

97. John McCray to Robert E. Hannegan, June 22, 1946, PDP file, Clement Papers, SCL.

98. Brooks, "From Hitler and Tojo to Talmadge and Jim Crow," 91.

99. Quoted in ibid., 30. See also Bates, *Long Shadow of Little Rock,* 44.

100. See Sullivan, *Days of Hope,* chap. 7.

101. Ibid., 215–16; Egerton, *Speak Now against the Day,* 391–92.

102. Hamilton, *Lister Hill,* 144–45.

103. Memorandum, "Citizenship in the South," November 8, 1948, p. 4, and Voting Rights Campaign, 1916–1950, pt. 4, reel 7, NAACP Papers (mf).

104. "Negro Vote in Southern States: 1946," p. 8, pt. 4, reel 8, and Daniel E. Byrd to Thurgood Marshall, July 3 1946, Voting Rights Campaign, 1916–1950, pt. 4, reel 9, ibid.

105. "Affidavit of Etoy Fletcher," June 15, 1946; also see "Affidavit of V. R. Collins," n.d., Voting Rights Campaign, 1916–1950, pt. 4, reel 9, ibid.

106. "Affidavit of Charles Donaville Jr. and Steve Hunter Jr.," August 5, 1947, ibid.

107. Quoted in Skates, *Mississippi,* 155.

108. Sullivan, *Days of Hope,* 225, 235, 243.

109. Brooks, "From Hitler and Tojo to Talmadge and Jim Crow," 17–18.

110. Lester, *Man for Arkansas,* 19–30.

111. For the caning of Charles Sumner, see Potter, *Impending Crisis,* 209–11; Simkins, *Pitchfork Ben Tillman.*

112. For Thurmond's early life, see Cohodas, *Strom Thurmond,* 26–36.

113. For Thurmond's early political career, see ibid., 37–125, and press release, May 15, 1946, box 1, Speeches Series, Thurmond Papers, CU.

114. Quoted in Bass and Thompson, *Ol' Strom,* 75.

115. Cohodas, *Strom Thurmond,* 86.

116. Ashley, "Selected Southern Liberal Editors and the States' Rights Movement of 1948," 100–101.

117. *Charleston News and Courier,* July 24, 1946. For Eugene Talmadge's 1946 gubernatorial campaign, see Anderson, *Wild Man from Sugar Creek,* 226–33.

118. Osceola E. McKaine to J. Strom Thurmond, March 12, 1947, file 26, box 2, McCray Papers, SCL.

119. J. Strom Thurmond, address, Louisville, Kentucky, October 2, 1947, box 1, Speeches Series, Thurmond Papers, CU.

120. Billington, *Political South,* 88–90.

121. Berman, *Politics of Civil Rights,* 54. According to Berman, African Americans had begun to lose faith in the present government's commitment to civil rights and were discouraged by the number of "Deep Southerners," like Secretary of State James F. Byrnes, in the Truman administration, men who could not possibly have sympathy for them. Black leaders reasoned that the removal of southern Democrats from committee chairmanships could conceivably lead to the passage of civil rights legislation.

122. Kellogg, "Civil Rights Consciousness in the 1940s," 24.

123. Press release, speech transcript, June 28, 1947, NAACP speech file, box 17, Elsey Papers, HSTL.

124. McCoy and Ruetten, *Quest and Response,* 43–44; O'Brien, *Color of the Law.*

125. President's Committee on Civil Rights, *To Secure These Rights,* 22; *New York Times,* August 4, 1946; Wallace H. Warren, " 'The Best People in Town Won't Talk:' The Moore's Ford Lynching of 1946 and Its Cover-Up," in Inscoe, *Georgia in Black and White,* 271–72, 273–74, 281–82.

126. Quoted in Numan V. Bartley, *Creation of Modern Georgia,* 202.

127. Quoted in Wallace H. Warren, " 'The Best People in Town Won't Talk:' The Moore's Ford Lynching of 1946 and Its Cover-Up," in Inscoe, *Georgia in Black and White,* 273.

128. Eleanor Morehead, "Negro Vet Tells How Dixie Cops Gouged Out Both Eyes with Club," *PM,* July 17, 1946, clipping, Isaac Woodard file, box 36, Nash Papers, HSTL.

129. John McCray, "The Isaac Woodard Story," typed manuscript, n.d., box 7, McCray Papers, SCL.

130. Franklin H. Williams to Lincoln Miller, August 6, 1946, and Robert L. Carter to Harold R. Boulware, August 13, 1946, Woodard file, box 219, series B, group 2, NAACP Papers.

131. Walter White to Robert P. Patterson, May 6, 1946, ibid.

132. Walter White to Orson Welles, July 24, 1946, ibid., Legal files.

133. *New York Times,* August 9, 1946. See unidentified news clipping, August 12, 1946, and Hope Spingarn to John Crosby, September 6, 1946, Orson Welles file, box 671, series A, group 2, NAACP Papers; *Aiken Standard and Review,* July 26, August 2, 14, 1946.

134. Memo, Robert L. Carter to Walter White, July 19, 1946, Woodard file, box 219, series B, group 2, NAACP Papers.

135. Lincoln Miller to Walter White, July 27, 1946; Robert L. Carter to Harold R. Boulware, August 13, 1946; and telegram, Oliver W. Harrington to Orson Welles, August 14, 1946, ibid.

136. Robert L. Carter to Walter White, August 19, 1946, and to A. D. Smith, August 21, 1946, ibid.

137. Telegram, Walter White to Orson Welles, c/o Charles Wilson, American Broadcasting Company, August 19, 1946, and telegram, Walter White to Orson Welles, September 27, 1946, Orson Welles file, box 671, General Office files, series A, group 2, NAACP Papers.

138. Press release, September 26, 1946, Isaac Woodard file, box 36, Nash Papers, HSTL.

139. *New York Times,* November 6, 1946.

140. John H. McCray to David Lachenbruch, November 13, 1946, file 8, box 1, McCray Papers, SCL.

141. Franklin H. Williams to Ollie Harrington, August 2, 1946; "31,000 at Woodard Rally," news clipping; and "Memorandum to Walter White re. Isaac Woodard Tour," October 16, 1946, Woodard file, box 219, series B, group 2, NAACP Papers.

142. See, for example, Dan T. Carter, *Scottsboro,* 249–50.

143. Harry S. Truman to E. W. [Ernie] Roberts, August 18, 1948, file C, box 306, PSF, HSTL; also see J. C. Turner interview transcript, Washington, D.C., August 1972, OH 116, p. 18, Oral History Collection, HSTL.

144. Members of the committee included Walter White and Leslie Perry of the NAACP, Boris Shishkin of the American Federation of Labor and former member of the FEPC, CIO Secretary James Carey, Dr. Herman Reissig of the Federal Council of the Churches of Christ in America, and Channing Tobias, director of the Phelps-Stokes Fund. See Garson, *Politics of Sectionalism,* 200–201; Berman, *Politics of Civil Rights,* 50–51. Also see Walter White to Branch Officers, January 14, 1947, box 10, Correspondence with Organizations, NAACP file, Federal Record Group 220, PCCR Papers, HSTL.

145. White, *Man Called White,* 330–31.

146. Berman, *Politics of Civil Rights,* 51.

147. Harry S. Truman to Tom Clark, September 20, 1946, and interoffice memo, Harry S. Truman to David K. Niles, September 20, 1946, Civil Rights/Negro Affairs file, box 26, 1945–June 1947, Niles Papers, HSTL.

148. Berman, *Politics of Civil Rights,* 53; Tom C. Clark to Harry S. Truman, October 11, 1946, OF 596A, WHCF.

149. Executive Order 9808, "Establishing the President's Committee on Civil Rights," Civil Rights/Negro Affairs file, 1945–June 1947, box 26, Niles Papers, HSTL.

Members of the committee included Sadie T. Alexander, James B. Carey, John S. Dickey, Morris L. Ernst, Rabbi Roland G. Gittelsohn, Frank P. Graham, the Most Reverend Francis J. Haas, Charles Luckman, Francis P. Matthews, Franklin D. Roosevelt Jr., the Right Reverend Henry Know Sherrill, Boris Shishkin, Dorothy Rogers Tilly, and Channing Tobias. See "Members of Committee on Civil Rights Legislation," Civil Rights/Negro Affairs file, 1945–June 1947, box 26, Niles Papers, HSTL. Also see Dorothy Rogers Tilly, biographical information, Tilly Papers, EU. The appointment of Wilson as the committee's chairman drew criticism from United Electrical, Radio and Machine Workers Local 201 in Lynn, Massachusetts. Twenty thousand union members, employees of the General Electric Company, complained that GE had been unresponsive to their desire to include a nondiscrimination clause in their contract. See Frederick M. Kelley to Harry S. Truman, January 22, 1947, box 1510, OF 596A, "Comments in Favor of President's Civil Rights Committee," WHCF.

150. "Draft of statement by president with reference to the President's Committee on Civil Rights," January 7, 1947, Civil Rights/Negro Affairs file, 1945–June 1947, box 26, Niles Papers, HSTL. In the final report the committee commented, "This report deals with serious civil rights violations in all sections of the country. Much of it has to do with limitations on civil rights in our southern states. To a great extent this reflects reality; many of the most sensational and serious violations of civil rights have taken place in the South" (President's Committee on Civil Rights, *To Secure These Rights,* x).

151. *P.M.,* February 18, 1947, Willie Earle Lynching file, box 55, Philleo Nash file, WHCF; *New York Times,* February 18, 1947; *The State,* February 18, May 14, 1947; telegram, Walter White to Charles E. Wilson, February 17, 1947, Willie Earle file, box 2, PCCR Papers, HSTL.

152. *The State,* February 18, 1947; press release, February 18, 1947, file 23, box 1, Speeches Series, Subseries A, General File, Thurmond Papers, CU.

153. Testimony of J. Edgar Hoover, transcript, March 20, 1947, Proceedings of the Committee, Records Relating to Meetings, Hearings, and Staff Interviews of the Committee, box 12, and Testimony of Tom Clark, transcript, April 3, 1947, Proceedings of the Committee, April and May 1947, box 13, PCCR Papers, HSTL.

154. Osceola E. McKaine to J. Strom Thurmond, March 12, 1947, file 26, box 2, McCray Papers, SCL.

155. Testimony of J. Edgar Hoover, transcript, March 20, 1947, Proceedings of the Committee, Records Relating to Meetings, Hearings, and Staff Interviews of the Committee, box 12, PCCR Papers, HSTL. Warrants charging the thirty-one men with murder were sworn out on February 21, 1947, four days after Earle's body was discovered. See *The State,* February 23, 1947.

156. For a provocative account of the Earle lynching trial, see West, "Opera in Greenville"; *The State,* March 5, May 15–16, 1947.

157. *The State,* February 22, 1947.

158. Alice Spearman to Rosamonde Wimberly, March 31, 1947, file 3, box 1, SCCHR Papers, SCL.

159. *The State,* March 13, 1947.

160. Anonymous to John McCray, March 4, 1947, file 26, box 2, McCray Papers, SCL.

161. *Houston Informer,* March 22, 1947, news clipping in Philleo Nash file, WHCF; also see *The State,* May 12, 1947.

162. *The State,* February 22, 1947.

163. Ibid., February 24, 1947.

164. Ibid., February 21, 1947.

165. Charles E. Wilson to Walter White, February 17, 1947, Willie Earle file, box 2, PCCR Papers, HSTL.

166. Robert K. Carr to David K. Niles, February 18, 1947, and David K. Niles to Matt Connelly, February 18, 1947, box 1510, OF 596A, "President's Committee on Civil Rights," WHCF; also see Juhnke, "Harry Truman's Committee on Civil Rights," 598.

167. Walter White to Robert K. Carr, February 17, 1947, NAACP file, box 10, PCCR Papers, HSTL.

168. Memorandum, Robert L. Carter to Walter White [cc Robert K. Carr], March 12, 1947, ibid.

169. Testimony of J. Edgar Hoover, transcript, March 20, 1947, Proceedings of the Committee, Records Relating to Meetings, Hearings, and Staff Interviews of the Committee, box 12, and Testimony of Tom Clark, transcript, April 3, 1947, Proceedings of the Committee, April and May 1947, box 13, PCCR Papers, HSTL.

170. *The State,* May 13, 1947; West, "Opera in Greenville," 55.

171. *The State,* May 13, 20, 1947.

172. Ibid., May 16, 1947.

173. Ibid., May 20, 1947.

174. Davis, Gardner, and Gardner, *Deep South,* 57; O'Brien, *Color of the Law,* 130.

175. Gilbert and Samuels, *Taxicab,* 79–85.

176. West, "Opera in Greenville," 45.

177. Olivier, "Jess Mitchell's Private War."

178. Simon, "Guilt."

179. *The State,* May 14, 1947.

180. Ibid., May 21, 1947.

181. Ibid.

182. West, "Opera in Greenville," 60.

183. Mark A. Smith to PCCR, June 9, 1947, Willie Earle file, Correspondence and Administration Records, box 2, PCCR Papers, HSTL.

184. Robert K. Carr, memo to Members of the President's Committee on Civil Rights, May 29, 1947, Civil Rights/Negro Affairs file, 1945–June 1947, box 26, Niles Papers, HSTL. See also telegram, Roy Wilkins to Charles E. Wilson, May 22, 1947; Roy Wilkins to NAACP Branch Presidents, May 22, 1947; and Roy Wilkins to Harry Truman, May 22, 1947, box 406, General Office files, series A, group 2, NAACP Papers; "Anti-lynching legislation" file, Correspondence and Administration Records, box 1, and Lou Ella Miler to Charles E. Wilson, June 5, 1947, Willie Earle file, Correspondence and Administration Records, box 2, PCCR Papers, HSTL.

185. Memorandum, Robert K. Carr to PCCR, February 19, 1947, Willie Earle file, box 2, and memorandum, Robert K. Carr to PCCR, February 21, 1947, box 16, PCCR Papers, HSTL.

186. Channing H. Tobias to Robert K. Carr, June 5, 1947, box 7, PCCR Papers, HSTL.

187. Walter Brown to Burnet R. Maybank, May 27, 1947, file 647, Byrnes Papers, CU.

188. David K. Niles to Matthew J. Connelly, June 16, 1947, and press release, speech transcript, June 28, 1947, NAACP Speech File, box 17, Elsey Papers, HSTL; Berman, *Politics of Civil Rights,* 61–62.

189. Press release, October 29, 1947, box 12, Record Relating to the Meetings of the Committee, PCCR Papers, HSTL.

190. President's Committee on Civil Rights, *To Secure These Rights,* 139–73.

191. Press release, "Statement by the President," October 29, 1947, box 80, Report of the Civil Rights Committee File, Subject File, DNC Papers, HSTL.

192. Harry S. Truman to Dorothy Rogers Tilly, November 3, 1947, file 7, box 1, Tilly Papers, EU.

193. Unidentified clippings, November 9, 11, 1947, p. 2, States' Rights Scrapbook, 1948, Workman Papers, SCL.

194. Lillian Smith to Dorothy Rogers Tilly, November 25, 1947, file 7, box 1, Tilly Papers, EU.

195. Robert K. Carr to Dorothy Rogers Tilly, November 8, 1955, file 6, ibid.

196. *Jackson Advocate,* January 10, 1948.

CHAPTER THREE

1. Berman, *Politics of Civil Rights,* 73–74; *Public Papers of the Presidents: Harry S. Truman, 1947,* 480–82.

2. McCullough, *Truman,* 590; "Memorandum for the President," pp. 1–4, 12–13, 40, political file, box 23, Clifford Papers, HSTL.

3. *New York Times,* December 30, 1947, and January 19, 1948.

4. Moon, *Balance of Power,* 198.

5. *Public Papers of the Presidents: Harry S. Truman, 1948,* 3; Ross, *Loneliest Campaign,* 60–61.

6. Berman, *Politics of Civil Rights,* 82.

7. Personally, Carr felt Truman should recommend to Congress "a substantial, but minimum, program for immediate action and then call for further study of many additional items." Carr's minimum recommendations included anti–poll tax and antilynching legislation; the creation of a permanent FEPC, as well as strengthening of the existing civil rights laws; and an executive order outlawing segregation of the armed forces. Elsey recommended that Truman only paraphrase the report. Above all, Elsey noted, the "President *must* retain his freedom of action." The message "ought to be a *wholly* Truman document, not just a feeble citing of certain recommendations of a committee" (Robert Carr to George Elsey, January 16, 1948, and George Elsey, handwritten notes, n.d., Civil Rights Message file, box 20, Elsey Papers, HSTL).

8. Ayers Diaries, 1945–48, set 3, entry for January 23, 1948, p. 16, Ayers Papers, HSTL.

9. *Jackson Daily News,* January 4, 1948.

10. *Jackson Clarion-Ledger,* January 17, 1948.

11. Fielding L. Wright, inaugural address script, Fielding L. Wright Subject File, MDAH. Also see, *Jackson Clarion-Ledger,* January 21, 1948.

12. *Jackson Clarion-Ledger,* January 21, 22, 24, 30, 1948.

13. *Jackson Daily News,* January 20, 25, 1948; Tuggle, "Dixiecrats as 'Stepping Stone,'" 31.

14. Key, *Southern Politics,* 229.

15. Sixty of the state's 82 counties in 1940 were more than 30 percent black; 35, more than 50 percent; 17, more than 70 percent (ibid., 229–30). Also see Charles N. Fortenberry and F. Glenn Abney, "Mississippi: Unreconstructed and Unredeemed," in Havard, *Changing Politics of the South,* 475–76.

16. McMillen, *Dark Journey,* 5, 9–10.

17. Ibid., 289.

18. Key, *Southern Politics,* 230.

19. Cobb, *Most Southern Place on Earth,* 150–51.

20. Woodward, *Origins of the New South,* 261. According to Woodward, for example, the populist movement in Mississippi was extremely weak.

21. Holmes, *White Chief.* Vardaman won election to the U.S. Senate in 1912 with a campaign advocating repeal of the Fourteenth and Fifteenth Amendments.

22. Chester M. Morgan, *Redneck Liberal,* chap. 1, 49. Percy is quoted p. 5.

23. Quoted in Cobb, *Most Southern Place on Earth,* 146.

24. Ibid., 146–52.

25. Anonymous source quoted in Charles G. Hamilton Oral History, March 3, May 11, 1983, Aberdeen, Miss., vol. 242, MOHP, USM.

26. Melton, "Mr. Speaker," 7–8, 87, 20–23.

27. Stanford Young interview, August 24, 1991, and Judge Lucy Somerville Howorth interview, May 30, 1984, p. 17, MOHP, USM.

28. Dorothy Lee Black to Walter Sillers, November 12, 1942, file 7A, box 29, Sillers Papers, DSU.

29. Judge L. B. Porter interview, May 13, 1985, pp. 12, 22, and Maurice R. Black interview, July 25, 1991, p. 8, MOHP, USM.

30. Sumners, *Governors of Mississippi,* 122–25; Hilliard, "Biography of Fielding Wright," 1–61.

31. "Message from the President of the United States Transmitting His Recommendations for Civil Rights Program," February 2, 1948, in box 20, Elsey Papers, HSTL.

32. *Congressional Record,* 976.

33. *Jackson Daily News,* February 3, 1948; *New York Times,* February 3, 1948.

34. *Anderson Independent,* February 7, 1948; *The State,* February 4, 7, 1948; Strom Thurmond to William Jennings Bryan Dorn, February 5, 1948, box 23, Public Papers, Dorn Papers, SCL.

35. *Jackson Daily News,* February 4, 1948.

36. Harold C. Fisher Jr. and Don Fisher to Harry S. Truman, March 2, 1948, PPF 200, HSTL.

37. W. B. Dowell Jr. to Harry S. Truman, February 10, 1948, ibid.

38. Virginia Hart Lide to Harry S. Truman, March 10, 1948, ibid.

39. M. F. Stack to James F. Byrnes, February 6, 1948, file 701 (4), Byrnes Papers, CU.

40. *Hattiesburg American,* February 4, 1948.

41. Ayers Diaries, set 3, p. 26, Ayers Papers, HSTL.

42. Ferrell, *Off the Record,* 122.

43. Minutes, Board of Directors Meeting, February 9, 1948, p. 12, pt. 1, reel 3, NAACP Papers (mf); *Jackson Advocate,* February 21, 1948.

44. Walter White, press release, "The President Means It," February 12, 1948, box 27, Niles Papers, HSTL.

45. James M. Hinton to President Truman, February 3, 1948, box 37, Dorn Papers, SCL. Civil rights activists' hopes for civil rights legislation were soon put on hold. Truman backed away from his plan to send an omnibus civil rights bill to Congress and to issue an executive order ending discrimination in the federal government. See Pemberton, *Harry S. Truman,* 116.

46. *New York Times,* February 4, 1948.

47. *Jackson Clarion-Ledger,* February 4, 6, 7, 1948.

48. Ibid., February 8, 9, 1948; Key, *Southern Politics,* 331; Chesteen, " 'Mississippi Is Gone Home!,' " 50.

49. Bendiner, "Dixie's Fourth Party," 174.

50. Walter Brown to James Byrnes, February 9, 1948, file 681 (1), Byrnes Papers, CU.

51. "Motion of J. Strom Thurmond, Governor of South Carolina, at Southern Governors' Conference," February 7, 1948, States' Rights Democrats file, box 2, Workman Papers, SCL.

52. *Albany Sunday Herald,* February 8, 1948, in Thurmond Scrapbook, vol. 1, Thurmond Papers, CU.

53. James M. Hinton to J. Strom Thurmond, February 8, 1948, file 3198, Gubernatorial Series, Thurmond Papers, CU.

54. *Atlanta Journal,* February 7, 1948.

55. *New York Times,* February 10, 1948.

56. J. Strom Thurmond to "Congressmen," February 9, 1948, file 3217, Gubernatorial Series, Thurmond Papers, CU.

57. "Digest of Replies Received From: Southern Governors, Southern Senators, Southern Congressmen, General Public, South Carolina Democratic Party," n.d., box 13, Figg Papers, SCL. Also see Richard B. Russell to Strom Thurmond, February 17, 1948, file 3230, Gubernatorial Series, Thurmond Papers, CU.

58. "Digest of Replies Received From: Southern Governors, Southern Senators, Southern Congressmen, General Public, South Carolina Democratic Party," n.d., box 13, Figg Papers, SCL.

59. *Jackson Clarion-Ledger,* February 7, 1948; *New York Herald Tribune,* February 20, 1948, news clipping in clipping file, box 193, DNC Papers, HSTL; *New York Times,* February 29, 1948. Jack Redding, director of public relations for the DNC, confirmed that the southern revolt was potentially costly because it "cut the party off from a large source of its contributions" (Redding, *Inside the Democratic Party,* 132).

60. *The State,* February 19, 1948.

61. Redding, *Inside the Democratic Party,* 136–37.

62. *New York Times,* February 24, 1948.

63. "Transcript of Conference of Southern Governors with Senator J. Howard McGrath, Chairman of the Democratic National Committee," February 23, 1948, Southern Governors' Conference 1948 file, box 26, McGrath Papers, HSTL.

64. *Charlotte News,* February 24, 1948; *Washington Daily News,* February 24, 1948, in South Carolina State Political file, box 169, DNC Papers, HSTL.

65. McCullough, *Truman,* 593.

66. Ayers Diaries, set 3, p. 37, Ayers Papers, HSTL.

67. *New York Times,* February 27, 1948; Garson, *Politics of Sectionalism,* 243.

68. *Jackson Clarion-Ledger,* February 13, 1948.

69. "Resolution adopted by Mississippi Conference of Democrats, February 12, 1948," Minutes of the Meeting of the Mississippi State Democratic Executive Committee, February 19, 1948, Democratic Executive Committee Papers, vol. 2, MDAH; *Jackson Clarion-Ledger,* February 13, 1948.

70. Ness, "States' Rights Democratic Movement," 58.

71. *Oxford Eagle,* January 29, 1948.

72. Mitchell, "Frank E. Smith," 90.

73. *Jackson Advocate,* February 21, 1948; *Jackson Clarion-Ledger,* February 12, 1948.

74. Representatives attended from Alabama, Arkansas, Florida, Georgia, Louisiana, Mississippi, North Carolina, South Carolina, Tennessee, and Texas. See *Jackson Clarion-Ledger,* February 21, 1948.

75. *Jackson Daily News,* February 23, 1948; *Jackson Clarion-Ledger,* February 23, 1948.

76. Minutes, Mississippi State Democratic Executive Committee, March 1, 1948, Democratic Executive Committee Papers, vol. 2, MDAH; *Jackson Daily News,* March 2, 1948; *States' Righter,* April 1948.

77. Minutes, Mississippi State Democratic Executive Committee, March 1, 1948, Democratic Executive Committee Papers, vol. 21, MDAH; John Oliver Emmerich interview, April, May 1972, vol. 16, p. 53, MOHP, USM.

78. *Jackson Clarion-Ledger,* March 9, 1948.

79. *Jackson Daily News,* March 16, 1948.

80. *Jackson Clarion-Ledger,* April 14, 16, 1948.

81. Ibid., April 16, 1948.

82. *Jackson Daily News,* March 21, 1948; *Jackson Clarion-Ledger,* March 21, 1948; *States' Righter,* April 1948.

83. Transcript, radio address of Governor Fielding L. Wright, May 9, 1948, Wood Scrapbook, MDAH.

84. *Jackson Advocate,* May 15, 1948.

85. Minutes, Board of Directors Meeting, 10 May 1948, p. 8, pt. 1, reel 3, NAACP Papers (mf).

86. "Revolt Grows," quote on p. 18; *Charlotte Observer,* February 20, 22, 1948; *Greenville News,* February 22, 1948.

87. *Atlanta Journal,* February 24, 1948.

88. "Democrats in Jasper Quit Party," unidentified clipping, February 24, 1948, p. 37, States' Rights Scrapbook, 1948, Workman Papers, SCL.

89. The Dorchester County Democratic Executive Committee, as well as the Bluffton Democratic Club of Beaufort County, recommended withdrawal from the national

party. See *Charlotte Observer,* February 25, 1948; *Charleston News and Courier,* February 26, 1948.

90. Simon, *Fabric of Defeat,* 15; Graham and Moore, *South Carolina Politics and Government,* 10–11.

91. Simon, *Fabric of Defeat,* 182.

92. William P. Baskin to State Executive Committeemen, February 6, 1948, file L 647, and "Resolution," adopted by State Democratic Executive Committee, Democratic Party of South Carolina, Columbia, S.C., March 1, 1948, file L 633, Brown Papers, CU; Cohodas, *Strom Thurmond,* 136; *Greenville News,* March 1, 1948; *Charleston News and Courier,* March 2, 1948.

93. J. Strom Thurmond, "President Truman's So-Called Civil Rights Program," March 17, 1948, Speeches Series, Thurmond Papers, CU.

94. Borsos, "Support for the National Democratic Party," 14; *Greenville News,* May 6, 1948.

95. "Committee Report Adopted by Southern Governors' Conference," March 13, 1948, States' Rights file, box 2, Workman Papers, SCL.

96. Ibid. The report was signed by Thurmond, Jester, Laney, and Tuck. Governors Lane and Cherry, although present at the meeting with McGrath, indicated neither approval nor disapproval of the document.

97. *Charlotte Observer,* March 14, 1948; *New York Times,* March 13, 14, 1948.

98. Rogers et al., *Alabama,* 524–25.

99. Ibid., 530.

100. Frank Dixon biographical sketch, n.d., file 1, box 1, Personal Papers, Dixon Papers, ADAH; Grafton and Permaloff, *Political Power in Alabama,* 119.

101. Frank Dixon, speech, "Crossroads Democracy," December 11, 1942, file 2, box 4, personal papers, Dixon Papers, ADAH.

102. Frank Dixon to A. G. Ewing, March 8, 1943, file 16, box 1, Personal Papers, Dixon Papers, ADAH.

103. Frank Dixon to B[enjamin] B. Gossett, August 2, 1944, file 17, box 1, personal papers, Dixon Papers, ADAH.

104. Glenn Feldman, *From Demagogue to Dixiecrat,* x.

105. Ibid., 8–11, 20.

106. Ibid., xiv.

107. Nunnelley, *Bull Connor,* 9–10.

108. Ibid., chap. 1 generally.

109. Ibid., 30.

110. John Sparkman to Eugene (Bull) Connor, May 11, 1948, box 94, Sparkman Papers, UA.

111. Key, *Southern Politics,* 332–33; Gessner McCorvey to "all candidates for delegate to Democratic National Convention," April 6, 1948, file 1, box 2, Personal Papers, Dixon Papers, ADAH.

112. Feldman, "Horace Wilkinson and Alabama Politics," 255–57. For an introduction to Alabama's political divisions in the twentieth century, see Key, *Southern Politics,* 36–57; Barnard, *Dixiecrats and Democrats.* Folsom quoted in *Montgomery Examiner,* February 12, 1948, clipping, box 15, Sparks Papers, ADAH.

113. Hamilton, *Lister Hill,* 149.

114. See Lister Hill, campaign statement, April 15, 1948; Horace Wilkinson to Lister Hill, April 19, 1948, file 20; Lister Hill to Horace Wilkinson, April 21, 1948, file 21, box 367, Hill Papers, UA.

115. See Hugh W. Cardon to Gould Beech, January 28, 1948; Hugh W. Cardon to Lister Hill, January 28, 1948; Lister Hill to Hugh W. Cardon, February 2, 1948, file 20, box 367, Hill Papers, UA. Also see *Alabama,* January 30, 1948, 1.

116. Hamilton, *Lister Hill,* 153; William M. Beck to Lister Hill, February 10, 1948; Clarence Allgood to Lister Hill, March 15, 1948, file 10, box 367, Hill Papers, UA.

117. John Sparkman to Reese Amis, May 8, 1948, Sparkman Papers, UA.

118. Hamilton, *Lister Hill,* 156–57.

119. *New York Times,* May 6, 1948; Garson, *Politics of Sectionalism,* 252–55.

120. No published book-length treatment of the 1948 campaign of the States' Rights Democratic, or Dixiecrat, Party exists. For summaries, see Ader, "Why the Dixiecrats Failed," 356–69; Heard, *Two-Party South?,* chap. 2; Key, *Southern Politics,* chap. 15; Numan V. Bartley, *Rise of Massive Resistance,* chap. 2, and *New South,* chap. 3; Garson, *Politics of Sectionalism,* chap. 9. Particularly useful dissertations include McLaurin, "Role of the Dixiecrats in the 1948 Election," and Ness, "States' Rights Democratic Movement."

121. *Jackson Clarion-Ledger,* May 9, 1948.

122. "Bryson Feels South Should Not 'Bolt,'" unidentified clipping, March 6, 1948, p. 48, States' Rights Scrapbook, 1948, Workman Papers, SCL.

123. Walter Sillers to Millsaps Fitzhugh, June 16, 1944, file 13, box 1, Sillers Papers, DSU. Also see Gilmore, *Gender and Jim Crow,* 13–14.

124. See, for example, "Birthpains of Southern Independence," unidentified clipping, p. 73, States' Rights Scrapbook, 1948, Workman Papers, SCL.

125. *McComb Enterprise-Journal,* February 17, 1948.

126. *Jackson Clarion-Ledger,* January 21, 1948.

127. J. Strom Thurmond, speech before the States' Rights Democratic Convention, May 10, 1948, in *States' Rights Information and Speakers' Handbook.*

128. "The Rebel Yell, 1948," in file 5, box 318, Colmer Papers, USM.

129. Unidentified cartoon, file 3241, Gubernatorial Series, Thurmond Papers, CU.

130. See Buck Gordon to Walter Sillers, July 18, 1948, file 16, box 28, Sillers Papers, DSU.

131. *Jackson Clarion-Ledger,* March 9, 1948.

132. "Rice Asks Uninstructed Delegates," unidentified clipping, February 19, 1948, p. 31; "Bethea Urges South Carolina Democratic Mass Meeting," unidentified clipping, February 20, 1948, p. 32; "Real Showdown Will Come in 1952," unidentified clipping, August 6, 1948, p. 136, States' Rights Scrapbook, 1948, Workman Papers, SCL.

133. Telegram, Harry C. Brown to J. Strom Thurmond, July 12, 1948, file 3286, Gubernatorial Series, Thurmond Papers, CU.

134. See, for example, *Charleston News and Courier,* March 17, 1948; *Greenville News,* March 18, 1948; *The State,* May 11, 1948; *Anderson Independent,* February 10, 1948.

135. John Bell Williams, speech transcript, February 12, 1948, States' Rights Scrapbook, MDAH.

136. For the concept of honor and its historical applications, see Ayers, *Vengeance and Justice;* MacLean, *Behind the Mask of Chivalry;* Wyatt-Brown, *Southern Honor.*

137. Workman, "Take Their Stand in Dixie," unidentified clipping, August 15, 1948; "Jasper Resolution Declares Party Outrages the South," unidentified clipping, February 22, 1948; "Firm Stand by South for Its Principles Urged by Warren," unidentified clipping, March 17, 1948; "Complete Abandonment of Primary May Be Necessary," unidentified clipping, August 10, 1948, all in States' Rights Scrapbook, 1948, Workman Papers, SCL; *Charleston Evening Post,* March 18, 1948; *The State,* May 11, 1948; Strom Thurmond, address, Florida State Labor Day Celebration, Wildwood, Florida, September 6, 1948, Speeches, Subseries A, General File, Thurmond Papers, CU.

138. Quoted in Cohodas, *Strom Thurmond,* 89.

139. William Jennings Bryan Dorn to Grace Dorn, July 25, 1947, correspondence file, box 23, Dorn Papers, SCL.

140. Bass and Thompson, *Ol' Strom,* chap. 6, quote on p. 70.

141. *Life,* November 17, 1947, 44–46.

142. Dorn and Derks, *Dorn,* 117.

143. For the political language of the white working class, see Simon, *Fabric of Defeat,* chap. 4.

144. Virginia was not represented. See "Advance Registration Lists," Wood Scrapbook, MDAH; *New York Times,* May 11, 1948; *Jackson Clarion-Ledger,* May 11, 1948; "South Constructs Political Freedom," unidentified clipping, May 12, 1948, p. 79, States' Rights Scrapbook, 1948, Workman Papers, SCL.

145. "South Constructs Political Freedom," unidentified clipping, May 12, 1948, p. 79, States' Rights Scrapbook, 1948, Workman Papers, SCL.

146. Fielding L. Wright, "Address of Welcome," Conference of States' Rights Democrats, May 10, 1948, in *States' Rights Information and Speakers' Handbook,* 36–38.

147. J. Strom Thurmond, speech before the States' Rights Democratic Convention, in ibid., 25–35.

148. "Declaration of Principles adopted at States' Rights Conference," May 10, 1948, Wood Scrapbook, MDAH.

149. *Jackson Daily News,* May 11, 1948; *New York Times,* May 11, 1948.

150. "Statement of James S. Peters," States Rights Conference, May 10, 1948, in "Delegates to the 1948 National Convention," Georgia State Democratic Party Executive Committee Papers, UGA; *New York Times,* May 11, 1948; *Columbia Record,* May 10, 1948; *Jackson Clarion-Ledger,* May 11, 1948.

151. James S. Peters to Frank Dixon, May 20, 1948, in "Delegates to the 1948 National Convention," Georgia State Democratic Party Executive Committee Papers, UGA.

152. Herman Talmadge to Richard E. Dodd, May 15, 1948, in ibid.

153. James S. Peters to Horace Wilkinson, May 22, 1948, in ibid.; James S. Peters to Frank Dixon, May 20, 1948, file 1, box 2, Personal Papers, Dixon Papers, ADAH.

154. States' Rights Democratic Campaign Committee, "Complete Campaign Organization," in Speeches: 1948 file, Godwin Collection, MSU; Jeansonne, *Leander Perez,* 178.

155. Key, *Southern Politics,* 329–44; Garson, *Politics of Sectionalism,* 242; *Jackson Daily News,* June 4, 1948.

156. Ibid.

157. *Jackson Clarion-Ledger,* May 21, 1948.

158. *Jackson Daily News,* June 17, 1948.

159. Ibid., June 22, 1948.

160. "Address of Governor Olin D. Johnston," in South Carolina General Assembly, *Journal of the Senate,* 3–5.

161. *Greenwood Index-Journal,* July 12, 1947.

162. Clay Rice was an election manager in Richland County's Ninth Ward. The suit actually named a total of sixty defendants, including John I. Rice, chairman of the Richland County Democratic Party, and the members of the county party's executive committee. See Cohodas, *Strom Thurmond,* 103.

163. This front group helped the NAACP get around the hesitancy of blacks to support the association. See John McCray interview, January 11, 1986, PDOHI; William D. Workman, handwritten notes, "Interview with John McCray," n.d., box 50, Workman Papers, SCL.

164. See *Elmore v. Rice,* 72 F. Supp. 516 (1947); *Greenwood Index-Journal,* July 12, 1947.

165. *Charleston News and Courier,* July 16, 1947.

166. *Gaffney Leader,* July 22, 1947, in Thurmond Scrapbook, vol. 3, Thurmond Papers, CU.

167. *Charleston Evening Post,* July 16, 1947.

168. *The State,* August 20, 1947.

169. *Columbia (S.C.) Record,* December 30, 1947.

170. William P. Baskin, memorandum, Feb. 11, 1948, file L 647, Brown Papers, CU.

171. "Gauging the South's Revolt," 23.

172. *Greenville News,* January 23, 1948.

173. *Charleston Evening Post,* April 22, 1948.

174. *Charlotte Observer,* April 23, 1948.

175. See *Anderson Independent,* May 19, 1948; Borsos, "Support for the National Democratic Party," 16.

176. *Columbia Record,* May 20, 1948; *Greenville News,* May 20, 1948.

177. *Columbia Record,* May 20, 1948.

178. *Greenville News,* May 21, 1948; *The State,* May 20, 1948.

179. *The State,* May 27, 1948.

180. Unidentified clipping in Thurmond Scrapbook, vol. 1, Thurmond Papers, CU. For PDP fund-raising, see memorandum to executive officers and chairmen of PDP, May 31, 1948, PDP file, Clement Papers, SCL.

181. John McCray to William L. Dawson, June 7, 1948, file 27, box 2, McCray Papers, SCL.

182. John McCray to J. Howard McGrath, June 10, 1948, ibid.

183. John McCray to Joseph Lawrence, June 24, July 2, 1948, ibid.

184. *The State,* May 30, 31, 1948.

185. John McCray to Alice Spearman, May 28, 1948, file 7, box 1, SCCHR Papers, SCL.

186. Arthur Clement to John McCray, June 22, July 3, 1948, file 13, box 3, McCray Papers, SCL.

187. "Columbia Trio Signs Letter Urging New Democratic Party," unidentified clipping, June 2, 1948, p. 89, States' Rights Scrapbook, 1948, Workman Papers, SCL.

188. "Truman Program Not Endorsed by Proposed Party," unidentified clipping, June 6, 1948, p. 90, ibid.

189. *The State,* June 9, 1948.

190. William P. Baskin to Edgar Brown, June 17, 1948, file L 646, Brown Papers, CU.

191. Statement of Citizen's Committee, June 20, 1948, file 683, Byrnes Papers, CU; Cohodas, *Strom Thurmond,* 152; Mrs. J. Richard Allison et al. to "Fellow Citizens," June 23, 1948, Allison Papers, SCL.

192. *Greenville News,* June 17, 1948; *Anderson Independent,* June 30, 1948; *Columbia Record,* June 30, 1948.

193. Garson, *Politics of Sectionalism,* 254–55; Key, *Southern Politics,* 109–10; Cortez M. Ewing, "Southern Governors," in Cole and Hallowell, *Southern Political Scene,* 404–9; Numan V. Bartley, *Creation of Modern Georgia,* 204–5; Ness, "States' Rights Democratic Movement," 80–81.

194. See, for example, William Jennings Bryan Dorn to Hermand Talmadge, February 24, 1948, box 37, Dorn Papers, SCL.

195. Kurtz and Peoples, *Earl K. Long,* 147.

196. Jeansonne, *Leander Perez,* 2–11.

197. Ibid., 12–29.

198. Ibid., 74–106.

199. Kurtz and Peoples, *Earl K. Long,* 148.

200. Jeansonne, *Leander Perez,* 166.

201. Kurtz and Peoples, *Earl K. Long,* 148.

202. Gremillion, *Tidelands Controversy;* Ernest R. Bartley, *Tidelands Oil Controversy; U.S. v. California,* 332 U.S. 19 (1947); Germany, "Rise of the Dixiecrats," 29–30.

203. Kurtz and Peoples, *Earl K. Long,* 128.

204. Germany, "Rise of the Dixiecrats," 39–40.

205. Kurtz and Peoples, *Earl K. Long,* 150–51.

206. Jeansonne, *Leander Perez,* 175.

207. Quoted in Ness, "States' Rights Democratic Movement," 73.

208. Key, *Southern Politics,* 184–200; Garson, *Politics of Sectionalism,* 255–57. Also see Morton, "Report on Arkansas Politics in 1948," 35–39.

CHAPTER FOUR

1. Historians in general have written favorably of the 1948 fight over civil rights. See, for example, Sitkoff, "Harry Truman and the Election of 1948," 611; McCoy and Ruetten, *Quest and Response,* 125–27.

2. "Mutineers and the Firm Hand," 17.

3. Garson, *Politics of Sectionalism,* 263–69; McCoy, *Presidency of Harry S. Truman,* 153–55.

4. Olin D. Johnston to Fielding Wright, March 22, 1948, box 11, Johnston Papers, SCL.

5. *Montgomery Advertiser,* July 1, 3, 4, 1948. Also see Ross, *Loneliest Campaign,* 109–11.

6. J. Strom Thurmond to James Roosevelt, July 3, 1948, file 3221, Campaign Series, Gubernatorial Papers, Thurmond Papers, CU.

7. *Jackson Clarion-Ledger,* June 30, July 2, 1948. Wilkinson ridiculed the Eisenhower boom as "bunk" and a "smoke screen" to nominate the more liberal William O. Douglas. See Horace Wilkinson to Chauncey Sparks, July 6, 1948, box 10, Sparks Papers, ADAH.

8. Olin Johnston to John B. Culbertson, March 25, 1948, box 240, Johnston Papers, SCL.

9. McCorvey quoted in Garson, *Politics of Sectionalism,* 271. Also see Marion Rushton to Chauncey Sparks, April 19, 1948; Gessner McCorvey to James Roosevelt, July 3, 1948; and E. C. Boswell to Chauncey Sparks, June 29, 1948, box 10, Sparks Papers, ADAH.

10. *Montgomery Advertiser,* July 6, 1948.

11. *Jackson Clarion-Ledger,* July 7, 1948.

12. Olin D. Johnston to Colonel Jacob Arvey, July 6, 1948, and Olin D. Johnston to Harry Carlson, July 6, 1948, box 11, Johnston Papers, SCL; J. Strom Thurmond to Charles Lucey, July 8, 1948, file 3222, Campaign Series, Thurmond Papers, CU.

13. McCoy, *Presidency of Harry S. Truman,* 155.

14. Ross, *Loneliest Campaign,* 90–109.

15. "Mutineers and the Firm Hand," 19.

16. Bendiner, "Route of the Bourbons," 93.

17. McCullough, *Truman,* 629–30; Ross, *Loneliest Campaign,* chap. 5.

18. *Jackson Clarion-Ledger,* July 12, 1948.

19. *New York Times,* July 11, 12, 1948.

20. *Montgomery Advertiser,* July 12, 1948; Ness, "States' Rights Democratic Movement," 134; *New York Times,* July 12, 1948; *Jackson Clarion-Ledger,* July 13, 1948; *Greenwood Delta Democrat-Times,* July 12, 1948.

21. Ness, "States' Rights Democratic Movement," 135; *Atlanta Constitution,* July 12, 13, 1948.

22. *Montgomery Advertiser,* July 14, 1948.

23. Ibid.

24. Ralph McGill to Hardy Lott, August 26, 1948, box 3, McGill Papers, EU.

25. Garson, *Politics of Sectionalism,* 271.

26. Ross, *Loneliest Campaign,* 117. The plank stated, "The Democratic party commits itself to continuing its efforts to eradicate all racial, religious and economic discrimination. We again state our belief that racial and religious minorities must have the right to live, the right to work, the right to vote, the full and equal protection of the law, on a basis of equality with all citizens as guaranteed by the Constitution. We again call upon the Congress to exert its full authority to the limit of its constitutional powers to assure and protect these rights."

27. Ibid.

28. Walter White to J. Howard McGrath, July 11, 1948, box 225, series A, group 2, NAACP Papers.

29. *New York Times,* July 11, 1948; Borsos, "Support for the National Democratic Party," 37.

30. *Charleston News and Courier,* clipping, ca. June 1948, in PDP file, Clement Papers, SCL.

31. Transcript, Democratic National Committee Meeting, July 10, 1948, box 3, DNC Papers, HSTL.

32. Ibid., 20–21.

33. Minutes, PDP Caucus and National Convention, July 10, 14, 1948, in PDP file, Clement Papers, SCL; Borsos, "Support for the National Democratic Party," 38–39; *Greenville News,* July 11, 12, 1948; *Anderson Independent,* July 14, 1948; *Charleston News and Courier,* July 14, 1948; *The State,* July 12, 14, 1948; *Birmingham World,* July 16, 1948.

34. Statement of L. A. Fletcher, pp. 16–17, in "Proceedings of Credentials Committee, Philadelphia, Pa., July 13, 1948," Democratic National Committee, Records of Meetings, 1944–1952, DNC Papers, HSTL.

35. Statement of David Baker, p. 23, in ibid.

36. Ibid., 25.

37. Ibid., 26.

38. Ibid. 28–29; Borsos, "Support for the National Democratic Party," 39–40.

39. Statement of A. J. Clement Jr., pp. 38–39, in "Proceedings of Credentials Committee, Philadelphia, Pa., July 13, 1948," Democratic National Committee, Records of Meetings, 1944–1952, DNC Papers, HSTL.

40. Ibid., 30–32.

41. Ibid., 30, 33.

42. *Greenwood Delta Democrat-Times,* July 13, 1948.

43. Ibid., July 14, 1948.

44. Statement of Charles Hamilton, pp. 77–79, in "Proceedings of Credentials Committee, Philadelphia, Pa., July 13, 1948," Democratic National Committee, Records of Meetings, 1944–1952, DNC Papers, HSTL.

45. Statement of A. J. Clement Jr., pp. 41–43, 46, in ibid.

46. Statement of Olin Johnston, pp. 47–48, in ibid.

47. Ibid., 46–52.

48. Ibid., 57–58.

49. *Charleston News and Courier,* July 14, 1948.

50. "Proceedings of Credentials Committee, Philadelphia, Pa., July 13, 1948," Democratic National Committee, Records of Meetings, 1944–1952, DNC Papers, HSTL, 51–52, 63–64.

51. Ibid., 95–96.

52. "Statement by John McCray," July 14, 1948, box 2, Workman Papers, SCL.

53. Ness, "The States' Rights Democratic Movement," 137; *Democracy at Work,* 102–5.

54. Gessner McCorvey to Albert Stapp, July 21, 1948, file 2, box 2, Personal Papers, Dixon Papers, ADAH.

55. "Minority Report, Committee on Resolutions and Platform, by Former Governor Dan Moody, of the State of Texas"; "Minority Report, Committee on Resolutions and Platform, by Mr. Cecil Sims, Delegate from the State of Tennessee"; "Minority Report, Committee on Resolutions and Platform, by Mr. Walter Sillers, Delegate from the State of Mississippi"; "Remarks of the Honorable Dan Moody, Ex-Governor, of the State of Texas"; "Remarks by Mr. Cecil Sims, a Delegate from the State of Tennes-

see"; "Remarks by Mr. Walter Sillers, a Delegate from the State of Mississippi," all in *Democracy at Work,* 178–86.

56. Ferrell, *Off the Record,* 143.

57. "Minority Report of the Committee on Platform and Resolutions Submitted by the Honorable Andrew J. Biemiller, a Delegate from the State of Wisconsin," in *Democracy at Work,* 181; Garson, *Politics of Sectionalism,* 277. The full plank reads,

> The Democratic Party is responsible for the great civil rights gains made in recent years in eliminating unfair and illegal discrimination based on race, creed, or color.
>
> The Democratic Party commits itself to continuing its efforts to eradicate all racial, religious, and economic discrimination.
>
> We again state our belief that racial and religious minorities must have the right to live, the right to work, the right to vote, the full and equal protection of the laws, on a basis of equality with all citizens as guaranteed by the Constitution.
>
> We highly commend President Harry S. Truman for his courageous stand on the issue of civil rights. We call upon the Congress to support our President in guaranteeing these basic and fundamental rights—
>
> (1) The right of full and equal political participation;
> (2) The right to equal opportunity of employment;
> (3) The right of security of person;
> (4) The right of equal treatment in the service and defense of our Nation.

See "The 1948 Platform of the Democratic Party," adopted by the Democratic National Convention at Philadelphia, Pa., July 14, 1948, in Campaign Platforms, 1948 file, box 62, Nash Papers, HSTL.

58. Ross, *Loneliest Campaign,* 121; *Democracy at Work,* 189–92.

59. *Montgomery Advertiser,* August 2, 1948.

60. *New York Times,* July 15, 1948; *Montgomery Advertiser,* July 15, 1948; Ross, *Loneliest Campaign,* 124; *Democracy at Work,* 229.

61. *New York Times,* July 15, 1948.

62. Quoted in Burns, "Alabama Dixiecrat Revolt," 162.

63. Katie Louchheim interview transcript, Washington, D.C., September 27, 1973, OH 137, pp. 26–27, 29–30, Oral History Collection, HSTL.

64. John Oliver Emmerich interview, April, May 1972, vol. 16, pp. 53, 70, MOHP, USM.

65. Garson, *Politics of Sectionalism,* 280.

66. Ross, *Loneliest Campaign* 125; "Address of President Harry S. Truman in Accepting the Democratic Presidential Nomination," in *Democracy at Work,* 300–306.

67. *New York Times,* July 16, 1948; *Montgomery Advertiser,* July 16, 1948.

68. Feldman, "Horace Wilkinson and Alabama Politics," 265.

69. Starr, "'Dixiecrat' Convention," 31; *Jackson Clarion-Ledger,* July 18, 1948; *Columbia Record,* July 17, 19, 1948; *New York Times,* July 16, 1948; Burns, "Alabama Dixiecrat Revolt," 166.

70. *New York Times,* July 17, 1948. The thirteen states included Virginia, North and South Carolina, Oklahoma, Louisiana, Mississippi, Alabama, Tennessee, Texas, Geor-

gia, Florida, Kentucky, and Arkansas (*New York Times*, July 18, 1948). Estimates of attendees vary. The *Denver Post* reported that approximately 7,500 attended the July 17 rally. See *Denver Post*, July 18, 1948, in Thurmond Scrapbook, vol. 6, Thurmond Papers, CU; quote in Starr, "'Dixiecrat' Convention," 31.

71. Ness, "States' Rights Democratic Movement," 172; Starr, "'Dixiecrat' Convention," 33; *New York Times*, July 16, 17, 19, 1948; Garson, *Politics of Sectionalism*, 282.

72. *Greenville News*, July 16, 1948; *New York Times*, July 16, 1948.

73. Burns, "Alabama Dixiecrat Revolt," 161; *New York Times*, July 16, 1948.

74. Starr, "'Dixiecrat' Convention," 40. Wallace Wright was appointed to serve as the liaison between the steering body and the rest of the assembly, the press, and the general public. Horace Wilkinson was designated head of the resolutions committee and charged with drafting specific principles to illuminate and guide the rebels' future political activities. See *Jackson Clarion-Ledger*, July 18, 1948.

75. *Montgomery Advertiser*, July 18, 1948; *New York Times*, July 18, 1948; *Columbia Record*, July 17, 1948.

76. *Birmingham News*, July 18, 1948.

77. *New York Times*, July 18, 1948.

78. *Clarksdale Register*, July 19, 1948; *Jackson Clarion-Ledger*, July 18, 1948.

79. *Montgomery Advertiser*, July 18, 19, 1948; *Columbia Record*, July 17, 1948.

80. *Jackson Clarion-Ledger*, July 18, 1948.

81. Address of Frank Dixon, States' Rights Democratic Convention, July 17, 1948, Birmingham, Alabama, in *States' Rights Information and Speakers' Handbook*, 41–47.

82. *Newsweek*, July 26, 1948, 21–22.

83. *Montgomery Advertiser*, July 18, 1948.

84. Ibid., July 20, 1948.

85. Ibid., July 17, 19, 1948.

86. Ness, "States' Rights Democratic Movement," 161–62; Starr, "'Dixiecrat' Convention," 39–44; *Jackson Clarion-Ledger*, July 18, 1948.

87. Cohodas, *Strom Thurmond*, 179–80.

88. *Birmingham News*, July 18, 1948; *Jackson Clarion-Ledger*, July 18, 1948; "Statement of Principles," in *States' Rights Information and Speakers' Handbook*, 4–5; Starr, "'Dixiecrat' Convention," 44.

89. "Statement of Principles," in *States' Rights Information and Speakers' Handbook*, 4–5.

90. *Jackson Clarion-Ledger*, July 18, 1948.

91. *Montgomery Advertiser*, July 22, 1948.

92. Unidentified clipping, 23 July 1948, p. 118, States' Rights Scrapbook, 1948, Workman Papers, SCL.

93. *Jackson Clarion-Ledger*, July 17, 1948; Garson, *Politics of Sectionalism*, 282.

94. *Greenville News*, July 18, 1948.

95. *Jackson Clarion-Ledger*, July 18, 1948; Garson, *Politics of Sectionalism*, 283.

96. Garson, *Politics of Sectionalism*, 287–88, 294; The South's other two weapons were the Senate filibuster and "her almost certain ability to prevent the Constitution from being amended" (Collins, *Whither Solid South?*, ix).

97. Collins was a graduate of the University of Chicago and had served as law librarian of Congress, librarian of the Supreme Court, and general counsel of the bud-

get bureau and the controller of currency. See Robert Howard, "Attorney Maps States Rights Drive of South," *Chicago Daily Tribune,* August 9, 1948, news clipping in Dixiecrat file, box 193, DNC Papers, HSTL; Collins, *Whither Solid South?,* 260–63.

98. *Washington Post,* July 19, 1948, news clipping in Birmingham Convention file, box 194, DNC Papers, HSTL.

99. *Columbia Record,* July 19, 1948; press release, July 20, 1948, vol. 1, States' Rights Papers, CU.

100. *New York Times,* July 17, 1948; Ness, "States' Rights Democratic Movement," 155.

101. Rogers et al., *Alabama,* 535.

102. *The State,* July 17, 19, 1948.

103. *Jackson Clarion-Ledger,* July 18, 1948; Germany, "Rise of the Dixiecrats," 74.

104. *Montgomery Advertiser,* July 20, 1948.

105. Ashley, "Selected Southern Liberal Editors and the States' Rights Movement of 1948."

106. *New York Times,* July 19, 1948.

107. Ibid., July 18, 1948; *New York Star,* August 15, 1948, news clipping in Thurmond Scrapbook, vol. 7, Thurmond Papers, CU.

108. Quoted in Gessner T. McCorvey to J. Strom Thurmond, September 30, 1948, file 3336, Campaign Series, Thurmond Papers, CU; see *Time,* October 4, 1948.

109. *Louisville Courier-Journal,* October 18, 1948, news clipping in Dixiecrat file, box 193, DNC Papers, HSTL.

110. *Montgomery Advertiser,* July 29, 1948.

111. "Report on States' Rights Democrats Meeting," July 24, 1948, file 3255, and J. Strom Thurmond to John V. Dodge, December 2, 1948, file 3360, Campaign Series, Thurmond Papers, CU; *Montgomery Advertiser,* July 25, 1948.

112. *Montgomery Advertiser,* July 24, 30, 1948.

113. *Jackson Clarion-Ledger,* August 3, 1948.

114. Ibid., August 4, 1948.

115. *The State,* July 17, 1948; *Columbia Record,* July 16, 1948.

116. *The State,* July 20, 1948; *Savannah Morning News,* July 20, 1948, news clipping in Thurmond Scrapbook, vol. 6, Thurmond Papers, CU; Cohodas, *Strom Thurmond,* 153, 169–72.

117. Borsos, "Support for the National Democratic Party," 48–49; *Anderson Independent,* July 23, 1948.

118. William P. Baskin to all State Democratic Executive Committeemen, July 29, 1948, file L 1401, Brown Papers, CU; *Greenville News,* August 8, 1948.

119. Heard, *Two-Party South?,* 54–73. Heard points out that Republicanism was stronger in North Carolina than in any other southern state. In 1944 Dewey had received one-third of North Carolina's popular vote.

120. J. Strom Thurmond, "Address at the Watermelon Festival," July 31, 1948, Cherryville, North Carolina, file 135, Speeches Series, Thurmond Papers, CU.

121. J. Strom Thurmond to Tom W. Ferguson, July 23, 1948, file 3391, Campaign Series, Thurmond Papers, CU; Ness, "States' Rights Democratic Movement," 190; Thurmond address, July 31, 1948, Speeches Series, Thurmond Papers, CU.

122. *Charlotte News,* August 3, 4, 1948.

123. *Columbia Record,* August 18, 1948.

124. *Charlotte Observer,* August 21, 1948.

125. *Charleston Evening Post,* September 9, 1948.

126. *Houston Post,* August 11, 1948, news clipping in Thurmond Scrapbook, vol. 7, Thurmond Papers, CU.

127. Spectator [J. K. Breedin], "Comments on Men and Things," August 19, 1948, clipping in States' Rights file, box 2, Workman Papers, SCL; *Atlanta Journal,* August 13, 1948; *Houston Post,* August 11, 1948, in Thurmond Scrapbook, vol. 7, Thurmond Papers, CU. The *Atlanta Journal* estimated 6,000, while the *Post* estimated a crowd of 10,000.

128. Ness, "States' Rights Democratic Movement," 197–98; *Houston Press,* August 11, 1948, news clipping in Thurmond Scrapbook, vol. 6, Thurmond Papers, CU.

129. Address of Fielding L. Wright and Address of J. Strom Thurmond, August 11, 1948, Houston, Texas, in *States' Rights Information and Speakers' Handbook.*

130. *Houston Post,* August 12, 1948, in Thurmond Scrapbook, vol. 7, Thurmond Papers, CU.

131. Garson, *Politics of Sectionalism,* 240.

132. *Montgomery Advertiser,* August 12, 1948.

CHAPTER FIVE

1. The Dixiecrats appeared on the ballot in Alabama, Arkansas, Florida, Georgia, Kentucky, Louisiana, Mississippi, North Carolina, North Dakota, South Carolina, Tennessee, Texas, and Virginia. See George MacNabb to Mrs. Henry Philip Staats, May 16, 1949, file 3289, Campaign Series, Thurmond Papers, CU.

2. *New York Times,* August 15, October 9, 1948; *Montgomery Advertiser,* July 22, October 7, 1948; Preston Lane to J. Strom Thurmond, October 1, 1948, and L. Mell Glenn to Carolina W. Stump, October 21, 1948, file 3369, Campaign Series, Thurmond Papers, CU.

3. Donovan, Gatewood, and Whayne, *Governors of Arkansas,* 203; Lester, *Man for Arkansas,* 97.

4. Key, *Southern Politics,* 183.

5. Ibid., 186–89, 191–95; Richard E. Yates, "Arkansas: Independent and Unpredictable," in Havard, *Changing Politics of the South,* 233–38.

6. *New York Times,* September 13, 1948; Morton, "Report on Arkansas Politics in 1948."

7. John L. Daggett to Frank Dixon, May 28, 1948, folder 1, box 2, Personal Papers, Dixon Papers, ADAH.

8. Lester, *Man for Arkansas,* 102.

9. Donovan, Gatewood, and Whayne, *Governors of Arkansas,* 208.

10. Strom Thurmond, Address to States' Rights Democrats, Marianna, Ark., Aug. 26, 1948, file 137, Speeches Series, Subseries A, General File, Thurmond Papers, CU.

11. *New York Times,* September 24, 25, 1948; Ness, "States' Rights Democratic Movement," 206.

12. Thurmond received support from Thomas G. Burch of Martinsville, a former member of the state boards of agriculture and education and both houses of congress;

state senator Frank Richeson of Richmond; and Thomas D. Odom of Suffolk, president of the Young Democrats of Virginia. See Grant, "1948 Presidential Election in Virginia," 320; *New York Times,* September 2, 13, 1948.

13. Grant, "1948 Presidential Election in Virginia," 322, 324.

14. Miller, *Mr. Crump,* 322–24; *New York Times,* August 7, 1948.

15. *New York Times,* August 24, 1948; *Montgomery Advertiser,* October 7, 1948; Miller, *Mr. Crump,* 331–34.

16. *New York Times,* September 12, 26, 1948.

17. Pleasants, "Claude Pepper, Strom Thurmond, and the 1948 Presidential Election in Florida," 439–41; Key, *Southern Politics,* 82; Colburn and Scher, *Florida Gubernatorial Politics in the Twentieth Century,* 23–26. Colburn and Scher note, however, that the urban-rural cleavage has often been blurred and that the state's cities have been unsuccessful in cobbling together an urban bloc.

18. See David R. Colburn, Steven F. Lawson, and Darryl Paulson, "Groveland: Florida's Little Scottsboro," in Colburn and Landers, *African American Heritage of Florida,* 298–325.

19. Danese, "Claude Pepper and Ed Ball," 289.

20. *Augusta Chronicle,* August 26, 1948, in Thurmond Scrapbook, vol. 7, Thurmond Papers, CU.

21. *The State,* September 3, 9, 1948; *New York Times,* September 8, 1948.

22. *Tallahassee Daily Democrat,* September 8–16, 1948.

23. *Gainesville Sun,* October 11, 17–19, 1948.

24. *New York Times,* October 30, 31, 1948.

25. Ibid., July 25, 1948.

26. Ibid., August 10, 1948.

27. *Jackson Clarion-Ledger,* August 10, 1948.

28. *New York Times,* September 2, 8, 9, 1948.

29. Ibid., September 15, 1948 Ness, "States' Rights Democratic Movement," 212–13.

30. Germany, "Rise of the Dixiecrats," 76–77.

31. Jeansonne, *Leander Perez,* 178; Vaughan and Deener, *Presidential Politics in Louisiana,* 60–61; Kurtz and Peoples, *Earl K. Long,* 150.

32. Germany, "Rise of the Dixiecrats," 82.

33. John U. Barr to J. Strom Thurmond, August 26, 1948, file 3255, Thurmond Papers, CU; Vaughan and Deener, *Presidential Politics in Louisiana,* 61.

34. Germany, "Rise of the Dixiecrats," 90.

35. Vaughan and Deener, *Presidential Politics in Louisiana,* 61.

36. Jeansonne, *Leander Perez,* 179; Vaughan and Deener, *Presidential Politics in Louisiana,* 61–62.

37. Jeansonne, *Leander Perez,* 179; Vaughan and Deener, *Presidential Politics in Louisiana,* 62.

38. Germany, "Rise of the Dixiecrats," 95.

39. *New York Times,* September 11, 1948; Jeansonne, *Leander Perez,* 180.

40. *New York Times,* September 11, 12, 1948.

41. Jeansonne, *Leander Perez,* 181.

42. *New York Times,* September 24, 25, 1948.

43. Jeansonne, *Leander Perez*, 180–81; *New York Times*, October 2, 1948; Germany, "Rise of the Dixiecrats," 114.

44. Jeansonne, *Leander Perez*, 183.

45. Key, *Southern Politics*, 341.

46. Quoted in Harold P. Henderson, "M. E. Thompson," in Henderson and Roberts, *Georgia Governors*, 53.

47. Quoted in Numan V. Bartley, *Creation of Modern Georgia*, 205.

48. Harold P. Henderson, "M. E. Thompson," in Henderson and Roberts, *Georgia Governors*, 64–65.

49. Talmadge with Winchell, *Talmadge*, 148, 179.

50. Wallace D. Malone to James S. Peters, September 9, 1948, and to Herman Talmadge, September 9, 1948, in May 31, 1948, meeting, Macon, Georgia, volume, Georgia State Democratic Party Executive Committee Papers, UGA.

51. *Augusta Chronicle*, September 10, 1948.

52. *New York Times*, September 10, 12, 1948.

53. *Augusta Chronicle*, September 14, 17, 1948.

54. *Atlanta Journal*, September 17, 1948.

55. *New York Times*, September 10, 12, 1948.

56. Unidentified news clipping, September 23, 1948, 1948 electors file, box 4, Gubernatorial Series, Talmadge Papers, UGA.

57. J. Robert Elliott to James S. Peters, September 21, 1948, in ibid.

58. Gessner T. McCorvey to Herman Talmadge, September 21, 1948, file 3336, Campaign Series, Thurmond Papers, CU.

59. Unidentified news clipping, September 23, 1948, 1948 electors file, box 4, Gubernatorial Series, Talmadge Papers, UGA.

60. James S. Peters to J. Robert Elliott, September 23, 1948, "County Committeemen" volume, 1948 Georgia State Democratic Party Executive Committee Papers, UGA.

61. *Augusta Chronicle*, September 24, 1948.

62. *Atlanta Constitution*, September 25, 1948; *New York Times*, September 26, 1948.

63. *Augusta Chronicle*, September 30, 1948.

64. *Atlanta Journal*, October 1, 1948.

65. *Augusta Chronicle*, October 3, 1948.

66. James S. Peters to Gessner T. McCorvey, September 29, 1948, file 3336, Campaign Series, Thurmond Papers, CU.

67. James S. Peters to J. Howard McGrath, September 27, 1948, May 31, 1948, volume, Georgia State Democratic Party Executive Committee Papers, UGA.

68. *Augusta Chronicle*, October 15, 1948.

69. James S. Peters to C. B. H. Moncrief, September 27, 1948, May 31, 1948, volume, Georgia State Democratic Party Executive Committee Papers, UGA.

70. J. Strom Thurmond to Gessner T. McCorvey, October 1, 1948, file 3336, Campaign Series, Thurmond Papers, CU.

71. Transcript, "Meet the Press," October 15, 1948, folder 2, box 5, Personal Correspondence Series, Talmadge Papers, UGA.

72. Talmadge with Winchell, *Talmadge*, 148–49.

73. *Montgomery Advertiser,* October 13, 14, 1948.

74. J. Strom Thurmond, address, Macon, Georgia, October 19, 1948, file 161, Speeches Series, Thurmond Papers, CU.

75. Henry McIntosh to Richard Russell, October 27, 1948, and Richard Russell to Henry McIntosh, October 28, 1948, political file 1-A, subseries B, series 6, Russell Papers, UGA; *New York Times,* October 28, 1948.

76. *Augusta Chronicle,* October 17, 1948; *New York Times,* October 31, 1948.

77. Half of this amount was to be forwarded to the national headquarters in Jackson. See W. W. Wright to J. Strom Thurmond, August 13, 1948, file 3255, Thurmond Papers, CU.

78. *New Orleans Times-Picayune,* October 22, 1948, news clipping in Dixiecrat file, box 193, DNC Papers, HSTL; also see "Resume of States' Rights Democratic Party Financial Report for Period August 4, 1948, to October 19, 1948," States' Rights file, Minor Papers, MSU.

79. *Newsweek,* November 1, 1948.

80. Unidentified news clipping, July 25, 1948, States' Rights Scrapbook, 1948, Workman Papers, SCL.

81. J. Strom Thurmond to John Temple Graves, published in *Birmingham Post,* July 26, 1948.

82. *New York Times,* July 18, 1948.

83. McLaurin, "Role of the Dixiecrats in the 1948 Election," 84.

84. Ross, *Loneliest Campaign,* 218.

85. Ness, "States' Rights Democratic Movement," 178.

86. *Newsweek,* October 25, 1948, 34.

87. Dameron H. Williams to J. Strom Thurmond, October 23, 1948, and John W. Hinsdale to J. Strom Thurmond, October 16, 1948, file 3392, and Nowlin Randolph to J. Strom Thurmond, October 7, 1948, file 3341, Campaign Series, Thurmond Papers, CU.

88. E. H. Ramsey to J. Strom Thurmond, November 4, 1948, file 3350, Campaign Series, Thurmond Papers, CU. Also see *Montgomery Advertiser,* October 20, 1948; *Jackson Clarion-Ledger,* July 18, 1948; Carl W. Kirkman to J. Strom Thurmond, November 7, 1948, file 3406, Thurmond Papers, CU.

89. John Oliver Emmerich, April, May 1972, vol. 16, MOHP, USM.

90. W. W. Wright to J. Strom Thurmond, September 6, 1948, file 3255, and Sam S. Farrington to George MacNabb, September 29, 1948, and Glenn Saunders to George MacNabb, October 6, 1948, file 3255, Thurmond Papers, CU. Gibson quoted in Cohodas, *Strom Thurmond,* 183.

91. Walter Brown to J. Strom Thurmond, January 4, 1949, file 3348, Campaign Series, Thurmond Papers, CU.

92. J. Strom Thurmond to Robert Figg, August 23, 1948, file 3287, ibid.

93. J. Strom Thurmond, presidential nomination acceptance speech, August 11, 1948, in *States' Rights Information and Speakers' Handbook,* 10.

94. Mississippi State Democratic Party, *Know All the Facts about Truman's So-Called "Civil Rights" Program and What It Means to You,* pamphlet (n.p., 1948), 2–3.

95. J. Strom Thurmond, address, Florida State Labor Day Celebration, Septem-

ber 6, 1948, Wildwood, Florida, file 139, Speeches Series, Thurmond Papers, CU. Also see Mississippi State Democratic Party, *You Have Been Betrayed,* pamphlet (n.p., 1948).

96. A. P. Shoemaker to Chambers of Commerce, Biloxi and Gulfport, April 12, 1948, folder 2, box 318, Colmer Papers, USM. Copies of this letter were sent to members of Mississippi's congressional delegation and to the governor.

97. For attacks by industrialists on a permanent FEPC, see *Alabama,* February 27, 1948, 16–17.

98. *Time,* October 11, 1948, 24; Caroline H. Stokes to J. Strom Thurmond, July 22, 1948, file 3286, Campaign Series, Thurmond Papers, CU; *Greenville News,* October 29, 1948.

99. *Nashville Banner,* October 13, 22, 1948, and *Nashville Tennessean,* October 2, 1948, news clippings in Thurmond Scrapbook, vol. 8, Thurmond Papers, CU; Hubert Gene Wright to J. Strom Thurmond, July 10, 1950, file 3357, Campaign Series, Thurmond Papers, CU.

100. Quoted in John M. Coski, "'The Dixiecrat Banner': The Emergence of the Confederate Battle Flag in American Popular Culture" (paper delivered at the Organization of American Historians meeting, March 30, 1996, Chicago, Ill., in author's possession), 9.

101. J. Strom Thurmond to Paul Quattlebaum, October 8, 1948, file 150, Quattlebaum Papers, CU.

102. Glenn Saunders to Rex Magee, September 26, 1948, file 3255, Campaign Series, Thurmond Papers, CU.

103. *New Orleans Times-Picayune,* n.d., news clipping, Dixiecrat file, Minor Papers, MSU; Worrell ?? to George Godwin, August 27, 1948, 1948–49 Correspondence file, Godwin Collection, MSU.

104. *Montgomery Advertiser,* August 28, 1948.

105. *Washington Post,* July 19, 1948, news clipping in Birmingham Convention file, box 194, DNC Papers, HSTL; Walter White, "Statement to the Associated Press," July 15, 1948, box 27, Niles Papers, HSTL; Chester Bowles to Walter White, July 22, 1948, Democratic National Committee file, box 225, series A, group 2, NAACP Papers; "Shape of Things," 85.

106. Sullivan, *Days of Hope,* 249–72.

107. *Montgomery Advertiser,* July 18, 20, October 12, 1948; *Birmingham News,* October 17, 1948.

108. *Montgomery Advertiser,* July 2, 1948.

109. See, for example, B. D. Dunlap to James E. Folsom, September 29, 1948, SC 13427, administrative files, gubernatorial files, Folsom Papers, ADAH. See file generally for other complaints.

110. *Montgomery Advertiser,* July 21, 22, August 19, 1948.

111. Ibid., July 31, August 16, 1948.

112. Ibid., August 19, 1948; "Statement of Gessner T. McCorvey," September 1948, political file 1-A, subseries B, series 4, Russell Papers, UGA.

113. James E. Folsom to C. B. Brickwith, September 5, 1948, SC 13427, administrative files, gubernatorial files, Folsom Papers, ADAH.

114. *Montgomery Advertiser,* October 8, 17, 1948.

115. Hamilton, *Lister Hill,* 159.

116. Ibid., 159–60; "Statement of Chauncey Sparks," August 1, 1948, box 10, Sparks Papers, ADAH.

117. *Montgomery Advertiser,* October 19, 1948.

118. Ibid., November 2, 1948. For Folsom and the 1948 election, also see Grafton and Permaloff, *Big Mules and Branchheads,* 110–23; Sims, *Little Man's Big Friend.*

119. See George Andrews to Frank Dixon, August 2, 1948; George Grant to Frank Dixon, August 6, 1948; Carter Manasco to Frank Dixon, August 6, 1948; Edward deGraffenreid to Frank Dixon, August 7, 1948; Albert Rains to Frank Dixon, August 9, 1948; Robert E. Jones Jr. to Frank Dixon, August 9, 1948; Laurie C. Battle to Frank Dixon, August 10, 1948, all in file 3, box 2, Personal Papers, Dixon Papers, ADAH.

120. Mitchell, "Frank E. Smith," 90.

121. *Jackson Clarion-Ledger,* September 4, 19, 1948; Charles Hamilton to Walter White, July 26, 1948, box 225, series A, group 2, NAACP Papers.

122. Borsos, "Support for the National Democratic Party," 51–52; *Greenville News,* August 19, September 2, 1948; *Anderson Independent,* September 2, 1948; *The State,* September 2, 1948; *Montgomery Advertiser,* September 4, 1948.

123. *Columbia Record,* August 17, 1948; *Newberry Observer,* August 17, 1948, news clipping in Thurmond Scrapbook, vol. 7, Thurmond Papers, CU.

124. *Charleston Evening Post,* October 6, 1948.

125. "Suggested Organizational Plan," South Carolina Thurmond-Wright Campaign Steering Committee, September 1948, file 3268, Campaign Series, Thurmond Papers, CU.

126. "Contributions—Thurmond-Wright Campaign Fund," July 29–October 22, 1948, file 3250, ibid.

127. *Charleston News and Courier,* July 25, 1948.

128. *Columbia Record,* September 28, 1948.

129. Kitty M. Wilson to Edgar A. Brown, September 6, 1948, L 646, Brown Papers, CU.

130. *Spartanburg Herald,* October 21, 498; *Anderson Independent,* August 12, November 5, 1948.

131. James F. Byrnes to R. M. Hitt, July 28, 1948, file 688, Byrnes Papers, CU.

132. *The State,* August 10, 1948.

133. Burnet R. Maybank, typed statement, n.d., 1948, election file, Maybank Papers, Smalls Library, College of Charleston, Charleston, S.C.

134. Unidentified news clipping, August 24, 1948, p. 153, States' Rights Scrapbook, 1948, Workman Papers, SCL.

135. *Washington Post,* October 4, 1948, news clipping in South Carolina file, DNC Papers, HSTL.

136. *Charleston Evening News,* August 30, 1948, in Thurmond Scrapbook, vol. 7, Thurmond Papers, CU.

137. *The State,* September 3, 1948; press release, Democratic National Committee, September 2, 1948, box 169, DNC Papers, HSTL.

138. *Providence Bulletin,* September 2, 1948, news clipping in Civil Rights file, McGrath Papers, HSTL; *Montgomery Advertiser,* September 4, 1948.

139. J. Howard McGrath to Mrs. J. Richard Allison, October 28, 1948, Allison Papers, SCL; *The State,* September 2, 26, 1948; unidentified news clipping, September 4, 1948, p. 165, States' Rights Scrapbook, 1948, Workman Papers, SCL.

140. *Montgomery Advertiser,* September 4, 1948. For Thurmond's resignation from the DNC, see J. Strom Thurmond to William P. Baskin, July 20, 1948, file 3347, Campaign Series, Thurmond Papers, CU.

141. Borsos, "Support for the National Democratic Party," 58.

142. Clark M. Clifford, Memorandum for the President: The 1948 Campaign, August 17, 1948, political file, box 23, Clifford Papers, HSTL. For other opinions on Truman and the Dixiecrats, see Katie Louchheim interview transcript, Washington, D.C., September 27, 1973, OH 137, pp. 26–27; Oscar R. Ewing interview transcript, Chapel Hill, N.C., April 29–30, May 1, 2, 1969, OH 69, vol. 2, p. 327; Kenneth M. Birkhead interview transcript, Washington, D.C., July 7, 1966, OH 27, pp. 58, 69, all in Oral History Collection, HSTL.

143. *Columbia Record,* July 31, 1948.

144. Ibid., August 3, 1948.

145. *New York Times,* August 12, 1948.

146. Unidentified news clipping, October 11, 1948, p. 220, States' Rights Scrapbook, 1948, Workman Papers, SCL; typed manuscript for *Lighthouse and Informer,* ca. 1948, box 7, McCray Papers, SCL.

147. John McCray, form letter to PDP members, n.d., box 4, McCray Papers, SCL.

148. John McCray, address to Orangeburg Democrats, Mt. Pisgah Baptist Church, Orangeburg, South Carolina, October 1, 1948, ibid.

149. See "Politics, August–December 1948" file and typescript, ca. 1948, box 7; John McCray to Govan Wilson, August 18, 1948, Horry County file, box 4; H. B. Sharon and Martha K. Sharon to John McCray, August 25, 1948; and box 4 generally, all in McCray Papers, SCL.

150. Arthur Clement to John McCray, July 19, 1948, box 3, McCray Papers, SCL; unidentified news clipping, October 1, 1948, p. 198, States' Rights Scrapbook, 1948, Workman Papers, SCL.

151. Cohodas, *Strom Thurmond,* 188.

152. Heard, *Two-Party South?,* 251–55; Phillips, *Emerging Republican Majority,* 198; Grant, "1948 Presidential Election in Virginia," 324.

153. Key, *Southern Politics;* 329–44; Heard, *Two-Party South?,* 251–52.

154. Fowler, *Presidential Voting,* 17–19; Scammon, *America at the Polls.*

155. Sundquist, *Dynamics of the Party System,* 254.

156. Ashmore, "South's Year of Decision," 2.

157. Key, *Southern Politics,* 671; Numan V. Bartley, *New South,* 103; Garson, *Politics of Sectionalism,* 315; Hodding Carter, "Southern Liberal Looks at Civil Rights," 10, 20–25; Ader, *Dixiecrat Movement.*

158. Quoted in Cohodas, *Strom Thurmond,* 189.

CHAPTER SIX

1. Truman quoted in McCoy, *Presidency of Harry S. Truman,* 167.

2. Berman, *Politics of Civil Rights,* 137.

3. *New York Herald Tribune,* January 14, 1949, in poll tax file, box 180, DNC Papers, HSTL.

4. Telegram, James M. Hinton to J. Strom Thurmond, November 3, 1948, file 3347, Gubernatorial Series, Thurmond Papers, CU.

5. Ayers Diaries, set 3, entry for November 6, 1948, p. 190, Ayers Papers, HSTL.

6. *Charleston Evening Post,* November 9, 1948, in Thurmond Scrapbook, vol. 8, Thurmond Papers, CU. For criticism of Eleanor Roosevelt, see Ned Haverly to J. Strom Thurmond, November 9, 1948, file 3403, Gubernatorial Series, Thurmond Papers, CU.

7. *The State,* January 2, 1949.

8. McCoy and Ruetten, *Quest and Response,* 182.

9. Olin D. Johnston to Calhoun Thomas, November 22, 1948, box 11, Johnston Papers, SCL.

10. Ashton Williams to Calhoun Thomas, November 20, 1948, ibid.

11. *Jackson Clarion-Ledger,* January 29, 1949.

12. Berman, *Politics of Civil Rights,* 162.

13. Harry S. Truman to James M. Cox, December 9, 1948, PPF 27, HSTL.

14. *Columbia Record,* January 21, 1949.

15. J. Strom Thurmond to Harry A. Neal, January 27, 1949, file 3360, Gubernatorial Series, Thurmond Papers, CU.

16. Reichard, *Politics As Usual,* 47.

17. *New York Times,* January 6, 1949.

18. *Atlanta Journal,* October 25, 1948.

19. Charles W. Collins to J. Strom Thurmond, December 6, 1948, file 3347, and W. W. Wright to J. Strom Thurmond, October 16, 1948, file 3351, Gubernatorial Series, Thurmond Papers, CU; "Attendance list," States' Rights Democrats meeting, October 24, 1948, Memphis, Tennessee, file 9, box 2, and "A Resolution Adopted by the Memphis Meeting," October 24, 1948, file 5, box 2, Personal Papers, Dixon Papers, ADAH.

20. *The State,* January 13, 1949.

21. J. Strom Thurmond to Horace Wilkinson, November 17, 1948, file 3337, Gubernatorial Series, Thurmond Papers, CU.

22. J. Strom Thurmond to John C. Sheffield, November 12, 1948, file 3340, ibid.; J. Strom Thurmond to Frank Dixon, November 11, 1948, file 5, box 2, Personal Papers, Dixon Papers, ADAH.

23. Frank Dixon to John U. Barr, January 19, 1949, and W. W. Wright to Frank Dixon, December 3, 1948, file 5, box 2, Personal Papers, Dixon Papers, ADAH; W. W. Wright to J. Strom Thurmond, December 3, 1948, file 3374, and John U. Barr to Frank Dixon, January 21, 1949, file 3408, Gubernatorial Series, Thurmond Papers, CU. Active members of the subcommittee included Ed Ramsey of Florida; Horace Wilkinson; Leander Perez; W. W. Wright; James Murphy, an attorney from Columbia; and Charles Collins. See James B. Murphy to J. Strom Thurmond, January 31, 1949, file 3325, Gubernatorial Series, Thurmond Papers, CU. Also see Horace Wilkinson to Ben Laney, December 21, 1948, and Charles W. Collins to Frank Dixon, January 29, 1948, file 5, box 2, Personal Papers, Dixon Papers, ADAH.

24. John Temple Graves to J. Strom Thurmond, December 27, 1948, file 3337, Gubernatorial Series, Thurmond Papers, CU; *The State,* February 7, 1949.

25. J. Strom Thurmond to John Temple Graves, December 31, 1948, file 3337, Gubernatorial Series, Thurmond Papers, CU.

26. The controversy revolved around the amendment of Rule 22. Adopted by the Senate in 1917, Rule 22 held that termination of debate on a "pending measure" required a two-thirds vote. Presiding over the special session in 1948, Republican senator Arthur Vandenburg had narrowed significantly the interpretation of the rule when he sustained a point of order by Georgia senator Richard Russell that cloture could only be applied to debate on the measure itself and not to debate on a "motion." This worked to the advantage of southern Democrats, since a motion to consider a bill had to precede a vote on the measure. In effect, then, Vandenburg's ruling gave southern Democrats carte blanche to filibuster on motions to consider civil rights bills. See McCoy and Ruetten, *Quest and Response,* 171.

27. Telegram, A. Philip Randolph to Harry S. Truman, January 28, 1949, President's Program file, OF 596-A, box 1510, WHCF.

28. Nash quoted in Berman, *Politics of Civil Rights,* 152.

29. Vivian Truman to Harry S. Truman, April 6, 1949, and Harry S. Truman to Vivian Truman, April 8, 1949, box 332, family correspondence file, J. V. Truman file 2, PSF, HSTL.

30. Anti–poll tax legislation was introduced in the House on March 3; Senator McGrath introduced an omnibus civil rights bill, an antilynching bill, an anti–poll tax bill, and an FEPC bill on April 28; Representative Adam Clayton Powell introduced the administration's FEPC bill to the House on April 29; and Representative Emanuel Celler of New York introduced an omnibus civil rights bill and an antilynching bill in the House on May 16.

The omnibus civil rights bill included provisions for the creation of a civil rights commission in the executive branch, as well as a civil rights division in the Department of Justice; called for a joint congressional committee on civil rights; "strengthened existing civil rights statutes; further protected the right of suffrage; and prohibited discrimination and segregation in interstate transportation." See Berman, *Politics of Civil Rights,* 157–58; Civil Rights file, box 41, Senatorial Records, McGrath Papers, HSTL; memorandum, Stephen J. Spingarn to Clark Clifford, May 17, 1949, Civil Rights file, box 36, Nash Papers, HSTL.

31. *New York Herald Tribune,* June 5, 1959, news clipping in Civil Rights file, box 179, DNC Papers, HSTL.

32. Barton J. Bernstein, "Ambiguous Legacy," in Bernstein, *Politics and Policies of the Truman Administration,* 295–96, 299; McCoy, *Presidency of Harry S. Truman,* 168.

33. See telegram, Adam Clayton Powell Jr. to Harry S. Truman, January 19, 1950, OF 596–A, box 1510; telegram, Walter White to Harry S. Truman, March 20, 1950, OF 413, box 125; telegram, Roy Wilkins to HST, April 12, 1950, OF 413, box 1235, WHCF.

34. *The State,* February 6–8, 1949.

35. Ibid., February 8, 1949; Merritt Gibson to W. W. Wright, April 20, 1949, file 7, box 2, Personal Papers, Dixon Papers, ADAH.

36. Horace Wilkinson to Frank Dixon et al., February 10, 1949, file 5, box 2, Personal Papers, Dixon Papers, ADAH.

37. Palmer Bradley to W. W. Wright, March 14, 1949, ibid.

38. Former Arkansas governor Ben Laney was elected chairman; vice-chairmen were Leander Perez and W. W. Wright. Ed S. Lewis Jr. and George C. Wallace, both of Mississippi, were elected secretary and treasurer, respectively. See National States' Rights Committee, "Constitution and Declaration of Principles," 1949, file 3375, Gubernatorial Series, Thurmond Papers, CU; *The State,* May 11, 1949.

39. "Report of the Jackson Meeting of the National States' Rights Committee," May 10, 1949, file 11, box 2, Personal Papers, Dixon Papers, ADAH.

40. Ben Laney to W. W. Wright, March 28, 1949, file 5, box 2, ibid. W. W. Wright confided to Dixon that he did not believe Laney had ever been "thoroughly sold on our program." See W. W. Wright to Frank Dixon, March 30, 1949, file 5, box 2; Frank Dixon to Wallace D. Malone, April 28, 1949; Frank Dixon to W. W. Wright, June 24, August 27, 1949; Frank Dixon to John Temple Graves, October 20, 1949, file 7, box 2, ibid.

41. Robert McC. Figg Jr. to J. Strom Thurmond, June 30, 1949, Thurmond file, box 12, Figg Papers, SCL.

42. Walter Brown to J. Strom Thurmond, June 27, 1949, States' Rights file, box 13, ibid.

43. J. Strom Thurmond to W. W. Wright, July 11, 1949, file 3375, Gubernatorial Series, Thurmond Papers, CU.

44. *New York Times,* July 16, 1949.

45. Minutes, National Democratic Party of South Carolina, July 27, 1949, box 1, SCCHR Papers, SCL.

46. Ashton H. Williams to J. C. Long, December 11, 1948, box 15, Democratic Party file, Johnston Papers, SCL.

47. *The State,* August 10, 1949.

48. *Jackson Clarion-Ledger,* January 12, 1949.

49. Ibid., January 16, 1949. McGrath met with Clarence E. Hood of Meridian, the national committeeman; John W. Scott, secretary-treasurer; and Curtis Rogers of Sylverina, Miss.

50. Ibid., January 28, 1949; *New York Times,* May 24, 1949.

51. *The State,* August 14, 15, 1949.

52. Ibid., August 19, 1949.

53. Ibid., August 20, 1949.

54. Ibid.

55. Ibid.

56. "Statement of Maxie Collins," transcript, p. 138, Credentials Committee Meeting, August 23, 1949, box 3, DNC Papers, HSTL. Also see Maxie Collins to Ashton Williams, July 15, 1949, box 1, SCCHR Papers, SCL.

57. "Statement of J. B. Snider," transcript, p. 53, Credentials Committee Committee Meeting, August 23, 1949, box 3, DNC Papers, HSTL.

58. "Statement of Anne Agnew," transcript, p. 120, ibid.

59. Unidentified news clipping, August 24, 1949, OF 1644, box 1673, WHCF. McCoy and Ruetten, *Quest and Response,* 182; *The State,* August 25, 1949.

60. *The State,* August 26, 1949.

61. Ibid., August 27, 1949.

62. Ibid.

63. Ibid., September 2, 1949.

64. Unidentified news clipping, November 25, 1949, OF 52B, WHCF; *New York Times,* December 1, 1949.

65. *New York Times,* January 2, 15, 1950.

66. *The State,* October 17, 1949.

67. Ibid., November 23, December 25, 1949.

68. James Doyle to James F. Byrnes, 24 February 1950, file 757, Byrnes Papers, CU.

69. Marion Wright to Editor, *Asheville Citizen,* April 6, 1951, box 1, SCCHR Papers, SCL.

70. *The State,* December 20, 1949.

71. National States' Rights Committee, "National States' Rights Program, 1950–1951–1952," file 3375, Gubernatorial Series, Thurmond Papers, CU.

72. J. Strom Thurmond to W. W. Wright, ca. 14 February 1950, ibid.

73. *New York Times,* January 2, 1950.

74. *Washington Post,* April 19, 1950, news clipping, in OF 52B, WHCF.

75. Frank Dixon to Ed S. Lewis, September 22, 1950, file 8, box 2, Personal Papers, Dixon Papers, ADAH.

76. Each of Alabama's nine districts sent eight representatives to the SDEC, and the loyalists and States' Righters organized slates of eight candidates each. See *Birmingham News,* March 13, 1950.

77. John Temple Graves quoted in Rogers et al., *Alabama,* 536.

78. Paul Anthony Smith Jr., "Loyalists and States' Righters," 29; *Birmingham News,* March 3, 11, 12, 1950.

79. *Birmingham News,* March 7, 21, 1950. Curiously, the governor's race failed to attract the attention that the SDEC garnered. See Paul Anthony Smith Jr., "Loyalists and States' Righters," 34.

80. William Mitch to Lister Hill, March 8, 13, 1950, and Lister Hill to William Mitch, March 10, 1950, box 368, Hill Papers, UA; *Birmingham News,* March 5, 6, 1950.

81. Paul Anthony Smith Jr., "Loyalists and States' Righters," 39–40.

82. Lister Hill to Ralph Silver, April 18, 1950, and "Democrats of Alabama Radio Spots," [April 1950], box 368, Hill Papers, UA.

83. *Birmingham News,* April 9, 1950.

84. Ibid., April 25, 1950.

85. Ibid., April 13, 1950.

86. Quoted in Paul Anthony Smith Jr., "Loyalists and States' Righters," 44.

87. *Birmingham News,* April 29, 1950.

88. Ibid., May 5, 1950.

89. Paul Anthony Smith Jr., "Loyalists and States' Righters," 52; *Montgomery Advertiser,* May 6, 1950; *Birmingham News,* May 4, 1950.

90. *Birmingham News,* June 1, 1950.

91. Paul Anthony Smith Jr., "Loyalists and States' Righters," 55.

92. Robert McC. Figg to Thomas R. Miller, March 27, 1950, States' Rights file, box 13, and J. Strom Thurmond to Walter Brown, April 1, 1950, Thurmond file, box 12, Figg Papers, SCL.

93. *New York Times,* May 10, 1950.

94. Quoted in Pleasants and Burns, *Frank Porter Graham,* 148.

95. Pepper with Gorrey, *Pepper,* chap. 7.

96. Pleasants and Burns, *Frank Porter Graham,* chaps. 1, 3.

97. Ibid., 219, 223, 244.

98. Ray Lasley to Charles Ross, June 26, 1950, OF 281, box 911, WHCF.

99. Walter Sillers to J. Strom Thurmond, June 25, 1950, file 3375, Gubernatorial Series, Thurmond Papers, CU.

100. *The State,* April 4, 1950; *Columbia Record,* April 4, 1950.

101. *The State,* April 5, 1950.

102. Ibid., April 20, 1950.

103. *Columbia Record,* April 14, 1950.

104. *New York Times,* April 1, 14, 1950.

105. See, for example, *The State,* October 18, 1949.

106. M. F. Stack to James F. Byrnes, June 1, 1950, file 716; George W. McFadden to James F. Byrnes, June 29, 1950, file 720; also see Caroline D. Gerardeau to James F. Byrnes, January 19 1950, file 761; S. Glenn Love to James F. Byrnes, January 19, 1950, file 768; Louis P. Good to James F. Byrnes, January 10, 1950, file 761, Byrnes Papers, CU.

107. *New York Times,* January 15, 1950.

108. Ibid., January 20, 1950.

109. *The State,* July 7, 1950.

110. See, for example, Numan V. Bartley, *Rise of Massive Resistance,* 36; Heard, *Two-Party South?,* 164; Klarman, "How *Brown* Changed Race Relations," 93.

111. *The State,* May 3, 1950.

112. Wayne Freeman to Roger C. Peace, June 10, 1947, Byrnes Papers, CU. Although Freeman, a correspondent for the *Greenville News,* wrongly predicted that Thurmond would run for the U.S. Senate in 1948, he nevertheless recognized Thurmond's national ambitions. See William D. Workman, typed manuscript, *Time,* October 11, 1948, States' Rights file, box 2, Workman Papers, SCL; Faggart, "Defending the Faith," 12, 15–16.

113. *The State,* April 30, 1950.

114. Kluger, *Simple Justice,* 299; "Address of Governor Olin D. Johnston," in South Carolina General Assembly, *Journal of the Senate,* 3–5.

115. *Charleston News and Courier,* January 8, 1948; *The State,* February 4, 1948; *Anderson Independent,* February 7, 1948. For a highly favorable political biography, see Huss, *Senator for the South;* also see Anthony Barry Miller, "Palmetto Politician."

116. Advertisement, 1950, Thurmond Senate Race file, box 13, Figg Papers, SCL.

117. Robert McC. Figg to Palmer Bradley, July 12 1950, ibid.

118. *The State,* May 24, 26, 27, June 3, 9, 1950.

119. Ibid., May 24, 1950.

120. Ibid.

121. Ibid., June 3, 1950.

122. Ibid., June 7, 1950.

123. Ibid.; Kluger, *Simple Justice,* 284.

124. *The State,* June 6, 1950.

125. Ibid., May 24, 1950.

126. Ibid., June 29, July 5, 1950.

127. Ibid., June 27, 1950. For PDP county and precinct organization information, see box 4, McCray Papers, SCL.

128. J. F. Stewart to James F. Byrnes, June 3, 1950, file 716; J. B. Gibson to Byrnes, June 8, 1950, file 723; Thomas R. Miller to Byrnes, May 16, 1950, file 727; James T. Richey to Byrnes, June 3, 1950, file 729, Byrnes Papers, CU. See also Progressive Democrats, sample ballot, "Candidates Recommended for July 11 Primary," ca. 1950, Politics 1949–50 file, box 2, McCray Papers, SCL. The sample ballot illustrates support for Johnston and for Byrnes's opponent Lester Bates.

129. John McCray, address, Mount Pisgah Baptist Church, Orangeburg Progressive Democrats, October 1, 1948, Speeches file, box 5, McCray Papers, SCL; Faggart, "Defending the Faith," 155–57.

130. *Greenwood Index-Journal,* August 9, 1949.

131. Ibid., August 10, 12, 1949.

132. Ibid., August 11, 12, 1949.

133. Ibid., August 19, 1949.

134. Ibid., September 13, 1949; J. Cal White to Federal Bureau of Investigation, August 15, 1949, in *State v. Willie Tolbert.*

135. *Greenwood Index-Journal,* September 13, 1949.

136. Ibid., August 13, September 14, 1949.

137. Ibid., September 14, 1949.

138. Ibid., October 27, 28, 1949. No appeal was attempted due to lack of funds. See memorandum, John McCray to Carl Murphy, January 7, 1950, Greenwood Libel folder, box 4, McCray Papers, SCL; Execution File 301, Records of the Department of Corrections, South Carolina Department of Archives and History, Columbia.

139. See "Memorandum from Harold R. Boulware," re: State vs. Willie Tolbert, n.d., box 4, McCray Papers, SCL. It was standard practice for NAACP attorneys to furnish such information to the *Lighthouse and Informer.*

140. Memorandum, John H. McCray to Carl Murphy, January 7, 1950, box 4, McCray Papers, SCL; *Greenwood Index-Journal,* January 4, 1950; *Anderson Independent,* October 28, 1949; copy of indictment, *State v. John H. McCray.*

141. *Greenwood Index-Journal,* January 4, 1950; copy of indictment, *State v. John H. McCray.*

142. *Chicago Defender,* January 21, 1950.

143. *Greenwood Index-Journal,* April 11, 1950.

144. John McCray to C. A. Scott, ca. August 1950, box 4, McCray Papers, SCL.

145. John H. McCray to T. Carl McFall, May 8, 1950, ibid.

146. John McCray to Guerny E. Nelson, May 6, 1950, ibid.

147. Richard E. Fields to John McCray, February 16, 1950, ibid.

148. John McCray to C. A. Scott, ca. August 1950, ibid.; *New York Times,* June 20, 1950; sentence, *State v. John H. McCray,* June 19, 1950.

149. See Greenberg, *Crusaders in the Courts,* 54–55.

150. D. Arnett Murphy to John McCray, February 13, 1950; Carl Murphy to John McCray, February 15, 1950; Emory O. Jackson to John McCray, May 17, 1950; John H.

Sengstacke to D. Arnett Murphy et al., May 18, 1950; John H. Sengstacke to John H. McCray, July 7, 1950; telegram, John H. McCray to John H. Sengstacke, July 11, 1950, box 4, McCray Papers, SCL. The National Negro Press Association paid for Thurgood Marshall's services.

151. See, for example, Luther T. Purvis to John McCray, May 10, 1950; D. Ireland Thomas to John McCray, May 10, 1950; James H. Rodolph to John McCray, May 12, 1950; Mr. and Mrs. William Hamilton to John McCray, May 13, 1950; Lela Haynes Lindsay to John McCray, May 13, 1950; R. O. Grant to Mrs. Liverman, May 13, 1950; J. B. Buchanan to John McCray, May 17, 1950, ibid.

152. "Funds Collected at Special Rally for John H. McCray at Progressive Democrat Institute," May 12, 1950; W. A. Baron to John McCray, May 15, 1950; J. S. Randolph to John McCray, May 15, 1950; Marion County Progressive Democrats to Mrs. Liverman, May 17, 1950; Mrs. LaVicia McDowell to Harriet Liverman, May 24, 1950; S. J. McDonald to Harriet Liverman, May 27, 1950; flyer, Progressive Democrats mass meeting, Charleston, June 7, 1950, ibid.

153. J. C. Parler to John H. McCray, May 24, 1950, ibid.

154. J. S. Randolph to John McCray, May 15, 1950; Joseph M. Wright to Harriet Liverman, May 27, 1950; L. M. Green to John McCray, June 24, 1950, ibid.

155. Modjeska Simkins, campaign letter, July 8, 1950; R. K Wise to Olin D. Johnston, March 30, 1950, 1950 Campaign File, box 111, Johnston Papers, SCL.

156. John H. McCray, "The Way It Was," *Charleston Courier,* January 30, 1982.

157. Strom Thurmond advertisement, file 24, box 4, McCray Papers, SCL.

158. *Greenwood Index-Journal,* July 3, 1950; advertisement, Olin D. Johnston Senate Campaign, in *The State,* July 7, 1950.

159. Bartley and Graham, *Southern Elections,* 201.

160. *Charleston News and Courier,* July 14, 1950; *The State,* July 13, 1950; George M. MacNabb to Robert M. Figg, July 18, 1950, and Robert M. Figg to Palmer Bradley, July 12, 1950, 1950 Senate race file, box 13, Figg Papers, SCL; Faggart, "Defending the Faith," 138.

161. *The State,* July 12, 1950.

162. Bartley and Graham, *Southern Elections,* 385, 387.

163. Robert McC. Figg to Palmer Bradley, July 12, 1950, J. Strom Thurmond, candidate for U.S. Senate 1950 file, box 13, Figg Papers, SCL.

164. Marion County, in eastern South Carolina, is a prime example. Marion ranked among the strongest counties for Thurmond in 1948. In 1950 Thurmond received only 40 percent of the vote, and Marion County boasted a strong PDP county organization. See *The State,* July 13, 1950; Marion County folder, box 4, McCray Papers, SCL.

165. W. W. Wright to Leander Perez, November 24, 1950, file 8, and "Agreement," ca. 1950, file 10, box 2, Personal Papers, Dixon Papers, ADAH.

166. Frank Dixon to W. W. Wright, December 2, 1950, file 8, ibid.

CHAPTER SEVEN

1. *The State,* August 20, 1952.
2. *New York Times,* November 14, 1951.
3. *The State,* January 25, 1951.

4. Ibid., March 17, 1951.

5. The voters eventually approved the referendum in the November election. See Blick, "Beyond 'The Politics of Color.' "

6. *The State,* April 7, 1951.

7. *New York Times,* September 9, 1954.

8. Ibid., June 6, 1950.

9. Numan V. Bartley, *Rise of Massive Resistance,* 41.

10. John Temple Graves to J. Strom Thurmond, May 1, 1951, and Thurmond to Graves, May 4, 1951, file 3420, Gubernatorial Series, Thurmond Papers, CU.

11. *The State,* May 20, 1951.

12. Jeansonne, *Leander Perez,* 188.

13. J. Strom Thurmond to E. Steuart Vaughan, January 16, 1952, file 3423, Gubernatorial Series, Thurmond Papers, CU.

14. *The State,* January 22, 1952.

15. Strom Thurmond to James F. Byrnes, March 19, 1951, file 3420; also see John Temple Graves to Thurmond, July 14, 1951, file 3421, Gubernatorial Series, Thurmond Papers, CU.

16. Strom Thurmond to John Temple Graves, April 3, 1951, file 3420, ibid.

17. James F. Byrnes to Strom Thurmond, March 22, 1951, ibid.; *The State,* March 24, 1951.

18. J. Strom Thurmond to Thomas R. Miller, November 26, 1951, file 3422, Gubernatorial Series, Thurmond Papers, CU.

19. J. Strom Thurmond to Horace Wilkinson, November 27, 1951, ibid.

20. *The State,* September 17, 1951.

21. Ibid., October 3, 1951.

22. Ibid., February 7, 1952.

23. Ibid., October 7, 1951.

24. Ibid., October 16, 1951.

25. Ibid., May 16, 1951.

26. Ibid., June 13, July 6, 1951; Black, *Southern Governors and Civil Rights,* 39–40; Fielding Wright to J. Strom Thurmond, September 6, 1951, file 3422, Campaign Series, Thurmond Papers, CU.

27. Quoted in McCoy, *Presidency of Harry S. Truman,* 300–301.

28. Reichard, *Politics As Usual,* 78.

29. *The State,* March 30, 1952.

30. Reichard, *Politics As Usual,* 78; McCoy, *Presidency of Harry S. Truman,* 302–3.

31. Numan V. Bartley, *New South,* 99.

32. *New York Times,* January 8, 1952.

33. *Birmingham News,* January 11, 1952.

34. Ibid., January 3, 1952.

35. Ibid., January 25–26, 1952.

36. Ibid., January 23, 1952.

37. Ibid., January 15, 1952.

38. Ibid., January 24, 1952.

39. Ibid., January 25–27, 1952.

40. Ibid., January 29, 1952.

41. Ibid., February 5, 1952.

42. Ibid., January 28, 1952.

43. Ibid., January 30–31, 1952.

44. Ibid., February 6–7, 1952.

45. Ibid., February 12, 1952.

46. Ibid., February 29, 1952.

47. Ibid., March 1, 1952.

48. Ibid., March 11, 1952.

49. Ibid., March 7, 9, 1952.

50. Ibid., April 3, 1952.

51. Ibid., April 4–5, 1952.

52. Ibid., April 6, 1952.

53. Ibid., April 1, 1952.

54. Ibid., April 24, 1952.

55. Ibid., May 8, 1952.

56. Ibid., May 28, 1952.

57. *The State,* April 17, 1952.

58. *Birmingham News,* July 1, 1952.

59. *The State,* April 17, 1952.

60. Ibid., June 27, 1952.

61. Press release, "A Statement of Mississippi's Position," May 11, 1952, Democrats 1948–1963 file, Minor Papers, MSU.

62. *The State,* May 16, 1952.

63. *Birmingham News,* February 9, 1952.

64. Ibid., March 9, May 10, 1952.

65. Reichard, *Politics As Usual,* 80.

66. *Birmingham News,* July 22, 1952.

67. Ibid., July 23, 26, 1952.

68. Ibid., July 30, 1952.

69. Ibid., February 23, July 22, 1952.

70. Rogers et al., *Alabama,* 385.

71. Key, *Southern Politics,* 292–93.

72. *Baltimore Sun,* August 7, 1952, and *Washington Star,* August 7, 1952, in South Carolina file, box 169, DNC Papers, HSTL.

73. *The State,* August 14, 1952.

74. Ibid., August 7, November 3, 1952.

75. Ibid., September 4, 1952.

76. Ibid., September 19, 1952.

77. Ibid., August 19, 1952.

78. Ibid., September 17, 1952.

79. H. K. Koebig to L. Mendel Rivers, November 12, 1952, box 2, Workman Papers, SCL.

80. *The State,* November 1–2, 1952.

81. Ibid., August 15, 1952.

82. Jeansonne, *Leander Perez,* 193.

83. Ibid., 194.

84. *The State,* November 3, 1952.

85. Numan V. Bartley, *New South,* 101.

86. *The State,* October 1, 1952.

87. Numan V. Bartley, *New South,* 102; also see Strong, *1952 Presidential Election in the South;* Lamis, *Two-Party South,* 3, 25–26.

88. Response of Bernard Manning, December 3, 1953, "Survey of South Carolinians for Eisenhower," Campaign Files, box 2, Workman Papers, SCL.

89. Kluger, *Simple Justice,* 700–710, 779–85.

90. Eastland quoted in Cohodas, *Strom Thurmond,* 254.

91. *The State,* May 18, 1954.

92. *Charleston News and Courier,* May 18, 1954.

93. *The State,* May 18, 1954; *Jackson Clarion-Ledger,* May 18, 1954.

94. *New York Times,* June 9, 1954; Numan V. Bartley, *Rise of Massive Resistance,* 67. Neopopulist Governor James Folsom of Alabama was elected to a second term prior to the May 1954 desegregation decision.

95. *New York Times,* July 7, 1954.

96. Quint, *Profile in Black and White,* 103–4.

97. For White Citizens' Councils and the massive resistance movement in general, see McMillen, *Citizens' Councils;* Numan V. Bartley, *Rise of Massive Resistance,* 82–107; Halberstam, "White Citizens' Councils," 293–302; Hodding Carter, *South Strikes Back.*

98. Tom P. Brady, "A Review of Black Monday," quote on p. 5, file 6, box 3, Subject Correspondence, Thurmond Papers, CU.

99. *Birmingham News,* February 23, 1952; Numan V. Bartley, *Rise of Massive Resistance,* 87–89.

100. McMillen, *Citizens' Councils,* 117–18; Jeansonne, *Leander Perez,* 235–36.

101. William D. Workman to George Warren, August 9, 1955, and William D. Workman, handwritten notes, August 20, 1955, "Committee of 52" file, box 50, Workman Papers, SCL; Dan F. Laney Jr. to Heyward Clarkson, November 5, 1954, file 1, box 6, and "Key Thurmond Men," list, ca. 1954, file 1, box 3, Campaign Series, Thurmond Papers, CU.

102. Memorandum to Strom Thurmond, ca. 1955, file 8, box 3, Subject Correspondence, Thurmond Papers, CU.

103. *The State,* September 8, November 3, 1954; Cohodas, *Strom Thurmond,* 255–67; *New York Times,* March 13, 1956.

104. See J. L. Coker to William D. Workman, September 21, 1955, and Bernard Manning, October 19, 1955, in 1955 general file, Campaign Files, box 2, Workman Papers, SCL.

105. Phillips, *Emerging Republican Majority,* 221; Lamis, *Two-Party South,* 15–16; Aistrup, *Southern Strategy Revisited,* 7.

106. Lamis, *Two-Party South,* 17; Garson, *Politics of Sectionalism,* 319.

107. Phillips, *Emerging Republican Majority,* 224; Black and Black, *Vital South,* 149–52; Cosman, *Five States for Goldwater.*

108. Charles N. Fortenberry and F. Glenn Abney, "Mississippi: Unreconstructed and Unredeemed," in Havard, *Changing Politics of the South,* 496.

109. Ibid., 498.

110. Black and Black, *Vital South,* 158–69, and *Politics and Society in the South,* 259–75; Garson, *Politics of Sectionalism,* 320.

111. Bain, "South Carolina: Partisan Prelude," in Havard, *Changing Politics of the South,* 613–14. Wallace and Nixon divided the South, with Wallace winning Alabama, Mississippi, Louisiana, Georgia, and Arkansas; Nixon won five rim South states and, with Thurmond's help, South Carolina.

112. Sundquist, *Dynamics of the Party System;* Bartley and Graham, *Southern Politics and the Second Reconstruction,* 25, 185–87.

BIBLIOGRAPHY

PRIMARY SOURCES

Manuscripts

Athens, Georgia
- Richard B. Russell Library for Political Research and Studies, University of Georgia
  - Georgia State Democratic Party Executive Committee Papers
  - Richard B. Russell Jr. Papers
  - Herman E. Talmadge Papers

Atlanta, Georgia
- Robert Woodruff Library, Atlanta University
  - Southern Regional Council Papers
- Robert Woodruff Library, Emory University
  - Ralph McGill Papers
  - Dorothy Rogers Tilly Papers

Charleston, South Carolina
- The Citadel
  - L. Mendel Rivers Papers
- Robert Smalls Library, College of Charleston
  - Burnet Rhett Maybank Papers

Cleveland, Mississippi
- Charles W. Capps Jr. Archives, Delta State University
  - Walter Sillers Jr. Papers

Clemson, South Carolina
- Clemson University Libraries, Clemson University
  - Edgar G. Brown Papers
  - James F. Byrnes Papers
  - Paul Quattlebaum Papers
  - States' Rights Papers
  - J. Strom Thurmond Papers

Columbia, South Carolina
- South Carolina State Archives
  - Gubernatorial Papers of James F. Byrnes
  - Gubernatorial Papers of George Bell Timmerman
  - Records of the Department of Corrections

South Caroliniana Library, University of South Carolina
- Mrs. Richard J. Allison Papers
- Arthur C. Clement Jr. Papers
- William Jennings Bryan Dorn Papers
- Robert McC. Figg Papers
- Olin D. Johnston Papers
- John H. McCray Papers
- South Carolina Council on Human Relations Papers
- William D. Workman Papers

Durham, North Carolina
- Perkins Library, Duke University
  - William Watts Ball Papers

Hattiesburg, Mississippi
- McCain Library and Archives, University of Southern Mississippi
  - William C. Colmer Papers
  - Mississippi Oral History Project

Independence, Missouri
- Harry S. Truman Library
  - Eben Ayers Papers
  - Oscar L. Chapman Papers
  - Clark Clifford Papers
  - Democratic National Committee Papers
  - George Elsey Papers
  - J. Howard McGrath Papers
  - Philleo Nash Papers
  - David K. Niles Papers
  - Oral History Collection
  - Papers of the President's Committee on Civil Rights
  - Stephen Spingarn Papers
  - Harry S. Truman Papers
    - President's Personal Files
    - President's Secretary's Files
  - White House Central Files

Jackson, Mississippi
- Mississippi Department of Archives and History
  - James C. Coleman Papers
  - Mississippi State Democratic Party Executive Committee Papers
  - States' Rights Scrapbook
  - John Bell Williams Papers
  - Walker Wood Scrapbook

Montgomery, Alabama
- Alabama Department of Archives and History
  - Alabama State Democratic Party Executive Committee Papers
  - Frank Dixon Papers, Personal
  - Frank Dixon Papers, Gubernatorial

James E. Folsom Papers, Personal
James E. Folsom Papers, Gubernatorial
James Simpson Papers
Chauncey Sparks Papers
Rock Hill, South Carolina
Dacus Library, Winthrop University
Progressive Democrats Oral History Interviews
Modjeska Simkins Papers
Jean Crouch Thurmond Scrapbooks
Alice Spearman Wright Papers
Marion Wright Papers
Starkville, Mississippi
Mitchell Memorial Library, Mississippi State University
Godwin Advertising Agency Collection
Wilson F. Minor Papers
Tuscaloosa, Alabama
William Stanley Hoole Special Collections Library, University of Alabama
Carl Elliott Papers
Lister Hill Papers
John Sparkman Papers
Washington, D.C.
Library of Congress
Papers of the National Association for the Advancement of Colored People
Moorland-Spingarn Research Center, Howard University
J. Waties Waring Papers
Microfilm Editions
Papers of the National Association for the Advancement of Colored People

Newspapers and Periodicals

Aiken Standard and Review
Alabama: News Magazine of the Deep South
Anderson Independent
Atlanta Constitution
Atlanta Journal
Augusta Chronicle
Birmingham News
Birmingham Post
Birmingham World
Charleston Evening Post
Charleston News and Courier
Charlotte News
Charlotte Observer
Chicago Defender
Clarksdale Register
Columbia Record
Gainesville Sun
Greenville News
Greenwood Delta Democratic-Times
Greenwood Index-Journal
Hattiesburg American
Jackson Advocate
Jackson Clarion-Ledger
Jackson Daily News
McComb Enterprise-Journal
Macon Telegraph
Montgomery Advertiser
Natchez Democrat
New York Times
Oxford Eagle

Southern Textile Bulletin
The State
States' Righter
Tallahassee Daily Democrat

Government Publications

Abney, Glen. *Mississippi Election Statistics, 1900–1967*. Oxford: University Press of Mississippi, 1968.
Congressional Record. 80th Cong., 2d sess., 1948, vol. 86, pt. 2.
Elmore v. Rice, 72 F. Supp. 516 (1947).
Facts about Arkansas. Little Rock: Arkansas Resources and Development Commission, 1944.
President's Committee on Civil Rights. *To Secure These Rights*. Washington, D.C.: U.S. Government Printing Office, 1947.
Public Papers of the Presidents: Harry S. Truman, 1947. Washington, D.C.: U.S. Government Printing Office, 1964.
Public Papers of the Presidents: Harry S. Truman, 1948. Washington, D.C.: U.S. Government Printing Office, 1964.
South Carolina General Assembly. *Journal of the Senate*. 85th General Assembly, special session, 1944.
The State v. John H. McCray, January 4, 1950, General Sessions, Greenwood County, S.C.
The State v. Willie Tolbert, case file, Greenwood County, S.C.

Pamphlet

States' Rights Information and Speakers Handbook. Jackson, Miss., 1948.

Articles

Arnall, Ellis. "The Democrats and the Future." *Yale Review* 37 (1947–48): 9–17.
———. "The Democrats Can Win." *Atlantic Monthly,* October 1948, 33–38.
"As Georgia Goes." *Newsweek,* October 1, 1948, 29.
Ashmore, Harry S. "The South's Year of Decision." *The Southern Packet: A Monthly Review of Southern Books and Ideas* 4 (November 1948): 2.
Bendiner, Robert. "Dixie's Fourth Party." *Nation,* February 14, 1948, 174–75.
———. "Route of the Bourbons." *Nation,* July 24, 1948, 91–93.
———. "Tour of the Border Country." *Nation,* October 9, 16, 23, 1948, 393–95, 424–25, 456–58.
Carleton, William G. "Why Call the South Conservative?" *Harper's Magazine,* July 1947, 61–68.
Carter, Hodding. "Civil Rights Issue As Seen in the South." *New York Times Magazine,* March 21, 1948, 15.
———. "Dixiecrat Boss of the Bayous." *Reporter* 2 (January 17, 1950): 10–12.
———. "Southern Liberal Looks at Civil Rights." *New York Times Magazine,* August 8, 1948, 10.

"Civil Rights Issue in Election." *U.S. News and World Report,* February 20, 1948, 22–23.
"Cooling of South's Anti-Truman Revolt." *U.S. News and World Report,* May 21, 1948, 24–25.
"Counterattack Begins." *New Republic,* December 27, 1948, 9.
"Cracker Boy's Vote: Presidential Election." *Christian Century,* October 27, 1948, 143–44.
"Danger from Dixiecrats." *New Republic,* August 2, 1948, 7.
"Democracy in the South." *New Republic,* October 18, 1948, 5.
"Dixiecrats." *Newsweek,* May 24, 1948, 23.
"Dixiecrat Vote." *Life,* November 8, 1948, 40.
Fuller, Helen. "Civil Rights Split the Democrats." *New Republic,* March 8, 1948, 16.
———. "The Fourth Party." *New Republic,* March 15, 1948, 9.
———. "The New Confederacy." *New Republic,* November 1, 1948, 10–14.
"Gauging the South's Revolt." *U.S. News and World Report,* March 26, 1948, 23–25.
"High Cotton." *New Republic,* August 2, 1948, 10.
Jones, Sam H. "Will Dixie Bolt the New Deal?" *Saturday Evening Post,* March 6, 1943, 20–21, 42, 45.
Kennedy, Renwick D. "Nowhere to Go." *Christian Century,* May 26, 1948, 510–12.
"Long and the Dixiecrats." *Newsweek,* October 4, 1948, 25.
Long, Stuart. "Freak Year in Texas." *Nation,* October 16, 1948, 427–29.
McGill, Ralph, "Will the South Ditch Truman?" *Saturday Evening Post,* May 22, 1948, 15–17, 88, 89.
"The Mutineers and the Firm Hand." *Newsweek,* July 26, 1948, 17–19.
"New South: A Political Phenomenon Grips Dixie's Voters." *Newsweek,* October 25, 1948, 32–34.
Olivier, Warner. "Jess Mitchell's Private War." *New Republic,* March 31, 1947, 17.
"One Course to Save the Democratic Party." *New Republic,* July 7, 1947, 14–15.
"The Only Hope." *Time,* August 23, 1948, 16–17.
"Origins of the Democratic Revolt." *U.S. News and World Report,* March 12, 1948, 13–14.
"Outlook in the Third Party Fight." *U.S. News and World Report,* March 5, 1948, 15–16.
"Pardon My Filibuster." *Newsweek,* August 9, 1948, 17–18.
Peacock, Eugene. "Why the Dixiecrats?" *Christian Century,* September 22, 1948, 975–77.
Rainey, Glenn W. "What Happened in Georgia?" *Nation,* October 2, 1948, 371–72.
"Real Issues in South's Revolt." *U.S. News and World Report,* April 9, 1948, 28–29.
"The Revolt Grows." *Newsweek,* March 8, 1948, 18–19.
Root, Oren, Jr. "The Republican Revival." *Atlantic Monthly,* September 1948, 28–34.
Sancton, Thomas. "Slowly Crumbling Levees." *New Republic,* March 8, 1948, 18–21.
———. "Trouble in Dixie I: The Returning Tragic Era." *New Republic,* January 4, 1943, 11–13.
———. "Trouble in Dixie II: The Bloody Shirt Once More." *New Republic,* January 11, 1943, 50–51.
———. "White Supremacy: Crisis or Plot?" *Nation,* July 31, 1948, 125–28.
"Shape of Things: Birmingham's Rump Convention." *Nation,* July 24, 1948, 85–86.

"Southern Revolt." *Time,* October 11, 1948, 24–27.
"Split in the South." *Newsweek,* September 20, 1948, 29.
Straight, Michael. "Revolt in the South." *New Republic,* March 8, 1948, 14–15.
"Truman and the Stop-Truman Revolt." *Newsweek,* July 12, 1948, 19–20.
"Truman Dilemma over Revolt." *U.S. News and World Report,* April 2, 1948, 19–20.
"Tumult in Dixie." *Time,* July 26, 1948, 15.
"Two-Party Headway in South." *U.S. News and World Report,* July 30, 1948, 22–23.
"The Unsolid South." *Newsweek,* February 16, 1948, 34.
"War between Democrats." *Newsweek,* July 26, 1948, 21.
West, Rebecca. "Opera in Greenville." *New Yorker,* June 14, 1947, 31–65.

SECONDARY SOURCES

Books

Ader, Emile. *The Dixiecrat Movement: Its Role in Third Party Politics.* Washington, D.C.: Public Affairs Press, 1955.
Aistrup, Joseph A. *The Southern Strategy Revisited: Republican Top-Down Advancement in the South.* Lexington: University Press of Kentucky, 1996.
Anderson, William. *The Wild Man from Sugar Creek: The Political Career of Eugene Talmadge.* Baton Rouge: Louisiana State University Press, 1975.
Ashmore, Harry. *Arkansas: A Bicentennial History.* New York: Norton, 1978.
Ayers, Edward L. *The Promise of the New South: Life after Reconstruction.* New York: Oxford University Press, 1992.
———. *Vengeance and Justice: Crime and Punishment in the Nineteenth-Century American South.* New York: Oxford University Press, 1984.
Barksdale, E. C., George Norris Green, and T. Harry Williams. *Essays on Recent Southern Politics.* Austin: University of Texas Press, 1970.
Barnard, William D. *Dixiecrats and Democrats: Alabama Politics, 1942–50.* Tuscaloosa: University of Alabama Press, 1974.
Bartley, Ernest R. *The Tidelands Oil Controversy: A Legal and Historical Analysis.* Austin: University of Texas Press, 1953.
Bartley, Numan V. *The Creation of Modern Georgia.* 2d ed. Athens: University of Georgia Press, 1990.
———. *The New South, 1945–1980.* Baton Rouge: Louisiana State University Press, 1995.
———. *The Rise of Massive Resistance: Race and Politics in the South during the 1950s.* Baton Rouge: Louisiana State University Press, 1969.
Bartley, Numan V., and Hugh D. Graham. *Southern Elections: County and Precinct Data, 1950–1972.* Baton Rouge: Louisiana State University Press, 1978.
———. *Southern Politics and the Second Reconstruction.* Baltimore: Johns Hopkins University Press, 1975.
Bass, Jack, and Walter DeVries. *The Transformation of Southern Politics: Social Change and Political Consequence since 1945.* New York: Basic Books, 1976.

Bass, Jack, and Marilyn Thompson. *Ol' Strom: An Unauthorized Biography of Strom Thurmond.* Atlanta: Longstreet Press, 1999.
Bates, Daisy. *The Long Shadow of Little Rock: A Memoir.* New York: David McKay, 1962.
Berman, William C. *The Politics of Civil Rights in the Truman Administration.* Columbus: Ohio State University Press, 1970.
Bernstein, Barton J., ed. *Politics and Policies of the Truman Administration.* New York: Quadrangle, 1970.
Billington, Monroe Lee. *The Political South in the Twentieth Century.* New York: Charles Scribner's Sons, 1975.
———. *Southern Politics since the Civil War.* Malabar, Fla.: Robert E. Krieger, 1984.
Black, Earl. *Southern Governors and Civil Rights.* Cambridge, Mass.: Harvard University Press, 1976.
Black, Earl, and Merle Black. *Politics and Society in the South.* Cambridge, Mass.: Harvard University Press, 1987.
———. *The Vital South: How Presidents Are Elected.* Cambridge, Mass.: Harvard University Press, 1992.
Boylan, James. *The New Deal Coalition and the Election of 1946.* New York: Garland, 1981.
Braeman, John, Robert H. Bremner, and David Brody, eds. *The New Deal: The National Level.* Vol. 1. Columbus: Ohio State University Press, 1975.
Brinkley, Alan. *Voices of Protest: Huey Long, Father Coughlin, and the Great Depression.* New York: Knopf, 1982.
Carter, Dan T. *The Politics of Rage: George Wallace, the Origins of the New Conservatism, and the Transformation of American Politics.* Baton Rouge: Louisiana State University Press, 1995.
———. *Scottsboro: A Tragedy of the American South.* New York: Oxford University Press, 1971.
Carter, Hodding III. *The South Strikes Back.* New York: Doubleday, 1959.
Carter, Luther F. and David S. Mann. *Government in the Palmetto State.* Columbia: Bureau of Government Research and Service, University of South Carolina, 1983.
Cash, W. J. *The Mind of the South.* New York: Knopf, 1941.
Chafe, William. *Civilities and Civil Rights: Greensboro, North Carolina, and the Black Struggle for Freedom.* New York: Oxford University Press, 1980.
Cobb, James C. *Industrialization and Southern Society, 1877–1984.* Lexington: University Press of Kentucky, 1984.
———. *The Most Southern Place on Earth: The Mississippi Delta and the Roots of Regional Identity.* New York: Oxford University Press, 1992.
———. *The Selling of the South: The Southern Crusade for Industrial Development, 1936–1990.* 2d ed. Urbana: University of Illinois Press, 1993.
Cobb, James C. and Michael V. Namorato, eds. *The New Deal and the South.* Jackson: University Press of Mississippi, 1984.
Cohodas, Nadine. *Strom Thurmond and the Politics of Southern Change.* New York: Simon and Schuster, 1993.
Colburn, David R., and Jane L. Landers. *The African American Heritage of Florida.* Gainesville: University Press of Florida, 1995.

Colburn, David R., and Richard Scher. *Florida Gubernatorial Politics in the Twentieth Century.* Tallahassee: University Press of Florida, 1980.

Cole, Taylor, and John H. Hallowell, *The Southern Political Scene, 1938–1948.* Gainesville, Fla.: Kallman, 1948.

Collins, Charles Wallace. *Whither Solid South? A Study in Politics and Race Relations.* New Orleans: Pelican, 1947.

Cosman, Bernard. *Five States for Goldwater: Continuity and Change in Southern Presidential Voting Patterns.* Tuscaloosa: University of Alabama Press, 1966.

Daniel, Pete. *Breaking the Land: The Transformation of Cotton, Tobacco, and Rice Cultures since 1880.* Urbana: University of Illinois Press, 1985.

Davis, Allison, Burleigh G. Gardner, and Mary R. Gardner. *Deep South.* Chicago: University of Chicago Press, 1941.

Democracy at Work: Being the Official Report of the Democratic National Convention. Philadelphia: Democratic Political Committee of Pennsylvania, 1948.

Donovan, Timothy P., Willard B. Gatewood Jr., and Jeannie M. Whayne. *The Governors of Arkansas: Essays in Political Biography.* Fayetteville: University of Arkansas Press, 1995.

Dorn, William Jennings Bryan, and Scot Derks. *Dorn: Of the People, a Political Way of Life.* Orangeburg, S.C.: Sandlapper, 1988.

Eagles, Charles W. *Jonathan Daniels and Race Relations: The Evolution of a Southern Liberal.* Knoxville: University of Tennessee Press, 1982.

Egerton, John. *Speak Now against the Day: The Generation before the Civil Rights Movement in the South.* New York: Knopf, 1994.

Elliott, Carl, and Michael D'Orso. *The Cost of Courage: The Journey of an American Congressman.* New York: Doubleday, 1992.

Emmerich, J. Oliver. *Two Faces of Janus: The Saga of Deep South Change.* Jackson: University Press of Mississippi, 1973.

Fairclough, Adam. *Race and Democracy: The Civil Rights Struggle in Louisiana, 1915–1972.* Athens: University of Georgia Press, 1995.

Feldman, Glenn. *From Demagogue to Dixiecrat: Horace Wilkinson and the Politics of Race.* Lanham, Md.: University Press of America, 1995.

Ferrell, Robert H. *Choosing Truman: The Democratic Convention of 1944.* Columbia: University of Missouri Press, 1994.

———. *Harry S. Truman: A Life.* Columbia: University of Missouri Press, 1994.

———, ed. *Off the Record: The Private Papers of Harry S. Truman.* New York: Harper and Row, 1980.

Fite, Gilbert C. *Cotton Fields No More: Southern Agriculture, 1865–1980.* Lexington: University Press of Kentucky, 1984.

———. *Richard B. Russell, Jr., Senator from Georgia.* Chapel Hill: University of North Carolina Press, 1991.

Fowler, Donald. *Presidential Voting in South Carolina.* Columbia: University of South Carolina Press, 1966.

Fraser, Steve, and Gary Gerstle, eds. *The Rise and Fall of the New Deal Order, 1930–1980.* Princeton: Princeton University Press, 1989.

Freidel, Frank. *FDR and the South.* Baton Rouge: Louisiana State University Press, 1965.

———. *Franklin D. Roosevelt: The Triumph.* Boston: Little, Brown, 1956.

Garfinkel, Herbert. *When Negroes March: The March on Washington Movement in the Organizational Politics for FEPC.* Glencoe, Ill.: Free Press, 1959.

Garson, Robert A. *The Democratic Party and the Politics of Sectionalism, 1941–1948.* Baton Rouge: Louisiana State University Press, 1974.

Gilbert, Gorman, and Robert E. Samuels. *The Taxicab: An Urban Transportation Survivor.* Chapel Hill: University of North Carolina Press, 1982.

Gilmore, Glenda Elizabeth. *Gender and Jim Crow: Women and the Politics of White Supremacy in North Carolina, 1896–1920.* Chapel Hill: University of North Carolina Press, 1996.

Goldfield, David R., *Black, White, and Southern: Race Relations and Southern Culture, 1940 to the Present.* Baton Rouge: Louisiana State University Press, 1990.

Grafton, Carl, and Anne Permaloff. *Big Mules and Branchheads: James E. Folsom and Political Power in Alabama.* Athens: University of Georgia Press, 1985.

Graham, Cole Blease, Jr., and William V. Moore. *South Carolina Politics and Government.* Lincoln: University of Nebraska Press, 1990.

Grantham, Dewey. *The Democratic South.* Athens: University of Georgia Press, 1963.

———. *The Life and Death of the Solid South: A Political History.* Lexington: University Press of Kentucky, 1988.

———. *The South in Modern America: A Region at Odds.* New York: HarperCollins, 1994.

Greenberg, Jack. *Crusaders in the Courts: How a Dedicated Band of Lawyers Fought for the Civil Rights Movement.* New York: Basic Books, 1994.

Gremillion, Jack P. F. *A Primer on the Tidelands Controversy and Louisiana's Experience in the Dispute.* N.p., 1962.

Hamby, Alonzo L. *Beyond the New Deal: Harry S. Truman and American Liberalism.* New York: Columbia University Press, 1973.

Hamilton, Virginia Van der Veer. *Lister Hill: Statesman from the South.* Chapel Hill: University of North Carolina Press, 1987.

Havard, William C., ed. *The Changing Politics of the South.* Baton Rouge: Louisiana State University Press, 1972.

Hawley, Ellis. *The New Deal and the Problem of Monopoly.* Princeton: Princeton University Press, 1966.

Heard, Alexander. *A Two-Party South?* Chapel Hill: University of North Carolina Press, 1952.

Heard, Alexander, and Donald S. Strong. *Southern Primaries and Elections, 1920–1949.* University: University of Alabama Press, 1950.

Henderson, Harold P., and Gary L. Roberts. *Georgia Governors in an Age of Change: From Ellis Arnall to George Busbee.* Athens: University of Georgia Press, 1988.

Hine, Darlene Clark. *Black Victory: Rise and Fall of the White Primary in Texas.* Millwood, N.Y.: KTO Press, 1979.

Hoff, Joan. *Herbert Hoover: Forgotten Progressive.* Boston: Little, Brown, 1975.

Hofstadter, Richard. *The Age of Reform: From Bryan to FDR*. New York: Random House, 1955.
Hollingsworth, Harold M. *Essays on Recent Southern Politics*. Austin: University of Texas Press, 1970.
Holmes, William F. *The White Chief: James Kimble Vardaman*. Baton Rouge: Louisiana State University Press, 1970.
Howard, Lawrence Vaughan, and David R. Deener. *Presidential Politics in Louisiana, 1952*. New Orleans: Tulane University, 1954.
Huss, John E. *Senator for the South: A Biography of Olin D. Johnston*. New York: Doubleday, 1961.
Inscoe, John C., ed. *Georgia in Black and White: Explorations in the Race Relations of a Southern State, 1865–1950*. Athens: University of Georgia Press, 1994.
Jeansonne, Glen. *Leander Perez: Boss of the Delta*. Baton Rouge: Louisiana State University Press, 1978.
Jordan, Frank E. *The Primary State: A History of the Democratic Party in South Carolina, 1876–1962*. Columbia, S.C.: R. L. Bryan, 1968.
Kelley, Robin D. G. *Hammer and Hoe: Alabama Communists during the Great Depression*. Chapel Hill: University of North Carolina Press, 1990.
Kesselman, Louis C. *The Social Politics of FEPC: A Study in Reform Pressure Movements*. Chapel Hill: University of North Carolina Press, 1948.
Key, V. O., Jr. *Southern Politics in State and Nation*. New York: Knopf, 1949.
Killian, Lewis M. *White Southerners*. Amherst: University of Massachusetts Press, 1985.
Kirby, Jack Temple. *Rural Worlds Lost: The American South, 1920–1960*. Baton Rouge: Louisiana State University Press, 1987.
Kluger, Richard. *Simple Justice: The History of Brown v. Board of Education and Black Americans' Struggle for Equality*. New York: Knopf, 1976.
Kneebone, John T. *Southern Liberal Journalists and the Issue of Race, 1920–1944*. Chapel Hill: University of North Carolina Press, 1985.
Kousser, J. Morgan. *The Shaping of Southern Politics: Suffrage Restriction and the Establishment of the One-Party South, 1880–1910*. New Haven: Yale University Press, 1974.
Kurtz, Michael L., and Morgan D. Peoples. *Earl K. Long: The Saga of Uncle Earl and Louisiana Politics*. Baton Rouge: Louisiana State University Press, 1990.
Lachicotte, Alberta. *Rebel Senator: Strom Thurmond and South Carolina*. New York: Devin-Adair, 1966.
Lamis, Alexander P. *The Two-Party South*. New York: Oxford University Press, 1984.
Lander, Ernest M., Jr. *A History of South Carolina, 1865–1960*. Columbia: University of South Carolina Press, 1960.
Lawson, Steven F. *Black Ballots: Voting Rights in the South, 1944–69*. New York: Columbia University Press, 1976.
———. *Running for Freedom: Civil Rights and Black Politics in America since 1941*. Philadelphia: Temple University Press, 1991.
Lemann, Nicholas. *The Promised Land: The Black Migration and How It Changed America*. New York: Knopf, 1991.

Lester, Jim. *A Man for Arkansas: Sid McMath and the Southern Reform Tradition*. Little Rock, Ark.: Rose Publishing, 1976.

Leuchtenburg, William. *Franklin D. Roosevelt and the New Deal, 1932–1940*. New York: Harper and Row, 1963.

Lowitt, Richard, and Maurine Beasley. *One Third of a Nation: Lorena Hickok's Reports on the Great Depression*. Champaign: University of Illinois Press, 1981.

McCoy, Donald R. *The Presidency of Harry S. Truman*. Lawrence: University Press of Kansas, 1984.

McCoy, Donald R., and Richard Ruetten. *Quest and Response: Minority Rights and the Truman Administration*. Lawrence: University Press of Kansas, 1973.

McCullough, David. *Truman*. New York: Simon and Schuster, 1992.

McElvaine, Robert S. *The Great Depression: America, 1929–1941*. New York: Random House, 1984.

———, ed. *Down and Out in the Great Depression: Letters from the Forgotten Man*. Chapel Hill: University of North Carolina Press, 1983.

MacLean, Nancy. *Behind the Mask of Chivalry: The Making of the Second Ku Klux Klan*. New York: Oxford University Press, 1994.

McMillen, Neil R. *The Citizens' Council: A History of Organized Resistance to the Second Reconstruction*. Urbana: University of Illinois Press, 1971.

———. *Dark Journey: Black Mississippians in the Age of Jim Crow*. Champaign-Urbana: University of Illinois Press, 1990.

———, ed. *Remaking Dixie: The Impact of World War II on the American South*. Jackson: University Press of Mississippi, 1997.

Matthews, Donald R., and James W. Prothro. *Negroes and the New Southern Politics*. New York: Harcourt, Brace, 1966.

Meier, August, and Elliott Rudwick. *CORE: A Study in the Civil Rights Movement, 1942–1986*. New York: Oxford University Press, 1973.

Mertz, Paul E. *New Deal Policy and Southern Rural Poverty*. Baton Rouge: Louisiana State University Press, 1978.

Michie, Allan A., and Frank Ryhlick. *Dixie Demagogues*. New York, 1939.

Miller, William D. *Mr. Crump of Memphis*. Baton Rouge: Louisiana State University Press, 1964.

Moon, Henry Lee. *The Balance of Power: The Negro Vote*. New York: Doubleday, 1948.

Moreland, Laurence W., Tod A. Baker, and Robert P. Steed. *Contemporary Southern Political Attitudes and Behavior*. New York: Praeger, 1982.

Morgan, Chester M. *Redneck Liberal: Theodore G. Bilbo and the New Deal*. Baton Rouge: Louisiana State University Press, 1985.

Myrdal, Gunnar. *An American Dilemma*. Rev. ed. New York: McGraw-Hill, 1964.

Norrell, Robert J. *Reaping the Whirlwind: The Civil Rights Movement at Tuskegee*. New York: Knopf, 1985.

Nunnelly, William A. *Bull Connor*. Tuscaloosa: University of Alabama Press, 1991.

O'Brien, Gail Williams. *The Color of the Law: Race, Violence, and Justice in the Post–World War II South*. Chapel Hill: University of North Carolina Press, 1999.

Odum, Howard W. *Race and Rumors of Race: Challenge to American Crisis*. Chapel Hill: University of North Carolina Press, 1943.

Patterson, James T. *Congressional Conservatism and the New Deal.* Lexington: University Press of Kentucky, 1967.

Peirce, Neal. *The Deep South States of America.* New York: Norton, 1972.

Pemberton, William E. *Harry S. Truman: Fair Dealer and Cold Warrior.* Boston: Twayne, 1989.

Pepper, Claude Denson, with Hays Gorey. *Pepper: Eyewitness to a Century.* New York: Harcourt Brace Jovanovich, 1987.

Perkins, Van L. *Crisis in Agriculture: The Agricultural Adjustment Administration and the New Deal, 1933.* Berkeley: University of California Press, 1969.

Phillips, Kevin B. *The Emerging Republican Majority.* New Rochelle, N.Y.: Arlington House, 1969.

Pleasants, Julian M., and Augustus M. Burns III. *Frank Porter Graham and the 1950 Senate Race in North Carolina* Chapel Hill: University of North Carolina Press, 1990.

Potter, David M. *The Impending Crisis, 1848–1861.* New York: Harper and Row, 1976.

Quint, Howard. *Profile in Black and White: A Frank Profile of South Carolina.* Washington, D.C.: Public Affairs Press, 1958.

Redding, Jack. *Inside the Democratic Party.* Indianapolis: Bobbs-Merrill, 1958.

Reed, Merl. *Seedtime for the Modern Civil Rights Movement: The President's Committee on Fair Employment Practice, 1941–1946.* Baton Rouge: Louisiana State University Press, 1991.

Reichard, Gary W. *Politics As Usual: The Age of Truman and Eisenhower.* Arlington Heights, Ill.: Harlan Davidson, 1988.

Rogers, William Warren, Robert David Ward, Leah Rawls Atkins, and Wayne Flynt. *Alabama: The History of a Deep South State.* Tuscaloosa: University of Alabama Press, 1994.

Ross, Irwin. *The Loneliest Campaign: The Truman Victory of 1948.* New York: New American Library, 1968.

Ruchames, Louis. *Race, Jobs, and Politics: The Story of FEPC.* New York: Columbia University Press, 1953.

Sale, Kirkpatrick. *Power Shift: The Rise of the Southern Rim and Its Challenge to the Eastern Establishment.* New York: Random House, 1975.

Scammon, Richard M. *America at the Polls: A Handbook of American Presidential Election Statistics, 1920–1964.* Pittsburgh: University of Pittsburgh Press, 1965.

Schlesinger, Arthur M., Jr. *The Age of Roosevelt: The Crisis of the Old Order, 1919–1933.* Boston: Houghton Mifflin, 1957.

Schulman, Bruce. *From Cotton Belt to Sun Belt: Federal Policy, Economic Development, and the Transformation of the South.* New York: Oxford University Press, 1991.

Shannon, Jasper B. *Toward a New Politics in the South.* Knoxville: University of Tennessee Press, 1949.

Sherrill, Robert. *Gothic Politics of the Deep South: Stars of the New Confederacy.* New York: Grossman, 1968.

Simkins, Francis Butler. *Pitchfork Ben Tillman, South Carolinian.* Baton Rouge: Louisiana State University Press, 1944.

Simon, Bryant. *A Fabric of Defeat: The Politics of South Carolina Millhands, 1910–1948.* Chapel Hill: University of North Carolina Press, 1998.

Sims, George E. *The Little Man's Big Friend: James E. Folsom in Alabama Politics, 1946–58.* Tuscaloosa: University of Alabama Press, 1985.

Sindler, Allan P. *Change in the Contemporary South.* Durham, N.C.: Duke University Press, 1963.

———. *Huey Long's Louisiana: State Politics, 1920–1952.* Baltimore: Johns Hopkins University Press, 1956.

Sitkoff, Harvard. *A New Deal for Blacks: The Emergence of Civil Rights As a National Issue.* New York: Oxford University Press, 1978.

Skates, John Ray. *Mississippi: A Bicentennial History.* New York: Norton, 1979.

Smith, C. Calvin. *War and Wartime Changes: The Transformation of Arkansas, 1940–1945.* Fayetteville: University of Arkansas Press, 1986.

Smith, Frank. *Congressman from Mississippi.* New York: Pantheon, 1964.

Steed, Robert P., Laurence W. Moreland, and Tod A. Baker, eds. *The Disappearing South? Studies in Regional Change and Continuity.* Tuscaloosa: The University of Alabama Press, 1990.

Strong, Donald S. *The 1952 Presidential Election in the South.* Tuscaloosa: University of Alabama Press, 1956.

Sullivan, Patricia. *Days of Hope: Race and Democracy in the New Deal Era.* Chapel Hill: University of North Carolina Press, 1996.

Sumners, Cecil L. *The Governors of Mississippi.* Gretna, La.: Pelican, 1980.

Sundquist, James L. *Dynamics of the Party System: Alignment and Realignment of Political Parties in the United States.* Washington, D.C.: Brookings Institute, 1973.

Swain, Martha. *Pat Harrison: The New Deal Years.* Jackson: University Press of Mississippi, 1978.

Talmadge, Herman E., with March Royden Winchell. *Talmadge: A Political Legacy, a Politician's Life: A Memoir.* Atlanta: Peachtree Publishers, 1987.

Thompson, Julius E. *Percy Greene and the Jackson Advocate: The Life and Times of a Radical Conservative Black Newspaperman, 1897–1977.* Jefferson, N.C.: McFarland, 1994.

Tindall, George B. *Disruption of the Solid South.* Athens: University of Georgia Press, 1972.

———. *The Emergence of the New South, 1913–1945.* Baton Rouge: Louisiana State University Press, 1967.

———. *The Ethnic Southerners.* Baton Rouge: Louisiana State University Press, 1976.

Truman, Harry S. *Memoirs: Years of Trial.* Vol. 2. New York: Doubleday, 1956.

White, Walter. *A Man Called White: The Autobiography of Walter White.* New York: Arno, 1967.

Williamson, Joel. *A Rage for Order: Black-White Relations in the American South since Emancipation.* New York: Oxford University Press, 1986.

Woodward, C. Vann. *The Burden of Southern History,* Rev. ed. Baton Rouge: Louisiana State University Press, 1968.

———. *Origins of the New South, 1877–1912.* Baton Rouge: Louisiana State University Press, 1951.

Workman, William D. *The Bishop from Barnwell: The Political Life and Times of Senator Edgar A. Brown.* Columbia, S.C.: R. L. Bryan, 1963.

Wright, Gavin. *Old South, New South: Revolutions in the Southern Economy since the Civil War*. New York: Basic Books, 1986.
Wyatt-Brown, Bertram. *Southern Honor: Ethics and Behavior in the Old South*. New York: Oxford University Press, 1982.
Wynn, Neil A. *The Afro-American and the Second World War*. New York: Holmes and Meier, 1976.
Yarbrough, Tinsely. *A Passion for Justice: J. Waties Waring and Civil Rights*. New York: Oxford University Press, 1987.
Zieger, Robert H. *The CIO, 1935–1955*. Chapel Hill: University of North Carolina Press, 1995.

Articles

Ader, Emile. "Why the Dixiecrats Failed." *Journal of Politics* 15 (August 1953): 356–69.
Bailey, Robert J. "Theodore G. Bilbo and the Fair Employment Practices Controversy: A Southern Senator's Reaction to a Changing World." *Journal of Mississippi History* 42 (February 1980): 27–42.
Blick, David G. "Beyond 'The Politics of Color': Opposition to South Carolina's 1952 Constitutional Amendment to Abolish the Public School System." *Proceedings of the South Carolina Historical Association* (1995): 20–30.
Carleton, William G. "The Conservative South: A Political Myth." *Virginia Quarterly Review* 22 (Spring 1946): 179–92.
———. "The Dilemma of the Democrats." *Virginia Quarterly Review* 24 (July 1948): 336–53.
———. "The Southern Politician, 1900 and 1950." *Journal of Politics* 13 (May 1951): 215–31.
Chesteen, Richard D. " 'Mississippi Is Gone Home!': A Study of the 1948 Mississippi States' Rights Bolt." *Journal of Mississippi History* 32 (February 1970): 43–59.
Dalfiume, Richard M. "The 'Forgotten Years' of the Negro Revolution." *Journal of American History* 55 (June 1968): 90–106.
Finkle, Lee. "The Conservative Aims of Militant Rhetoric: Black Protest during World War II." *Journal of American History* 60 (December 1973): 692–713.
Grant, Philip A., Jr. "Eisenhower and the 1952 Republican Invasion of the South: The Case of Virginia." *Presidential Studies Quarterly* 20 (Spring 1990): 285–93.
———. "The 1948 Presidential Election in Virginia: Augury of the Trend towards Republicanism." *Presidential Studies Quarterly* 8 (Summer 1978): 319–27.
Green, Fletcher M. "Resurgent Southern Sectionalism, 1933–1955." *North Carolina Historical Review* 33 (April 1956): 222–40.
Halberstam, David. "The White Citizens' Councils: Respectable Means for Unrespectable Ends." *Commentary,* October 1956, 293–302.
Heaster, Brenda L. "Who's on Second: The 1944 Democratic Vice Presidential Nomination." *Missouri Historical Review* 80 (January 1986): 156–75.
Hoffman, Edwin D. "The Genesis of the Modern Movement for Equal Rights in South Carolina, 1930–39." *Journal of Negro History* 44 (October 1959): 346–69.

Hofstadter, Richard. "From Calhoun to the Dixiecrats." *Social Research* 16 (June 1949): 135–50.
Hon, Ralph C. "The South in the War Economy." *Southern Economic Journal* 8 (1941–42): 291–308.
Juhnke, William E. "Harry Truman's Committee on Civil Rights: The Interaction of Politics, Protest, and Presidential Advisory Commission." *Presidential Studies Quarterly* 19 (Summer 1989): 593–610.
Kellogg, Peter J. "Civil Rights Consciousness in the 1940s." *Historian* 42 (November 1979): 18–41.
Key, V. O., Jr. "A Theory of Critical Elections." *Journal of Politics* 18 (February 1955): 3–18.
Klarman, Michael J. "How *Brown* Changed Race Relations: The Backlash Thesis." *Journal of American History* 81 (June 1994): 81–118.
Koeniger, A. Cash. "Carter Glass and the NRA." *South Atlantic Quarterly* 74 (Summer 1975): 349–64.
Korstad, Robert, and Nelson Lichtenstein. "Opportunities Found and Lost: Labor, Radicals, and the Early Civil Rights Movement." *Journal of American History* 75 (December 1988): 786–811.
Lemmon, Sarah McCulloch. "The Ideology of the 'Dixiecrat' Movement." *Social Forces* 30 (December 1951): 161–71.
McGlothlin, William M. "The South Advances." *Journal of Higher Education* 21 (March 1950): 113–20.
Melton, Thomas. "Walter Sillers and National Politics, 1948–1964." *Journal of Mississippi History* 39 (August 1977): 213–25.
Mitchell, Dennis J. "Frank E. Smith: An Intellectual Journey." *Journal of Mississippi History* 52 (February 1990): 23–40.
———. "Frank E. Smith: Mississippi Liberal." *Journal of Mississippi History* 48 (May 1986): 85–104.
Moore, John Robert, "The Conservative Coalition in the United States Senate, 1942–45." *Journal of Southern History* 33 (August 1967): 368–76.
Morgan, Chester. "At the Crossroads: World War II, Delta Agriculture, and Modernization in Mississippi." *Journal of Mississippi History* 57 (Winter 1995): 353–71.
Morgan, Thomas S. "James F. Byrnes and the Politics of Segregation." *Historian* 56 (Summer 1994): 645–54.
Morton, Ward M. "Report on Arkansas Politics in 1948." *Southwestern Social Science Quarterly* 30 (June 1949): 35–39.
Neuchterlein, James. "The Politics of Civil Rights: The FEPC, 1941–1946." *Prologue* 10 (Fall 1978): 171–91.
Norrell, Robert J. "Labor at the Ballot Box: Alabama Politics from the New Deal to the Dixiecrat Movement." *Journal of Southern History* 57 (May 1991): 201–34.
Partin, John W. "Roosevelt, Byrnes, and the 1944 Vice-Presidential Nomination." *Historian* 42 (November 1979): 85–100.
Patterson, James T. "A Conservative Coalition Forms in Congress, 1933–1939." *Journal of American History* 52 (March 1966): 757–72.

———. "The Failure of Party Realignment in the South, 1937–1939." *Journal of Politics* 27 (August 1965): 602–17.

Pleasants, Julian. "Claude Pepper, Strom Thurmond, and the 1948 Presidential Election in Florida." *Florida Historical Quarterly* 76 (Spring 1998): 439–73.

Reed, Merl. "FEPC and the Federal Agencies in the South." *Journal of Negro History* 65 (Winter 1980): 43–56.

Shannon, Jasper B. "Presidential Politics in the South." *Journal of Politics* 10 (August 1948): 464–89.

———. "Presidential Politics in the South: 1938," pt. 1. *Journal of Politics* 1 (May 1939): 146–70.

———. "Presidential Politics in the South: 1938," pt. 2. *Journal of Politics* 1 (August 1939): 278–300.

Simon, Bryant. "Guilt: A Historical Miniature." *Rethinking History* 3 (Fall 1999): 79–80.

Sitkoff, Harvard. "Harry Truman and the Election of 1948: The Coming of Age of Civil Rights in American Politics." *Journal of Southern History* 37 (November 1971): 597–616.

———. "Racial Militancy and Interracial Violence in the Second World War." *Journal of American History* 58 (December 1971): 661–81.

Starr, J. Barton. "Birmingham and the 'Dixiecrat' Convention of 1948." *Alabama Historical Quarterly* 32 (Spring/Summer 1970): 23–50.

Woodruff, Nan E. "'Pick or Fight': The Emergency Farm Labor Program in the Arkansas and Mississippi Deltas during World War II." *Agricultural History* 64 (Spring 1990): 74–95.

Dissertations and Theses

Ashley, Frank Watts. "Selected Southern Liberal Editors and the States' Rights Movement of 1948." Ph.D. diss., University of South Carolina, 1959.

Autrey, Dorothy A. "The National Association for the Advancement of Colored People in Alabama, 1913–1952." Ph.D. diss., University of Notre Dame, 1985.

Banks, James G. "Strom Thurmond and the Revolt against Modernity." Ph.D. diss., Kent State University, 1970.

Behel, Sandra K. "The Mississippi Homefront during World War II: Tradition and Change." Ph.D. diss., Mississippi State University, 1989.

Borsos, John. "Support for the National Democratic Party in South Carolina during the Dixiecrat Revolt of 1948." Master's thesis, University of South Carolina, 1987.

Brooks, Jennifer Elizabeth. "From Hitler and Tojo to Talmadge and Jim Crow: World War Two Veterans and the Remaking of Southern Political Tradition." Ph.D. diss., University of Tennessee, 1997.

Burns, Gladys King. "The Alabama Dixiecrat Revolt of 1948." Master's thesis, Auburn University, 1965.

Chesteen, Richard D., "The 1948 States' Rights Movement in Mississippi." Master's thesis, University of Mississippi, 1964.

Clark, James C. "Road to Defeat: Claude Pepper and Defeat in the 1950 Florida Primary." Ph.D. diss., University of Florida, 1998.
Corely, Robert Gaines. "The Quest for Racial Harmony: Race Relations in Birmingham, Alabama, 1947–1963." Ph.D. diss., University of Virginia, 1979.
Crispell, Brian L. "George Smathers and the Politics of Cold War America, 1946–1968." Ph.D. diss., Florida State University, 1996.
Danese, Tracy E. "Claude Pepper and Ed Ball: A Study in Contrasting Political Purposes." Ph.D. diss., Florida State University, 1997.
Ethridge, Richard C. "Mississippi's Role in the Dixiecratic Movement." Ph.D. diss., Mississippi State University, 1971.
Faggart, Luther Brady. "Defending the Faith: The 1950 U.S. Senate Race in South Carolina." Master's thesis, University of South Carolina, 1992.
Farmer, James O., Jr. "The End of the White Primary in South Carolina: A Southern State's Fight to Keep Its Politics White." Master's thesis, University of South Carolina, 1969.
Feldman, Glenn. "Horace Wilkinson and Alabama Politics, 1887–1957." Master's thesis, Auburn University, 1992.
Germany, Kent Barnett. "Rise of the Dixiecrats: Louisiana's Conservative Defection from the National Democratic Party, 1944–1948." Master's thesis, Louisiana Tech University, 1994.
Hayes, Jack Irby. "South Carolina and the New Deal, 1932–1938." Ph.D. diss., University of South Carolina, 1972.
Hilliard, Elbert R. "A Biography of Fielding Wright: Mississippi's Mr. State's Rights." Master's thesis, Mississippi State University, 1959.
Lofton, Paul Stroman, Jr. "A Social and Economic History of Columbia, South Carolina, during the Great Depression, 1929–1940." Ph.D. diss., University of Texas, 1977.
McLaurin, Ann Mathison. "The Role of the Dixiecrats in the 1948 Election." Ph.D. diss., University of Oklahoma, 1972.
Melton, Thomas R. "Mr. Speaker: A Biography of Walter Sillers." Master's thesis, University of Mississippi, 1972.
Miller, Anthony Barry. "Palmetto Politician: The Early Political Career of Olin D. Johnston, 1896–1945." Ph.D. diss., University of North Carolina, 1976.
Ness, Gary Clifford. "The States' Rights Democratic Movement of 1948." Ph.D. diss., Duke University, 1972.
Richard, Miles. "Osceola E. McKaine and the Struggle for Black Civil Rights, 1917–1946." Ph.D. diss., University of South Carolina, 1994.
Robson, George L., Jr. "The Mississippi Farm Bureau through Depression and War: The Formative Years, 1919–1945." Ph.D. diss., Mississippi State University, 1974.
Smith, Paul Anthony, Jr. "Loyalists and States' Righters in the Democratic Party of Alabama, 1949–1954." Master's thesis, Auburn University, 1966.
Tuggle, John Anthony. "The Dixiecrats as 'Stepping Stone' to Two-Party Politics for Mississippi." Master's thesis, University of Southern Mississippi, 1994.
Wells, Raymond B. "The States' Rights Movement of 1948: A Case Study." Master's thesis, Mississippi State University, 1965.

INDEX